GW00694500

AUSTRALIAN
CINEMA
THE FIRST
EIGHTY YEARS

AUSTRALIAN
CINEMA
THE FIRST
EIGHTY YEARS

GRAHAM SHIRLEY
&
BRIAN ADAMS

First published in the United States in 1985.
Distributed by St. Martin's Press, New York.

ANGUS & ROBERTSON PUBLISHERS
AND
CURRENCY PRESS

To my parents,
who gave immense encouragement
GS

ANGUS & ROBERTSON PUBLISHERS AND CURRENCY PRESS

This book is copyright. Apart from any fair dealing for the purposes of private study, research, criticism or review, as permitted under the Copyright Act, no part may be reproduced by any process without written permission. Inquiries should be addressed to the publishers.

First published by Angus & Robertson Publishers, Australia, in association with Currency Press, 1983

Copyright © Graham Shirley and Brian Adams, 1983

National Library of Australia
Cataloguing-in-publication data.

Shirley, Graham, 1949-.
   Australian cinema, the first eighty years.

   Bibliography.
   Includes index.
   ISBN 0 207 14581 4.

   1. Moving pictures, Australian - History.
   I. Adams, Brian, 1934-. II. Title.

791.43 '0994

Typeset in 10pt Garamond by Setrite Typesetters

Acknowledgements

No work such as this could be compiled without reference to the original research of a great many people. The authors especially wish to acknowledge the kind permission of Ross Cooper and Andrew Pike to use their unpublished MA theses to provide a valuable basis for the sections dealing with the Australian cinema of 1896-1913 (Ross Cooper: "And the Villain Still Pursued Her: Origins of Film in Australia 1896-1913") and Cinesound (Andrew Pike: "The History of an Australian Film Production Company: Cinesound 1932-1970"). Grateful acknowledgement is also made for permission to use Lindsay Wasson's unpublished BA (Hons) thesis, "The Quota Question in the Film Industry in New South Wales, 1920-1940"; Barrett Hodsdon's unpublished Master of Economics thesis, "The Australian Film Industry: A Case Study"; for research by Joan Long into the 1920s production period, by Chris Long into the coming of sound, and by Brett Levy and John Hughes into the Waterside Workers' Federation Film Unit.

In addition to those named above, the authors wish to thank Ray Edmondson and the staff at the National Film Archive of the National Library of Australia for help with film screenings and for access to stills and other documentation; and Film Australia, the Research and Survey Unit of the Australian Film and Television School, and the Performing Arts Museum of the National Gallery of Victoria for granting access to research documents.

We are deeply indebted to Derek Barton for his long and patient editing of the manuscript; and to the following individuals for their sometimes extensive help over a number of years: Judy Adamson, Reginald Baker, Elsa Chauvel, John Daniell, Leslie Daniell, Miriam Davis, Trader Faulkner, Ken G. Hall, A. R. Harwood, Herbert Hayward, Cecil Holmes, Fred James, Crewick Jenkinson, Lyle Leeds, Hugh McInnes, Mel Nichols, Allan Osborne, Marjorie Osborne, James Pearson, Lee Robinson, Priscilla Rowe, Colin Scrimgeour, Ralph Smart, Mary and Elizabeth Smith, Clive Sowry, Albie Thoms and Sid Wood; and the late Fred Daniell, Norman Dawn, Paulette McDonagh and Syd Nicholls. Important background information has also been drawn from interviews funded by the Australian Film Commission under the Film Pioneers Oral History Project, in particular those with Shan Benson, Herbert Hayward, John Heyer, John Kingsford Smith, Gwen Oatley and Ralph Smart.

Photographs

The authors wish to thank the following people and organisations for permission to reproduce photographs in this book. Photographs are identified by number.

1, 2, 3, 4, 5, 6 National Film Archive; 7 Jack Tauchert; 8, 9 National Film Archive; 10, 11, 12 Dick Collingridge; 13, 14 National Film Archive; 15, 16 Paulette McDonagh; 17 Edythe Pratt; 18 Ian Hanna; 19 Edythe Pratt; 20, 21 National Film Archive; 22 Cinesound Productions; 23 Ian Hanna; 24 Cinesound Productions; 25 National Film Archive; 26, 27 Cinesound Productions; 28 Elsa Chauvel; 29 Lesley Daniell, John Daniell; 30 Elsa Chauvel; 31, 32 EMI Film Distributors Ltd; 33 Joan Sheil; 34 Film Australia; 35 Cecil Holmes; 36 Lee Robinson; 37 Elsa Chauvel; 38 By courtesy of The Rank Organisation PLC; 39 Sydney Filmmakers' Co-operative; 40 Hardings (Solicitors); 41 Columbia Pictures; 42, 43 Tim Burstall; 44 20th Century-Fox for Max L. Raab-Si Litvinoff Films (Pty) Ltd; 45 Smart Street Films; 46 McElroy and McElroy; 47 Michael Thornhill; 48 South Australian Film Corporation.

Introduction

On 19 September 1900 four thousand people crowded into the Melbourne Town Hall to see and hear a Salvation Army lecture — titled **Soldiers of the Cross**, a multi-media presentation of lantern slides, hymns, sermons . . . and moving pictures. The short film sequences showed chastening Biblical scenes shot on a suburban tennis court which had been cunningly disguised as the Colosseum and other Roman locations. This early example of narrative cinema was produced far from the influences of Europe and America, both half a world away.

Just around the corner from the Melbourne Town Hall stands the impressive facade of the Athenaeum Hall; its graceful mock-Grecian statuary, gazing down from the upper storeys, seems more appropriate to the stately clatter of the era of horse-drawn carriages than the cacophony of today's traffic. In 1906 **The Story of the Kelly Gang** opened there. At the time it was claimed to be the longest continuous narrative feature made anywhere in the world, and it led the way to a vigorous Australian silent cinema.

In nearby Collins Street, behind an austere office block, are the remnants of the Capitol Theatre; "the theatre magnificent" they called it when it opened in 1924 with Cecil B. De Mille's **The Ten Commandments**. Designed by the planner of the nation's capital, Walter Burley Griffin, the Capitol reflected in its luxury and scale the increasing dominance of the American film industry that was to threaten local Australian production for most of its history. Fifty years later and drastically reduced in size, the Capitol premiered an Australian film, **The Adventures of Barry McKenzie**, one of several films that were to rejuvenate confidence in local production. The Regent, another of Melbourne's flamboyant picture palaces built during that first wave of confidence and within sight of the three other monuments, the Capitol, the Athenaeum and the Melbourne Town Hall, is a reminder of the cinema boom of the late 1920s when Australians achieved one of the highest per capita attendance records in the world. Two blocks away stands Her Majesty's Theatre, which as *His* Majesty's, served as a studio for Efftee Film Productions, Australia's first successful maker of ''talkie'' features in the early 1930s. All of these buildings remained in existence at the time of Australia's production revival of the 1970s, and the Regent was classified to be preserved as part of Melbourne's heritage.

But preservation came too late to save a large proportion of the nation's film heritage for posterity. This neglect left many gaps, and over ninety per cent of the silent narrative features were lost. Now, however, the picture is a little brighter thanks to a new generation keen to conserve what remains. New discoveries will continue long after this book has made its appearance. Indeed, near the completion of the manuscript, Raymond Longford's 1914 one-reel film **Trooper Campbell** was located, bringing the number of surviving Longford titles to five from the original thirty. But the high rate of loss for other films of the silent era has meant that much of our commentary on films from that period has had to be drawn from contemporary published articles and reviews.

The revival of the local production industry has run parallel to the determination to retain links with the past. In the many decades since the Kellys first flickered onto the screen, the fortunes of the business have continued to ebb and flow with a cyclic pattern of growth, euphoria, despair and collapse. But from the mid-1970s, nourished by government funding and a growing measure of confidence on all sides, the Australian cinema began to take its place in an international context as never before. This journey through the first eighty years to 1975 documents some of the social, financial, political and artistic events which combined to make a fascinating story, culminating at a time when all these elements came together to provide a springboard for a more substantial and continuing Australian film industry.

We have employed the term "cinema" with full awareness of its use to denote a national cinema which, to borrow from the ABC's film critic John Hinde's definition, interacts with its home public for inspiration and support. We have also used the term knowing that the essence of a true national cinema has emerged and vanished repeatedly throughout Australia's film history. The division of this book into three parts, The Silent Era, Sound and Survival, and Revival, highlights the fact that the most sustained evidence of an Australian national cinema to date has been that of the silent era (1896-1929), and that the first three decades of sound (1930-60) were characterised by films which for the most part were guided by competition with Hollywood on their home territory. As will be seen, the 1960s revival brought a new confidence as well as unprecedented possibilities for a new national cinema. The industry is still exploring these new directions.

Our narrative ends in mid-1975, a time when the industry was to enter a period rich enough to demand a separate book. The industry is therefore covered up to the point where its formerly separate artistic and commercial achievements were merged in **Sunday Too Far Away**. This film was to mark yet another beginning for Australian cinema, not diminishing the age-old battle between art and commerce, but launching hopes for their permanent co-existence.

Graham Shirley and Brian Adams

Contents

PART ONE

The Silent Era

1

The first decade
1896 – 1906

Australians' first experience of "film" was the Edison Kinetoscope. From early 1895, this machine made its first appearances in Sydney, Melbourne and Adelaide. In March 1896 an "Edison Electric Parlour" with gramophones and Kinetoscopes was operating in Pitt Street, Sydney. People who dropped a penny in the slot and stooped to look through an eyepiece saw animated pictures running for up to ninety seconds. They included a James Corbett boxing match, a dramatised lynching and a hand-coloured film of "Annabelle" doing her "serpentine dance". Customers, however, soon lost interest in the contraption; the unreality of the small, jerky images was little competition for the flesh-and-blood stage performances that the device was claimed to reproduce. It was in the vaudeville houses and the music halls rather than penny arcades that the new medium of cinema began to emerge.

The 1880s had seen an economic boom in Australia and this prompted the building of many new theatres and the refurbishing of existing houses. Melbourne's fine Princess Theatre opened in 1887 with Gilbert and Sullivan's *Princess Ida*. A spirit of proud confidence pervaded both business and showbusiness as the centenary of Australia's European settlement approached. But the feeling was relatively short lived. By the beginning of the 1890s a chronic drought began to affect the wool trade — the nation's principal export — and land speculation, which had taken Melbourne by storm, collapsed with a series of bank failures. Economic uncertainty in the community was reflected in dwindling attendances at places of entertainment, and many small entrepreneurs went out of business, although there was still enough wealth in Melbourne and Sydney for outstanding attractions to prosper; Sarah Bernhardt's company played to packed houses in 1891 and both the music halls and popular melodrama kept their business. By the mid-1890s however, the entertainment scene was in a poor way; admission prices had to be reduced and something new was needed to tempt audiences back to the theatres. From the beginning film was enough of a novelty to fulfil this aim, but nobody could have foreseen that the new medium was to have an

3

effect on live theatre far more radical than that created by the vagaries of a passing economic depression.

The technical background to cinema had developed over sixty-five years of the nineteenth century. It began experimentally almost at the beginning of the century and had emerged as a medium of mass entertainment by its end. In early November of 1895 Max and Emil Skladanowsky gave the first public screening in Berlin of their Bioskop, a complicated projection device involving two parallel strips of film and two lenses. However, on 28 December, Auguste and Louis Lumière introduced their combination camera-projector to a paying audience in a basement below the Grand Café on the Boulevard des Capucines in Paris and it was this screening of scenes from single 35 mm film strips that is generally accepted as the birth of cinema.

Motion picture projection was based on the persistence-of-vision theory studied by a number of scientists, among them Peter Mark Roget and Michael Faraday, between 1824 and 1831. Developed from this, optical toys such as the Thaumatrope, the Zeotrope and the Praxinoscope had since the 1820s conditioned a public to the illusion of continuously reproduced movement with a series of drawings viewed in rapid succession. The concept of optically-reproduced motion was, therefore, not a total surprise to the first cinema audiences who were also familiar with high quality still photography. The one vital component that cinema alone added was dynamism. It was the combination of realism and movement that could cause early audiences to panic at the sight of a train apparently heading out of the screen towards them, and to brace themselves from being swept from their seats by **Sea Waves**, another ''scenic'' episode shown by the Lumière brothers.[1]

The most important events in cinema's development during the nineteenth century occurred in France and America. In 1826 Joseph Niepce was the first to succeed in recording a permanent image on a sensitised plate; Louis Daguerre's refinement of this process was perfected and demonstrated in 1839. In 1882 the physiologist Etienne Marey developed a photographic ''gun'' to study animal locomotion. His device was further developed by English-born Eadweard Muybridge for a study of horses in motion, under the patronage of Governor Stanford of California. Since the early 1880s Muybridge had been able to project his images, but his and Marey's experiments were considerably advanced by the introduction in 1889 of flexible celluloid roll film by the American, George Eastman.

Inspired by the Muybridge projector, Thomas Edison assigned his laboratory head, W. K. L. Dickson, to develop a more sophisticated machine using the new roll film to record as well as reproduce images. By September 1890 Dickson was filming rapid sequences of photographs on his Kinematograph. In August 1891 Edison's Kinetoscope was patented — a peepshow device running short strips of film with unsynchronised music. It was marketed throughout the world and gave the patrons of amusement arcades and Kinetoscope ''parlours'' the opportunity to individually view ''actuality'' and vaudeville items. Edison's failure to patent the machine outside the United States left the way open for others to copy and develop it.

4

Working separately, the Lumière brothers in France and R. W. Paul in England expanded the principle into the projection of motion pictures, and by the end of 1895 the Lumières and Edison had forged ahead with the production of short films. At the same time R. W. Paul and his collaborator, Birt Acres, had made their own short films and begun regular screenings on the bill at London's Alhambra Music Hall. Although Paul's initial engagement was for two weeks, he was to remain there for a total of four years. Among his projectionists was a former music hall musician, Franklyn Barrett, who was later to become a cameraman. Within two decades he would also be one of the leading directors of the Australian silent cinema.

The Cinématographe

During 1896 Lumière agents with their camera-projectors travelled as far afield as North and South America, Southern Europe, Russia, China, Scandinavia, the Middle East and Australia. Quick profits were made by these showmen as they built up an audience for short, topical scenes such as **A Sack Race Between Lumière and Sons Factory, Lyons, Negro Minstrels Dancing in the London Streets, The Fish Markets at Marseilles** and **The Electrical Carriage Race from Paris to Bordeaux**. The stagebound, virtually static product of Edison's Vitascope Company and other early producers suffered by comparison with the "actualities" of the Lumière brothers. A Lumière agent could photograph the people of a district and show them the results the same day. Sent back to the Lumière head office, prints of these films could then be distributed to other parts of the world. From the status of a vaudeville act, film had started to become a medium of information about faraway and fascinating places brought immediately to life. Cinema was working to shorten distances and widen human horizons well before the Wright brothers made their first powered flight in 1903.

However, it was not a Lumière agent who gave the Australian public its first experience of projected film but an American magician. In August 1896 the Melbourne Opera House advertised a variety bill headed by "the premier prestidigitator and illusionist of the world", a man called Carl Hertz. His programme, announced as "a conflux of apparent miracles and marvellous illusions" included "the great London sensation, the Cinématographe" which, it was claimed, would reproduce animated nature as if to bring it to life. Hertz's use of the Lumière trademark "Cinématographe" was, in fact, misleading because his projector was one of two "Kinematographs" constructed by R. W. Paul in London earlier that year.

It was really Paul's ingenuity rather than Hertz's magical powers that deserved the enthusiastic applause of the audiences that thronged to see the act. Hertz was thirty-seven, born in San Francisco, the son of Russian immigrants. He learned his stagecraft on the California goldfields and then toured the vaudeville circuits of the world, first playing in Australia in 1892. Visiting London in March 1896, he was entranced with screenings by the Lumière and Paul machines. Like other magicians who rushed to buy

5

projectors, Hertz considered the new invention the last word in magic and persuaded Paul to sell him a machine and a collection of films. The following day Hertz left London on the journey that would make him the first person to screen film in South Africa and many parts of Asia as well as in Australia. In South Africa he added to his library by acquiring twenty Kinetoscope shorts and had to laboriously adapt their incompatible sprocket holes to fit his projector. On the opening night of his twenty-minute film programme at the Melbourne Opera House on Saturday, 22 August 1896, Hertz shared the bill with an English vocalist, a comedian, a baritone, an Australian song and dance man, minstrels and dancers. But only Hertz, according to a poster, could present "The Original And Only Genuine Cinématographe Ever Exhibited In The Colonies".[2]

Hertz and his top-of-the-bill act quickly became the talk of the town. To audiences conditioned by the crude kinetic displays of the optical toys of the nineteenth century, these first motion pictures with their ability to simulate life with the accuracy of a still photograph must have seemed an extraordinary extension of the magician's powers. Journalists covering the event needed a new language to describe what they had experienced. The *Age*, in publishing Australia's first film review, declared:

As an up to date scientific novelty, the cinématographe which was introduced to Australians by Carl Hertz at the Opera House on Saturday night must be ascribed a leading position. It is a combination in which the effects of the kinetoscope are imparted to limelight views, producing scenes of amazing realism, and giving them all the characteristics of actual moving life.[3]

The "limelight views" referred to were the glass magic lantern slides that had become common throughout the world over the past two hundred years. Another reviewer wrote of the cinematograph not simply reproducing but actually *producing* every motion of real life with marvellous fidelity, while one writer imagined a sensation of coolness when viewing a water scene,[4] and another referred to the sound of a brass band and "the ceaseless tramp of a thousand feet" in describing a military subject.[5] A seascape screened by Hertz evoked "a storm of applause" from its Melbourne first-nighters.[6]

The *Age* account of the Melbourne screening reported that the "views" also included:

an Italian skirt dance, in which the *danseuse* was seen with the same clearness as if she had actually been on the stage; a pugilistic encounter; street scenes of London Bridge, showing hansoms, market waggons, buses and coster carts threading their way at various rates of speed through the maze of traffic, the drivers gesticulating and apparently reviling each other, just as they did, one morning, when the original photograph was taken.

The screening by Hertz of the seascape, "a flowing tide and rocky foreshore" was judged to be "the most perfect of the scenes". The audience was said to have responded to the intense naturalism of "the rhythmic motion of the waves, the spray and foam and broken water where the waves were reft by boulders".[7] After this, a scene from the play *Trilby* depicting the death of Svengali seemed rather pallid.

Marius Sestier

September 1896 saw the arrival in Sydney of the first Lumière agent. Although he was by then out of favour with his employers, the name of Marius Sestier was to outlive all but a handful of his associates. The Lumière brothers, disturbed by Sestier's previous ineptitude, had sent him a reprimand. While smarting at this rap in India, he was persuaded by the Australian portrait photographer Walter Barnett to try his luck in the Antipodes and was offered a partnership. Neither knew of Hertz's activities, nor were they aware that a showman named Joseph McMahon had been the first to screen film in Sydney at a preview early in September 1896.

On 19 September, the very week that Sestier and Barnett arrived, Carl Hertz opened Sydney's first public season of films. His now tried-and-true screenings were part of a variety bill at the Tivoli Theatre, so it was left to Sestier and Barnett to achieve the distinction of opening Australia's first auditorium devoted entirely to the showing of films. Their "Salon Lumière", as it was called, opened on 28 September with the same programme that had been shown at the Grand Café in Paris ten months before. The films were projected onto a large screen surrounded by a richly moulded frame and on several occasions during the first season an orchestra from the nearby Lyceum Theatre provided musical accompaniment. Because the Salon Lumière was far enough removed from the usual association between rowdy working-class audiences and the vaudeville houses, it attracted more élite patronage. In October they welcomed the Governor, Lord Hampden, and his entourage, followed a few days later by the Anglican Primate of Australia together with an ecumenical ensemble including the Roman Catholic Bishop of Goulburn and a large excursion group of boys and priests from Riverview College.

By the end of the month Sestier and Barnett decided to put their camera-printer-projector to more practical use. In late September and early October they filmed experimental footage around the shores of Sydney Harbour. It was the first motion picture film to be exposed in Australia. The Lumière brothers' estimation of their employee seemed to be justified when some of the material was destroyed during processing, but there was enough remaining to make up several shorts, each around sixty feet in length. The most successful of these, **Passengers Alighting from Ferry "Brighton" at Manly**, showed people leaving the ferry and walking along Manly Pier.[8] Exhibition was delayed until after Sestier's next venture.

It was Carl Hertz who first publicly announced an intention to film the 1896 Melbourne Cup, Australia's premier horse race. The motivation came from his success with a recent R. W. Paul film from Britain showing Persimmon, Prince Edward's horse, winning the Prince's Derby. But Hertz

7

lacked a camera and it was Sestier who committed the Melbourne Cup to film. He and Barnett arrived at Flemington Racecourse early on the first Tuesday in November, the day the race is traditionally run. Barnett served as director and public relations man. As the shuffling crowds stared with curiosity at Sestier's hand-cranked contraption, his partner persuaded many prominent people, including the Governor, Lord Brassey, to walk in front of the lens to be photographed. The film stock was unable to record the horses in motion beyond long-distance shots of the field galloping toward the camera, but this proved to be no hindrance to the film's massive audience appeal. As the *Bulletin* was to comment:

It is something beautifully appropriate that the first Australian picture presented by the new machine should be a horse race. Of course it had to be either that or a football match.[9]

Two weeks after the race the film had its premiere at the Princess Theatre, Melbourne, at a matinée given in aid of the blind asylum. Sydney first saw it at the Criterion Theatre at the end of November, and its popularity kept it there for three months. The "exhibition of the wonderful tableaux of the Melbourne Cup" included scenes of the arrival of the special train at the course and a crowd of well-dressed racegoers spilling onto the platform; views of the "lawn" at the racecourse; the entrance of the Governor; activity in the saddling paddock; weighing for the Cup; and the finish of the race itself with Newhaven the winner. The crowd shots convey a rich and fascinating glimpse of Melbourne society in the 1890s. Among those recognisable are a nervous viceroy, Lord Brassey and the photographer Walter Barnett, who appears in several scenes, each time with the wife of a different dignitary. During the screenings of 1896 and 1897, **Melbourne Cup** was shown with their Sydney film of October 1896. Other Sestier films on the same programme included the New South Wales Horse Artillery at Victoria Barracks, Government Printing Office employees leaving work, and a stream of people taking a Sunday walk from Hyde Park to the Domain by way of St Mary's Cathedral.[10] The programme ended with imported scenes of French infantrymen on the march. Eager audiences paid a substantial sum of up to two shillings to see the thirty-minute show. In 1897 the **Cup** also became the first Australian film seen abroad when it was included in Wybert Reeve's presentation "Cinématographe — Lumière Living Pictures" in New Zealand.

Sestier's **Melbourne Cup** is Australia's oldest surviving film — by default. A large number of the early Lumière films from all over the world were sent back to France and some of them were eventually lodged with the Cinémathèque Française. If Sestier's negative had not left Australia it would almost certainly have been lost, destroyed by over-use, affected by the climate or, in time, discarded, because of the general indifference to archival material. The National Film Archive in Canberra has a copy of the film presented by the Cinémathèque Française but several scenes, including the arrival of the train, are missing.

Between 1896 and 1900 cinema around the world remained a novelty, although several writers in the Australian press were able to predict a future for it. In October 1896 the *Australasian* observed:

Perhaps we shall one day combine with the cinematograph an improvement upon the present phonograph. Then we shall be able to hear the cries of the lucky winners as Persimmon gallops home, the murmur of the sea as it ripples upon the beach, and the roar of the London streets as vehicles and men scud across the canvas.[11]

The *Bulletin* even foreshadowed television:

What is badly wanted now is some device whereby the machine can be connected with the telegraph and made to represent events while they happen, so the public can sit in a theatre on Cup Day, and see the race in spectral guise on a white background as it progresses. This improvement is bound to come along sooner or later and when it does the 'graph will have a great future before it.[12]

Many of the earliest exhibitors had little faith in the ability of motion pictures to transcend the status of a vaudeville act and were in the process of selling their projectors after mid-1897 because of declining audiences. In America, the slump almost closed one of the most prolific of the early producers, Vitagraph, but the company managed to retrieve its fortunes by "gazettes" (a primitive form of newsreel) of the Spanish–American war. Few cared if some of the footage was faked.[13] Vitagraph's work in this area was one important step in the worldwide move toward covering unusual and newsworthy subjects. Gazette single items ("topicals") or series were incorporated in film programmes with "scenics" (mainly tourist attractions), "travelogues" (which went one step further than the scenics by incorporating travel between the attractions), "industrials" (productive processes of all kinds), and the staged "novel" and "comic" films. The English and French were among the earliest to realise the gazette's potential and its appeal was firmly established by the success of R. W. Paul's film of the Prince's Derby. Gazette cameramen covered some of the great events in the final years of the nineteenth century and among the subjects seen by Australian audiences in 1897 were the Greek–Turkish and the Spanish–American conflicts, Queen Victoria's Jubilee procession and, the first multi-reel film shown in Australia, an hour-long coverage of the Corbett–Fitzsimmons fight in Carson City. The Boer War, which was of direct local interest, was a consistent attraction between 1899 and 1901, but in the absence of further excitement, city exhibitors experienced a decline in attendances. Of the handful of films made locally, only major sporting events could be counted on to draw an audience. A new and more lasting emphasis was needed for film to become more than a novelty.

Origins of the "story" film

The Lumière brothers are generally credited with the first "story" film, **L'Arroseur Arrosé (Watering the Gardener)**, made in 1895. In the same year Alfred Clark, the director employed by Thomas Edison at West Orange in the United States, made several costume films, the most important of which was **The Execution of Mary Queen of Scots**, and at least one dramatised film (**Arrest of a Pickpocket**) was directed by R. W. Paul in England. But the most influential of the narrative pioneers was the Frenchman Georges Méliès who from 1897 used his camera to reproduce and enhance the effects he had achieved previously as a stage magician. The American Edwin S. Porter who joined the Edison Company in 1899 was impressed by Méliès's work but was prompted to go one step further by employing what he regarded as more straightforward storytelling. Porter's techniques were the first to advance film construction and editing. But before any of these developments were evident to audiences, filmmakers in Britain, France and America — many of whom, like Porter, were their own technicians — continued to turn out one minute dramas and comedies derived from the stage. If any of these producers thought about progress at all it was invariably about improving the technology of film, not aesthetic advancement.

The longest of the early American story films was **The Passion Play**, filmed on a New York rooftop in 1897. It was a remake of an unsatisfactory film of the Passion Play performed at Oberammergau in Bavaria the same year. The new version used 2100 feet of film, and ran for approximately thirty-four minutes. Staged in the tableau-style of magic lantern slides, the twelve scene shots, like all film dramas of the period, took a frontal perspective which was changed only by cutting to the next scene. No film of equivalent length was to be made in America for another fifteen years, except for a prize fight filmed in its entirety in 1899.[14]

The Salvation Army

The earliest story films in Australia were made in August 1897. These were the dramatised episodes of a series produced by the Limelight Department of the Salvation Army in Melbourne. The organisation was one of the many religious bodies of the period increasingly concerned with the morals of society. Through its Limelight Department, the Salvation Army proved to be more effective than the others in attempting a remedy. The population of Australia was approaching three and a half million and Melbourne was the largest city. So intense was the desire of a section of the community for social propriety that a new word ''wowser'' was invented by the journalist John Norton and became common currency. It described a puritanical enthusiast, a person of any denomination, usually a teetotaller, who wanted everyone to adopt abstemious standards.

At a time when the middle and upper classes in America, Europe and Britain regarded the cinema as entertainment fit only for their social inferiors, the most vigorous developments in Australian film production were being aimed at moral reform. Chief responsibility for the Salvation Army's faith in this new medium was Major Joseph Perry. Born in England and trained at

10

Dunedin in New Zealand, Perry had been placed in charge of the Limelight Department in 1892. From his earliest use of glass slides projected by magic lantern, Perry approached the task with a mixture of evangelical fervour and showbusiness acumen. The development of the magic lantern had reached its peak by the late nineteenth century; brilliant limelights could throw bright, sharp images across the largest hall. Lanterns could also produce a whole range of optical effects including simple animation by means of successive overlapping slides. Combined with words and music, they became a powerful means of increasing the Salvation Army's public impact, and the work of the Limelight Department was able to attract a popular following to religion without deviating from the intended aim of salvation.

In August 1896, Perry had attended Carl Hertz's first cinematograph screening in Melbourne. He sensed that, if used in conjunction with magic lantern slides, it could be unrivalled in its power to attract large congregations. His Commandant from 1896 onwards, General Herbert Booth, backed Perry and in early 1897 he bought a Lumière machine and a collection of films. Booth, the son of the Salvation Army's founder, was anxious to enlarge the scope and influence of the Limelight Department, and under his patronage it expanded in three years from one man with a single projector to a staff of four officers using three lanterns, three Cinématographes, six phonographs and three graphophones — an early type of gramophone. Booth expressed his own belief in the role to be played by the Cinématographe by stating in the Salvation Army's own publication, *War Cry*, that he had seen "at a glance that the living pictures, worked in conjunction with life-model slides would provide a combination unfailing in its power of connecting narrative".[15]

When audiences began to tire of the repetition of the Lumière subjects, Booth and Perry decided to make their own films about Salvation Army activities. An attic studio and laboratory were established at the back of the headquarters in Bourke Street and by August 1897 a number of short films were in production. Part of the intention was to seek public financial support for the expansion of social work and the films being made to promote it. Under the collective title of **Our Social Triumphs** these first Salvation Army films were premiered at the Melbourne Temple in May 1898, accompanied by lantern slides, graphophone records and hearty hymn singing from the congregation. The majority of the short films making up the programme were straightforward documentary items: one showed a Congress march and another women cadets selling copies of *War Cry*. At least one of them, however, was dramatised, including elements of enactment within a rudimentary narrative framework. In it a hungry man is seen stealing bread and then being arrested and imprisoned. On his release he is met by social workers from the organisation's Prison Gate Brigade.

Perry and Booth soon realised that story films could best convey their message and new strips of film were added later in 1898. When they took **Our Social Triumphs** to New Zealand in December, a well-received episode showed one of Mrs Booth's Slums Sisters, yet another division of the Salvation Army, taking an "unfortunate woman" into protective charge.

Others portrayed examples of the Army's Rescue and Maternity operations including — according to a Wellington report — one "in which a young girl was saved from the clutches of a villain by one lassie, while another was seen 'dealing it out' to the rogue. The audience waxed so enthusiastic that it had to be repeated."[16]

After 1898, new films formed part of Mrs Booth's **Social Lecture** which was presented all over Australia with considerable impact. This included a sequence showing an unmarried mother being rescued by an Army lassie after attempting suicide from the banks of Melbourne's Yarra River. During 1899 the **Social Lecture** grossed more than £1500 and by the turn of the century had established the Salvation Army as the most important Australian film producer. Major Joseph Perry, as the officer-in-charge of the Limelight Department, was responsible for buying new equipment for processing and printing, as well as the purchase and exchange of suitable films from local exhibitors. In the twelve months from the end of 1898 he was busy planning a new set of short films on a Biblical theme, together with the production of gazettes.

The Department's productions of 1898-99 laid important groundwork for the longer films which were to follow. Late in 1899 Perry's team produced thirteen shorts: Biblical subjects each of about seventy-five feet (just under three minutes). Known collectively as **The Passion Films,** they illustrated the life and death of Jesus.[17] Perry was able to state in January 1900 with justifiable pride:

We enjoy a monopoly of the business and manufacture of films for all the colonies. Only the other day I took a photo of the Victorian contingent in the morning, developed and printed a film 100 feet long, and six hours later it was shown before a crowded hall amidst great applause.[18]

The Salvation Army's initiative and its success with short dramatised films was outstanding for a country so remote from the cinema of Europe and America. The story films were particularly novel in Australia, where other producers with commercial rather than evangelical motives concentrated on actuality — scenics and gazettes.

It is possible that before embarking on **Soldiers of the Cross** in June 1900, Perry and Booth had seen, or at least heard of, the New York film version of **The Passion Play**.[19] In any case, they were now fully convinced of the propaganda potential of film and were beginning to recognise the need for a presentation that would exceed the scale of their previous efforts. At this time religious melodrama was drawing packed houses to the theatres with the staging of epics such as *The Christian* and *The Sign of the Cross*. In 1898 the latter was playing its 250th performance in Melbourne.

Taking this as their cue, and long before the Biblical spectaculars of the Italian and American cinema, Booth and Perry devised a lengthy religious epic. It was to be an episodic story using glass slides, motion pictures, hymns and a spoken commentary, to tell the story of the early Christian martyrs.[20] Unlike the mixed educational, evangelistic and entertainment motives of the

Department's earlier films, **Soldiers of the Cross** was planned from the start as propaganda. The general intention was still to preach the glories of salvation, but Commandant Booth announced that the prime purpose was to recruit two hundred young male and female cadets for the newly opened Commonwealth Training College in Melbourne. But the production was to have equal significance as a showbusiness event. Two hundred elaborately conceived slides were integrated with thirteen rolls of film running for about one minute each. The two were not intended to present a continuous narrative; the interspersed film segments were used either to repeat in motion the pictures first presented by the slides, or the slides were given added impact by following the film in the style of a "freeze" frame.[21] Most of them were location photographs, hand-tinted and where necessary touched-up with spectacular effects not within the scope of the motion picture. The visual elements were underscored by the singing of hymns, the integration of classical and original music, and the resonant, crowd-stirring oratory of Booth. One of the hymns, which began, "Am I a soldier of the Cross?" gave the event its title.

Most of the film and many of the lantern slides were photographed on tennis courts at the Salvation Army Girls' Home in the suburb of Murrumbeena. Perry and Booth painstakingly researched the records of early Christian times to authenticate the settings and costumes. Large painted backdrops were strung on wires around the courts and a contingent of Salvationists was dressed up as Romans and martyrs. For the Colosseum scenes, Perry integrated real lions from a circus with papier-mâché beasts operated by children. His son Reg, then aged ten, played the hindquarters of one of these with his brother Orrie as the front half. Reg Perry recalled details of the production:

Many incidents were portrayed, one being the Christians jumping into a burning lime pit rather than recant. Dressed in togas and positioned on a raised staging, they were prodded by cardboard spears until they jumped — onto a mattress five feet below where a smoke bomb burned. Also included were the life of Saint Peter and his martyrdom, and Saint Paul brooding over the stoning of Stephen. The lecture lasted for (nearly) two and a half hours and caused an immediate sensation. Nothing like it had been seen before — Christ writhing on the Cross, Stephen pounded to death with stones, and women going to their death in preference to the worship of Diana.[22]

The premiere was held on 13 September 1900 at the Melbourne Town Hall before an audience of four thousand guests. According to the Salvation Army publicity, the capacity crowd, which had defied threatening skies to attend, was fully absorbed, reacting with "involuntary interjections, moans of pity, sighs of relief".[23] The film and slides were projected with a clarity and integration which astonished most observers.

Soldiers of the Cross was an evangelist's compendium of horrors guaranteed to jolt audiences into an awareness of terrible suffering for the sake of Christianity. On the screen Perry thrilled his viewers with maulings at the Colosseum; there were crucifixions, beheadings, savage hackings and burnings at the stake, burnings in the limepit, and the spectacle of human torches in Nero's garden. Journalists attended the premiere in force, attracted by the promise of "soul-stirring stories of the martyrs, illustrated by the most beautiful living pictures by kinematograph and limelight and never before witnessed in this or any other country".[24] The *Argus* reported:

Bold as the lecture was in conception, the illustrations were even more daring. Their preparation reflected the highest credit upon Commandant Booth and his assistants.[25]

The *Age* stated:

To have some of the most tragic episodes of Christian history carried out in all savage but soul-stirring realism is an accomplishment essentially of today. It is a thrilling, novel and instructive lecture.[26]

The Salvation Army's own publication, *War Cry*, gave the liveliest comment on the presentation:

It was a knock-out. Possibly "knock-out" is slang, but it is rapidly becoming good English, and we like to be ahead of the times.

War Cry pointed out that more than the skilful handling of the display, the true success of the event lay in its ability to attract a full house in the face of the "bold announcement by the Commandant, that it was not his aim to entertain, but to rouse religious thought; that the object was not cash, but to recruit cadets for Christ". The objective, they claimed, had been amply achieved.[27]

Today, without the film segments available, the praise for **Soldiers of the Cross** as it appeared in 1900 cannot properly be evaluated. All that remains of the "knock-out" programme are the two hundred lantern slides and Robert McAnally's original score, passed for safe keeping to the National Film Archive in the 1950s. The film sequences left Australia in 1902 with Herbert Booth who resigned from the Salvation Army after a policy disagreement and became an independent evangelist in the United States. A print of the film was rumoured to have been stored at the Temple of the Salvation Army in London before its destruction by bombing during the Second World War.

The spread of cinema

Largely because of the appeal of the gazettes, cinema in Australia had reclaimed some of its appeal by 1900. But short films lacked the substance and continuity to warrant permanent picture theatres. Live theatres and halls, usually seating no more than three hundred people, were used for short seasons of films by entrepreneurs like J. C. Williamson, James McMahon and Harry Rickards but there was little sign yet of an exhibition industry. Most screenings were still part of vaudeville shows, although occasionally they made an appearance as part of more allegedly uplifting entertainments such as recitations and lectures. The public had little opportunity to experience film as a separate entity; the music hall, the concert platform and drama remained the principal forms of mass entertainment. In the United States, where most film screenings were part of vaudeville entertainment also, the first permanent auditorium for cinema did not open until 1902.

By then Australia's principal cities, Sydney and Melbourne, had a combined population of just over one million. Added to the population of other cities, country centres and New Zealand, this audience supported a theatre circuit lucrative enough to attract many of the world's leading performers. Strong cultural and political ties with Britain brought a constant flow of melodrama and musical comedies, most of which had earned the right to appear in Australia by earlier success on the London stage. Complete Italian opera companies made tours, Melbourne's own Nellie Melba returned in triumph for a concert tour, and large audiences were lured by other leading singers and instrumentalists. The managements of J. C. Williamson's, George Musgrove and the Tait brothers vied with each other for imported attractions, and also staged a wide variety of local plays spanning popular melodrama, comedy and domestic drama. Popular entertainment was big business everywhere and film was about to make an impression as an attraction in its own right.

With the supply of films from France, England and the United States increasing after 1904, a stable exhibition industry began to appear. There was a world-wide burgeoning of permanent cinemas in 1905, and substantial growth in Australia during 1905-6 was heralded by the appearance of four exhibitors who were soon to achieve prominence — Charles Cozens Spencer, Johnson and Gibson, and T. J. West. The London-born Spencer began his cinema career by touring with films through Canada, New Zealand and Australia in 1905. In Australia his two-hour programme, with admission prices ranging between sixpence and two shillings, was accompanied by a "full orchestra and mechanical effects". T. J. West, a Scotsman who by 1910 controlled one of the biggest cinema circuits in Britain, opened Australia's first purpose-built cinema soon after his arrival in early 1906. From 1905, Millard Johnson and William Gibson, partners in a pharmacy business at St Kilda, Melbourne, progressed from screenings at St Kilda Beach and various open air concerts, to a regular circuit of city and suburban halls. After continued success, they established an exchange from which they hired projectors and films, most of them imported. As chemists they moved into photography and processing with comparative ease, supplementing the imports with local short films and the development of their business soon incorporated a projection staff and repair service. Among their rivals in exhibition were those who, like John H. Tait, had hired films from them.

Australians in the country areas, often huge distances from the cities, were also introduced to film during this rapid growth in exhibition. The emergence of the touring showman was to be the link in this consolidation. His one-night stands usually began with a parade through the town's main street to attract attention and then, as darkness fell, the roar of a tractor harnessed to his lighting generator shattered the customary rural calm and a searchlight probed the night sky. As the flickering films reached the screen, a lecturer would brave the audiences's cheering and catcalls to explain the events to be shown. The repertoire might include a patriotic item like Queen Victoria's funeral, news about the end of the war in South Africa, the indispensable scenics and a dramatic or comedy turn derived from the theatre. The term "moving pictures" took on a double meaning as the travelling picture showmen would sometimes play six towns a week, and their publicity gimmicks — the parade and the searchlight — symbolised the coming of a new awareness, a breaking down of the old isolation, a moulding of opinions and, above all, an irresistible new form of entertainment.

The Story of the Kelly Gang

The five Tait brothers — Charles, Edward, Frank, Nevin and John — were best known for their work as theatrical entrepreneurs. From concert promotion, they expanded into theatrical enterprises, forming J. and N. Tait as a theatre management company before a merger with their main rival, J. C. Williamson, in 1920. But like Carl Hertz as a magician and Joseph Perry as a salvationist, the brothers soon recognised the value of cinema exhibition. Like Perry, they saw the need to supplement inadequate film supplies with their own production and their initiative in 1906 led to the first boom period of Australian feature production.

In March 1904 the Taits made their first substantial move into film exhibition by dividing one of the programmes they ran at the Melbourne Town Hall between imported newsreels and a series of gramophone recordings by Nellie Melba. The following year they lost money as exhibitors in Sydney but were back in Melbourne by early 1906; there they had a highly successful run with the documentary **Living London** and made their initial fortune. It began an association with film that would last for more than a decade.

As early as 1900 the Taits had noticed the impact of cinema with **Soldiers of the Cross**. In August 1905 they saw the huge success being enjoyed by the rival exhibitor Cozens Spencer with his screenings of Edwin S. Porter's **The Great Train Robbery**, re-titled for Australia as **The Great American Train Robbery**. It confirmed their belief in the potential of the narrative film and they realised the market was virtually untapped. The handful of dramatised Australian films made up to this time extended little beyond the Salvation Army's contributions and background segments integrated into such plays as *Besieged at Port Arthur*. (Performed in 1906, the play dealt with the Russo-Japanese War.) Only one narrative film is known to have been made in Australia during 1906 — the Taits' production of **The Story of the Kelly Gang**.

The background to this project was indigenous melodrama. One of several contradictory sources states that it was at the suggestion of Sam Crews, an old-time theatrical personality, that Charles and John Tait began in late 1906 to prepare a film version of the long-running play *The Kelly Gang*.

It celebrated the exploits of the horse thief and bank robber Ned Kelly, who twenty years earlier had been hanged for murder at the end of a sensational two-year hunt. Following Kelly's dramatic capture by siege at Glenrowan in the north-east of Victoria, his trial and subsequent execution in Melbourne Gaol were accompanied by public attention of the kind usually reserved for royalty, and he acquired the reputation of an antipodean Robin Hood.

The national predilection to favour the underdog certainly added to that image. In 1906 the *Kelly Gang* play, one of a number written about the outlaws, was still drawing large audiences on its tour through country centres. Charles and John Tait planned to raise most of the money for the screen version themselves but they approached Millard Johnson and William Gibson to provide technical work and share financially in the venture.

Every weekend for a period of several months the Tait family, together with Johnson, Gibson, a cast and a small crew, travelled to the Chartersville Estate at Heidelberg near Melbourne to re-enact the bushranger's most celebrated exploits. Direction was by Charles Tait, the eldest of the family and in later years referred to as "the main counsellor of his brothers and the power behind the Tait combine".[28] Camerawork was by Millard Johnson; technical supervision, laboratory processing and printing were handled by William Gibson. Ned Kelly was played initially by a Canadian stunt actor from the Bland Holt company. After his departure from Melbourne for other work he was replaced by an understudy, his face concealed by judicious camera placement or hidden by Kelly's steel helmet. Members of the Tait family took most of the remaining roles, including John Tait as the schoolmaster, and Mrs Charles Tait as Kate Kelly, Ned's sister.

Unlike most producers of Australian features between 1906 and the First World War, the Taits took the trouble to distinguish between stage artifice and the capacity of film for naturalism. This approach began with research into original records and was consolidated on camera by the use of outdoor locations, horses, guns, trains, and the burning of a building for the climax. Only small sections of the film survive to indicate the degree of editorial sophistication but the published synopsis indicates that the editing, by the standards of the period, was complex. During the first Adelaide season a journalist commented that the synopsis — provided in booklet form at the screenings — required careful study if the continuity of the film were not to become confusing.[29]

During its profitable country trial run **The Story of the Kelly Gang** was projected in silence, but for the Melbourne premiere on 26 December 1906 live sound effects were added for realism. They included blank cartridges as gunshots, pebbles shaken for rain, metal sheets wobbled for wind, and coconut shells beaten together to simulate hoofbeats. By mid-January 1907 a lecturer was explaining each scene from the side of the screen, following a pattern of presentation frequent from the earliest days of exhibition.

It is probable that more scenes were added between its Victorian and subsequent interstate screenings. The version shown during the first

Melbourne season was advertised as being 4000 feet, more than an hour long.[30] The total cost of around £1000 was recouped during the week's trial run in the country, and from the very first screenings the audience response was enthusiastic. They sympathised with Kate when she refused to embrace the trooper in return for her brother's safety; they cheered the gang when they doffed their hats over a constable they had killed and hissed the schoolmaster when he foiled the Kellys' plan to wreck a train. The film ran simultaneously in Melbourne, Adelaide and Sydney for a month and soon played all over Australia with five separate companies touring from March 1907. From the middle of that year it was screened in New Zealand, throughout Britain, and in the home country of Ned Kelly's emancipist father, Ireland.

The Story of the Kelly Gang aroused much critical and social comment. The *Age* declared:

The story provides sufficient sensationalism to satisfy the most exacting, and the whole of the miscreants' lawless career is covered from the first encounter between Constable Fitzgerald and the Kelly women to the fall of Ned Kelly outside the hotel at Glenrowan. Messrs J. and N. Tait, the promoters, had promised that no expense would be spared in securing an imposing combination of cinematograph films and by frequent outbursts of applause, the audience indicated that the quality of the entertainment had not been overstated.[31]

The *Bulletin* complained:

There is a deal too much racket about the show — sometimes you can't see the picture for the noise of horses, trains, gunshot and wild cries; but, all the same, it is the sort of bellowdrama that the lower orders crave for, and two-thirds of Australia will want to see it — the two-thirds that believe Ned Kelly was a greater man than George Washington.[32]

The Taits had scored with the old showbusiness maxim that you don't fail by underestimating audience taste. However, as the *Bulletin* reported, the social consequences might be serious:

The arrival in Ballarat of the Kelly Gang pictures was followed by the uprising of five Ballarat kids not yet in their teens who broke into a photo studio and stole a cash box containing £8.10s ... Next day two of them armed with loaded revolvers, bailed up some school kids in the best Kelly style while the other comic opera desperados went through the kids' pockets. The Children's Court will consequently have before it five infant burglars who are sorry they did it. Nobody has suggested arresting the Kelly Gang pictures for inciting a felony.[33]

In fact, the authorities did the next best thing. The film's alleged tendency to corrupt resulted in the first official censorship of Australian cinema. In April 1907, after The Story of the Kelly Gang was advertised to be shown in the town of Benalla, a scene of the Gang's operations, a firm of solicitors attempted to prevent the screening on the grounds that it could injure the reputations of people still living in the district. The result was a ban by the Victorian Chief Secretary on showings in Benalla and Wangaratta (another Kelly haunt) under a section of the Theatres Act of 1890 which, not surprisingly, made no reference to film shows. When re-released in revised form during 1912 the film was banned from the entire State of Victoria.

The Story of the Kelly Gang is important historically because of its length. In 1906 film exhibitors in the United States would have regarded its five reels as unthinkable. Even as late as 1909 the powerful Motion Picture Patents Company of America was forcing one of its member companies, Vitagraph, to release the five-reel Life of Moses one reel at a time; and in 1911 similar pressure caused the two-reel film His Trust, directed for Biograph by D. W. Griffith, to be released as two separate films running for twelve minutes. But by 1911 Italian films were running to five reels, and their durations grew even longer the following year. In 1913 French producers were making films that ran for eight or even twelve reels. The American distributors' resistance began to break down after the success of Adolph Zukor's well-publicised importation of the four-reel French production, Queen Elizabeth, during 1912. By 1913, when American audiences responded enthusiastically to the nine-reel Italian epic Quo Vadis?, five-reel features had been entering production in the United States for a year.

At least ten prints were made for the first release of The Story of the Kelly Gang and one was sent to Britain. However, all known copies had disappeared by the time of the Second World War. But with a growing interest in Australia's cinema history many years later, portions of the film were discovered in two private collections in the late 1970s and, although the brief sections are probably rejected takes or editing offcuts which were never seen in release form, they allow some judgement on the filmic style of the production.

Contemporary audiences no doubt expected a re-enactment of the Gang's exploits rather than a stylised or romantic interpretation. Actuality and dramatised films shot on location had already conditioned the audiences to a level of realism much in advance of live theatre and The Story of the Kelly Gang was intended to outclass its stage rivals. If several exaggerated performances are discounted, the impression given by the surviving fragments is that of period authenticity. The details of setting, costume and props convincingly evoke the times. The producers adopt a cinematic rather than a stage-based approach, with the action filmed in such a way as to be suitable for editing from a number of perspectives.[34]

The formation of an industry

Millard Johnson and William Gibson were becoming major figures within the film trade — distribution and exhibition — and were also involved in production work within the growing Australian film community. The Limelight Department of the Salvation Army had remained pre-eminent in all aspects of the business from the turn of the century until its closure in 1910.[35] Other producers included Franklyn Barrett, who made narrative shorts in

New Zealand before concentrating on scenics and newsreels both in New Zealand and Australia[36]; Harry Krischock; Albert J. ("Mons") Perier, who for the Sydney firm of Baker and Rouse combined with the Limelight Department to cover the Federation celebrations in 1901; and the anthropologist Professor Baldwin Spencer, whose unique films of tribal Aboriginals have survived in their entirety.[37] Another person attracted early to the new medium was the poet and short story writer Henry Lawson. In 1898 Lawson wrote a "scenario" in short story form, *The Australian Cinematograph*. By film standards of the time it was a revolutionary blending of narrative and ballad, containing literary equivalents of the fade, dissolve, and complex shifts in time. The story's title, its detailed visual descriptions and use of the present tense, leave the modern-day reader with little doubt that the tale of death among inland drovers was intended for cinematic interpretation. Lawson's "scenario", although published, was ignored by producers until the early 1970s when the Commonwealth Film Unit produced the story as **Where Dead Men Lie.**

Although the pace of film activity was picking up during the first decade of the new century, it was still possible for a visiting cameraman to travel the entire length of the continent, including the main cities, and hear little of other filmmakers' activities. Norman Dawn, for example, who first came to Australia as a freelance newsreel cameraman and returned in 1926 to direct the epic **For the Term of his Natural Life,** recalled having met no Australian engaged in film, or even hearing of much film activity, during a visit of several months in 1908.[38]

By the end of 1906, however, a number of key achievements favoured the growth of a healthy Australian production industry. Film had already been integrated prominently and with the great success into **Soldiers of the Cross.** That presentation partly encouraged the Taits to make **The Story of the Kelly Gang** and the enthusiastic response to an uninterrupted film of an hour's duration helped to create a favourable climate for further feature production. The regular production of lengthy features from 1906 to 1911 predated that of almost every other nation, and on the local market gave Australian films at least one advantage over competitors from abroad.

A large increase in capital city exhibition outlets occurred in 1907 when shows consisting entirely of films were running at permanent locations in Sydney and Melbourne. Similarly, distributors were finding that business was good enough to establish companies that did nothing else but hire out films. The growth of domestic production and distribution over the next few years gave little hint of the differences that would grow between the two activities. The disadvantages of a small population and geographical isolation were offset by large urban concentrations and a protective insulation from other film producing nations. If an Australian producer wanted to export his product, silent film had a universal appeal. For acceptance in the local market all he had to do was select and produce story themes that could compete with the infrequent imports.

2

The growth of an industry
1907 – 13

International developments

By 1910 film production was continuous in at least fourteen countries. In America, film "factories" turning out an ever-expanding amount of product, were increasingly linked to distribution and exhibition interests. Boosted by the popularity of Nickelodeons, a generic term for the first movie theatres, the leading American companies built their centres in New York, Philadelphia and Chicago. Each studio produced an average of two titles a week and their films ran for one reel — anything between five and fifteen minutes. Many short films now owed less to the theatre and more to story ideas developed expressly for the screen. Exclusively film actors, or stars, emerged together with a new generation of directors whose skills were those of the film medium rather than the stage. One such director was D. W. Griffith, who in 1908 began working at the Biograph studios in New York and within five years had produced over five hundred films. Australia's only known narrative contender in 1908 was **For the Term of his Natural Life** and its subject was drawn from a novel by way of the stage.

The years 1911 to 1913 saw a worldwide transition in narrative film construction or "screen grammar". The uninterrupted frontal stage perspective of early film dramas was replaced by variation in angles to enhance tempo and involvement; acting was transformed from melodrama to a realism that invited the close-up. Judging by the few narrative films that survive from pre-war Australian cinema, it can be assumed that the work of only one or two directors — and only Raymond Longford for certain — was keeping pace with the developments in American filmmaking. Australia was not alone in this. For well over a decade, the English cinema, like the Australian, drew its inspiration and many of its techniques from the theatre. After 1910 the inventive pre-eminence of French cinema was exhausted and in Italy nothing matched **Cabiria** (1913) for several decades as the climax of all its costume spectacles.

In spite of the United States' early lead in quality and technique, a

21

torrent of American films into Australia was not immediate. Pre-war American films made up less than half of the total imported, and Australian filmmakers had seven years of local market freedom between **The Story of the Kelly Gang** of 1906 and the consolidation of outlets which began in 1913.

The growth of exhibition and distribution

The exhibition business in Australia boomed, and organised distribution (film hiring) was not far behind. In Melbourne and Sydney, the year 1907 saw exhibitors begin to show films on a regular basis at the one theatre. A number of full-time film distribution companies were also formed in that year. The group of show business entrepreneurs soon to make their presence felt in exhibition circles included Cozens Spencer and his wife Eleanor, J. D. Williams, T. J. West, the Taits, and Hoyts Pictures. Spencer, West and Williams were to do more than anyone else to revolutionise exhibition. They and their rivals bid for the latest pictures from overseas and often screened the same film. Some also backed local production and built studios.

Australia's first notable exhibitor was T. J. West, a Scotsman who in March 1906 began his Australian operations in Sydney by combining a film show with the musical troupe, "the Brescians". By April he was running the show simultaneously at two theatres (swapping the first and second halves at interval) and incorporating locally-shot short film items like **The Audience Leaving the Theatre Royal** and **Fire in Clarence Street**. West then moved to Melbourne, screening in several theatres between May and October, and shooting what was probably the first film of a Melbourne football match. From October 1906 until late 1907, he returned for a further season in Sydney, and then embarked on an extensive tour of New Zealand and all of Australia. In December 1907, he felt sufficiently assured of his capital city markets to purchase the leases of the Sydney Glaciarium and Melbourne Olympia. As West was a key figure, this was considered a major decision, and it helped to bring about the move to permanent cinemas, intensified in the years 1910 and 1911. By 1910 West controlled fourteen permanent cinemas throughout Australia and was estimated to have a nightly audience of 20 000 patrons. One of his cinemas in Melbourne seated 5000, and was claimed to be "the largest picture hall in the world".[1]

In 1909 Pathé Frères became the first overseas company to establish a distribution agency in Australia. For the previous six years the Frenchman Charles Pathé, the firm's founder, had been the leading figure in the world's film industry and was the first to control an organisation which linked production, distribution and exhibition interests. In Australia, Pathé Frères was later joined by West, under whose auspices the business was continued. By late 1912 the main distributors were Spencer, West, Williams and Amalgamated Pictures — the latter comprising a combination of J. and N. Tait with Johnson and Gibson. The linking of the distribution and exhibition interests of these companies brought a firmer assurance of film supply to their outlets, but it also posed a potential threat to the Australian producer.

As the supply of films increased and a weekly change of programme could be assured, the touring shows in hired halls gave way to permanent venues. Commenting on the proliferation of cinemas, the *Lone Hand* wrote:

The theatres are all placed where there is a large and increasing foot passing traffic. The gay exterior, the light and the music, all attract the people. The splendid vestibule, with marble steps, marble ticketboxes, splendid doors, and the vast marble staircases, with railings of burnished brass make an alluring bait. And when all this splendour is available for sixpence and threepence the places are naturally rushed. It's worth a shilling an hour just to sit there and rest, but when the world's best photoplays are laid on the value received for the money becomes overwhelming.[2]

The most striking of the early cinemas was The Crystal Palace built by J. D. Williams and opened in June 1912, and later reduced in size and re-named The Century. The *Bulletin* noted that:

The Crystal Palace is easily the handsomest photoplay theatre in Sydney, and the plays are shown by a greatly improved process. This theatre is a symphony in dark green with pictures painted on the walls, and framed heavily in old gold.[3]

In 1909 J. D. Williams opened Australia's first continuous cinema at the Colonial Theatre, Sydney. Admission was 3d and the show ran non-stop from 11.00 a.m. to 11.00 p.m. Williams also introduced special matinées and a twice-weekly change of programme, and from five luxurious cinemas in Sydney, he expanded throughout Australia and New Zealand. Very quickly he became a major trade figure alongside Cozens Spencer and T. J. West. In mid-1912 he established a newsreel, **Williams Weekly**, with Bert Cross and Bert Ive as cameramen. From 1910, Williams's innovations in exhibition were eagerly absorbed by a junior employee, Stuart F. Doyle. In the next thirty years, both men were to become international figures in the film industry. The year 1911 saw over a hundred permanent and temporary picture shows in Sydney employing about 2000 people, and the following year twenty-five permanent cinemas were listed in Melbourne with a combined seating capacity of 50 000. By 1913 in Melbourne 65 000 people were attending city and suburban cinemas on a Saturday night, in addition to the 14 000 who went regularly to stage productions.[4]

Moving pictures tapped a new, egalitarian market. As early as 1909, the *Bulletin* observed that "Pictures have become a habit, not to say a vice, and there are people going around who would sooner miss two meals a week than their regular 'picture night'."[5] A typical programme included five or six short non-fiction films made up of travelogues and "industrials", a couple of one-reel comedies, a newsreel, a story feature (two reels maximum) and another comedy to end the two-hour show. The programmes developed to include the screening of two short dramatic films, two comedies, a "topical" and main feature. None exceeded two reels.

By 1910 the Australian production of short films was flourishing, with newsreel coverage of local events especially popular. But audiences were tiring of the "rag-bag" makeup of cinema programmes. Remembering the success of productions like **The Story of the Kelly Gang**, they began to demand longer films than the average "two-reelers". Public interest after 1906 encouraged local producers to embark on making five or six-reel films, running for eighty to ninety minutes.

Production's golden age

Before the outbreak of the First World War came the few golden years of Australian production. The number of local features released in 1911 and 1912 reached a level unequalled until 1975, a peak year in the much later revival. The year 1911 saw the most prolific output, with no less than fifty-two narrative fiction films making their appearance. Their length (shot and projected at different speeds) varied between 1000 and 5000 feet.

It was a brief moment sandwiched between the freewheeling days of open market competition and the closed shop control of what would soon be known as "the combine". There was a ready audience for Australian outdoor subjects, especially the colonial tales that had captured the public's attention on stage. The main companies, in order of output, were the Australian Photo-Play Company, Spencer's Pictures, Australian Life Biograph, Lincoln-Cass Films, Amalgamated Pictures and West's Pictures. The leading directors were Raymond Longford, Franklyn Barrett, John F. Gavin, W. J. Lincoln, Alfred Rolfe and Gaston Mervale. Between them, these six directors were responsible for at least thirty-four narrative films released in 1911.

Before the existence of the major film exchanges, films could often be financed even before production began by sales to local exhibitors. Half the main producers were also their own exhibitors, striving to supply their own programmes. Shooting schedules varied but most films were shot in six to seven days. Properties, players and production costs were relatively inexpensive and it was not unusual for a popular film to recoup its cost within a few weeks.

Favourable scenic and climatic conditions created a precedent for location shooting. This could bring authenticity to even the most stage-bound material, and suited the early dominance of convict and bushranging subjects. Avoiding the expense and inconvenience of studio work, most "interiors" were filmed out-of-doors, on sets built under muslin cloth stretched out to diffuse the sunlight.

A crew usually consisted of no more than the director, a camera-man and one assistant. The cameraman would process, print and edit the film in a home laboratory. Prominent cameramen in the years before the First World War included the brothers Ernest, Arthur and Tasman Higgins, Franklyn Barrett, Orrie and Reg Perry, Lacey Percival, George Young, Alf J. Moulton, Alfred Segerberg, A. J. Perier, Maurice Bertel and Bert Ive. They began and would usually continue as all-rounders — photographing, processing and screening. If not involved in a feature production, they might film newsreels or tour country towns shooting small sponsored films. It was little wonder that such continuity of work allowed them to develop their craft to a level that few directors were able to share, though the director-cameraman Franklyn Barrett was an exception.

Popular screen actors were scarce. The first Australian "star" was Lottie Lyell, who until the early 1920s appeared in nearly all the features directed by Raymond Longford. Small budgets prevented big stage names from being lured to the screen unless it was to repeat a theatrical triumph for wider exhibition. The close link between film and theatre was reinforced by stock companies filming their own repertoires.

Early features

In 1911 only one-third of the population of Australia lived in cities. With bush subjects close to the lives and hearts of most Australians, the outback was to remain dominant on Australian film screens for almost half a century. It was typical of the industry that after the nation's official birth at Federation in 1901, the first stories chosen were those of the early colonial years.

Australia's second feature, **Eureka Stockade** (1907), portrayed the 1854 Ballarat goldfields rebellion that crystallised early hopes of Australian nationalism. The film was produced, directed and photographed by George and Arthur Cornwall, whose budget of £1500 came from Melbourne businessmen. The directors aimed at historical accuracy, and their publicity worked hard to build up the audience's expectations:

A picture story of the most memorable event in Australian history; throbbing with the pulse and memories of the Roaring Fifties. Goldseekers leaving London ... On the road to the diggings ... the gold rush ... lost in the bush ... the gold robbery ... diggers chained to logs ... building the Eureka Stockade ... Murder at Bentley's Hotel ... and storming Eureka Stockade ... the unveiling of Lalor's Monument with a grand Military March Past. Undoubtedly, the most realistic combination of pictures ever produced in the annals of animated art.

The *Bulletin* reviewer commented: "However short of the possible the Eureka scenes might be, they stirred me to the core ... What tremendous possibilities there are in the biograph!"[6] From 19 October, **Eureka Stockade** had a premiere season of two weeks at Melbourne's Athenaeum Hall. Although the Eureka Stockade subject would be revived by at least three later filmmakers, the 1907 version failed to excite as much interest as its Kelly Gang predecessor had the year before.

The subjects of the third and fourth Australian features were also to be favoured by filmmakers for decades to come. **Robbery Under Arms** (1907) and **For the Term of his Natural Life** (1908) were direct adaptations from the novels by Rolf Boldrewood and Marcus Clarke, from which Alfred Dampier had prospered by presenting stage versions in the early 1890s. His actress daughter Lillian and her husband, the actor-director Alfred Rolfe, were not far behind with a screen rendition of the Dampier version in 1911. Production of the 1907 and 1908 films was by Charles McMahon, the theatrical entrepreneur who had been involved with film exhibition since its beginnings in 1896. McMahon's co-producer on **The Term** was E. J. Carroll, who had entered the film business by touring with **The Story of the Kelly Gang** and was later to play a substantial role in Australian exhibition and production. The budget of the 5000-feet **Robbery Under Arms** was £1000, and **The Term**, with its sprawling plot admirably condensed into 2000 feet, cost an immense £7000. Audiences, which regarded the stories as national legends, responded enthusiastically to the elaborate scale of the films. McMahon's **Robbery** was successfully shown for the next three years, and **The Term** until the First World War. During **Robbery**'s premiere season in Sydney, the Oxford Theatre management exuberantly claimed its ticket office "was almost wrecked by patrons in a remarkable crush".

The pioneering initiative of the Salvation Army's Limelight Department continued in 1909 with its production of two 5000-feet features, **Heroes of the Cross** and **The Scottish Covenantors**. The Army's interest in film had intensified after 1905, as it produced an increasing number of non-fiction films, and expanded distribution. By 1908 it had Limelight branches in Sydney, Adelaide, Brisbane and Christchurch, New Zealand. The great event of that year was the filming of the arrival of the American Great White Fleet, consisting of sixteen warships, in Auckland, Sydney and Melbourne. February 1909 brought the completion of the Department's elaborate new studio in Khartoum Street, Malvern, a Melbourne suburb.[7] It was Australia's first film studio to be specially constructed and was glass-walled and glass-roofed for natural lighting, had adjoining dressing rooms, dark rooms, a carpenter's shop and props storage area.

Both **Heroes of the Cross** and **The Scottish Covenantors** were truly feature films, although neither was to exert as much impact as **Soldiers of the Cross** had in 1900. The fact that screenings were scarce and only *War Cry* reviewed the first does imply they were no match for their secular contemporaries. With script, direction and camerawork by Joseph Perry, **Heroes of the Cross** contained events almost identical to those of **Soldiers**. A limited number of slides seems to have been interspersed, but the greater part of the film narrative was unbroken. **The Scottish Covenantors** continued the theme of martyrdom with the hunting down and murder of Christians by Cromwell's Roundheads in the seventeenth century. The film appeared in New Zealand in late 1909 but there is no record of an Australian release.

Early in 1910 the Limelight Department was abruptly closed down. Commissioner Jason Hay and others at the Melbourne headquarters of the Salvation Army were, it seems, concerned that the bulk of films being distributed were likely to corrupt rather than save souls. At the same time the regular screening of films in Salvation Army halls was discontinued. Joseph Perry resigned from the Salvation Army, working for a time with Johnson and Gibson, and subsequently devoting himself to film distribution, mainly in the Dutch East Indies, until his retirement in 1930. He died in 1943. Johnson and Gibson also employed two of Joseph Perry's sons, Orrie and Reg, as cameramen. In 1910 Orrie Perry was to photograph an adaptation of Bert Bailey and Edmund Duggan's play *The Squatter's Daughter.*

On stage, *The Squatter's Daughter* had enjoyed commercial success since 1905. The story of two sheep stations linked by rivalry and romance, integrated the exploits of the courageous daughter with those of the bushranger Ben Hall. Just as audiences had revelled in the authentic backgrounds in the films of **Robbery Under Arms** and **For the Term of his Natural Life**, those familiar with *The Squatter's Daughter* on stage admired the exteriors and "real rides" of the 5400-feet feature.[8] The film's authenticity and action incorporated bushrangers' haunts at the Jenolan Caves in the Blue Mountains, a shearing match, an Aboriginal wedding, ordeal by flood, and the scaling of precipitous cliffs. The climax was the hero's wild gallop to rescue the abducted heroine. The *Bulletin* reported that the filming of **The Squatter's Daughter** would save the William Anderson Dramatic Company from having to further "shriek their way north, south, east and west", and save Bert Bailey's "clergyman's sore throat" which was by now red-raw from live performances.[9] Having once more worked from a proven source, the film became immensely popular.

Two years later saw the arrival of Gaston Méliès, probably Australia's first "visiting" maker of fiction films — a filmmaker from abroad who briefly used local settings for stories of exotic appeal before moving on. Visiting filmmakers did not arrive in Australia in significant numbers until the dying days of the indigenous industry in the 1950s, but it is appropriate that in the year 1912, when Méliès filmed in Australia, the industry suffered its first major setback with the withdrawal of at least three major producers — Australian Photo-Play, Australian Life Biograph and Amalgamated Pictures. Gaston Méliès was an older brother of the French film pioneer Georges Méliès. In September 1908, Gaston had established a production company in America on behalf of his brother. In 1912 and 1913, he toured through Tahiti, New Zealand, Australia and South-East Asia filming single reel and two-reel fiction films as well as documentaries. In addition to four non-fiction subjects, his Australian titles (all one-reelers) were: **A Buried Treasure, The Black Trackers, Gold and the Gilded Way, The Foster Brothers, The Stolen Claim, Captured by Aboriginals** and **Cast Amid Boomerang Throwers**. Nearly all were released in the United States and Britain during 1913, but there is no record of their appearance in the country that provided their backgrounds.

Spencer's pictures and Alfred Rolfe

The Life and Adventures of John Vane, the Notorious Australian Bushranger (1910) had marked the entry into feature production by the distributor and exhibitor, Cozens Spencer. Spencer, a Londoner, had entered film exhibition in Canada and first travelled to Australia with his wife in 1905. Predating J. D. Williams, he was the first to bring real showmanship to local film promotion. The *Bulletin* of 23 January 1913 dubbed him "the Cinematocrat", for Spencer was indeed the most outstanding of Australia's early film exhibitors. He fitted the description of a "movie mogul" more perfectly than any of his rivals, and eventually died a millionaire. His exchange (distribution branch office) business was the biggest in Australia, and he proudly claimed to charge the highest hiring fees. His principal cinema, the Sydney Lyceum Hall, and his exhibition techniques, were watched closely by all the other showmen.

Spencer had started his Australian exhibition career at the Lyceum Hall late in June 1905 and enjoyed success from the beginning. What was originally to be a brief season was extended to eight weeks and his drawing power, like that of T. J. West later, was consolidated by the inclusion of locally made topical items. His financial stability had been established by **The Great American Train Robbery** and at the end of August he set off on an Australian tour and travelled the continent until early 1908 with consistently good takings. Again like T. J. West, whose own touring had indicated a good local market potential for film, he decided to embark on permanent exhibition, and for this purpose opened the remodelled Lyceum Hall. To capitalise on the popularity of Australian films, he formed a permanent production unit under the cameraman Ernest Higgins in June 1908, initially making actuality (non-fiction) shorts and a newsreel. For several years Spencer billed his wife Eleanor as "Señora" Spencer, "the only lady operator (projectionist) in the world". Along with T. J. West and J. D. Williams, Spencer was also among the first to show sound films in Australia.

Eager to embark on the production of local fiction films, Spencer began in 1910 with **The Life and Adventures of John Vane, the Notorious Australian Bushranger.** Vane, a member of Ben Hall's gang, was seen as that least-typical of bushrangers, a penitent who gave himself up and exchanged his life of crime for fifteen years in prison. The *Bulletin* judged the film to be "a rare hash of saintliness and sensation".[10]

Although Spencer was reportedly dissatisfied with the production, he was determined to persist. He employed the actor Alfred Rolfe to direct three films from the repertoire of his father-in-law, the late actor-manager Alfred Dampier. **Captain Midnight, The Bush King, Captain Starlight** and **The Life of Rufus Dawes** were all released in 1911. They starred what then remained of the Alfred Dampier Company, including Rolfe, his wife Lillian Dampier, and Raymond Longford. Making her film debut as second lead of **Captain Midnight** was Lottie Lyell.

Spencer had initially contracted a young Englishman, Alan J. Williamson, as the producer. A son of James Williamson, a British film pioneer, he had participated in some of the earliest English films and was managing his father's London office when he met Cozens Spencer in 1910. Later in life he was to record a vivid account of what he experienced after his arrival in Sydney in October 1910.

Spencer had misled me into thinking I was to take charge of all production and that he had no one very capable of helping me. I found Ernest Higgins virtually in charge of photography and darkrooms, and it took time to overcome his opposition to my "intrusion". Ernest was a far better cameraman and film processor than I was by a great margin, and later with all I had to do, this was a great boon to me and we worked well together.[11]

Williamson was given the job of reorganising Spencer's darkroom on the fourth floor of the Lyceum Theatre. Work was then begun on **Captain Midnight** with a budget of £300. Of this and subsequent Spencer features, Williamson recalled:

Having secured a suitable story, carefully selected so that no interior shots were necessary as no studio existed at that time, the plot was then carefully written in sequences ... The finished plot, or as it is now called the scenario, probably covered half a dozen pages ... We then collected our cast and having previously chosen a suitable spot, which in this particular production was French's Forest, out from Narrabeen, Sydney, the whole of the company including cameraman, producer, and all the artists would be taken to the spot and after a hurried consultation between the producer and the cameraman it was decided which scenes should be shot first. Rehearsals would then take place with many heated arguments as to how the scenes should be photographed, acted and generally arranged and eventually, having arrived at a fair amount of agreement, the scene would be photographed, probably only to find that there was a doubt as to whether the camera had functioned properly and it would all be done over again.

Five or six scenes were shot on an average per day and the cameraman and the whole company would return to Sydney. The cameraman would develop the negative so that on the next day anything unsatisfactory could be retaken. This process would be repeated each day until it was considered that sufficient negative had been secured to be joined up into something approaching a consecutive story.

By the time all the film had been developed and printed and the good shots separated from the bad, probably many of the artists had dispersed to other states with theatrical companies and a situation had been reached where retakes were impossible. In this instance the title writer, who instead of being a specialist or title expert, might be anybody available who was considered good at saying as much as possible, would be brought in to invent a good title or caption which would bridge the gap.[12]

Spencer knew the kind of film he wanted **Captain Midnight** to be, but had little idea of the expense involved. Williamson continued:

To impress Spencer I arranged that the early shots would contain as many horses and as much action as I felt I could afford ... When he saw my police and bushranger shots he raved and shouted and said he wanted dozens, for these horses were just a handful — all for £300 inclusive of everything![13]

The film eventually cost £800 and, as Alan Williamson observed, "Spencer survived, and the film made its cost out of the Lyceum run alone".[14]

Although Spencer was not renowned for his calmness, his faith in Australian production was unshakable and well-founded. He later claimed that the success of his company's productions had had a "great deal" to do with his attaining pre-eminence in distribution and exhibition. He backed this up with the observation:

...any showman will tell you that he can make more out of an Australian subject than any imported film – except, perhaps, a star spectacular picture, the production of which is restricted to a few European countries.

Spencer observed that the film showman in almost every country of the world

must have at least a fair proportion of films made in the country in which he is in business. Patrons insist upon it. They want to see in the pictures something of their own people and their own country. So showmen have to frame their programmes accordingly. Why should not Australian showmen have Australian films?

He also had great faith in the export potential of local productions, stating that:

The change, the variety, the freshness that would be got in an Australian picture would ensure its being welcomed by picture lovers all over the earth. For anything with a new atmosphere or note about it — and an Australian picture would have these recommendations — there is always a market in the picture world.[15]

Under Spencer's auspices, **Captain Midnight** was followed by Alfred Rolfe's **Captain Starlight** and **The Life of Rufus Dawes**, and in 1911 Alan J. Williamson wrote and directed **Captain Moonlite**, a subject also filmed the previous year by John F. Gavin. After the departure of Alfred Rolfe to Australian Photo-Play, Spencer gave Raymond Longford — an actor and assistant on **Captain Midnight** and **Captain Moonlite** — a first chance at direction. Alan Williamson was in turn to assist Longford on the latter's second feature, **Margaret Catchpole**, before being assigned to continue Spencer's regular production of short subjects. Among the films Williamson made with the cameraman Arthur Higgins over a six-month period was the actuality film, **State Education**, made in conjunction with the New South Wales Department of Education, and a film on Sydney Harbour for the Australian Travel Bureau.

Raymond Longford

Raymond Longford, who had made his screen debut in **Captain Midnight** and played the cannibalistic convict Gabbett in **The Life of Rufus Dawes**, was to become the most important and prolific director of the Australian cinema's silent era. He was born in Sydney in 1875, the son of a prison warder. While still in his teens, he sailed as a crewman aboard the windjammers making their swift voyages from London to Sydney and back. It was a life of adventure that involved him in a Chilean revolution and the Boer War. In England he took his second mate's ticket and worked in the British merchant marine. Ever mobile, he then accepted a job as an official in the

Indian medical service, but while in Calcutta abandoned medicine to join a theatrical company. On returning to Sydney, he became a full-time actor, touring with a number of companies, among them Alfred Dampier's, around Australia and New Zealand. It was while travelling as leading actor with the Edwin Geach Touring Theatrical Company that Raymond Longford met their new leading lady, Lottie Lyell, then aged seventeen, and from this first meeting sprang a rich creative partnership.

Longford's first involvement in film was working on Cozens Spencer's feature-length documentary **The Burns–Johnson Fight** in 1908. When Alfred Rolfe left Spencer for Australian Photo-Play, Longford was chosen as his successor. His directing debut came with **The Fatal Wedding** (1911), a domestic drama starring himself, Lottie Lyell and Walter Vincent. It had enjoyed great success as a stage play, and Longford and Lyell had toured New Zealand in the leading roles. Although Longford was subsequently to favour location work, **The Fatal Wedding** was shot mostly indoors. His "studio" for this film was a Bondi artist's studio with its roof removed. Making his debut as feature cameraman was the nineteen-year-old Arthur Higgins, the younger brother of Spencer's first cameraman Ernest Higgins. From an outlay of £4000, **The Fatal Wedding** returned £18 000, and these profits, together with the returns from Longford's following three films, enabled Cozens Spencer in September 1912 to open a £10 000 studio complex at Rushcutters Bay in Sydney. Glass-roofed and with its own laboratory, it was more elaborate and was to see longer service than the Salvation Army's Melbourne studio built three years earlier. The studio, and indeed the film industry, were considered important enough for the building to be opened by the Premier, J. McGowan, and film coverage of the event was screened at the Lyceum that night. The first two films to use Rushcutters Bay for interiors were under Longford's direction — **The Midnight Wedding** (1912) and **Australia Calls** (1913).

Following **The Fatal Wedding** in 1911, Longford's second film was drawn by way of a novel and stage play from the real-life saga of "Margaret Catchpole". **The Romantic Story of Margaret Catchpole** told of the heroine's transportation to New South Wales in 1801 after being twice sentenced to death for horse-stealing and escaping captivity. The scenes set in Australia are now lost but much of the surviving "English" footage — filmed, of course, in Australia — is infused with a sense of doom and foreboding, and this derives force from the inclusion of towering coastal cliffs and inlets as backgrounds. The use of locations contributes a naturalism that was to enhance Longford's later surviving features **The Sentimental Bloke** (1919) and **On Our Selection** (1920). Performances, except those of Longford and Lyell, are rudimentary but are redeemed by the film's pacing, especially an action sequence where Margaret frantically rides her stolen horse along a country road.

Longford's next four productions for Spencer were **Sweet Nell of Old Drury** (1911), a theatre-to-film translation of the actress Nellie Stewart's crowning achievement; **The Tide of Death** (1912), an epic melodrama spanning several years of life in the bush and city; **The Midnight Wedding** (1912), a costume melodrama set in Europe; and **Australia Calls** (1913), a prophecy of Asiatic invasion. All were elaborate productions, indicating Spencer's determination to compete with the best of imported films.

The scenario of **Australia Calls** was written by two *Bulletin* journalists, J. Barr and C. A. Jeffries. It was typical of the weekly's racist campaign against the "yellow peril", pursued through its editorials, short stories and outrageous cartoons. **Australia Calls** included events in city and country, opening with scenes of leisure-loving urbanites at the races, playing football and wallowing in the surf. Above each successive scene rose an image of the greedy Asiatic invader. While Sydney was the centre of the attack, human interest was focused not surprisingly on a sheep station. Invading Asiatics were shown overrunning adjacent country stations, while in the city, Australians armed for the defence, and troops marched through cheering crowds. According to a *Bulletin* synopsis:

And then the boom and smoke of battle; Sydney a sea of fire where tower and spire come toppling down. Hereabouts the rejected suitor turns traitor, and in return for the girl, £5000 cash and a passage out of the country, he undertakes to guide the Mongolian forces. The girl is captured and brought into the Chinese camp, but the Australian aeroplane, manipulated by [Capt. W. E.] Hart, happens through the air, rescues her, and carries her off amid a storm of bullets and a typhoon of applause.[16]

Further patriotic elements included the rallying of bush soldiers and a charge by the New South Wales Lancers.

This was Longford's final production for Spencer's Pictures, and his most ambitious. It took a year to complete — although production was not continuous — and the filmmakers had the cooperation of the Australian Defence Department. Extras were drawn from Sydney's Chinatown, and the Sydney air raid was an ingenious fabrication of cardboard planes swooping down wires onto a large-scale model, skilfully intercut with actual scenes of the city. The visiting American fleet doubled as the Japanese Imperial Navy, and to avoid giving offence to the Japanese the invaders were portrayed as Japanese, Chinese and "Asiatics" in general.

The scale and blatant propaganda of **Australia Calls** made it the least typical of Longford's thirty narrative films. Most of his 1911-1918 productions were intimate melodramas enlivened by a variety of settings and action sequences. But not until **The Sentimental Bloke** and **On Our Selection** does he seem to have laid aside melodramatic convention to pursue realism. What happened to Longford after **Australia Calls** was to set the pattern for the rest of his career. It explains a disparity between subjects, available budgets and quality, and led to a professional insecurity that sometimes verged on the paranoid.

On 6 January 1913 "the combine" — the exhibitor Union Theatres and an associated production and distribution company, Australasian Films — was formed by the merger of key Australian exhibition, distribution and production companies. The first move had been the merging on 4 March 1911 of Johnson and Gibson with J. and N. Tait to form Amalgamated Pictures. In November 1912, the General Film Company of Australasia was formed to control the merged interests of West's Pictures, Spencer's Pictures and Amalgamated Pictures. The addition of the Greater J. D. Williams Amusement Company in January 1913 brought a centralising of the four partners under Union Theatres and Australasian Films.

The "combine" was to retain industry dominance until it faced rivalry from Hoyts Proprietary Ltd (later Hoyts Theatres) and the appearance of American film exchanges during the First World War.[17] Before this amalgamation, there had not been enough films to serve the separate companies that had proliferated from 1906 onwards. The competition had forced up the price of films bought in London and New York to the extent that the elaborate duplication in film buying, distribution and exhibition back home became less justified. If further persuasion was needed, there were the successful examples of amalgamated cinema interests in other countries, especially America.

Cozens Spencer was opposed to his company's decision to merge. Because the combine was now assured a supply of imported film, Australasian Films and Union Theatres saw no reason for the former Spencer studio to continue feature production. Accordingly, Raymond Longford was dismissed and the studio's output virtually confined to the **Australasian Gazette**, a newsreel successor to **Spencer's Gazette**. Spencer persuaded a reluctant Australasian Films to back the production of one more feature, **The Shepherd of the Southern Cross** (1914), directed by an English visitor, Alexander Butler. The film's failure ensured that Australasian only occasionally engaged in feature production for the next decade. Cozens Spencer, remaining at odds with his board on non-production and other policies, resigned and travelled abroad. Before his departure, he told the *Theatre Magazine* in October 1914:

Picture production has been killed. Today it is dead as the proverbial doornail. Can you believe that this is the only place in the world where pictures are not being made? Such is, indeed, the case. Australia has become the dumping-ground for all the producers in the world, when it could most profitably be taking its place side by side with other picture-producing countries, and providing work in Australia for thousands of its own people.[18]

Alan J. Williamson, who in mid-1911 had been sent to establish a film exchange and the production of shorts for Spencer in Melbourne, found that after the amalgamation he was responsible to a board of five people instead of to Spencer alone. In mid-1913 he resigned to serve as a London buyer for the Cooperative Film Exchange Ltd. This company had been formed to supply film to independent exhibitors, who like producers, suddenly found themselves no part of the combine's future plans.[19]

The Cozens Spencer story had a bizarre ending. While there is evidence that his enforced withdrawal from the Australian film scene left him deeply disturbed, his settling on a Canadian ranch seemed peaceful enough. In September 1930, his finances and nerves frayed by the Wall Street crash the year before, Spencer ran amuck, shooting several employees before disappearing. Six weeks later his body was dragged from a nearby lake.

The Fraser Film Company

After his retirement from Australasian, Spencer had joined Raymond Longford, J. D. Williams and the managing director of Lincoln-Cass Films, H. Dean Stewart, in advocating a revival of the Federal Government's import duty on film. Already by 1911, the Sydney *Sun* considered:

Now there are half a dozen firms manufacturing photo plays in Australia, while hundreds of people are thereby securing employment, the question is being asked as to whether it isn't time the Federal Government imposed a duty on imported films.[20]

In early 1915, J. D. Williams pointed to how such a tariff had placed the American film industry on its feet. He concluded:

Now, when Australia is in imminent danger of being literally swamped with millions of feet of cheap film from abroad, this tariff will prove not only a beneficial measure but an absolute necessity.[21]

But a high film tariff imposed by the Fisher Government in 1914 was to be short-lived. Four years later, following a plea from importers that the tariff only compounded wartime difficulties, it was substantially reduced. Raymond Longford was to claim later at the Royal Commission of 1927 that the combine's antipathy to his own film output dated from "certain representations to Mr Fisher" that he had made in support of the 1914 tariff.

After his departure from Spencer's Pictures, Longford obtained a brief respite with the Fraser Film Release and Photographic Company, a small distribution firm established in late 1912 to handle European and British films which would not otherwise have obtained a release in Australia. The co-founders were the Sydney businessmen Colin and Archie Fraser, with additional finance from the Italian hat manufacturer Giuseppe Borsalino whose involvement stemmed from his investment in Italian features and a desire to see these films obtain an outlet in Australia. After the production of a highly-successful Australian short, **Whaling in Jervis Bay**, the Fraser brothers employed Franklyn Barrett to direct two features, **A Blue Gum Romance** and **The Life of a Jackaroo** (1913). Raymond Longford's features for Fraser Films were the comedy **Pommy Arrives in Australia** (1913) and an adaptation of the novel and stage play **The Silence of Dean Maitland** (1914). In 1915 he also adapted a Victor Hugo poem, **We'll Take Her Children in Amongst Our Own**, as well as making the comedy short, **Ma Hogan's New Boarder** (1915).

According to evidence in the *Theatre Magazine* and at the 1927 Royal Commission into the Moving Picture Industry, the combine was not kindly disposed to Fraser Films for two reasons. The first was its existence as a business rival in distribution; the second was the combine's opposition to any feature production apart from its own occasional output. Longford was to be especially resisted because of his part in obtaining the 1914 film import duty. He was repeatedly refused the use of the Rushcutters Bay studio, and the combine rejected **The Silence of Dean Maitland** in spite of a good preview reception. When Colin Fraser secured the Palace Theatre, Sydney, for the premiere the combine cancelled its further supply of films to the theatre's leaseholder and threatened other exhibitors with similar action if they showed the film. Managements surrendering to the demand were also asked to guarantee not to screen any non-combine film over 1000 feet. On behalf of Fraser Films, Longford in late 1914 attempted to sue an executive of Australasian Films, Henry Gee, for £1000 damages. The case was heard in the New South Wales Supreme Court and High Court, but Longford was defeated under a state law stipulating that a distributor could refuse to trade with an exhibitor unless that exhibitor "block booked" or traded exclusively with the distributor.

Ironically, while the combine's **Shepherd of the Southern Cross** did poor business wherever it was shown, **The Silence of Dean Maitland** was an instant success and was screened repeatedly for years to come. But this was of little direct aid to Longford. As published in the *Theatre Magazine*, the evidence in the case of Longford *v*. Gee illustrates vividly the predicament he faced for the rest of his career. In recalling a conversation with Gee, Longford told the Court:

He (Henry Gee) said, "The position is this — we do not intend to produce any more stars in Australia, and with the exception of the Gazette-work, we won't touch anything in the future .... To be candid with you, I've stopped Fraser from carrying out his contract with you, and clearly let him understand that I would boycott him or anybody else in Australia who made similar contracts. If you like to run your head against a brick wall, that's your lookout". I said, "That's an end to me after four years' service, and making thousands for the firm". He said, "That's our policy old man; and I can assure you that Fraser and the Corporation's end is not far off. You're up against a tough proposition."[22]

Although Longford's contract of May 1914 with the Frasers had requested that he make twenty-four films in two years, these plans evaporated after the court case. A lack of outlets for Australian features meant the Frasers' inability to honour their contract, and Longford left to seek other work. Between **Pommy Arrives in Australia** and **Dean Maitland**, he had directed an Anglo-Australian drama, **'Neath Austral Skies** (1913) and a short drama of city and bush differences, **The Swagman's Story** (1913), for the Commonwealth Film Producing Company. Afterwards, for Higgins-Longford Films, he scripted and directed two one-reel adaptations from Henry Lawson's poems, **Taking his Chance** and **Trooper Campbell** (1914). The latter, recently rediscovered, shows an advance on **The Romantic Story of**

Margaret Catchpole, not so much in performance, which is still haunted by melodrama, as in the use of depth of field and positioning within the frame. **Trooper Campbell** seems to have been hurriedly made (it was never listed among Longford's major achievements), and displays nowhere near the polish of Alfred Rolfe's **The Hero of the Dardanelles,** completed halfway through the next year.

According to his later Royal Commission evidence, Longford attempted in 1915 to hire the Australasian Films studio for an adaptation of Allen Doone's stage success **The Rebel.** The combine rejected the application until he was replaced by American director John Matthews. Fraser Films, however, made at least three more features after Longford's departure. **The Day** (1914), an adaptation of the patriotic poem by Henry Chappell, and **The Sunny South** (1915), from George Darrell's smash-hit play of 1884, were both directed by Alfred Rolfe. John Matthews then directed **Murphy of Anzac** (1916), based on the heroic deeds of Private Simpson (of "Simpson and his donkey" fame), an AIF ambulance officer who used a donkey to carry the wounded from the front at Gallipoli. By 1918, the war had reduced the Frasers' supply of European and English films to a trickle, and the company went into liquidation.

Actuality (nonfiction) films

The only areas of production where films were guaranteed a release were newsreels and documentaries. By 1910, among the prominent Australian newsreels were **Spencer's Gazette, Pathé Animated Gazette, West's Journal of Daily Events,** and a regular reel from Johnson and Gibson. Cameramen were rarely idle in their work for these companies and they included Lacey Percival, Maurice Bertel, Albert Segerberg, Orrie Perry and Bert Cross. With the consolidation of the combine in early 1913, various newsreels, principally Spencer's, were absorbed into the newly formed **Australasian Gazette** and until the coming of sound nearly twenty years later, **Australasian Gazette** remained the most important Australian newsreel. Its only substantial rivals were the international reels of major overseas companies. Cameramen around Australia contributed items to the Gazette, which had national distribution, and each State's edition was varied by the inclusion of material of local interest.

In December 1911 the Commonwealth Government appointed J. P. Campbell as its first full-time official cameraman, responsible to the Department of External Affairs. However, personal conflicts with the bureaucracy led to Campbell's replacement in May 1913 by Bert Ive. In 1916, Ive's responsibilities were transferred to the Department of Home and Territories and he remained through several more departmental changes, shooting film to promote Australia and record important occasions, until 1939.

Among the documentary series that had emerged by 1911, titles like **Australia Today, Real Australia** and **Know Australia** joined the newsreels in presenting the only consistent film record of day-to-day life. However, feature-length documentaries, usually of a scenic nature, often managed to find outlets when narrative features continued to encounter difficulties.

The best-known Australian documentary filmmakers of the silent era were Frank Hurley and Francis Birtles. Hurley was a visual perfectionist while Birtles, primarily an explorer, regarded the cinema as a useful device to publicise an expedition and to raise funds for the next. Initially both were celebrated adventurers, Birtles for his marathon bicycle and car tours across Australia and Hurley for his exploits as a cameraman in Antarctica with Douglas Mawson and Ernest Shackleton. By the time they collaborated on the feature-length Into Australia's Unknown (1914), Hurley had risen to prominence through his photographs and a 4000-foot documentary on the Mawson expedition, Home of the Blizzard (1913). The film was acclaimed in Australia and Britain; subsequently Hurley's name was to be an essential ingredient in Ernest Shackleton's fund-raising efforts.[23]

Frank Hurley's record of the gruelling Shackleton expedition, In the Grip of the Polar Ice (1917), was his most famous film. The film, together with still photographs, showed how the explorers had spent over half of the two-year expedition marooned on pack-ice. The coverage included the slow crushing by ice of their ship *Endurance*. After Hurley had dived into the ship's flooded interior to recover film negative, it was developed and dried using a refrigerator heated by Primus stoves. Faced with the ensuing trek across the ice, Hurley had to sort and deliberately destroy — ''to obviate all temptation'' — four-fifths of his glass-plate still photographic negatives.[24]

Francis Birtles' first encounter with film had been on Gaumont's 3000-foot documentary Across Australia with Francis Birtles (1912). Photographed by Gaumont's staff cameraman Richard Primmer, it showed a long bicycle journey from Sydney to Darwin, and was predominantly scenic but included dramatised interludes such as a battle between early settlers and Aboriginals. In 1913 Birtles became the first person to drive a motor car between Sydney and Perth. In planning another motor trip to the Northern Territory and the Gulf of Carpentaria the following year, he persuaded Australasian Films to pay for hiring Frank Hurley as the expedition's cameraman. The resulting film, Into Australia's Unknown, was an objective account of Aboriginal customs on Carpentaria (many of which were filmed for the first time) as well as local Aboriginal and station life, and the flora and fauna of the Northern Territory. During the four months of filming Birtles served as director, with Hurley a frequent collaborator. The film's negative was developed and despatched en route, and Australasian Films paid a total of £300 (at 1/6d per foot) for 4000 feet of acceptable material. One year later, Birtles himself was to film Across Australia in the Track of Burke and Wills (1915).

Birtles' three later feature documentaries were Through Australian Wilds: Across the Track of Ross Smith (1920), Australia's Lonely Lands (1924), and the dramatised Coorab in the Island of Ghosts (co-directed by

Torrance McLaren, 1929). Although he continued to travel and capture public attention until the early 1930s, the infrequency of Birtles' films after 1915 can perhaps be attributed to poor box office returns.[25] He had, however, been the first to commercially popularise factual films of outback adventure and pioneering — a genre that continues today.[26]

Other prewar directors and companies

The growth of the combine was connected with the decline of at least six feature production companies in addition to Spencer's Pictures and the Fraser Film Company. Four of them, Pathé Frères, West's Pictures, Amalgamated Pictures and Australian Photo-Play, were absorbed by the combine, and both Australian Life Biograph and Lincoln-Cass blamed their demise on the impossibility of obtaining outlets.

Pathé Frères, after the opening of its Melbourne distribution agency in 1909, employed Australian and New Zealand cameramen to shoot industrial documentaries and items for the Australian and European editions of the **Pathé Animated Gazette.** Two of its principal cameramen were Maurice Bertel and Franklyn Barrett. Their output included **The Real Australia** (1909-10), a series for the Commonwealth government containing such episodes as **Mining In Newcastle.** In 1911, with Bertel as cameraman, Pathé Frères produced thirteen 1000-feet dramas featuring the repertoire of Edwin I. Cole's Bohemian Dramatic Company. Cole specialised in action dramas of the American west, and it is likely that one of his films, **Buffalo Bill's Love Story,** now survives in the National Film Archive under a different title: **A Maiden's Distress.** The film, basically a backyard production, has its "Red Indians" garbed in waistcoats and trousers, hurling knives while encircling a portly heroine. Far more convincing is **A Miner's Luck,** a 1000-feet drama produced by the Photo Vista Company for Pathé Frères in 1911. Although direction is not credited, this tale of a miner swindled out of his gold claim makes similar realistic use of bush settings as Franklyn Barrett's two later surviving features, **The Breaking of the Drought** and **A Girl of the Bush.** In the midst of mysterious goings-on in thickly timbered country, an interlude of bush workers clearing land for a new selection is conveyed through several spectacular images that have the power of real events as lived rather than those re-created.

After the company's demise, Pathé Frères' production was continued under the auspices of T. J. West after West's takeover in early 1911. Franklyn Barrett remained as the principal cameraman and within a year had photographed six features for his new employer. Barrett is known to have directed at least one (and possibly three) of these features before leaving to work for Fraser Films.

Like Longford, Barrett had a more adventurous background than other contemporary Australian filmmakers. Born in England in 1874, he had worked at a wide range of jobs including musician, press photographer, film exhibitor and newsreel cameraman before directing an 800-feet adaptation of the play **A Message from Mars** in Wellington in 1903. For the next eight years he concentrated on scenics and newsreels, working all over Australia, New Zealand, Canada, America and Europe.

As part of the careful preparation for their first feature, West's offered a £25 prize in mid-1911 for the best scenario on "Australian life". Bushranging themes were barred: a clear indication of disenchantment with "colonial" stories. The prizewinner was the comedian W. S. Percy, whose contemporary story, **All for Gold** (1911), concerned an attempted murder over a disputed gold claim. Barrett began the film's climactic race between heroine and villain with a bold use of split-screen. The heroine, seen telephoning to order a speedboat on the left of screen, was separated by an expanse of water from a boatman receiving the call on the right. Barrett's visual ingenuity was to be the highlight of all his work, but as his two surviving later films showed, his direction of actors was less assured.

Whether Barrett directed any of the West productions other than the last (**The Silent Witness**, 1912) is not known, but he would certainly have brought his film expertise to the other productions that featured stage artists, particularly those who made more than an average contribution to Australian films. The second West production, **The Christian** (1911), was probably self-directed by the cast of the William Anderson Dramatic Company which, but for the inclusion of exterior shots, simply repeated its oft-played performance on stage at Sydney's Palace Theatre. The four remaining features contained script input and performances by Cyril Mackay, Leonard Willey and Sydney Stirling. As films with contemporary stories made on a joint writer-director-technician basis, they were unique. Just how successful the collaboration was can only be judged by the fact that **The Silent Witness**, the last of the four, was under the sole direction of Barrett.

In the meantime, other Pathé Frères staff had gone into independent production. In early 1911 Pathé's Australian manager, Stanley Crick, and one of his cameramen, Herbert Finlay, resigned to form a partnership. Their first four films — **Ben Hall and His Gang; Frank Gardiner, King of the Road; The Assigned Servant** and **Keane of Kalgoorlie** — were all made by the director and actor John F. Gavin.

While Gavin's output was prolific his later surviving work shows that his entrepreneurial talent outweighed any he might have had as a director. Bushranging captured most of his initial attention and his first films, produced by the exhibitor H. A. Forsythe, were **Thunderbolt** and **Moonlight, the Bushranger** (1910). Gavin later claimed that these films "were really the first pictures of consequence to be made in New South Wales, and they earned a fortune for the Forsythe investors".[27] **Thunderbolt** was filmed partly in the Lithgow district with striking coal miners hired as extras. With a personal background in Outback and Wild West stage extravaganzas, Gavin was to continue filming Australian colonial themes until the end of his career.

Nearly all Gavin's films were written by his wife Agnes, with Gavin himself as the hero or character heavy. The success of his four productions for Crick and Finlay encouraged the partners to float the Australian Photo-Play Company with a nominal capital of £20 000. Two production units were established — one under the direction of Gavin, the other under Alfred Rolfe. By July 1911 Australian Photo-Play had distribution outlets throughout Australia and New Zealand and in less than a year they produced twenty known features — all but one of them directed by Alfred Rolfe. After making only **The Mark of the Lash** for Australian Photo-Play, John Gavin resigned to form his own company, claiming that their plans would exceed the capacity of the local market.

Alfred Rolfe was to be the most prolific of the Australian silent era directors, making no less than twenty-nine narrative fiction films between 1911 and 1918. Today only **The Hero of the Dardanelles** (1915) survives, but it indicates a director skilled in the type of visual and naturalistic sophistication later attributed to Raymond Longford. The conventions of spectacle melodrama so favoured in late nineteenth century Australian theatre, with their realistic settings and real chases on horseback and train wrecks, played a large role in the films he made for Australian Photo-Play in 1911-12. They were conventions at which his late father-in-law, Alfred Dampier, had excelled in his stage productions of *Captain Midnight, the Bush King, Captain Starlight* and *His Natural Life*, and which Rolfe appears to have carried intact into his adaptations of these (with the latter re-titled **The Life of Rufus Dawes**) for Spencer's Pictures. If **The Hero of the Dardanelles** and reviews of other films are an indication, Rolfe's work for Spencer and Australian Photo-Play had helped refine the achievement of naturalistic performances for the screen, not to say the basis of a screen grammar that vividly captured setting and spectacle.

The Australian Photo-Play formula was a string of sensational incidents climaxed by a chase, with actuality footage sometimes cunningly incorporated, as in the climax of **The Cup Winner**, which intercut the hero's ride to victory at the Melbourne Cup with coverage of the real race run on the day of the film's premiere. In **Moora Neeya, or The Message of the Spear** (1911), the highlight was an Aboriginal tribe's "Death Dance" around the captured hero which was intercut, according to the synopsis, with a ride to the rescue by stockmen. Nearly all the APP films made use of popular conceptions of the bush, peopling their stories with marauding Aboriginals, venegful settlers, English outcasts and shamed women. Revenge melodramas were the staple, with **The Lady Outlaw** (1911) notching up crimes to avenge the presumed death of her convict lover, Aboriginals being shot for the abduction of a settler's daughter in **Caloola, or The Adventures of a Jackeroo** (1911), and a miner avenging his brother's death in **Cooee and the Echo** (1912).

Australian Photo-Play's bankruptcy in 1912 came from the over-production John Gavin had predicted and an inability to recoup money from the local market. After APP was bought by the local branch of the Gaumont Company, it eventually fell into the hands of the combine.

Another Sydney company, Australian Life Biograph, was established in early 1911, and produced eight features under the direction of the actor Gaston Mervale: **A Tale of the Australian Bush; One Hundred Years Ago; A Ticket in Tatts; The Colleen Bawn** (1911), **Hands Across the Sea; A Daughter of Australia; Conn, the Shaughraun;** and **The Ticket of Leave Man** (1912). The stock company working at Australian Life Biograph's glass-roofed studio in Manly included Jerome Patrick, Godfrey Cass, Harry Beaumont and Louise Carbasse (later to become the American star Louise Lovely). The subjects chosen were predominantly colonial, with no less than six featuring prison themes, usually with an innocent man receiving a pardon or making his escape. The first three scripts were originals, and three of the remainder were adaptations from plays, including two by Dion Boucicault. After the company's closure, Mervale directed one further feature, **The Wreck of the Dunbar** (1912), before leaving to work in America. He returned later to direct stage comedies and musicals before acting in several Australian films of the late 1920s.

The other two principal production companies of the period were Melbourne-based. The director for Amalgamated Pictures and Lincoln-Cass Films was W. J. Lincoln, a former playwright, stage actor and exhibitor. Amalgamated Pictures was formed by a combination of the production and exhibition firm of Johnson and Gibson with their 1906 **Kelly Gang** partners, J. and N. Tait. In late 1910, prior to the establishment of Amalgamated, the Taits had backed W. J. Lincoln's first feature, **It Is Never Too Late to Mend.**

As a novel, Charles Reade's *It Is Never Too Late to Mend* (published 1856) had helped revolutionise the English penal system and influenced Marcus Clarke's writing of *For the Term of his Natural Life*. Reade's story began and ended in England and while the rigours of his hero's suffering were not as extreme as Clarke's, it supplied strong fare for a stage adaptation by Reade and ultimately Australian (1911) and British (1916) film versions. W. J. Lincoln's 1911 film was praised for its ambitious scale and the unforced quality of its performances.

During 1911 and until its closure in early 1912, Amalgamated Pictures produced a newsreel and eight known features. All but one of the features were adaptations from either a novel, story, stage play, or, as in one case (**The Lost Chord**, 1911), a song. The highlight of the exception, **Breaking the News** (1912), inspired by John Longstaff's painting of that name, was the flooding of a mine. Judging by the subjects chosen, the average length (4000 feet) and the scale of Amalgamated's productions, the company was second only to Spencer's Pictures in its resolve to build a quality reputation for Australian features. Four of what were possibly the largest productions, **The Luck of the Roaring Camp, Called Back, The Bells** and **Rip Van Winkle**, had overseas period settings, and their stories departed from the standard fare of Australian colonialism. The company's first film, **The Mystery of a Hansom Cab** (1911), was the first Australian feature to use a predominantly urban background.

The camerawork on most of the Amalgamated features was by Orrie

Perry, son of the Salvation Army's Joseph Perry. Having shot each film — with the exception of **The Bells** — in the courtyard studio behind Johnson and Gibson's oxygen and boracic works in St Kilda, Orrie Perry and his brother Reg would complete the laboratory work, titling and editing. They then projected the films at their Melbourne premiere season, which in summer was conducted at the city's vast Glaciarium, using a portable projection booth.

W. J. Lincoln was the first of the very few experienced writers to direct Australian films. While the production scale of his Amalgamated films was grand he remained, for all his experience, firmly attached to stage conventions if his **The Sick Stockrider** (1913) and **The Life's Romance of Adam Lindsay Gordon** (1916) are any indication. It is probable that all his Amalgamated and subsequent Lincoln-Cass films were more like stage tableaux than films. However, with the right ingredients at their disposal the best of Lincoln's early productions were well-received. The epics **It Is Never Too Late to Mend, The Mystery of a Hansom Cab, Called Back** and **Breaking the News** all drew good houses and were favourably reviewed.

Following Amalgamated's absorption by the combine, W. J. Lincoln formed Lincoln-Cass Films with Godfrey Cass, an actor who had appeared regularly for Australian Life Biograph. Between July and October of 1913 they produced eight features at their small glass-roofed studio in suburban Cole Street, Elsternwick. Location exteriors were shot in bushland not far from the city at Healesville. Their length ranged between 1200 and 4000 feet, the most ambitious productions being the final two, **The Reprieve** and **The Crisis**. The majority were made swiftly with low budgets, and the subjects chosen reworked the familiar themes of convicts, goldmining, urban evil and bush nostalgia. Two examples of the latter were adaptations of the Adam Lindsay Gordon poems, ''The Sick Stockrider'' and ''The Wreck''. Of the company's total output only **The Sick Stockrider** survives. Compared with Longford's **Margaret Catchpole** and Pathé Frères' **A Miner's Luck**, it is stolid and stagey with shaking canvas sets, an exaggerated alcoholic scene and a bull-goring sequence in which an actor tumble-turns across an animal all too obviously at rest.

Crude though they may have been, these films at first did good business. The company's managing director, H. Dean Stewart, claimed that the Lincoln-Cass closure in late 1913 was caused by ''the pernicious system of Australasian Films Ltd, in binding the showmen to take their full programme from them, and not allowing a picture to be hired from an outside source if over 1000 feet in length''. While **The Sick Stockrider** screened to thirty full houses in Victoria, the later Lincoln-Cass films were scarcely booked at all and interstate screenings were rare.[28]

Dissent

The period from 1907 to 1913 had seen the growth of Australian film production, distribution and exhibition on a scale that was revolutionary after the sporadic activity between 1896 and 1906. The transition of cinema from novelty to industry showed the faith of the emerging filmmakers, their backers and release outlets. Between 1907 and 1911, the production, distribution and exhibition interests had developed simultaneously with Australian films complementing the exhibitors' erratic supply of product from abroad.

The post-1911 division into hostile camps between production and distribution-exhibition had two causes. The first, and more readily identifiable, was the formation of the combine and the organised supply of overseas films. In 1909 Pathé Frères had introduced the concept of the distributor, or middleman between producer and exhibitor. From now on, it was easier for the exhibitor to regularly book imported films from the distributor than it was to pour comparatively large amounts of money into local production.

The second reason, already apparent by 1911, was the lack of originality in most Australian films. Australian filmmaking owed its initial success — as has each ''new wave'' since — to the novelty of its existence. The lengths of the films, the longest of them averaging 4000 to 5000 feet, undoubtedly helped. But after the adaptations from popular stage plays had justified their investment, a continued reliance on theatre properties and miscellaneous bush themes developed a monotony that palled beside the increasingly accomplished imports.

Of the six main producers, the only three to effectively test ways in which Australian films could challenge the imports were Spencer's Pictures, Amalgamated Pictures and Australian Photo-Play. Amalgamated and Spencer lavished money on projects like **The Mystery of a Hansom Cab** and **Australia Calls** that were clearly intended to lift the expertise and reputation of Australian filmmaking. Australian Photo-Play made racy action dramas that had far greater cinematic potential than the theatrical subjects which other producers preferred.

Had Spencer and Longford remained in production under the auspices of the combine, they would have had more than a good chance of building on the joint success they had established with Spencer's Pictures. They might easily have continued to make money for AF–UT and build investment confidence for other producers, at the same time drawing creative work away from the over-familiar.

Supporters of local production had no doubt as to where the source of the industry's ills lay. The author Henry Fletcher wrote in May 1915:

It is true that C. Spencer had proved there were great possibilities of profit, both locally and overseas, for home-made films. With intelligence a great industry might have been built up . . .
But the small minds saw the bird in the hand only, and now [the combine] has raised up enemies all round it, ruthless and persistent, who will never rest till [its] power for ill . . . is broken.[29]

3

Reaching towards nationalism
1914 - 24

The ten-year period from 1914 to 1924 brought with it new concepts of Australian nationalism through the momentous upheaval of the First World War and the difficult period of postwar readjustment. The valour of Australians on the battlefield kindled the spark of nationalistic fervour; later a nationalism of a more complex kind was inflamed amid sharp community divisions over conscription and a questioning of Imperial ties. Within Australia's film industry, two periods of boom were followed by signs of irreversible decline. During these years, world cinema was transformed into an industrialised cultural force more potent and popular than any other medium. In purely local terms, the nationalistic impulse of filmmakers and audiences was enough to keep the industry alive throughout most of the 1920s. But increasingly, the industry fell prey to the dominance of imported film, and it approached the latter half of the decade fragmented and unsure of future directions.

The appearance in 1915 of D. W. Griffith's two-and-a-half-hour epic **The Birth of a Nation** revolutionised the style and thematic preoccupations of the American cinema. Here for the first time was a film which aimed to make a definite, if contentious, statement about the nation to every class of filmgoer. In September 1915, returning to Australia after a trip to America, Harry Musgrove, the general manager of Australasian Films, told the *Theatre Magazine* that the "displacement of smaller films by feature films" was bringing "outstanding change" to the American film industry.[1] Union Theatres had already reaped rich returns with the Italian multi-reel spectacles **Cabiria** and **Quo Vadis?**, the latter running for an unprecedented ten weeks at the Sydney Lyceum and eleven weeks at West's Picture Palace in Melbourne. By the end of 1915 there was a feature film on every programme exhibited by the company together with a news gazette, a "scenic" and perhaps an "industrial". Some of the nonfiction actuality footage represented the only continuous production by Australasian Films.

After the outbreak of war in August 1914, the severe restrictions on production in England and Europe gave the American film industry an easy advantage in its world markets. In December 1915 Barrington Miller, the general manager of Union Theatres, announced:

I do not think it would be an overestimate to say that eighty per cent of the world's pictures are made in America. So, as we have all along been in the habit of drawing largely on America, the war has made little or no difference in the programmes we are able to offer patrons and exhibitors.[2]

The previous year had seen the United States supply just over fifty per cent of the value of films imported to Australia and the American producer-distributors clearly realised the value of the Australian market. The first American film exchange was opened in Australia during 1915 and by the end of the war Paramount, Fox, First National and Metro had all opened offices in various Australian state capitals. By late 1915, Australasian Films employed five full-time agents to screen and select films in both New York and London.

At that time *Theatre Magazine* continued a campaign of support for Australian production:

Is Australia going to be a mere dumping ground for pictures made in other parts of the world? The national disease is to import everything ... It is about time someone with brains, pluck and backing gave picture producing a run.[3]

But some salvation had already arrived along with the war.

Patriots

The start of the "Great War" was greeted with enthusiasm by some and a vocal public vigorously proclaimed its support for Britain as the Prime Minister elect, Andrew Fisher, voiced his celebrated promise to "help defend the Mother Country to our last man and our last shilling". Barely a decade earlier, some 16 000 Australian soldiers had taken part in the Boer War, but it was the heroism of the Anzacs at Gallipoli and in France that helped bring about a change within Australia, a step into what the Melbourne *Argus* called "the world of great manhood". Parallels were drawn between the honourable defeat at Gallipoli and the experience of failure on Australia's pioneering frontiers. But the real sacrifice was much greater. Of the 330 770 troops sent abroad to fight during the First World War, about one in five did not return.

For a short period, the decline in European film production meant more screen time for the local product. In late 1914, the Higgins brothers, with **It's a Long, Long Way to Tipperary**, and Alfred Rolfe, with **The Day**, dramatised aspects of the European war. From the following year, Rolfe was employed by Australasian Films to revive the company's production of features and fiction shorts. At least one observer, "Picture Lover", writing in *Theatre Magazine*'s issue of 1 February 1915, felt that Australasian's "miserable pretence at interesting itself in Australian-made pictures" was part of its attempts to obtain a reduction in the 1914 federal film duty — an accusation to be echoed in the mid-1920s, when the combine embarked on a further scheme of production.

Alfred Rolfe's first dramatised short for Australasian Films, **Will They Never Come?** (1915), was, like two of the features that followed, made with the assistance of the Department of Defence. The first feature, **The Hero of the Dardanelles** (1915), was billed as a sequel to **Will They Never Come?** and endorsed by the Department of Defence as "The Official Recruiting Film". **The Hero of the Dardanelles** is the only one of the early wartime propaganda narrative features to survive. Naturalistically, and with some sensitivity, the film shows its hero Will (Guy Hastings) forsaking the pleasures of family life to enlist in the armed forces and embark on rigorous training; the film aims to convince its audience that the hero's family and fiancée will react to the war's demands with a sensible patriotic calmness. Alfred Rolfe makes fine use of flashbacks and parallel action, and one of his more memorable sequences shows Will's memory of his girl as, far away, he reads her letter beside a flowing, sunlit sea. Unhappily, footage of the climactic Anzac landing at Gaba Tepe is now lost.

J. C. Williamson Ltd entered production late in 1914 as a protective measure to film plays from their repertoire which they knew were to be adapted as films in America. Like Australasian Films, "the Firm" then temporarily abandoned their antipathy to original Australian stories in order to cash in on wartime patriotism. **Within Our Gates, or Deeds that Won Gallipoli** (1915, directed by Frank Harvey), combined another portrayal of the landing at Gaba Tepe with a theme that was soon to be popular among wartime filmmakers — the activities of German spies within Australia.

Fear of outward threat by Asia or Europe or subversion from within were inevitable products of a nineteenth century Australian nationalism that was tied closely to British ideals. German expansion in the Pacific had caused great concern in Australia, for the country now shared its allies' fears of rising German militarism. Just before the war, the German trading vessel *Pfalz* was apprehended as she left Port Phillip Bay carrying concealed naval guns for a career of commerce raiding. From the earliest war days, spy rumours grew; scare stories told of alien signal lights flashing out to sea, of hostile submarines and aircraft. By September 1914, all German island possessions in the Pacific had been occupied and on 9 November, the Australian Navy won its first sea battle with the destruction of the German cruiser *Emden* by the *Sydney*.

By late 1915 the *Sydney—Emden* encounter had been re-told in two separate features — **How We Beat the Emden** (Australasian Films), directed by Alfred Rolfe, and **For Australia** (JCW), directed by Monte Luke. The latter, and inferior, film traded on fears of German infiltration at home, beginning in prewar Sydney as a newspaper reporter trails German spies. Later, the hero and the villains fight it out on an uncharted island conveniently close to a view of the *Emden*'s defeat. All the subsequent films showing the German menace were set on the mainland, mostly in Sydney or Melbourne. Both **If the Huns Come to Melbourne** (1916), directed by George Coates, and **Australia's Peril** (1917), directed by Franklyn Barrett, reflected the hysterical tone adopted by the political drive for compulsory conscription in which posters showed "the Hun" slaughtering Australians in their own backyards.

In 1917, **Australasian Gazette** took part in the conscription drive with its employment of the cartoonist Harry Julius to produce a series of animated propaganda subjects. One that survives shows a monstrous German ripping apart the buildings and populace of beleaguered Europe and Australia. Prime Minister Hughes's conscription referendum campaigns in time led to national divisions between working class and middle class, Catholic and Protestant, and a split within the Labor Party. In his lead-up to the second referendum of December 1917, Hughes issued a proclamation under War Precautions Regulations compelling exhibitors to screen whatever slides or films they were sent concerning the Government's views on the referendum. The proclamation divided exhibitors, one of whom wrote that audiences attended picture-shows:

to avoid rather than get politics. Further, it is mixed audiences that they attract — men and women of all shades of political opinion. Consequently there was a desire on the part of picture-men (in this instance, at any rate) to exclude the political element from their programmes.

Theatre Magazine went on to relate that on the Saturday before the referendum "the audience literally howled the roof off" one Balmain (Sydney) cinema that had been forced to show pro-conscription slides.[4]

In July and August 1917, divided opinion in Australian society, spurred on by opposition to the war, forced a nation-wide general strike involving 95 000 workers. **The Great Strike**, a film that sympathetically covered some of the more rousing events, was suppressed for several months and heavily censored by the New South Wales Government before being released as **Recent Industrial Happenings in New South Wales**. Another film, showing Russian revolutionaries and which had been cheered during a Sydney suburban screening, was also banned for the duration of the strike.[5] In December of 1917, several months after the strike had ended, production began on **The Enemy Within**, the first of five films made locally to showcase the prowess of sports all-rounder Reg L. "Snowy" Baker. Although it was a tale of German infiltration into Australian society, it was cautiously advertised as "not a war picture". It modelled the activities of its gang of subversives on popular beliefs about the International Workers of the World (the "Wobblies"), then widely held to be responsible for the Great Strike as well as for attempted arson and German collaboration. **The Enemy Within** had its hero's quarry infiltrating all levels of society from garden party élite to the working class. The gang plan their actions from a concealed room, later emerging to sow the seeds of social discontent with soapbox oratory in the Sydney Domain. They pursue the hero — a special agent — across rooftops, along city streets and through bush tracks. Writer-director Roland Stavely was able to incorporate a real incident of German hostility by blaming his fictional spy ring for the destruction of the trading vessel *Cumberland* which was mined off the southern New South Wales coast in

July 1917. The German raider *Wolff* had laid the mines and was still claiming headlines at the time of the film's release. This helped make the events "seem more probable", according to one reviewer but among the faults the same writer found were the film's length and the unreality of the concealed room: "Its hidden entrances, and walls with mysterious trapdoors, are as out of place, at least in Australia, as the slinking walk of the conspirators".[6]

Actuality film of the Australian war effort continued to be shot and exhibited throughout the conflict. In October 1914 the Commonwealth cinematographer, Bert Ive, had travelled from Melbourne to Fremantle filming aboard the troopship carrying the First Expeditionary Force to Egypt and Gallipoli. Covering the war at home, Ive filmed recruiting scenes, German internees and the 1918 French mission to Australia. In June 1917 Frank Hurley, who had recently returned from the Antarctic, was appointed as the country's first official photographer to the AIF. Hurley and his assistant, Hubert Wilkins, filmed in the trenches of France, and in the Middle East; Hurley also covered the manoeuvres of the Australian Light Horse and a number of battles including the capture of Jericho. Actuality that showed contrasting aspects of the war at home included **Broken Hill New Year's Day Massacre** (1915), **Australia at War** (1916), **Making Wool into Khaki Cloth** (1916) and a 1918 **Australasian Gazette** item that "showed the clever manufacture of artificial limbs at Victoria Barracks, Sydney". *Theatre Magazine* regarded the latter as "interesting, but hardly entertaining".[7]

Since propaganda had proved to be unpopular in the latter part of the war, narrative filmmakers turned to producing escapist comedy. Like American screen comedy, which did not really develop significantly until after 1912, Australian comedy films were not made regularly until late in the piece. There had been isolated early examples of local screen humour, such as the shorts made by the comedian W. S. Percy (**Percy Gets a Job**, 1912, and **Percy's First Holiday**, 1914) and Raymond Longford's feature **Pommy Arrives in Australia** (1913). But indigenous producers showed no lasting faith in comedy until 1915 — a year that brought the filming of two stage comedies by J. C. Williamson and comedy shorts by Raymond Longford (**Ma Hogan's New Boarder**) and John F. Gavin (**Charlie at the Show**).

The J. C. Williamson film enterprise was more than usually promising, as it had the advantage of popular players and local screen rights to a string of well-known titles. In early 1915, the Firm commissioned the visiting American actor-producer Fred Niblo to direct film adaptations of two comedies from among the nine plays he had toured around Australia and New Zealand for three years. The release of both films was delayed until after Niblo's return to America, but the surviving **Officer 666** confirms the impression that they were considered to be small by-products of the triumphant tour. Their entertainment value lies entirely in the timing of long-performed stage farce, and its contemporary audience reaction was probably similar to that for the filmed version of **Get-Rich-Quick-Wallingford**, which *Theatre*'s critic noted had been followed:

with interest by a large audience; but with little of the amusement evoked by the same company on the stage. It was interesting as a proof of how much the Niblo farces relied for their success on smart dialogue, and subtle touches of business impossible on the film.[8]

Apart from its propaganda features, JCW's two other films of the period were also based on popular plays. **Within the Law** (1916), a drama of a woman trying to clear her name of a charge of theft, and **Seven Keys to Baldpate** (1916), another play from the Niblo repertoire, featured respectively the prominent actresses of the day, Muriel Starr and Dorothy Brunton. Monte Luke, the director of these two features and of **For Australia**, was an actor who had turned to still photography, and was appointed film producer-director for JCW following the departure of Fred Niblo.

After the production of **Seven Keys to Baldpate**, Luke signed a year's contract with the company which was to commence on 26 January 1916 with his sailing to America to study film production and still photographic work.[9] The highlight of Luke's trip was his observation of work on D. W. Griffith's **Intolerance**. Awe-struck, he returned home to suggest that JCW should leave filmmaking to Hollywood. The Firm took his advice and embarked upon no further films until the 1930s.[10] Fred Niblo, in the meantime, had begun an important Hollywood career directing films that included **The Mark of Zorro** (1920), **Blood and Sand** (1923), and **Ben Hur** (1927).

Despite the pessimistic attitudes of Monte Luke and JCW, 1916 was the second most prolific year for Australian features released during the 1914-24 period. In 1918 — the peak year — nearly a third of the eighteen features made were comedies. All had bush backgrounds, and owed their existence to the success of Beaumont Smith's debut film as a director, **Our Friends the Hayseeds** (1917).

Beaumont Smith

Among Australian filmmakers, Beaumont Smith was a rare combination of creative craftsman and entrepreneur. He had worked in journalism and publicity, and his most notable films shrewdly incorporated a strain of nationalism with the melodrama and comedy calculated to draw audiences. Smith was much less concerned than Raymond Longford or Franklyn Barrett to express a personal vision through filmmaking. His grounding in nationalistic literature and art, however, was solid. He knew and had worked with Steele Rudd, bought subjects for stage and film adaptation from Henry Lawson and Banjo Paterson, and in the early 1900s worked with C. J. Dennis on *The Critic* and *Gadfly* magazines. He was a collector of Australian paintings, eventually owning "one of the most representative selections of this country's art".[11] But in his films, as in earlier stage productions, his interest in nationalism was guided more by business and less by the artistic impulse that motivated Longford and Barrett.

After working briefly on the *Bulletin*, Smith became publicity manager for the theatre producer William Anderson, and in 1911 showed a flair for exploiting novelty with his operation of "Tiny Town", a European midget circus which he toured through Australia, New Zealand, Canada and Africa. In 1914 he became a theatrical entrepreneur with the importation of English plays and his own adaptations of Ethel Turner's *Seven Little Australians* and Lawson's *While the Billy Boils*. In 1917, a depressed theatre trade led him to abandon that field and turn to film production. His **Hayseeds** film series was a clever imitation of the rural stories by Steele Rudd, and for a while cornered the market for rural comedy on the screen. Smith had worked initially with Bert Bailey and Edmund Duggan on the stage dramatisation of Steele Rudd's *On Our Selection* stories, and in his writing and direction of the knockabout romp **Our Friends the Hayseeds**, he closely moulded his characters on Rudd's, even to the extent of having "Dad" as one of the leads together with "Ma" and a boisterous family. The box office returns were so good that two more Hayseed pictures were made that year — **The Hayseeds Come to Town** and **The Hayseeds' Backblocks Show**, and these were followed by **The Hayseeds' Melbourne Cup** in 1918. Two more titles within the same formula followed in 1923 — **Prehistoric Hayseeds** and **Townies and Hayseeds** — both of which revived the convention of comparing gawky rural life with slick city ways.

Smith was the complete filmmaker/showman. He wrote, directed and distributed his productions, and they were among the most quickly and cheaply made; his earliest productions cost between £600 and £1200. Longford's **The Sentimental Bloke** (1919) had cost £2000. After writing a first draft script, Smith often sought comments from his wife Elsie who, according to relatives, shared his creative flair. His brother Gordon attended to company finances and assisted with production[12], and *Everyones* noted that on location Beaumont Smith was:

more often than not taken for the chief mechanist, as he was busy here and there arranging props, adjusting lights and doing a hundred and one other things that a producer ought not to do.[13]

When he had built up a sufficient package of films, Smith would personally tour them around Australia and New Zealand, frequently enhancing their regional appeal by filming part or all of a story against local landmarks. His production schedule, from first shots to post-production, was usually no more than a month; and while his films were often criticised for thin, unoriginal plots and technical indifference, his survival lay in lacing formula stories with lively and exploitable gimmicks. A typical example was the melodrama **Desert Gold** (1919), in which events surrounding a champion racehorse included a desert gun battle, a spectacular steeplechase pile-up and an attempt on the horse's life in which a wire is stretched across the track.

With **Satan in Sydney** (1918), Smith linked Australia's anti-German attitude with another war theme recurrent throughout Australian films — a city under alien threat. The bigotry of the plot earned it many headlines and high box office returns: Australia's anti-German stance was linked with the traditional discrimination against the resident Chinese. The story begins before the war with a country girl who, having been socially embarrassed by a German choirmaster, is driven from home by a narrow-minded parent and forced to live in Sydney. The German follows her and his attentions cost the girl job after job. She goes to the battlefront at the outbreak of war, while her lover from the country, who has come to Sydney to enlist, is enticed into a Chinese opium den that has been founded by the German in order to tempt newly enlisted troops to desert. In this unlikely and convoluted plot the German, as portrayed by Charles Villiers, was the film's most obvious "Satan"; but the title and also the publicity — particularly after a temporary ban by the police — could leave few in doubt that Satan was part of the wicked city itself and to be found specifically within its Chinese community. Prompted by the opium den scenes the police suppressed the film pending judgement by the Censorship Board. **Satan in Sydney** was, however, soon released uncut when the Board decreed that it would bring no offence to the Chinese community and that furthermore it provided a valuable warning to soldiers. Most reviewers praised the pace and social concern, although the *Lone Hand* considered it "a poor production, with a drab plot of the penny novelette type".[14] The *Green Room* judged it to be "right up to the minute, and deals with affairs that are of paramount importance to men and women who live in these troublesome times".[15] *Theatre Magazine* praised its use of locations and the *Green Room* added, "It analyses whether the city is more immoral than the country — whether Satan lives in Sydney more than he does in the country".[16]

Only one of Smith's seventeen silent films survives today and of the hallmark **Hayseed** series, only the sound version is known to exist. The quality of the 1933 **Hayseeds** and a portion of **The Digger Earl** (1924), compared with the other two surviving productions — **The Adventures of Algy** (1925) and **Splendid Fellows** (1934) — is probably an indication of the haste and consequent lack of finesse that characterised most of his work. The *Bulletin*'s reaction to **The Gentleman Bushranger** (1922) emphasises this:

Cobb and Co's coach with the gold escort leaves the wild, lawless diggings from the door of a fine two-storey brick pub in a very modern street. A motor-car is in the offing, and the woman in the case prances around wearing Centennial Park riding breeches.[17]

By shooting swiftly, if at times carelessly enough to earn himself the nicknames "One-take Beau" and "That'll Do Beau", Smith was responding realistically to the uncertain marketing and low returns in Australian film production. The film trade journal *Everyones* commented:

There are some who sneer at Beau Smith's films, but it is a fact that they have all made money for him and for the showmen who have screened them, and what more could any man ask?[18]

Despite the successes, little over two years after entering the field Smith seriously questioned whether it was worthwhile continuing to make films and in May 1919 he announced that he would suspend production until the more equitable exhibition terms being sought by himself and other local producers had been secured. He regarded the inequity in the terms offered for Australian and imported films by the large city exhibitors to be the main deterrent to local production.[19] The next month he put it far more strongly:

Australian picture production cannot stagger along any more. It has a place in our life today, and this fact must be recognised. The industry can only be built up with the cooperation of all parties concerned — the producer, the exhibitor and the public. . . . There are many other people who would be willing to interest themselves in local production if they saw a certainty of their films being shown on equitable terms.

He went on to point out that, "A good Australian picture never fails to attract big houses, and wise picture showmen book them".[20] This opinion, upheld by other producers, was to be hotly contested at the 1927 Royal Commission by distributors, who claimed that too many Australian films were "not up to standard".

In October 1919, planning to combat the adverse reputation of Australian films, Beaumont Smith announced a new series of "Australian super-films" whose high budgets would ensure, not to say necessitate, a release in England, beginning with **The Man from Snowy River** and **While the Billy Boils**. Although the scale of Australian production had revived in the second half of the year, Smith delayed these plans until he and his fellow producers had secured better exhibition terms. He concluded optimistically: "Before the present month is done it is hoped satisfactory arrangements will be made."[21]

New approaches

By the war's end, the old sense of comfortable isolation and innocence had left Australia. Battlefield achievements and first-hand contact with Britain had dispelled many illusions and a new sense of nationhood was confirmed when Australia signed the Treaty of Versailles as a separate nation. The economy had improved since the beginning of the war, although unemployment remained high throughout the 1920s. Social conflict, aggravated by the wartime conscription issue, continued throughout 1919, a year in which returned soldiers fought ferociously in the streets with militant trade unionists. But while many Australians embraced the new nationalism with confidence, many others still considered England to be the only true "home". As the recent war glories became enshrined beside the old and durable bush ideals, it became apparent that the fresh sense of national identity would not survive too far into the 1920s.

In Australian film production the war years had brought not only propaganda and comedy but also costume drama. Longford's **The Mutiny of** the **Bounty** (1916) and Barrett's **The Monk and the Woman** (1917) were two such films. There was also a re-telling of the Eureka Stockade saga — Alfred Rolfe's **The Loyal Rebel** (1915); a revival of convictism in John F. Gavin's **His Convict Bride** (1918), and the story of a famous Australian poet, **The Life's Romance of Adam Lindsay Gordon** (W. J. Lincoln, 1916). One notable absence was bushranging. Under a 1912 amendment to the 1908 New South Wales Theatres and Public Halls Act, bushranging film scenes were expressly banned in that State. Since no less than fifteen bushranging films had been made between 1906 and 1912 (and most were profitable) the removal of screen bushranging from New South Wales, the State with the largest film audience, created a minor crisis. New national cinema subjects were obviously needed, but the stop-start nature of the industry brought no solution.

From the end of the war until the early 1920s, the perpetuation of old nationalist ideals provided a temporary answer. There was a ready local audience for this type of film, and at least two key filmmakers responded with confidence and maturity. The first was Raymond Longford, who in 1918 commenced his rich cycle of Australian subjects with the production of **The Woman Suffers** and **The Sentimental Bloke**.

Longford and Lyell

"Veering from the beauty of the bush to the sorrow of the city", **The Woman Suffers** showed the family retribution that followed the jilting of a woman. The *Bulletin* praised the blending of melodrama with authentic backgrounds, stating that it "never descends to the pathetic incongruities of imported fiction and tries to picture our life without fanciful embellishments".[22] The Adelaide *Mail* noted the "beauty and rugged grandeur"[23] of the country scenes, and the *Bulletin* alluded to this when it noted approvingly that the "local colour throughout" was "full of good Australian sunlight".[24] A decade later, "KDS" in the *Bulletin* recalled that **The Woman Suffers** had captured some of the Australian nationalist painters' love of the countryside when he declared:

No truer picture of the "blue and gold" days has been made.... The film showed the Murray in flood, sheep-droving, lamb-marking, cattle-mustering, and dust, a burning hut, kangaroos, a child lost in the ranges, a demented mother ... lost and picked up by a real swaggie, and a dinkum parson with a sulky — all this true to life.[25]

Of Longford's earlier films, three had dealt with contrasts between the Australian city and the bush, and three with differences between England and Australia. In real life, both distinctions had been intensified by the experience of war. Growing urbanisation and a nostalgic longing for the bush were elements of C. J. Dennis's book of verse, *Songs of a Sentimental Bloke*, of which more than 60 000 copies were sold within eighteen months of its publication in 1915. It is the story of a city barrowman redeemed from his larrikin ways by the love of a good woman — but always on the brink of being lured back by his mates into another bout of heavy drinking and a flutter at two-up. Special pocket editions of the book were printed for troops in the trenches of Europe and its sequel, *The Moods of Ginger Mick* (1916), had Mick, the Bloke's cobber, forsaking the urban alleyways to enlist in the army and die gloriously at Gallipoli.

Longford's version, **The Sentimental Bloke**, received better reviews and made more money than any other Australian feature before it, yet the director had great difficulty in raising the money for its production and waited almost a year after its completion for a release. At first it was rejected outright by Australasian Films, but later made a good proportion of its profit for that company alone. The idea of adapting C. J. Dennis's story-poem for the cinema first came from the film executive J. D. Williams, who gave Longford a copy of the book to read soon after its publication. Longford asked Lottie Lyell for an opinion and she thought it could have success as a film because of the uncomplicated plot and the simple love story; no potential investor shared her views, even though Longford had a reputation as a good director, and one whose films made money. Finance came eventually from an Adelaide company, The Southern Cross Feature Film Company, which had employed Longford to make **The Woman Suffers**. Once the budget was secured another obstacle presented itself: the author himself, who feared that any miscasting of his hero would ruin future sales of the book. Dennis's reluctance to sell the screen rights was ultimately overcome after prolonged negotiations and a royalty payment of £1000 — half the film's budget. Dennis, however, refused to participate in the production although, ironically, its success eventually led him to collaborate closely with Frank Thring on the vastly inferior sound remake of 1932.

C. J. Dennis's verse had achieved instant fame with its quaint use of colloquialisms and colourful characterisation, but it lacked a narrative structure that the filmmakers needed. In writing their scenario, Longford and Lyell developed a rich and perceptive story from Dennis's verse (much of which is used in the film as inter-titles).

The events of the book take place in Melbourne's "Little Lon" district in the city's centre, but Longford's locale was working-class Woolloomooloo in Sydney, a teeming inner city area adjacent to Darlinghurst where he had spent his formative years. All the actors benefited from the director's encouragement to familiarise themselves with slum living before filming began. The *Green Room* journal related that the actors:

talked Woolloomoolese by day, and slept at night with a book of the verses under their pillows. They sought Doreens among the mazes of Strawberry Hill and Chippendale, and embarked on strange and adventurous enterprises with wild rabbit men in the highways and byways of the Waterloo.[26]

Longford explained to the *Lone Hand*:

The true art of acting is not to act ... That's what I have drummed into the ears of my characters and I think it has had its effect in the naturalness of my pictures . . . It is the little things that count, the little human touches that build up a big production, and to these I have given the most thought.[27]

It is familiarity with many such touches that gives **The Sentimental Bloke** a strong sense of place and character. Although the film mainly concerns Bill (the Bloke) and Doreen, there is a firm background sense of others living exactly as the central characters live. Arthur Higgins, one of Australia's leading cameramen, worked on most of Longford's productions and contributed significantly to this impression. Sets were used sparingly and the "interiors" were filmed out-of-doors to avoid paying the excessive rentals charged by Australasian Films for their Rushcutters Bay studio.

In contrast to the large American film teams of the period, the technical crew numbered no more than four. Lottie Lyell's behind-the-scenes collaboration was vital, for she co-wrote the scenario with Longford, assisted with the costumes, art direction, editing and business matters. The art direction reinforces the social impact of the settings, particularly the cluttered parlours with their Edwardian bric-a-brac.

The performance of Arthur Tauchert as the Bloke was the most immediate sign of Longford's success, but Lottie Lyell brought equal strength and added sensibility to her role as Doreen. Lyell was already an experienced film actress but Tauchert's only previous screen appearances had been in two undistinguished short comedies directed by John F. Gavin. In **The Sentimental Bloke** Tauchert's comic talent is most evident in the way he communicates the conflict between the Bloke's easy ways and the leaden respectability he has to accept as part of his infatuation for Doreen. His performance is instinctive rather than the mugging burlesque it might have been, and he builds a rapport with the audience through repeated touches — such as nudging his hat back, digging friends and foes in the ribs, and unbuttoning his waistcoat for action. He brings comic subtlety to small moments — even the way the Bloke cuddles Doreen on the beach, enthusiastically squeezing her mouth and cheeks.

The Sentimental Bloke gives some sense of Longford's mastery of film technique. In the introduction to the Bloke's rival, the Stror 'at Coot, the director draws attention to the Bloke's feigned indifference, followed by his mounting fury at the intimacy between the Coot and Doreen by skilful framing and cutting between the characters. The film's distance from melodramatic convention he emphasises with an exaggerated dream sequence in which the Bloke imagines he has hurled the Coot to his doom over a sea cliff — then awakens to find himself tumbling out of bed.

The film's only perceivable fault is its concluding descent into lush pastoral romanticism as the Bloke and Doreen move to an orchard inherited from a country uncle. Although serving the period's collective Australian dream, its effect remains that of a postscript.

The Sentimental Bloke was first screened privately at the Adelaide Wondergraph in November 1918 and the *Advertiser* regarded it as "deeply human and true to the nature of a big class of city dwellers".[28] The public premiere took place exactly a year later in the same city with the Governor of

South Australia in attendance. Within weeks of its subsequent release in Melbourne all box office records had been broken and **The Sentimental Bloke** played to packed houses all over Australia. In Sydney, patrons paid the unheard-of price of 3/3d for standing room at the Theatre Royal. The literary journal the *Triad* commented that it was "very easily the best Australian picture yet . . . It is a blessed relief and refreshment after much of the twaddlesome picturing and camouflaged lechery of the films that come to us from America".[29] The good reviews and attendance continued in England where the *Daily Express* wrote, "If Australia can keep up this standard, a new and very serious competitor will enter the world's film markets."[30] The *Referee* stated that, "The film makes an instant appeal to high and low, rich and poor . . . there has been nothing quite like it before . . . wholesome, humorous, pathetic . . . the sort of thing one feels better for having seen."[31] The *Daily Mail* classified it as one of "the two greatest pictures ever produced in the British Empire". No clue was given as to the identity of the other film.[32]

Five years after the Gallipoli events it dramatised, Longford's next production, **Ginger Mick** (1920), brought humour and a sense of loss to Australia's intense pride in its war achievements. The casual slum mateship and scepticism about the war gives way under fire to heroic individualism. Mick's initial response to Gallipoli is ironic — after enlisting to escape the monotony of "'awkin' rabbits", he finds himself engulfed in the dreariness of a "bunny's" life in the trenches. Reviewing the film, the British *Kine Weekly* stated that during the story's climax Ginger Mick shows:

real merit and grit by heading the charge when all the officers have been killed. Wounded in the neck, he finally dies, leaving behind him his broken-hearted sweetheart and his sorrowing friends, who have only the thought of his bravery and courage with which to comfort themselves.

In relating social background to character, the reviewer wrote that the

endurance and strength of the new virile life in Australia is painted with vivid, sturdy strokes, which help to explain the personality of the hero.[33]

Unfortunately no copy of the film survives.

Longford's **On Our Selection** (1920) was made at a time when the belief that Australia could continue to be a nation of small farmers still held sway. Immediately after the war, the Commonwealth and States collaborated on a Soldier Settler Scheme under which 37 000 returned soldiers took up land holdings across the country. The failure of the scheme over the next two decades was final confirmation, if any were needed, that Australia's future lay with urban secondary industry and the growth of cities and suburbs.[34]

Bert Bailey's stage adaptation of Steele Rudd's *On Our Selection* stories enjoyed constant success from the time of its premiere at the Palace Theatre, Sydney, in May 1912. Steele Rudd (whose real name was Arthur Hoey Davis) had originally created his durable "Dad and Dave" characters for the *Bulletin*, and from 1895 they appeared in a series of short stories in that paper. These were eventually published as *On Our Selection* in 1899. Rudd's characters were based on the experiences of his own family and their neighbours slogging away on small blocks of land — their "selections" — on the Darling Downs of southern Queensland. Davis was always quick to point out that his homely people, battling against the unpredictable hazards of rural life were real, drawn from his own life.

Bailey was the writer, producer and star (as Dad) of the first stage adaptation. He was a New Zealander who began his theatrical life in the 1880s as a singer, later becoming a touring actor. With Edmund Duggan, he wrote many Australian plays, among them the original *The Squatter's Daughter*, *The Man from Outback* and *The Native Born*. After the stage version of *On Our Selection*, the characters of Dad and Dave quickly became famous all over Australia and in London. In 1919 Longford began work on a screen version of *On Our Selection* for E. J. Carroll when Wilfred Lucas, an American director employed by Carroll, decided he could not do justice to a subject so intrinsically local. Since the Bert Bailey–Steele Rudd agreement had barred a filmed version of the play, Carroll negotiated for a direct adaptation of the original Rudd stories. In any case, Longford claimed that he preferred

the starkly true Australian characters of the book to the puppets of the play, with all its old trappings of mortgages, flinty-hearted moneylenders, black-moustached heavies in polo suits, and the various other borrowed stage traditions.[35]

In Longford's faithful interpretation, the bush, for once, was not used as the moral antithesis of the city, but was shown as a hard, uncompromising region which forced its settlers to constantly re-work their strategy in order to survive. The entire production was shot just outside the Sydney metropolitan area at Baulkham Hills which at that time was farming country. The interiors were filmed in a roofless bark hut with muslin stretched over it to diffuse the sunlight. The cast, a mixture of seasoned professionals and newcomers, included Percy Walshe as Dad, Beatrice Esmond as Mum, and Tal Ordell as Dave.

At the time of **On Our Selection**'s release, the Sydney *Sun* commented:

Mr Longford has been content to depict men and things as they are rather than as they might be, and the result, though aesthetically disappointing, is thoroughly convincing.[36]

Smith's Weekly was similarly overwhelmed by Longford's accuracy:

Whether so much realism is advisable in a picture is a mixed question. The ugliness of bush life is presented without the saving grace of kindliness and good nature ... This "holding the mirror up to nature" needs discretion.[37]

The intervening years have enhanced the film's aesthetic as well as its sociological value. Scatterbrain farce breaks out here and there, but for the most part **On Our Selection** is an authentic, deeply human evocation of a pioneering period. The story tells of the family's difficult adjustment to bush life, including the trials of fire and famine. The settlers' indignity at having to beg the neighbours for a bag of flour is handled with a touching restraint that demonstrates the affection shown by Longford for his characters both in this film and in **The Sentimental Bloke**.

Longford subsequently directed a sequel called **Rudd's New Selection** which was released in 1921. The farm scenes were shot at the Megalong Valley in the Blue Mountains and the interiors at the Palmerston Studios operated by E. J. and Dan Carroll in Sydney. Longford informed the *Picture Show* magazine that **Rudd's New Selection** would be

something of a satire on bush folk — a friendly satire, mind you. It shows the Rudds in their prosperous days, and has given the players and myself greater chances than **On Our Selection** did.[38]

The leading players were J. P. O'Neill as Dad, Tal Ordell as Dave with Lottie Lyell supplying the romantic interest as Nell Rudd. The main elements, again episodic, were Dave's return from his honeymoon and his struggles at the new selection, and Nell's choice between two equally persistent suitors. The success of **Rudd's New Selection** was to equal that of its predecessor, but it is impossible to judge it as the film no longer survives.

While Raymond Longford was earlier making the transition from actor to producer and director, Lottie Lyell was becoming the most prominent and consistently successful of Australian screen actresses. Not only was she the nation's first film star, she appeared in at least seventeen of the thirty films made by Longford, and shared with him a creative collaboration unequalled by any later Australian filmmaking team. She contributed, both as scenario writer and business manager, on nearly every film made by Longford between 1910 and 1925. Later in her career, while working on **The Blue Mountains Mystery** (1921), the actress Marjorie Osborne said of Lottie Lyell:

I like brains in a woman, and she has them. Her work on this picture is more on the directing side than the acting. She assists Mr Longford, and the two of them have plenty of healthy argument when their ideas about a scene are different.[39]

In later years, Marjorie Osborne amplified this by stating that Lyell's suggestions were an essential part of Longford's work as a director.[40] The *Picture Show* in November 1921 praised Lottie Lyell as "enthusiastic, original, possessing charm and common sense", while the same magazine had earlier observed:

Her name is closely linked with the early struggles of the picture pioneers, and she must always be regarded as the first girl who really had faith in locally-made movies.[41]

The Blue Mountains Mystery was Longford's third production for E. J. Carroll and the first to provide Lyell with a formal co-direction credit. The subject matter was far removed from the line taken by **Sentimental Bloke** and the **Selection** films. Lottie Lyell's script, adapted from Harrison Owen's novel *The Mount Marunga Mystery*, involved the alleged murder of a wealthy businessman and the eventual discovery that the victim was an underworld look-alike impersonator. John Faulkner played the dual role of millionaire and criminal, and Marjorie Osborne one of the prime murder suspects. The company spent several months on location filming in and around the fashionable Carrington and Hydro Majestic Hotels in the Blue Mountains, and the budget was almost double that of **The Sentimental Bloke**.

When it was released the reviews and financial returns were good in Australia, England and America. The London *Bioscope* wrote:

The Blue Mountains Mystery by its restrained acting, shows the force which a story gains in the telling. As a consequence, suspense is held throughout.[42]

The variety of locations included Katoomba and Echo Point in the Blue Mountains, Sydney Harbour and the jungles of a South Sea island. *Everyones* praised the film for getting "off the beaten bush track".[43] The nationalistic *Bulletin* could still approve of **The Blue Mountains Mystery** as being "real Australian, acted by healthy, good-looking Cornstalk men and women . . . The views of Echo Point are a masterpiece; in the valleys a mist breaks like a surf and curls against the rugged fissure of a rent tableland."[44] *Everyones* again declared that it deserved "every support, not only from the standpoint of Australian sentiment, but because it shows our own producers to be capable of the best in film production when given the opportunity."[45] Along with the majority of Longford's finest achievements, the film is now lost.

Franklyn Barrett

A similar fate awaited the films of Franklyn Barrett: only two complete silent feature films by Barrett survive from among the great number he made — a total of thirteen in eleven years — **The Breaking of the Drought** (1920) and **A Girl of the Bush** (1921). These two films may well have been his best and like Longford's finest surviving films they were made during one of the Australian silent cinema's most nationalistic periods. Barrett's strength was his documentarist's perception of everyday events (deriving from his work as an actuality cameraman), and in the films that survive he crafted a richly authentic and affectionate response to the values of rural Australia. "We were for Australia first, last and always", Barrett recalled many years later. "We decided if it was not possible to make interesting pictures about our own country then we would give up the ghost".[46]

After working on films for T. J. West in 1911-12, Barrett directed **A Blue Gum Romance** and **The Life of a Jackeroo** (1913), the first features backed by Fraser Films. The former, a romantic drama set against the hardwood timber industry, and the latter, an English "new chum" tale, both enjoyed local success and also performed well in England and the United

States. After a period as an overseas film buyer for the Frasers, Barrett returned to local production as a director and cameraman on his own and other people's projects. In 1916 he directed **The Pioneers**, adapting the script from a competition-winning novel by Katharine Susannah Prichard. A colonial bush story spanning two generations, its climax focuses on attempts to silence a blackmailer who has discovered that a respected community figure is an escaped convict. Like Longford's later version of the story (1926), Franklyn Barrett's **Pioneers** suffered from being over-ambitious on a limited budget.

Between 1916 and 1920, Barrett directed two costume dramas, **The Monk and the Woman** (1917) and **Struck Oil** (1919) as well as the contemporary propaganda piece, **Australia's Peril** (1917). Only **The Monk and the Woman**, aided by church controversy, moved into profit, and **Struck Oil** (in its stage form, an early triumph for J. C. Williamson and his wife Maggie Moore, which had brought them to Australia in 1874) seems to have shared the basic budget and release problems of **The Pioneers**.

The scale, topicality and background of **The Breaking of the Drought** was much more promising. Before reaching the screen it had a long gestation period. In 1902 Bland Holt first presented his play of the same name in Sydney; it was so successful that for a long time Holt refused to release the rights for the screen. Finally, in 1919, Barrett was able to secure agreement and begin production, and the scale was impressive. Shooting took place in Sydney, Narrabri, Mulgoa and Kangaroo Valley, and the real drought scenes — which were to make this the first Australian film censored for export because it showed the nation in an unfavourable light — included a catastrophic dust storm and plagues of mice devouring wheat stored in silos. The cast was drawn from leading stage performers including Rawdon Blandford, Nan Taylor, Marie La Varre, John Faulkner and Charles Beetham, along with the up-and-coming film regular, Dunstan Webb.

The son of a country family, portrayed as sturdy self-sacrificing citizens battling against drought, is disowned after siphoning away the family fortune to corrupt society friends in Sydney. After the family has first been ruined and then saved, the down-at-heel son returns to the bush in time to witness, with almost divine retribution, a soul-searing bushfire. After rescue, reunion and forgiveness, the drought is broken.

The original play had been staged at a time of severe drought. The making of the film coincided with another drought in 1919 and the film, according to Barrett, helped to "illustrate to our city dwellers the brave fight of the man on the land, and make them a little more tolerant of their country cousins". The film is a true epic, worthy of comparison with Longford's **Sentimental Bloke** and **On Our Selection** but covering much more in its contrasting of the extremes of country and city life. The documentary record of the drought is vivid, and the city slum life surrounding the family in its doldrums includes such authentic details as ragged children sitting on a worn doorstep and the unemployed bedding down in Sydney's Domain park. The inter-titles, like those for **A Girl of the Bush**, are littered with rich examples of Australian argot.

The twist of fortune that returns the family to its farm, while even less credible than the ending of **The Sentimental Bloke**, again evokes a nostalgia for rural ways. The city is given no redeeming features; it is a place of high society, loose living and corruption contrasted starkly with poverty. The return of the prodigal son from city to country is realised through several classic images once more recalling the "blue and gold" ideals of the nationalist painters. One in particular is memorable — the son seated in front of a boiling billy beneath a majestic gum, while beyond him the road stretches away to a lonely farmhouse and mountains.

Barrett's weakness was his inability to curb the excesses of stage-trained actors, and both **The Breaking of the Drought** and **A Girl of the Bush** contain some exaggerated posturing. Nevertheless, he did give his actors the benefit of lengthy rehearsal on **Know Thy Child**, and an indication of his methods on that film is contained in a statement by Fred James, brother of the actress Vera James who appeared in both **A Girl of the Bush** and **Know Thy Child**.

He was a very kind man. There was no ranting and raving of the kind I later saw in Hollywood. He pretty much let people have their own head. He'd give them an idea of what he wanted, and say "Go ahead and see what you can do".[47]

Made directly after **The Breaking of the Drought**, Barrett's **A Girl of the Bush** was technically superior, although its naturalism was again at odds with occasional moments of melodrama. Documentary observations of rural life are interwoven with the central story of Lorna, a young woman who manages and eventually inherits her uncle's property while saving it from the clutches of a scheming cousin. He is a more direct link with urban evil than is the prodigal son of **The Breaking of the Drought**, but provides little more than a larrikin subplot until his death brings an accusation of murder to Lorna's suitor Tom, one of the station hands. As the story develops, the film's tempo quickens, climaxing in the intercutting between the deliberations of a murder jury and a wild coach ride bringing vital evidence. Barrett's editing is both taut and exciting, and although his frequent use of flashbacks confuses the tightly-packed plot, this and the cross-cutting indicates that as a director he was well-versed in the editorial sophistication of D. W. Griffith. In the role of Lorna the inexperienced actress Vera James gives a performance of ease and natural charm which under Barrett's guidance she would later surpass in **Know Thy Child** before leaving to pursue a career in Hollywood.

Know Thy Child (1921) recalled the abandoned mother theme of **The Woman Suffers**, but here there was no retribution and no convenient escape to the country. Instead, salvation of sorts comes from the moneyed city class who were to appear in angelic or comic contrast in almost every other slum film of the period. Having been snubbed by other women who won't let their children play with her illegitimate daughter, Sadie (Vera James) is befriended by a socialite charity-worker. Later on the daughter, having grown up, is employed and eventually propositioned by the socialite's husband. At this point all is revealed: he is her father. **Know Thy Child** was praised on its release for an unblinkered yet subtle handling of illegitimacy and incest. Indeed, taste must have been one of its virtues, for the publicity boasted of a film that "Every Man, Woman and Child Will Enjoy".

Although it was regarded by some reviewers and later remembered by Vera James as superior to **A Girl of the Bush, Know Thy Child** was criticised by others for not emphasising Australian life at a time when it was considered necessary to oppose the dominance of Hollywood. But the *Bulletin*, normally the champion of inland myth, defended Barrett with:

A bush story might be more healthy than the **Know Thy Child** one but, after all, the story is in a better frame for Australian vision in home surroundings, than in the artificial background of USA problem-drama films; and it has the advantage of keeping money in the country that would otherwise be paid abroad for a similar picture. And life in Australia, anyway, is not all Bush.[48]

Barrett's abandonment of Australiana for this film came at a time of increased uncertainty for him and for other Australian producers. **Know Thy Child** failed to return money, and his next film, the racing drama **A Rough Passage** (1922), was his last. Barrett withdrew entirely from production and for the rest of his career worked as an exhibitor. He died at the age of ninety-one in July 1964.

The stranglehold of the exchanges

For Franklyn Barrett, Raymond Longford and Beaumont Smith, increased nationalism had become an economic strategy as much as an ideal and for several years after 1920 it was linked with higher budgets to encourage overseas sales and allow them to remain solvent. In Barrett's view this was part of a concerted effort to overcome the stranglehold of the overseas exchanges set up in Australia during the war years. Where exhibitors had previously been able to select films on merit alone — including cheaply-made Australian productions — the exchanges' new contract system compelled exhibitors to accept everything sight-unseen by "blind" and "block" booking a pre-sold package. (As early as 1914, Longford had confronted the combine over this system with his **Silence of Dean Maitland**.) To cover themselves in case of an unsatisfactory film, most exhibitors entered into a second contract, and the market for Australian films declined rapidly. From this period onward, related Barrett,

Australian pictures even at £1000 began to be an unprofitable speculation. Attempts were made to improve the Australian film by spending lots more money on them with the hope of sales abroad making up the difference. Unfortunately the same contract system had been introduced almost everywhere and our little pictures cannot even push in. There are several exceptions, of course, but they only prove the rule.[49]

From 1920, the capital involved in the vertical integration of American production, distribution and exhibition interests was making the widespread sale of its output even more necessary than before. As the size and power of Hollywood studios grew, so did the cost of maintaining their "stars", production values and publicity. Several times during the 1920s, Australia ranked second to North America as the industry's best customer. By 1922-23, the USA supplied ninety-four per cent of the total value of films imported into Australia. But the impact of America had already been evident by 1915 when the American actress Josephine Cohan (Mrs Fred Niblo) wrote:

In Australia they look upon going to the movies as they do to the theatre. They know all the American players, and they are particularly fond of the Wild West films, for that phase of life is strange to them. They have built fine moving-picture theatres, patterning them after American playhouses, I imagine, for they like American things.[50]

In early 1918, Joseph P. Darling, visiting Australia as a "representative-at-large" for Fox Films, voiced early faith in Australia's ability to build a film industry, provided it looked to high capital investment and an overseas market.[51] Nearly two years later, Beaumont Smith prepared to give more than a head start to his plans for "super productions" by sailing from Sydney with the intention of making the bulk of **The Man from Snowy River** in Hollywood. He explained to the *Picture Show* that his aim was to learn about American production techniques as well as acquire insight into the American film industry at large:

I think, too, that being on the spot I will be able to secure an American release for my films far more readily than if I remained here and had to conduct all my negotiations by letter or cable.[52]

Although Smith intended to employ an American director, he denied that the **Snowy River** characters would become Americanised

. . . because Mr Smith is too keen a showman to overlook those points. He is taking a complete Australian equipment with him, even including the saddles.[53]

Four months later he returned to Australia having filmed nothing more than a documentary on Hollywood. Exchange rates and the expense of film production in America had ended his plans for feature production there, but he had at least been able to observe film production at all the major studios. Smith seemed more determined than ever before to upgrade his work: "America has plenty of mediocre films already, and she isn't so interested in Australia as to want second-rate pictures from here."[54]

Carroll-Baker Australian productions

If American expertise was to be used, then the alternative to Beaumont Smith's plan was to bring the Americans to Australia. Earlier importations by other concerns had not been particularly happy; they included the Englishman Alexander Butler, who followed Longford as Spencer's one-off director after the formation of Australasian Films–Union Theatres and the American Walter C. Plank, who preceded Longford as director of productions for Southern Cross Feature Films. But in September 1919 the importation by E. J. Carroll of the American director Wilfred Lucas and his wife, the writer Bess Meredyth, promised something more eventful.

Carroll's partner in this venture was Snowy Baker who, after appearing in **The Enemy Within**, had starred in Claude Flemming's **The Lure of the Bush** (1918), which Carroll distributed. Later, Baker travelled to Hollywood and met Lucas during a period of several months' observation and work. When at first it seemed that Lucas would be unavailable, Baker returned with the announcement that the Carrolls and he would form a syndicate with Beaumont Smith to feature Baker himself as **The Man from Snowy River**. In voicing his belief in the viability of an overseas market for bush films, Snowy Baker stated:

We could weave a romance about the bush that would make Australian bush films sought after just as eagerly as the pictures dealing with Western life in America. We can stamp out our type the same as the Western type. There is a wonderful field. Even our Aboriginals have not yet been exploited as they should. The field is vast.[55]

Despite the production philosophy shared by Baker and Beaumont Smith, it was Wilfred Lucas who became involved in the Carroll-Baker productions. Lucas was originally a stage performer and had entered film production as one of D. W. Griffith's stock company of actors at American Biograph in 1908. By 1914 he was directing at Universal Studios and in 1915 was one of their most prolific directors. In the same year he moved to Triangle where he appeared in a number of productions directed by Allan Dwan and it was possibly through Dwan that Lucas met Snowy Baker, because he was among Baker's contacts during Baker's first stay in Hollywood.

Bess Meredyth had also worked at Universal and in 1915 wrote the scenario for the Australian Louise Lovely's first Hollywood film, **Stronger Than Death**. Lucas's career as a director was probably on the decline by the time the couple visited Australia, but Bess Meredyth was just rising to prominence. After their return to Hollywood Meredyth co-scripted Fred Niblo's version of **Ben Hur**, wrote the 1926 **Don Juan** and remained in demand as a scriptwriter well into the 1940s.

Speaking at the 1927 Royal Commission, Dan Carroll stated that, encouraged by the success of **The Lure of the Bush** and **The Sentimental Bloke**, he and his brother E. J. Carroll had decided to embark on a comprehensive schedule of production. The rights for *On Our Selection* and *On Our New Selection* — filmed as **Rudd's New Selection** — were purchased and it was intended that at least one sequel to **The Sentimental Bloke** be produced. However, the Carrolls admitted to doubts about their overseas marketing operation. Dan Carroll told the Commission:

Being entirely Australian in character, we doubted the overseas value of The

Sentimental Bloke, Ginger Mick and the Steele Rudd films, and the idea of bringing an American producer and scenario writer was to endeavour to make pictures which would be entirely cosmopolitan in their appeal.

In July 1920 the *Picture Show* reported that E. J. Carroll's intention was "to send film footage *out* of Australia as against the foreign film mileage which now comes in".[56] Bess Meredyth was sent to search for suitable story material but she admitted, after studying Australian history, literature and national character, that she had found little that would be uniquely marketable for the audiences they had in mind. The only remaining option, Dan Carroll later reported, was for stories set in a station or bush environment. The result was three such films starring Snowy Baker — The Man from Kangaroo, The Shadow of Lightning Ridge and The Jackeroo of Coolabong, all produced in 1920. Among the imported personnel were the actress Brownie Vernon, cameraman Robert Doerrer and a film editor. Lucas himself played the part of a loutish villain in The Man from Kangaroo and during his appearances in front of the camera, he was directed by his wife.

The Man from Kangaroo is the only one of the three Lucas–Baker films to survive, and succeeds largely as an escapist action thriller which displays examples of small-town charm and Baker's agility. At the outset, Baker, playing the local parson, faces ostracism for teaching several of his young flock the art of fist-fighting. His sweetheart, played by Brownie Vernon, is first seen playfully tying knots in Baker's discarded clothes as he demonstrates his athletic prowess by high diving into the local swimming hole. Miss Vernon is soon revealed to be the victim of a swindling guardian with influence in the town who has arranged to have the parson transferred to the city.

Once in the city, Baker apprehends two snatch-and-grab thieves after a wild chase along traffic-filled streets, up walls and over bridges. Expressing his gratitude, the victim of the theft offers Baker a posting in his country parish, where all recent attempts to encourage religion have failed and the parson terrorised into leaving the town by the local bully — played by Wilfred Lucas. Baker accepts the appointment and encounters not only the bully, but also the re-located Miss Vernon and at first allows himself to be intimidated by both. He renounces his position and becomes a shearer, but his heroic stance is restored in the finale when he gives chase to a wildly careering coach containing Vernon and the villainous Lucas. The film's most spectacular stunt is Baker and Vernon's leap from the coach as it crosses a bridge spanning a deep gully and river.

The Man from Kangaroo is essentially a conventional Western melodrama incorporating a few recognisable Australian landmarks and some moderately engaging performances. While there is no doubting the acting ability of Vernon and Lucas, Baker is seldom given the opportunity to prove that his forte lies anywhere but in action. As the *Bulletin* wrote about one of his film performances in America: "He has an unscrupulous enemy — the man who told him he could act".[57] The same magazine wrote of **The Man from Kangaroo**:

Uncle Sam soon gets in his dirty work, and the Australian story becomes starred and striped ... It simply *couldn't* happen in Australia. In our backblocks the parson is as inevitable as the drought ... When *will* we get an Australian film? Barring the "Bloke" pictures, they all have the flavour of chewing-gum.[58]

The *Bulletin* was no less critical of the company's next production:

The only Australian thing about **The Shadow of Lightning Ridge** is the setting. The scenery is dinkum, but the story itself is a mistake of melodrama and Wild West movie.[59]

Everyones, however, reported that the ingredients were more diverse:

For several hundred feet he (Baker) is a lion hunter in Africa, for several hundred more he is on an American ranch, and he finished up as an outlaw in Australia.[60]

The stunt work was similarly ambitious. Baker was required to ride his horse over a high cliff and land through a cottage roof, repeat the action into a pool of water, jump the horse off a moving train and carry the heroine along a swaying cable above jagged rocks.

The Carrolls were particularly impressed with the qualities of **The Shadow of Lightning Ridge**. They renewed their contract with Lucas and Meredyth and sent them on a visit to America to sign up a new leading lady as well as to obtain new equipment and additional technical staff. The company also invested in Palmerston, a large Waverley mansion as their studio base. On his return to Australia Lucas announced that he intended to "aim at presenting Australians in their true light — as people with a little dignity, rather than as half-savage bush folk". His next Snowy Baker film would, he claimed, "show Australia from every aspect".

The Jackeroo of Coolabong turned out to be another English "new chum" action comedy. According to the publicity, Baker as an Englishman "arrived at an outback station, complete with monocle. But the fun started when someone called him 'dear' ''. The *Bulletin* wrote that the film:

contains all the features that went into the making of **The Lure of the Bush**, and Snowy Baker is once again demonstrator of how Young Australia can ride and drive and shoot and fight with his fists. Kathleen Kay, the quaint little American importation, does not even contrive to look like an Australian girl.[61]

To date, all the Carroll-Baker films had been box-office successes. They were released in the United States, and **The Shadow of Lightning Ridge** appeared on Broadway. But **The Jackeroo of Coolabong** was a turning point for the company. Arguments during production over alleged excessive expense led to the employment of Lucas and Meredyth being terminated and they returned with Baker to America where Baker enjoyed a short career as a star of Westerns before settling down as manager of a Hollywood country club.

Australian distribution for the Carroll-Baker films — in spite of their success — had been proving harder to achieve. **The Jackeroo of Coolabong** was released in Sydney in October 1921, but it failed to obtain an interstate release for another six months. Deciding to concentrate on films specifically for the Australian and British markets, E. J. Carroll placed Raymond Longford in charge of the Palmerston studio, where he successfully produced **Rudd's New Selection** and **The Blue Mountains Mystery**; but after that Carroll ceased regular production. This action was a serious blow to the industry. At the Royal Commission, Longford reported that Carroll as an exhibitor had been told that unless he left the production field, Australasian Films would terminate his overseas film supplies. Longford stated:

As part-owner of some Queensland theatres he (E. J. Carroll) depended on the combine for his supply of film, and, as they were opposed to local production, it would be impossible for him to continue should they cease supplies.

A more ironic discovery, made some years later, was that not only had **The Blue Mountains Mystery** enjoyed success in America, but all the Carroll-Baker films earned substantial profits in both the American and European markets. By means of some shady accounting, the Chicago corporation handling overseas distribution had sent the Carrolls only the smallest returns. By the time this was realised, it was years too late.

Other American visitors

In late 1919 E. J. Carroll had justified the importation of his American team as being necessary "to give the industry a fair start".[62] It might be argued that the popularity of the films sustained public awareness of Australian production, but in cultural and industrial terms they contributed little. When Charles Chauvel, who began his career as an assistant and bit-part player on the Carroll-Baker films, was asked at the Royal Commission whether they had been unduly "Americanised", he replied "unfortunately they were neither Australian or American". Following Lucas and Meredyth's departure the *Bulletin* commented:

Australia owes Lucas nothing. A great deal of Australian capital was meted — chiefly in big salaries — to the American bunch, Lucas and wife drawing £150 from shore to shore.

The writer contrasted Lucas with Longford:

Longford, so far, seems to be the only one who has given much practical encouragement to the industry; he has produced films at a profit, and thereby made the industry look healthy. Lucas, apart from wearing an extraordinary get-up and shouting through a megaphone, has left behind him a feeling of discouragement among people who would like to invest in the film industry.[63]

Far more sympathetically received than Lucas's efforts was **Silks and Saddles** (1921), produced and directed by the American John K. Wells, who worked as an assistant director on **The Man from Kangaroo** and was co-director of Beaumont Smith's **The Man from Snowy River** (1920). Perhaps the reception was due to the more English atmosphere of **Silks and Saddles**, although it might have emerged from either side of the Atlantic — or Pacific. W. G. Faulkner of the London *Evening News* wrote during the film's British release: "**Silks and Saddles** is a story of the great outdoors of Australia — how very English many of the locations are!"[64] A year later the *Bulletin* reported that the American company Robertson Cole was exploiting the production under its new title **Queen of the Turf**, "as a South American film".[65]

The subject was hardly new to Australians as locally-produced racing films had appeared regularly since **The Cup Winner** and **The Double Event** in 1911. Lucas and Meredyth had baulked at the idea of producing racing films because of their over-familiarity to British producers, but in spite of the predominance of formula material in **Silks and Saddles**, the direction is fresh and even the most mechanical situations are played naturalistically. An intimate approach lends great effect to Brownie Vernon's central performance, as well as to Tal Ordell's villain and the jovial neighbour played by John Cosgrove. Unhappily, Wells had no further opportunity to show his talents, for his backer, fearing losses if they continued after one success, forced the production company into liquidation. He tried hard to raise money to make further films in Australia but failed and returned to America.

The **Silks and Saddles** storyline was written by the actor John Cosgrove, who shortly afterwards supplied another story and performance for **Sunshine Sally** (1922). Lawson Harris, the film's director, was an American who had come to Australia in 1920 to work as production manager on Arthur Shirley's **The Throwback**. Under the auspices of Austral Super Films, his first production was **Circumstance** (1922), and it featured Yvonne Pavis, who was to star in all three of the company's films. In the second, **A Daughter of Australia** (1922), Harris himself appeared as an English migrant humping his bluey across Australia to escape a murder charge back home. Next came **Sunshine Sally**.

Viewed today, the social values of **Sunshine Sally** are more acutely perceived than those of **The Sentimental Bloke**. Its characters are tougher and hold fewer illusions about improving their lot. Sally's adopted parents are gin-soaked layabouts with a genuine resentment against the Potts Point upper class from whom, it is later revealed, they abducted Sally as an infant. Behind their reason for turning her out after she has lost her job in an oppressive steam laundry, is the indelible "difference" between Sally and the general run of slum people. As one class-conscious title puts it, Sally's "better nature revolts at anything cheap or tawdry". She is eventually restored to her rightful upper-crust family when a coincidence leads them to offer her an education as a lady.

While it is perceptive and entertaining, **Sunshine Sally** gives a condescending view of slum life. The upper class, living at Potts Point on the hill above, are shown as refined, poised and complete; the lower orders of Woolloomooloo are ignorant and accept the third rate as a matter of course.

"It's 'ell to be poor", Sally tells her friend Tottie as she remembers a meeting with the rich family's adopted son. As the realisation of her social restriction grows, she tells her Potts Point hostess, "It's awful ter be common".

A comedy-melodrama of manners, **Sunshine Sally** is one of the key films of the 1920s to reflect the role of women in society. While in reality the average working class woman was more oppressed than Sally herself, she is surrounded by a number of conventions which make the plight of her fellow women abundantly clear. Even in whimsical terms, the women are referred to by their men as "tarts", and at a picnic a medley of rich character vignettes includes an exhausted mother with screaming children and a husband who commands her to keep the "brats" quiet so he can pick a winner. Sally puts on male clothes on two occasions — one at the scene of a robbery; the second time to blend into a crowd at the Sydney Stadium. None of the male 'Loo friends is presented as an ideal marriage prospect and the pub provides consolation for one of them when Sally's reply to his proposal is that she "ain't ready for double harness".

The delayed and sporadic exhibition of the Austral Super output was ominous. For reasons of marketing difficulties and an unstable personal relationship between Harris and Pavis, the couple failed to return to Australia from what was claimed to be a sales trip back home to America.

More bushranging

The variety of filmmakers and the types of film being made increased in the early 1920s. Among the miscellaneous products of the early and mid-1920s was the expected quota of adaptations from popular plays and poems, together with a completely new phenomenon — features directed by principals of acting schools. Notable in this regard was P. J. Ramster, who for almost a decade after 1918 made short and feature length dramas starring pupils from his school in Sydney. Films financed by the wealthy through charities were another new growth area. Funds for **His Only Chance** and **Cupid Camouflaged** (1918) were originally raised by the Red Cross with the intention that returns would aid the war effort and **The Twins** (1923), set up on a similar basis, helped to raise funds for various Melbourne charities. Among not-so-wealthy producers was Mary Mallon who in 1924 courageously made a single feature, **The Price**. As a lone female producer (one not working with a husband or other women as Louise Lovely and the McDonagh sisters were to do), her closest parallel in the 1920s was Juliette De La Ruze, who in 1928 financed P. J. Ramster's last film, **The Russell Affair**.

Inexplicably avoiding the New South Wales ban on the subject, two new directors made and released bushranging films in 1920. The first was Harry Southwell, a Welshman who had come from America in 1919 after scenario work for Vitagraph. **The True Story of the Kelly Gang** (1920), the first of his three films about the Australian outlaw Ned Kelly, is the earliest bushranging feature to survive virtually intact. Its greatest asset is location

69

work filmed in the Warburton district near the Dandenong Ranges close to Melbourne. Otherwise, the standard of direction and performance is low and there are some alarming continuity gaps. As seen today, the film is sensation thinly disguised as moral guidance. The lesson, which included Ned Kelly's unlikely final words, "What fools we've been!", failed to save it from eventual censorship because the film was refused a screening by the citizens of Kelly's native Glenrowan and it was banned in Adelaide. Reviewers howled at the historical inaccuracies and when Southwell asked his cameraman Tasman Higgins to make fresh prints for its re-release, Higgins persuaded him to make a new version. The result, filmed in the Burragorang Valley west of Sydney, was **When the Kellys Were Out**, first released in July 1923. It was only a marginal improvement on the earlier film and suffered official intervention immediately after its completion. While, to the confusion of the New South Wales Police, that State's censors had passed the 1920 version, they banned **When the Kellys Were Out** in October 1922.

Smith's Weekly commented:

Although it is hard on the Southwell Co., the banning of the **Kelly Gang** should teach producers to aspire to higher things than the mere raking up of our best forgotten history.[66]

In early 1923 Southwell re-cut the film at the censor's recommendation with the result, stated *Everyones*, "that a good deal of the better work was necessarily deleted".[67] Two years later it was banned again in New South Wales, but by 1929 was still earning money on the country circuits of other States. Godfrey Cass, who played Ned Kelly in the first Southwell version, was in real life the son of the governor of Melbourne Gaol at the time of Kelly's execution in 1880. Neither this nor the actor's fat and fiftyish form were any aid to authenticity. During its British release one London critic summed up his impressions by saying:

We feel bound to say that, while this film might be attractive enough as a sensational story founded on fact, as an historical record of the deeds of the Kelly Gang it is ludicrous.[68]

Eight months after the premiere of **The True Story of the Kelly Gang** in 1920, an infinitely superior version of **Robbery Under Arms** made its appearance. The director was Kenneth Brampton, a stage character actor who later played several roles in films of the 1930s. To arrange finance for **Robbery Under Arms**, Brampton and the actress Tien Hogue, who played the part of Aileen, persuaded the mining magnate Pearson Tewksbury to serve as the producer and raise a budget of £3000. Tewksbury took part enthusiastically in the making of the film, but the experience of its release through Union Theatres left him reluctant to engage in further production. With the advantage of considerably more influence than the average producer, he told a specially assembled gathering of federal government ministers that the first immensely successful week of **Robbery Under Arms** at the Strand Theatre in Melbourne had brought him nothing save a bill for

16/1d to cover screening costs. Eventually, after the film had grossed £16 000, he managed to cover all costs with a small margin.[69]

Robbery Under Arms co-starred Brampton as the outlaw Starlight, with Roland Conway and Dunstan Webb as the Marsden brothers. As a director, Brampton conveys well the privations and sensibilities of awkward bush-born characters. His goldfields and farming backgrounds filmed at Braidwood near Canberra are realistically and moodily evoked; but pedantic, sometimes shoddy story construction and a censor-deflecting morality (which appears to have worked) lose much of the excitement of the Rolf Boldrewood novel. The action is at its best before and during the hold-up of a coach. Preceded by the bushrangers' preparations and intercut with the coach lumbering around hairpin bends, the hold-up itself is depicted with almost *cinema-verité* casualness.

Three years later brought the release of Kenneth Brampton's second feature, a family drama called **The Dingo**. While critically praised, it failed to return its money and Brampton directed no more films.

Increasing insecurity

Following E. J. Carroll's withdrawal from production, Raymond Longford lost little time in setting himself up in independent production. But the industry's constriction from mid-1922 and Longford's increasing bad luck cast a pall over his achievements. At the 1927 Royal Commission he attributed many of his industrial difficulties to Australasian Films–Union Theatres (AF–UT) whom he claimed had discriminated against him since the early 1910s. While it could never be proved that the combine did deliberately conspire against Longford, their rejection of nearly all his post-1914 films added weight to the claim.

In May 1922, Longford and Lottie Lyell formed Longford-Lyell Australian Productions with initial capital of £50 000. Their first project for this company, at a cost of just under £5000, was **The Dinkum Bloke**, an original story by Longford and Lyell inspired by **The Sentimental Bloke** characters. The *Sunday Times* considered:

This simple tale owes most of its attraction to the acting of Arthur Tauchert, the Bloke himself. In this film he surpasses his work in **The Sentimental Bloke**, which is saying a great deal.[70]

To ensure that **The Dinkum Bloke** was released through the combine, Longford made use of their studio and cameraman at what he regarded to be an "excessive rental". Nevertheless, the film was rejected by AF–UT and when subsequently bought by Paramount it was screened through Hoyts seven months after its completion. It soon returned £6000 to its backers and was sold in Britain to Gaumont for a further £2300. But in spite of the success Longford and Lyell's financiers did not wish to remain in production and liquidated the company

Longford next made two migration-incentive films for the Australian

Government which were screened during 1924 at the British Empire Exhibition in London. Following these, Longford and Lyell persisted as independents with a new company, Longford-Lyell Productions, which was to make three films on low budgets. The first, **Fisher's Ghost** (costing £1000), was based on actual Campbelltown (New South Wales) events in 1826. The combine rejected it for the unlikely reason of its gruesomeness, and Longford sold it outright to Hoyts for £30 to cover a one-week season. The film's strong commercial results, beginning with £1200 in that single week alone, were continued throughout Australia and Britain.

Unexpectedly at first, Australasian Films bought Longford-Lyell's next film, **The Bushwhackers** (1925), an Australian city-and-bush story based on Tennyson's "Enoch Arden". At the Royal Commission, Longford claimed that Australasian's purchase was to persuade him into heading their own mid-1920s feature production schedule which had not fared well under the Hollywood import F. Stuart-Whyte. After Longford's agreement, Australasian refused to buy **Peter Vernon's Silence** (1926), the final Longford-Lyell production, which was instead accepted by Paramount on a percentage basis. Longford related that twelve months after its completion, "it was accorded a première at a third-rate city theatre [The Empress, Sydney] with inadequate publicity and very little if any newspaper publicity". With these final two independent films, it appeared that a combination of low budgets and industrial uncertainty had led Longford and Lyell to apply their talents too thinly, as faithfulness to Australian atmosphere was virtually all they had in common with the earlier triumphs. The *Bulletin* found The **Bushwhackers** "amateurish and disappointing", and "only saved from complete failure by the comedy touches".[71] The British trade magazine *Kine Weekly* said of **Peter Vernon's Silence**: "Apart from its Australian atmosphere, this feature has little appeal."[72] Longford's misfortunes intensified. In December 1925 Lottie Lyell died of tuberculosis at the age of thirty-four. Many years later he wrote of his partner: "She was universally loved by all and her death was not only a deep loss to me, but to the Australian Film World at the time."[73] Her loss was closely followed by Longford's creative decline.

Through adaptability and stringent economy, Beaumont Smith remained a regular independent producer for three years longer than Franklyn Barrett but was to cease regular filmmaking the year before Longford. Nevertheless, in the five years after his return from Hollywood in 1920 Smith was able to produce and direct ten features. Only three came anywhere near the "super-productions" he had envisaged before his Hollywood trip and two of these, **The Man from Snowy River** (1920) and **While the Billy Boils** (1921) were made in the peak years 1920-21. The third, **Joe** (1924), according to contemporary reviews, seems to have been Smith's best film to this time. Drawing its narrative from a series of Henry Lawson stories, it told of the struggle of Joe Wilson and his wife on their country selection and the assistance Joe gives to an old school mate in the city. The *Bulletin* found the film "a faithful reflection of the spirit of the pioneers who battle in the open spaces, with a broad vein of humour running through it''.[74] Apart from this, to judge from the reviews of his other films of the 1920-25 period, Smith's 1919 determination to raise the quality of his features had proved to be impossible. Rather than risk money on expensive projects he had continued his initial practice of minimising risk with the prolific production of sure-fire subjects. Even his much-touted **The Man from Snowy River** appeared cheap and packed with formula ingredients. Of **While the Billy Boils**, ''Dido'' in the *Bulletin* wrote: ''I have a more appropriate title for this film. I would call it *While the Belly Boils*''.[75]

Old ideas recycled by Smith at this time were the **Hayseed** comedies, the dilemma of the English ''new chum'' and, with greatest constancy, differences between city and bush. Commercialism aside, his strategy was one more sign that after the 1920-21 period of creative maturity Australian filmmakers were again deprived of security and the freedom to explore new subjects. Despite Smith's impressive production tally, he shared many insecurities with his fellow filmmakers. In April 1922, about to travel to England, where he hoped to market at least three of his films, he told *Everyones* that failing the assurance of an outside market, ''I will discontinue production indefinitely. We cannot now produce solely for the local market, the cost of production is too high.''[76]

Three years and six films later his outlook was unchanged and he added that any filmmaker seeking to survive on the imitation of imported films for an export market was wasting his time.[77] At this point, Smith was completing what was to be his final silent, **The Adventures of Algy**.

Eight months later, in November 1925, Smith announced he would leave film production for exhibition. For the next twelve years he was to be managing director of a new company, the J. C. Williamson Picture Corporation of New Zealand. As if to emphasise the permanence of withdrawal, all of his stored props and scenery were destroyed by a fire in February 1926.

4

The Royal Commission
1925 – 29

Among those who gathered on the steps of the new Parliament House to watch the official opening in the nation's capital on 9 May 1927 were seven members of a Select Committee which had been convened the previous month to inquire into the motion picture industry. As they gazed out across the thousands of people crowded around the huge tents erected on Canberra's Parliamentary front lawn, their minds might have turned to the moment at which their inquiry had been abruptly suspended a few days before. Scarcely a fortnight after they had begun, the investigations were terminated when William Gibson, a joint managing director of Australasian Films–Union Theatres, declined to divulge his earnings. Because this refusal revealed the Committee's limited powers, its members now sought reconstitution as a Royal Commission. Amid Canberra's pomp and ceremony they stood near the man who would make that decision, the Prime Minister, Stanley Melbourne Bruce.

The watching crowds included at least three motion picture camera teams filming the ceremonial opening performed by the Duke of York. Joining the Commonwealth's Cinema Branch and **Australasian Gazette** in the coverage was a comparative newcomer, De Forest Phonofilms (Australia), established in September 1925, three years after the development in America of the De Forest sound-on-film recording system. As De Forest had been forbidden to record on-site sound, they sent Walter Sully to shoot silent coverage in Canberra. On their sound recorder in Sydney they captured the radio broadcast of the speeches, including Prime Minister Bruce and the Duke and Duchess of York, together with a choral rendition of the National Anthem led by the ageing Dame Nellie Melba.

Printed together, sound and image were premiered in Sydney on Saturday 14 May. Although the item received an enthusiastic response, its significance to the film industry was largely ignored at the Royal Commission into the Moving Picture Industry which followed the Canberra ceremonies — and the assent of the Prime Minister. Nobody could have foreseen that within two years both sound and the Royal Commission would play their part in forcing Australian feature production to a halt.

The sittings commence

By 5 August 1926 there had been enough friction within the film industry for Senator John Grant to first move that a Royal Commission be appointed "to inquire into and report upon the moving-picture industry in Australia". The basis for dissent was growing opposition to what many saw as the corrosive effect of the American cinema. The three main groups calling for action were Empire loyalists (who advocated a greater proportion of English and Australian films), the Australian producers struggling to remain in business (which meant virtually all of them), and women's organisations pressing for stricter censorship and the appointment of a woman censor. Senator Grant told Parliament that it should follow the example of the British Parliament and "numerous commissions and committees in various parts of the world . . . to discover what action can be taken to prevent the United States of America having a complete monopoly of the business". Grant then proceeded to list all major issues that would later be examined in detail by the Commission. His speech dealt with the influence of American cinema and its distribution-exhibition combines in Australia, the restrictive nature of block-booking which reduced the distribution of British and Australian films, and the need for government film taxes, tariffs and quotas to protect them. The Senator evaded the broader question of censorship with a call for the Minister of Trade and Customs to prohibit the export of Australasian Films' version of a nineteenth century convict novel *For the Term of his Natural Life*, then about to enter production in Sydney. "The screening of that picture", he said, "will present Australian life in its most unfortunate light."

The Minister of Trade and Customs, Senator Herbert Pratten, was no stranger to the film industry, for he was by now one of the producers' firmest political allies. On 6 April 1927, he officially opened the De Forest Phonofilms studio at Rushcutters Bay, Sydney, and in his speech, which was filmed, declared:

Ninety-five per cent of the Federal Parliament is in sympathy with Australian-made films. We recognise that the film is a great means of instilling a national Australian spirit in the Australian people.[1]

Commonwealth tariffs aimed at aiding Australian filmmaking were enacted on an average of every eight years since 1902, but the revenue had never been directly passed on to producers. Following a world-wide advocacy of film quotas from the early 1920s, Pratten in 1925 received a deputation of Australian producers including Raymond Longford, Franklyn Barrett and Arthur Shirley, who called for a fifteen per cent quota of Australian and British films. The *Sydney Morning Herald* reported that the Minister "expressed sympathy with the deputation's aspirations, and promised to have all phases of the film industry investigated".

The quota question was already under review in 1923 by the parliaments of the main production States, New South Wales and Victoria. While the New South Wales Chief Secretary's Department delayed decisive action until the mid-1930s, Victoria passed a Censorship of Films Act in 1926 that required 2000 feet of Australian film per screening in each Victorian theatre. It proved ineffective because this could be made up with short films, and there was no obligation on distributors to buy the films in the first place. But the protests in New South Wales continued, and were influential in the Commonwealth's decision to appoint the Select Committee.

Fresh from the Imperial Conference of 1926, Prime Minister Bruce stated that the film needs not only of Australia but of the entire British Empire could be served. Because he considered British legislative measures would do more than enough to help the Australian film industry, he urged that a comparatively modest Select Committee rather than a Royal Commission was the most appropriate form of inquiry. The Imperial Conference, in expressing deep concern over the American cinema's world-wide dominance, had recommended film quota legislation for Britain and the Dominions. The Victorian quota was in response to this move, as were those in Great Britain, New Zealand and Canada's British Columbia.

By May 1927, however, Bruce's ideals had been overturned by William Gibson's truculence and the realisation of the Select Committee's severely limited powers. *Everyones* reported that:

Under present plans, the Royal Commission enquiring into motion pictures meets in Melbourne on 2 June, when a decision must be made as to whether evidence already given before the Committee is admissible by the Commission.[2]

The Committee's evidence was accepted, and a number of its witnesses, including William Gibson, returned to be questioned more deeply by the Royal Commission. The Committee members, who automatically became Commissioners under the chairmanship of Walter Marks, were Messrs Gregory, Forde and Nott, and Senators Grant, Duncan and Hayes. Between 2 June 1927 and 16 February 1928, they examined two hundred and fifty witnesses and travelled 17 000 miles, visiting all State capitals and many country centres.

When all the pages of discussion on such irrelevancies as playing the national anthem in cinemas were discarded, the Royal Commission's Minutes of Evidence stood as the most complete and valuable record of the Australian cinema's production, distribution, exhibition and censorship activities up to 1927. Those giving evidence included producers, directors, writers, actors, technicians, distributors and exhibitors. Commonwealth and State censors also appeared, together with twenty-one women representing such groups as the National Council of Women, the Women's Christian Temperance Union and the Women's Vigilance Society.

Veteran producers who appeared were Raymond Longford, John F. Gavin, Franklyn Barrett, and Frank Hurley; those who had entered production in the 1920s included Charles Chauvel, the McDonagh sisters, Dunstan Webb, Louise Lovely, Vaughan Marshall and Roy Darling. On the distribution and exhibition side were the executives Stuart Doyle, William Gibson and Gordon Balcombe (all of Australian Films–Union Theatres), George Griffiths (Hoyts), Bernard Freeman (MGM), Stanley S. Crick (Fox),

Herc C. McIntyre (Universal), John C. Jones (First National), John W. Hicks (Famous-Lasky), and Ralph Doyle (United Artists).

The most impassioned evidence came from Raymond Longford, who gave a detailed account of his career as well as recounting his frustrations at the hands of the Australasian Films–Union Theatres combine. The most carefully constructed defence, part of it in reply to Longford, came from AF–UT's Stuart Doyle, while his fellow managing director William Gibson was rarely less than arrogant. Probably the most colourful of all witnesses was John F. Gavin, who *Everyones* reported

turned comedian when he faced the Commission; they have travelled 15 000 miles without seeing a better show ... Even Senator Grant looked up from his proposed question list and eyed him over the top of his spectacles.

On Gavin's advocating a twenty per cent quota, a "deep chuckle came from the usually quiet and absorbent [sic] Raymond Longford in his reserved seat in the corner".[3]

The cinema boom

Longford had few other reasons for levity. The 1920s brought massive expansion to the American film industry, squeezing tighter still the release opportunities for Australian films in their home territory. At a time when political leaders and moral guardians fulminated against dwindling British and Australian sentiment, the Australian public showed no slackening of interest in American comedies, action serials, society romances and dramas, and both the small and elaborate Westerns, war pictures, costume stories in exotic settings, and Biblical spectaculars. They could read daily newspaper accounts of the lives of the stars, and newspaper display advertisements for American films were large and eye-catching.

Hollywood's films promoted American ideals in a way that no other medium of the period could. Motion pictures introduced the American way of dress, social behaviour, home design, speech and music. Few picturegoers would have given a second thought to Senator Reid's view that images of "extravagance and luxury" in American films were giving Australians "a feeling of discontent" and abnormal views of life.[4]

Although unemployment was never below five per cent, most Australians throughout the 1920s managed at least a weekly visit to the cinema. By 1927, it was estimated that 1250 picture theatres drew a combined total of 110 million admissions. The nation's population at this time was six million and since every man, woman and child made, on average, eighteen visits to the cinema annually, the attendance rate was one of the highest in the world. The bulk of the audiences were working class, to the extent that the trade and politicians could claim that film industry admission taxes and duties automatically became class taxes passed on in the form of more expensive tickets.[5]

During the decade's unparalleled suburban growth, cinemas were springing up in almost every large community. Rural centres shared the boom, with theatres being newly built or improvised in existing halls. Travelling showmen continued to flourish with each moving through a set territory to screen in a local hall or out of doors. Country and suburban patrons often booked their seats permanently for the weekly or bi-weekly change of programme. By 1921, suburban cinema attendances had outstripped those of the city.

The prestige of city cinemas was enhanced by the mass construction of new "picture palaces" in the latter half of the decade. The most elaborate of these was the State Theatre, Sydney, opened in June 1929. Its Gothic entrance hall, leading into a Grand Assembly, in imitation of Louis XIV style and dominated by mirrors and chandeliers, was complemented by a plush upstairs Gallery of Australian Art with paintings by William Dobell, Howard Ashton and Charles Wheeler. All six of the State's rest rooms were decorated in individual styles, described by their titles: Pompadour, Empire Builders', College, Futurist, Butterfly and Pioneers. A company brochure of the time said of the auditorium:

Contemplate the peerless luxury and comfort, the beautiful Louis interior in gold and ivory, the vast vista of countless velvet seats seating three thousand people, the immense sweep of the golden dome, the unparalleled magnificence and splendour of the giant proscenium arches, and you will get a very good idea of the tremendous strides made in theatre construction.

The first important developments in picture palace construction had occurred in late 1924 with the opening of the Wintergarden in Brisbane, the Prince Edward in Sydney, and the Capitol in Melbourne. The Melbourne Capitol, designed by Canberra's architect, the American Walter Burley Griffin, was regarded as "among the finest cinemas in the world".[6] According to the Melbourne *Herald* on the opening day in November 1924:

Architectural forms never before attempted here have been planned with a colour scheme of bronze and gold and the musical and lighting equipment have been installed to produce the perfect palace of moving pictures.

The main stimulus for the picture palace boom had come from American distributors seeking ways in which to maximise their film-revenues. Activity was spurred on by the determination of the business rivals Stuart Doyle, managing director of Australasian Films–Union Theatres, and Francis W. Thring, managing director of Hoyts Theatres, to outclass the achievements of each other. Both Doyle and Thring had entered the film industry by 1910 and were to remain rivals in exhibition and, eventually, production. For the most part their careers ran parallel. Five years after the formation of AF–UT in 1913, Doyle was promoted to the position of Union Theatres' general manager, and within a few years he was managing director of the company, a position he also held on the board of Australasian Films by the late 1920s. In 1915 Frank Thring moved, within three months, from being a humble projectionist to become a part-owner of Electric Theatres. In

1918 he became managing director of the distribution company, J. C.
Williamson Films; by the early 1920s his theatre interests had expanded
across the continent and in 1926 they were merged with Hoyts to form
Hoyts Theatres. Thring now controlled Australia's second largest film
exhibition chain, rivalled only by Union Theatres.

In 1921 Doyle launched Union Theatres' large-scale modernisation of its
older cinemas. In March 1923, *Smith's Weekly* announced that one of
Thring's exhibition companies would spend half a million pounds on new
theatres. Competition began in earnest three years later when Hoyts started
the construction of a string of Regent Theatre picture palaces in nearly all
State capitals and several major country centres. The Regent Theatres'
architectural styles were drawn from a mixture of classical Rome and early
French Renaissance. The biggest of the series, built at a cost of £360 000, was
in Melbourne, with the Sydney Regent ranked second at a cost of £250 000.
Union Theatres replied with the Capitol Theatre, Sydney, the State Theatres
of Sydney and Melbourne, the Ambassadors in Perth, and the total
reconstruction of the Brisbane Tivoli. The Sydney Capitol was the Southern
Hemisphere's first ''atmospheric'' theatre with the projection of a star-filled
sky and drifting clouds onto the ceiling of its auditorium.

Probably as a result of the Thring–Doyle rivalry, Doyle's State Theatres
outclassed Thring's Regents in scale — the Melbourne State was Australia's
largest theatre — and grandeur — the Sydney State was its most elaborate.
The publicity brochure for the opening of the Sydney State thundered that
Stuart Doyle had ''personally supervised every detail'' of the construction,
decoration and furnishing, and had ''twice travelled the world in search of
novelties and ideas''. In the two years from 1927, Union Theatres alone
spent over one million pounds on the construction of modern cinemas. In
April 1929 *Everyones* reported:

Approximately £31 000 000 is now invested in movies in Australia. Official
figures available to *Everyones* show that the Australian motion picture industry
has created an expansion record with which no other industry in the country can
compare.[7]

Union Theatres controlled eighty per cent of Sydney's city and suburban
cinemas by 1921. At the end of the decade, when Hoyts had overtaken Union
Theatres in cinema ownership, the domination by these combines provoked
scores of complaints from independent exhibitors and producers giving
evidence to the Royal Commission. They pointed out that the practice of
block-booking obliged an exhibitor to reserve his entire programme twelve
months ahead. This not only denied him knowledge of the majority of films
he would receive, but severely restricted release opportunities for Australian
films unless they were part of a block-booked package. To allow exhibitors a
freedom of choice and independent producers the right of release, the Royal
Commission was under pressure to include a clause that would allow a small
percentage of booked films to be rejected and replaced by ''Empire''
productions. Until then, as Charles Chauvel had shown, the only alternative a

filmmaker had was to bribe an exhibitor to replace a scheduled feature with his own.

Charles Chauvel

Chauvel had adopted this system in touring the country towns of Queensland and New South Wales with his first two productions, **The Moth of Moonbi** and **Greenhide**, in 1926. The tactic demonstrated his doggedness as an independent producer, especially a determination that films must continue to be made, even in the face of the severe restrictions imposed by distributors and exhibitors. Following the release of the Royal Commission's recommendations, Chauvel commented that distributors and exhibitors had been put on their "honour, so to speak, to play the game. Let us bury our dead past and from it call our experience".[8] This kind of resolve, fired by high creative confidence, nationalistic idealism and a shrewd business sense was to keep him in production for the next thirty years.

Charles Chauvel was born in Warwick, south-western Queensland, in 1897. His family had been rural pioneers, and the men served with distinction in the Australian Light Horse during the Boer War and the First World War. After a stint as a jackeroo, Chauvel travelled to Sydney where he trained as an artist with Dattilo-Rubbo. He had his first film experience as a horse and stable hand on two of the Snowy Baker features, and after further film work with Kenneth Brampton and Franklyn Barrett, Chauvel went to Hollywood for eighteen months to learn more about production. In 1923, after working his way up from property man to assistant director, he returned to Queensland and raised capital for a film company. His first feature, **The Moth of Moonbi**, was premiered in January 1926.

Although quickly and sometimes crudely filmed, **The Moth of Moonbi** and Chauvel's next film, **Greenhide** (1926), show him to be a director of talent and originality. The use of the Australian landscape is fresh, the characters have dimension, and the action scenes rhythm and impact. **The Moth of Moonbi** concerns a country girl who comes to the city and — like the hero of **The Breaking of the Drought** — returns home having lost money and romantic illusions to smart city society. On arriving back at her property, she discovers the house has been ransacked and the only reminder of former security is the portrait of her late father staring across the room. Doris Ashwin as the girl subtly portrays the move from back-country naivety to the city conditioning which makes her see everything through new eyes on her return home. The rigours of her post-city life are climaxed graphically with the savage attempt by cattle duffer Black Bronson (Arthur Tauchert) to smash his way into her home. Due to film deterioration, all that survives of the remainder is an escape on horseback and fragments of a cliff-dangling brawl.

Greenhide starred Elsie Sylvaney as the spoilt city girl, Margery Paton, who travels to her father's property hoping, as the title says, to be "sheiked by a bushranger". She meets the impatience and finally the love of the property's manager whose nickname "Greenhide" is drawn from the tough saddle leather he uses. Margery's city life is characterised by the social whirl of a garden party and her incessant eating of chocolates. Predictably, the country scenes contrast such frivolity with the harsh reality of a low-yield property.

Lighter in content than **The Moth of Moonbi** and, like the earlier films, not without its American Western influences, **Greenhide** again draws value from its locations. Both contained a sufficient degree of Australian-ness to support Chauvel's claim at the Royal Commission that, "the only way in which we can give a film an international appeal is to make it Australian".

Before embarking on the extended country exhibition tour with his two films, Chauvel married **Greenhide**'s leading lady. As Elsa Chauvel, she would play a key role behind the camera in all her husband's further productions. Seeking an American market for **The Moth of Moonbi** and **Greenhide**, they travelled to Hollywood in 1928. The coming of talkies destroyed any hopes of a release, and twelve months later the Chauvels returned to Australia to consider producing sound features.

Hollywood credentials

The impact of American film and the sporadic nature of Australian production made Hollywood the ultimate goal for most Australian actors, whether experienced or aspiring. In March 1919 Beaumont Smith wrote:

For every girl that becomes ambitious for the stage, fifty now pine to go into the movies. The cheap and screaming publicity of the American companies, the intimate stories of artists' lives, the whirlwind rise of unknown girls to stardom, the eternal struggle for notoriety by the stars — these and a host of other things distract our young women's and young men's (though in a considerably lesser degree with the men) attention from their everyday business and make them dream of fame and fortune in the movies.[9]

Two years earlier, Australian entrepreneur J. A. Lipman had written to *The Green Room*:

Quite a number of Australians are placed in current shows, whilst you meet many of them in the picture studios.

At the same time, he cautioned that the market for film actors was

glutted and practically only those with experience before the camera stand a chance, and unless a long and full purse accompanies the desire for fame, I would advise them to stay home.[10]

In the early 1920s, Lotus Thompson, an actress who had appeared in several Australian features and who had emigrated to Hollywood, poured acid over her legs in a desperate bid for notoriety and stardom. But during the previous decade, Arthur Shirley, Elsie Wilson, Louise Lovely, Enid Bennett, Rupert Julian, and Sylvia Bremer were some of the Australian actors and actresses that J. A. Lipman found looking "happy and prosperous" in Hollywood. His list could have included Annette Kellerman, Mae Busch, Jerome Patrick and Dorothy Cumming. Nearly all these stars had faded into obscurity by the time talking pictures had arrived. But during the 1920s, others, like Arthur Shirley and Louise Lovely (the former Louise Carbasse), returned to Australia with the intention of continuing their careers in their own productions.

Arthur Shirley had already been appearing in American films for a year by the time he joined Louise Lovely for her Hollywood debut in the 1916 release **Stronger Than Death**. After other feature roles in **The Fall of a Nation** (1916) and **Modern Love** (1918), Shirley returned to Australia in April 1920 amid lavish publicity, to set up a company to produce a South Seas saga, **The Throwback**. The project foundered and the company went into liquidation. Nearly three years later Shirley wrote, directed, and played two parts in a new screen version of Fergus Hume's novel **The Mystery of a Hansom Cab** (released 1925). Extensive location shooting took place in Melbourne and in country New South Wales, with interiors filmed at the Rushcutters Bay studio in Sydney. Exhibitors giving evidence at the Royal Commission stated it was a poor film, one claiming it would harm the industry if exported. Nevertheless it was well received by the critics, and after a grand premiere attended by the Governor of New South Wales, went on to net £15 000. Shirley immediately ploughed his profit into **The Sealed Room** (1926), a detective drama again featuring himself. The film once more returned money, but not sufficient for him to remain in production. His subsequent career was plagued by a series of misfortunes. Unable to sell his films in England, he was then unsuccessful in establishing a production company in Rhodesia, forbidden by immigration authorities to resume his acting career in Hollywood, and back in Australia had no luck in raising a budget for a talkie remake of **Hansom Cab**. Towards the end of his life, still clad in old-time spats, a long tweed coat and homburg hat, he drifted from stage door to stage door in Sydney telling tales of early Hollywood to anyone who would listen. He died in 1967.

After Louise Lovely's first American films, her international popularity became spectacular. She received fan mail from all over America, Canada, England, Australia and Japan. Her Pickford-style looks and strong dramatic flair helped her when playing opposite such matinee idols as Warren Kerrigan and William Farnum. Her work for Universal Pictures included **The Trail of the Sun** (1916), **Tangled Hearts** (1916), **The Gift Girl** (1917), **The Man Hunter** (1919), **The Last of the Duanes** (1919), **Bettina Loves a Soldier** (1919), and **The Orphan** (1920). In 1921 Louise Lovely made two films for Goldwyn, **Poverty of Riches** and **The Old Nest**; in the same year for Fox she made an Indian romance, **The Little Grey Mouse**. One of her last American features was **The Bride of the Gods** (1922). With her screen career in decline after 1922, stage work — which included top billing with Eddie Cantor at the Palace in New York — occupied more and more of her time. In 1923 she returned to Australia with her husband for a series of personal appearance tours.

It was while touring Tasmania that Louise Lovely read a pre-publication copy of Marie Bjelke-Petersen's mining romance, *Jewelled Nights*. After purchasing the screen rights, she prepared a scenario and formed a production company with backing from Melbourne society people. The filming of **Jewelled Nights**, under the direction of her husband Wilton Welch, was spread over eight months on locations including western Tasmania and Melbourne. Over a third of the £8000 budget was spent on converting Wirth's Hippodrome, Melbourne, into a studio for shooting elaborate interiors as well as a Tasmanian rainforest complete with epic storm. Besides acting and writing, Miss Lovely assisted with the direction and supervised the editing of the film which had been shot by Arthur Higgins and Walter Sully. Her ability to coordinate a team owed much to her Hollywood experience; at Universal she had studied the practicalities of camerawork and editing and from 1923 onwards her stage appearances included a demonstration of film direction.

The story of **Jewelled Nights** (1925) tells of an unwilling society bride (played by Louise Lovely) who rushes screaming from the church before her wedding is complete. Disguising herself as a boy, she seeks refuge in a rugged mining district and befriends a good-looking miner (played by Gordon Collingridge). After rescuing ''the kid'' from a ruffian who has tried to blind her, Collingridge guesses her secret, and the two are drawn together. Louise Lovely intended the film to be the first of a series drawn from further novels by Marie Bjelke-Petersen but her hopes were not fulfilled. Stimulated by Miss Lovely's personal appearances, **Jewelled Nights** received wide and popular Australian release, but failed to make a net profit. At the 1927 Royal Commission, Louise Lovely spoke in favour of the establishment of government studio facilities for independent producers and the importation of American expertise; but it was to no avail. She made no more films and after her second marriage lived mostly in Hobart until her death in 1980.

The McDonagh sisters

Of all the later-1920s Australian producers striving to emulate American cinema, the most successful in artistic as well as box office terms were Paulette, Phyllis and Isobel McDonagh. They had grown up in a theatrical atmosphere (their father was honorary surgeon to J. C. Williamson Theatres), and in their teenage years became ardent filmgoers. They dismissed most Australian films as ''Dad 'n Dave idiot stupidity'', and drew nearly all their creative inspiration from Hollywood. Paulette, the future director, was the most frequent cinema patron, and she studied the impact of framing, shot sizes and cutting. But the originality and depth of the McDonagh sisters' features placed the sisters as considerably more than imitators. Where too many other Australian films of the period suffered from limited creative input, the McDonaghs' pictures resulted from an intelligent collaborative unity between the sisters as co-writer/director, co-writer/art director and leading player. Isobel McDonagh was billed as ''Marie Lorraine'' for her film appearances.

The McDonaghs were not as nationalistic as Longford or Chauvel, although there are indications that they intended to move to indigenous and larger subjects once their commercial credibility was assured. Isobel McDonagh told the Royal Commission that the sisters considered an overseas market to be essential for Australian films, and "that at the start we should confine our production to simple stories. The more ambitious productions will come later".

To compete with American cinema in Australia, the McDonaghs' first three features — **Those Who Love** (1926), **The Far Paradise** (1928) and **The Cheaters** (1930) — were society dramas, essentially similar to those emerging from Hollywood quality studios like Paramount and MGM. Jack Fletcher, the cameraman on all three films, had in fact trained at Paramount in the early 1920s and the hallmarks of his work were a striking use of shadows, depth of focus and backlighting. The films made little attempt to portray everyday reality, looking instead to the prevailing romantic fantasies of social extremes. The plotlines of the McDonaghs' silent films are all variations on the contrasts between middle-class and underprivileged lives, with heroine and hero suffering the consequences of inter-family feuds. The protagonists move from opulent to squalid settings, or vice versa, as fortune takes them. In all the films love comes second to family loyalty. **Those Who Love** tells of a cabaret girl who leaves her rich lover when it becomes apparent that the affair might cost him his inheritance. **The Far Paradise** and **The Cheaters** both burden their heroines with criminal fathers to whom they remain loyal even when offered love by men from the "right" side of the law.

The Far Paradise is the more emotionally engaging It portrays the misadventures of Cherry, the unsuspecting daughter of a society swindler, who returns home from finishing school to fall in love with Peter, the son of one of her father's opponents. Not only does the father intercept Cherry's letters, but he allows his cadaverous business partner Karl Rossi (Arthur McLaglen) to foist his attentions on her. Eventually the father murders Rossi and, suddenly penniless, seeks refuge with Cherry on a poultry farm in the remote Paradise Valley. After tracking the couple down, Peter is rejected, but returns to claim Cherry after her father's death.

Although parts of **The Far Paradise** seem forced and dramatically off-key, several impressive sequences derive their power from an underlying tension. Cherry's despair at receiving no letters from Peter is beautifully underplayed as the camera lingers on her face during a breakfast scene; later on, as her father lies dying, the use of moonlight as primary illumination evokes the stark romanticism of contemporary European films. Special photographic effects add a further dimension: the identity of the villainous Rossi is revealed during a masked ball when his mask dissolves momentarily under Cherry's gaze; during Peter's first visit to the ramshackle farm, the fact that Cherry's coldness actually conceals embarrassment is adroitly conveyed by a shot of her overworked hands dissolving to the same hands toying with a rose during the ball.

Critical acclaim for **The Far Paradise** contained none of the compromise or forced encouragement often reserved for local films. The *Sydney Morning Herald* wrote:

Those Who Love was palpably an experiment; a rather timid imitation on the American mode. **The Far Paradise** shows decision in every detail, and both the scenario and the captions are straightforwardly forceful.[11]

Smith's Weekly commented:

This picture has a smoothness and finish rare in Australian films; apparently the astute sisters have realised that America has developed the technique of production to a fine art, and have been willing to learn ... This does not mean that their work has an American flavour. Far from it. But it has something of the art that conceals art; that makes you forget you are watching a film and so lets you judge the drama on its own merits.[12]

The Cheaters was comparatively detached, and sometimes sardonic, in its approach to a similar subject. The inclusion of a welter of startling revelations and derivative gangster elements seems to have clouded the reaction of most critics. Certainly the story is cluttered and the ending too pat, but it is the integration of an increasingly assured film technique with the new mood that makes **The Cheaters** stylistically superior. A jewellery shop swindle is calmly yet intricately unravelled, offering the audience several alternative conclusions within the space of five minutes. Colourful diversion is supplied by Leal Douglas as the heroine's bogus aristocratic mother who delightfully overdoes the ''tough'' image when two equally bogus detectives arrive. A spareness pervades the settings, and constant use is made of archways to lead the eye into rooms beyond the action, adding dimension to movement and the players' response to surroundings.

Produced at the time American talkies were making their initial impact on the Australian market, **The Cheaters** had no chance of repeating the success of its predecessors. A sound-on-disc music score and three synchronised sequences were added in early 1930, partly to improve its chances in the Royal Commission's Commonwealth production contest. Neither the judges nor the public were impressed by the disc additions, which seem to have thrown **The Cheaters** off balance. A subsequent plan to release only the silent version was shelved, and the McDonagh sisters entered full sound production with the making of documentary featurettes.

Tal Ordell

Tal Ordell's **The Kid Stakes** (1927), like the films of Charles Chauvel, had imaginative direction, economy of production, and a plot which, although partly derived from an American novel, showed recognisably Australian characters and situations. It is perhaps the most ebullient of all the surviving Australian silents, demonstrating just how dynamic a film without sound could be.

Ordell, a verse and short-story writer, playwright, painter and actor, had already directed one film, a two-reel comedy, **Cows and Cuddles**, in 1921. His background, particularly as a writer, had been more varied than most of his filmmaking contemporaries and his early career as an itinerant bush worker and writer was similar to that of Henry Lawson, with whom he was on friendly terms. By the late 1920s, Ordell was one of Australia's most experienced stage and film character actors. He had clearly absorbed a great deal about the medium through appearances in films by Beaumont Smith and Raymond Longford among others, and in **The Kid Stakes** appeared to be building on their observations of Australian character.

Its generic predecessors were the comedies and dramas shot in the Woolloomooloo district since the late 1910s by Longford, Franklyn Barrett and Lawson Harris, and the film's cameraman, Arthur Higgins, had worked on the Longford and Harris productions. **The Kid Stakes** was based on the Sydney *Sunday News* cartoon strip *Fatty Finn* by Syd Nicholls and owed some of its wilder children's humour to Hollywood's **Our Gang** series. Its episodic plot covers events up to and including a goat race. On the day of the race, one of Bruiser Murphy's gang frees Fatty Finn's goat, Hector, to eat its way through sundry clothes, wall posters and flower beds. Hearing that a crotchety millionaire has ordered the animal's destruction, Fatty's gang save Hector and rush him to the racecourse via street chases, a car ride and an aeroplane which loops the loop. Having built up the film through a series of confrontations, Ordell turns its final third into a continuous race — at first in a hot pursuit from the millionaire's mansion, and finally in the "kid stakes" itself, with goats and riders jostling for space along a dusty racecourse flanked by a cheering crowd. It is here that the excitability of his characters (including Ordell himself as a radio announcer) reaches its peak, matched by animated sub-titles that leap and twirl.

The Syd Nicholls cartoons were a relatively uncomplicated series showing children's pranks against each other and parental authority. Social values were rarely questioned and settings were generalised. **The Kid Stakes**, through its authentic and specific locations, is a film where even the wildest flights of fantasy are anchored to a believable milieu. The Woolloomooloo working-class settings and characters are again contrasted with the wealthier residents of Potts Point, though this time satirically rather than dramatically as in **Sunshine Sally**. The children are unmistakably from the district. Fatty is tougher, sometimes surlier, than his cartoon counterpart; Bruiser, his adversary, is every inch the hood of the future. Even in the slum context, a class difference is evident between the gangs. Bruiser and his toughs look less comfortably brought up, are worse dressed and more disposed to larrikinism. Fatty's tactics are those of a high-spirited rabble; Bruiser's are devious, aimed at further perpetuating the gang rivalry. Distinctions extend to girlfriends: Fatty's is demure and principled, Bruiser's a mean-faced moll who frequently resorts to violence.

Tal Ordell's use of his settings is similar to that of Longford in **The Sentimental Bloke**. The assumptions about slum larrikins are basically the

1
One of 200 slides interspersed
with film segments in *Soldiers of
the Cross* (1900).

2
Ned Kelly's last stand in *The
Story of the Kelly Gang* (1906). A
frame enlargement from
recently discovered footage.

3

The Fatal Wedding

3
Captain Midnight, the Bush King
(1911). An action scene filmed
at French's Forest.

4
Lottie Lyell and Raymond
Longford (second and fourth
from left) in Longford's

5
Cozens Spencer's Lyceum Hall,
Sydney, during the record
season of *The Fatal Wedding*.

6
*The Romantic Story of Margaret
Catchpole* (1911). A frame
enlargement showing Margaret
(Lottie Lyell) and her rejected
suitor (Augustus Neville).

7
The Sentimental Bloke (1919).
Doreen (Lottie Lyell) and the
Bloke (Arthur Tauchert) during a
visit to Manly.

8
The Blue Mountains Mystery
(1921). Hotel guests including
Billy Williams (left) and Marjorie
Osborne examine the
supposedly dead Henry Tracey
(John Faulkner).

9
A Girl of the Bush (1921). Vera James.

10
Prehistoric Hayseeds (1923). An anthropology student (Gordon Collingridge, second from left) accompanies the Hayseed family (J. P. O'Neill, James Coleman, Pinky Weatherley and Zilla Weatherley) in search of a prehistoric race.

11
Joe (1924). Gordon Collingridge
and Marie Lorraine.

12
On location in Tasmania for
Jewelled Nights (1925). The
group includes, in back row:
Godfrey Cass and Gordon
Collingridge; in left front row:
Wilton Welch and Louise Lovely;
extreme right: Arthur Higgins.

13
For the Term of His Natural Life
(1927). Maurice Frère (Dunstan
Webb) takes over as
commandant of Norfolk Island.

14
For the Term of His Natural Life.
Sylvia (Eva Novak) with the ill-
fated convict children (Jimmy
McMahon and Hartney Arthur).

15
The Far Paradise (1928).
Paulette McDonagh directs Paul
Longuet.

16
Family loyalty is under strain in
The Cheaters (1930), with Marie
Lorraine and Arthur Greenaway.

same, although conveyed with sharper slapstick humour that derives from the gangster rivalry in miniature. But this does not distance Ordell from his subject, for he remains in close empathy with his child cast — all non-professionals led by his son Robin playing Fatty — who give performances of spontaneous hilarity.

Curiously, **The Kid Stakes** made no great impact on its release. Its £4000 budget, provided by Queensland exhibitor Virgil Coyle, was returned with a slight margin, and the film had regular revivals at children's matinees for years afterwards. While Tal Ordell directed no further features, he continued to appear in films and on radio until his death in 1948.

Frank Hurley

For thirty years Frank Hurley was Australia's foremost actuality filmmaker, combining skill as a movie and stills cameraman with an explorer's enthusiasm. He was producer, director, cameraman, writer, editor and showman. As long as the exotic and unexplored remained to be filmed, Hurley excelled in all his capacities. While many Australian producers of the silent era worked with the hope of obtaining an international breakthrough, Hurley was the only one to establish an overseas reputation.

After his polar documentaries Hurley was appointed the first official photographer to the Australian Imperial Force in June 1917 and covered the Australian war effort in France and the Middle East. Afterwards, he filmed **The Ross Smith Flight** (1920), a record of Ross and Keith Smith's homeward run across Australia after their record-breaking flight from England. In late 1920 he shot two films in New Guinea. The first, a record of the Anglican Mission's work, was to pass almost unnoticed; the second, **Pearls and Savages** (1921), which eventually combined footage from two expeditions, firmly consolidated Hurley's fame.

Both the **Pearls and Savages** journeys trailblazed new territory. Nearly all the first trip was made by lugger and on foot around eastern Papua. The second, more scientifically based and with the added advantage of two seaplanes (the first aircraft to fly in New Guinea), concentrated on the native tribes of the Fly River and Lake Murray. Hurley's footage amazed audiences who had no previous knowledge of the societies and customs, and through its record of lifestyles, ceremonies and reactions to the first white explorers, **Pearls and Savages** retains its confrontational impact. The most impressive of the ethnographic material shows elaborately costumed, trance-like dancers, and villages built majestically out across the water, with galleries of human skulls in their long-houses.

Having hand-coloured every frame of **Pearls and Savages**, in August 1923 Hurley took the film and his photographs on a two-year overseas lecture tour that met with acclaim in the United States, Canada and Britain. The American tour alone took twelve months and Hurley lectured in almost every State. His adventures were featured in numerous magazines and newspapers, and during ten frantic days in New York, he wrote a best-selling book edition. The tour's most euphoric experience for Hurley was screening the film to leading producers, stars and critics in Hollywood. But while the lecture tours around Australia, Canada and England proved financially successful, the competition from Hollywood left box office takings in America far below expectation.

Determined to meet Americans at their own game, he began planning two films intended to combine the appeal of Hollywood's output with the exoticism of the **Pearls and Savages** locations. During his English tour, he induced the film and theatre magnate Sir Oswald Stoll to invest £10 000 and several British stars in two narrative features he would make back-to-back on Thursday Island and in New Guinea. **The Hound of the Deep** (1926) concerns the attempts of a Londoner to find a large pearl in the waters off Thursday Island, and **The Jungle Woman** (1926) is a goldfields romantic drama. Although Hurley's scripting and direction of actors was naive, the backgrounds, and especially the ethnographic content of **The Jungle Woman** were praised in reviews. Both films were profitable.

In 1927, along with other Australian producers, Frank Hurley suspended production to wait for the outcome of the Royal Commission. After he was unable to raise capital for further features, he resumed his career as explorer-cameraman in late 1929 when he joined the first of two research expeditions and headed once more for the chill of the Antarctic.[13]

Australasian Films

At the time of the first Royal Commission sittings in 1927, Australasian Films were completing the final project in a three-year schedule of feature production. Although their exact reason for entering production is not clear, these three years of activity laid the basis for the revival of continuous production under the auspices of Union Theatres and Cinesound Productions during the 1930s.

The managing director of the combine, Stuart Doyle, told the Royal Commission that Australasian Films–Union Theatres' rejection of certain independent features in the past had been for the sake of the entire Australian production industry. He argued that his companies could not be expected to play their part in salvaging the poor reputation of Australian films if they had to release every Australian feature made. Partly with the knowledge that good Australian films still made money, and partly — though Stuart Doyle would hardly have admitted it — to counter criticism of AF–UT's inactivity in feature production, the combine had decided to embark on a comprehensive campaign of production. In November 1924 Franklyn Barrett tartly observed:

It is a remarkable coincidence that the spasms of zeal on the part of Mr Doyle's two companies to "enter the field of Australian productions" have always come at a time when public opinion (tired of American trash) begins to inquire for British or Australian pictures, or when some revision of the tariff threatens a little protection and encouragement for an industry that is of national importance ... By a similar coincidence, these activities cease when all danger is passed.[14]

The principal investor was to be Australasian Films, with Union Theatres supplying the balance. Although Australasian had produced occasional features since 1913 (the greatest concentration during the war years), no continuity of production emerged until the new regular schedule was announced with the arrival in late 1924 of F. Stuart-Whyte. A Scotsman with some stage and marginal film experience in America, he was instructed by Australasian to produce a series of modern films, with international appeal. He told the *Sydney Morning Herald*: "The Australian atmosphere will not be eliminated; nor will it be unduly intruded".[15]

In spite of its "international" content, Stuart-Whyte's first film for the company, **Painted Daughters** (1925), missed its intended market. The film's modest local success was probably due more to publicity than directorial skill, for Stuart-Whyte left Australia before **Sunrise** (1926), his second Australasian assignment, was complete. While **Painted Daughters** emerged as a passable programme picture, the incompatibility of its internationalism and a limited budget led Australasian to inject enough national sentiment into their subsequent films to appeal to the home market at the very least.

The first step in this direction was the appointment of Raymond Longford to head the company's production activities. Longford and Australasian Films, traditional opponents since the closure of Cozens Spencer's production enterprise in 1913, seemed, surprisingly, to have settled their differences. In October 1925 William Gibson, one of the AF–UT combine's managing directors, told the *Daily Guardian*:

For Mr Longford we have the greatest regard and respect. We think that today he is the dominant figure in Australian picture production.

Partly admitting his organisation's antipathy to independent producers, Gibson continued: "For many years he has laboured under great difficulties, because he has had no big organisation behind him."[16]

However, what should have meant security to Longford brought only frustration. He later told the Royal Commission that AF–UT had given him no say in the subject or casting of his Australasian features, and that his budgets had been too "absurdly cheap and inadequate to secure even an English market". This had been central to the failure of **The Pioneers** (1926), a would-be epic whose rapid spanning of several generations baffled at least one critic[17], while others attacked evidence of a cheese-paring budget. In spending as little as they had, the *Bulletin* commented, Australasian Films were "helping to kill the sentiment in favour of local pictures by trading on it".[18]

Both **The Pioneers** and Longford's second Australasian film, **The Hills of Hate** (1926), used the company's new Bondi studio for interiors. Following the purchase and equipping of the former skating rink at a cost of £50 000, the first film to be shot there had been **Sunrise**, completed by Longford after the departure of F. Stuart-Whyte. In December 1925 the actor

Dunstan Webb joined Longford to direct two further films for the company, **Tall Timber** and **The Grey Glove**. Ironically **Tall Timber**, which cost only £3000, was the only one of Australasian's 1925-27 productions to obtain a release in England.

In mid-1926 Raymond Longford suggested that Australasian make a more realistically budgeted film for the English market. The project he recommended was a new adaptation of Marcus Clarke's novel, *For the Term of his Natural Life*. The AF–UT executives quickly warmed to the idea, as did Marion Marcus Clarke, the author's daughter and literary executor. Longford was assigned to direct the film on a budget of £15 000. With more cause for optimism than he'd had in years, he commenced preproduction, while his son Victor began writing a script with Dorothy Gordon.

The plain sailing was to be short lived. The AF–UT executives controlling production (Stuart Doyle, William Gibson and Gordon Balcombe) read the script and decided that more money and a wider market were needed. To ensure the American market, Longford was asked to relinquish the direction of **For the Term of his Natural Life** to a visiting American, Norman O. Dawn.[19] Longford agreed to the request in late June 1926. Gordon Balcombe assured him that Australasian, in appreciation of his sacrifice, would renew his contract in September and continue to employ him as director of future projects.

Norman Dawn had come to Australia with cameraman Len Roos to shoot backgrounds for a film they intended to complete in America. Roos, who had co-photographed the Stuart-Whyte–Longford collaboration **Sunrise** on a previous visit, introduced Dawn to various Australian film people including William Gibson. Eventually he met and befriended Frank Hurley, whose two narrative features were not dissimilar to the kind in which Dawn specialised. Though by no means a front-rank Hollywood name, Norman Dawn had two decades experience as an independent producer, director and cameraman making features in distant locations. As a pioneer of special photographic effects, he had saved major American studios thousands of dollars with his work on glass shots (where new ingredients of a shot were painted onto a sheet of glass carefully positioned between camera and set), matte shots (where two separate exposures on one piece of film combined elements difficult or impossible to film at the same time) and miniatures.

Even before linking up with Australasian, Dawn's presence as an American filmmaker drew criticism from the press. In two articles of late May and early June 1926, the Sydney *Sunday Truth* accused him of being "party to the slaughtering"of Australia's infant film industry through his (presumed) intention to involve American money and leading players. Demonstrating a xenophobia that was to last until the end of Dawn's second trip to Australia in the early 1930s, *Truth* concluded:

A new, fresh, and individualistic outlook is what Australian films want — and they have a hope of getting it if the American invasion will really demonstrate a willingness to make Australian pictures in Australia and not American pictures in Australia.[20]

90

Dawn was stung by this criticism, as well as by minor but vocal public opposition to his version of **For the Term of his Natural Life** depicting the country's convict origins on the screens of the world. Sight unseen, Tasmania's Royal Society and Bishop Dr Snowden Hay decided that the film would sensationalise the grislier aspects of the story and Senator Guthrie proclaimed that the theme was best forgotten. As mentioned earlier, Senator Grant had urged Customs Minister Pratten to ban its export. Sensitive as the issue remained, it was excellent publicity for an Australian film already planned as the biggest and best-publicised to date.

Contrary to *Truth's* assertion, the entire upgraded £40 000 budget was to come from AF–UT. Two "name" actors, George Fisher and Eva Novak, both of whom had been used by Dawn in previous American films, were now imported to improve **The Term**'s market appeal. Fisher, "an actor of fine spiritual quality", according to *Everyones*[21], was signed to play both the hero Rufus Dawes and the villainous John Rex, whose similar looks are the cause of Dawes's unjust transportation to Van Diemen's Land (Tasmania). Eva Novak, a star of Hollywood outdoor films, was to play the heroine Sylvia Vickers. Three other Americans were employed in supporting roles: Arthur McLaglen (as the cannibalistic convict, Gabbett); Dawn's wife, Katherine (who played Mrs Vickers and was to co-edit the film); and Steve Murphy. The only Australian leads were Jessica Harcourt (Sarah Purfoy) and Dunstan Webb (Maurice Frère). But numerous others appeared in bit parts, including Arthur Tauchert, Mayne Lynton and Marion Marcus Clarke (who had appeared on stage as Sarah).

Two months were spent on research and preproduction and then, on 10 August 1926, only three days after the arrival of its American leads, the cameras began to roll. After shooting initial interior sequences at Bondi Junction, the company moved to Port Arthur, the Tasmanian penal settlement featured in Marcus Clarke's novel. Even in remote locations, the film generated intense interest. Scores of spectators constantly had to be cleared from the set. In early September the company filmed at the desolate Macquarie Harbour on Tasmania's west coast, then moved back to Sydney for further interiors. Studio work then alternated with locations spread the full length of eastern New South Wales. Publicists enthusiastically reported such vivid events as a ship's fire filmed off Sydney Heads (encouraged by twenty-five pounds of dynamite and two tons of nitrate film saturated in crude oil!), and 500 "convicts" rioting at Dundas, west of Sydney, and a further hundred prisoners floating logs along a Parramatta River tributary. With huge sets representing gaol, tavern, ballroom and English manor house interiors, and a tank for the shipwreck sequence, jostling for space at the Bondi studio, the AF–UT board must have believed their investment in a truly world-class feature would be justified. As they allowed **The Term**'s budget to rise from £40 000 to £60 000 they watched, impressed, as Dawn stretched more of their money's worth with special effects. Final shots were taken in mid-December, ending a tightly organised schedule of four months. From a total of 100 000 feet of film, **For the Term of his Natural Life** was fine-cut to a duration of under two hours.

Everyones in its review of June 1927 observed there were occasions when Norman Dawn "seemed to shy away from the dramatic possibilities of his story. There were times when he showed a fine perception . . . But his principal strength lay in mob-stuff action". The magazine shared almost every other reviewer's opinion that the dramatic highlight of **For the Term of his Natural Life** was the suicide of two convict children at Port Arthur's Point Puer.[22] Beatrice Tildesley, writing in *Beckett's*, agreed that this was "the most poignant scene of all, though it was a rather obvious and prolonged play upon our feelings".[23] *Variety*, on the film's American release in June 1929, said that the scene furnished "a suspense gem rarely caught with such sincerity by American cameras".[24]

Most commented unfavourably on what remains **The Term**'s central flaw — its over-eventful plot. As Dawn had disregarded the Longford–Gordon script and worked directly from Clarke's book, the narrative too easily became a progression of extremes. Much more plot is said to have been filmed than the final cut contained, and this may have reduced Dawn's chances of faithfully juggling Clarke's original elements of mistaken identity, lost memory and long episodes of parallel action. Kenneth Wilkinson, the *Sydney Morning Herald* critic, wrote:

It may be said with confidence that **For the Term of his Natural Life** is a distinct advance on any film yet produced in Australia, with the exception perhaps, of **The Sentimental Bloke**; and **The Sentimental Bloke** was prepared on a much more modest scale. Yet the Australasian Films production . . . still leaves much to be desired. Against the inspiring, natural scenery to be found in it, and the truly skilful way in which the director (Mr Norman Dawn) has dealt with the figures in some of his sets, must be balanced a crudely written scenario and a multitude of weak captions.[25]

Variety correctly observed that "a jumbled story . . . and directorial laxity in keeping the threads of the yarn and the characters apart" allowed an otherwise first-rate production to fall short of the epic status to which it aspired.[26]

Yet *Variety* did find **For the Term of his Natural Life** "grippingly dark-hued and old-worldish from start to finish".[27] Indeed, it is the film's authenticity and mood that, along with the logistics of its production, make it one of the major achievements of the Australian silent era. Dawn and cameraman Len Roos make powerful use of locations, notably the forbidding "organ-pipe" coastal cliffscapes, the mountain tangle into which an axe-wielding Gabbett pursues his human quarry, and the vast sea cave from which John Rex escapes after his run across the Eaglehawk Peninsula. Impressive special effects supervised by Dawn include the use of paint on glass to provide ornate interior ceilings, and most notably, a replacement roof for the decaying Port Arthur penitentiary; matte shots combining scene components often hundreds of miles apart; and the shipwreck (actually a miniature filmed in a tank at the Bondi studio) that provides the film's catharsis. Through harsh lighting and deep shadows, the convict scenes convey an appropriate Gothic mood, and even the quieter moments have a foreboding quality. Performances range from the rudimentary to the inspired, indicating that Dawn worried little about the intricacies of casting and directing actors. Those given the best opportunities are George Fisher, Jessica Harcourt and Dunstan Webb. Eva Novak's role is a troublesome one, complete with amnesia and suffering; it was not until her second Australian film, **The Romance of Runnibede** (1928), that her talent was fully displayed.

Two months before the premiere of **For the Term of his Natural Life**, Norman Dawn began Australasian's second epic, **The Adorable Outcast** (1928) with a budget of £40 000. This was to be AF–UT's last production for several years because the combine needed all available capital for its theatre-building programme. It was also keen to await the outcome of America's sound revolution — sound became increasingly important after the New York premiere in August 1926 of **Don Juan**, which had recorded music and effects.

The Adorable Outcast took Australasian back to the cosmopolitanism of **Painted Daughters**. Its plot, which tells of a white girl who is raised by "natives" and who falls in love with a wealthy white trader, followed the pattern of several island pictures made by Dawn in the early 1920s. Dawn employed the star of one of the earlier films, Edith Roberts, together with his fellow Americans Edmund Burns, Walter Long and Arthur McLaglen. **The Adorable Outcast** was shot over several months in the Fijian Islands, and again visual impact was its mainstay. In the two reels that survive, the most impressive sequence is a brisk native attack on a slave-trader's hut perched on top of a small island.

On its home territory, **For the Term of his Natural Life** did better business than any Australian film before it. In its first week at the Crystal Palace, Sydney, it attracted 26 686 attendance. **The Adorable Outcast** did even better in its opening weeks, then fell behind, indicating high expectations on the strength of its predecessor. But if both films were expected to return the rest of their money on overseas markets, Australasian Films were quickly disappointed. Neither obtained a release in Britain, and had only limited exposure in America in early 1929. Ironically, in America both films were victims of block-booking and the spread of talkies. The fact that **Outcast** was given a music and effects track for its American run made little difference. In June 1930 Stuart Doyle told *Smith's Weekly* that £30 000 had been lost by his companies after an investment of £100 000 in the two Norman Dawn films. Of **The Term**'s overseas performance, Doyle stated:

Not one penny could be earned by us, with all the influence we could bring to bear, in either England or America, or any other part of the world, and today . . . [**For the Term of his Natural Life**] stands as not recouping to us one farthing, outside of the local sphere.[28]

Raymond Longford was another person to feel a considerable sense of loss.

When Australasian Films had not renewed his promised contract in late 1926, he was understandably bitter, and the following year, he tabled his grievances against AF–UT in his evidence before the Royal Commission. Norman Dawn and The Term were two of his main targets. ''Mr Dawn is not a producer'', Longford commented and then proceeded to revive the bugbear that Dawn had exploited the novel's least-savoury aspects. He stated that the film originally proposed by him could have made its money back on the Australian market alone. Perhaps it might have, replacing Dawn's grandeur and violence, as John Baxter has said, ''with something more moving, and more Australian''.[29] But for Longford, there were to be few other chances.

Final silents

''I am not bothering about the Australian market'', Frederick Phillips, American businessman and Managing Director of Phillips Film Productions, told the Royal Commission. After an expenditure of £12 000 on The Romance of Runnibede (1928), Phillips optimistically expected his company to net a minimum of £40 000 from overseas markets. In retrospect, Phillips Film Productions was seen by AF–UT's Stuart Doyle as one more ''mushroom'' company planted to take advantage of Australasian Films' initiative. Essentially he was correct. The company was formed in November 1926 when publicity for For the Term of his Natural Life was at its peak. Phillips signed Eva Novak as his leading lady, Len Roos as his cameraman, and another American, this time Scott Dunlap, as director.

The novel by Steele Rudd, from which the script was adapted, had sympathetically explored the differences between Queensland Aboriginals and early white settlers. The script adaptation by John M. Giles highlighted one of the book's several strands, the worship of the city-educated settler's daughter Dorothy (Eva Novak) as a reincarnated tribal princess. Australia's cities were portrayed as frontier metropolises, where, according to a title, ''the pavements ... end with the bewitching wilderness of the Never-Never''. The experience of the Sydney finishing school where Dorothy has spent ''four years putting social polish on her outback tan'' counts for little against her abduction twice by the Aboriginals. In moments of tranquillity, Dorothy's sophistication and that of a smitten trooper (Claude Saunders) are contrasted with the outback naivety of her childhood sweetheart, a farm manager played by Gordon Collingridge. In a conclusion of poetic justice, the trooper is speared during Dorothy's second rescue, leaving her to the attentions of the farmer.

Scott Dunlap's direction of The Romance of Runnibede was smooth enough. Len Roos's camera work carefully evoked lush pastoral beauty, and both Eva Novak and Gordon Collingridge gave warm, sincere performances. But in other respects it was a conventional Western, distinguished from its American model only by the gum trees and wildly melodramatic natives. In the matter of distribution and exhibition, chance again played a hand.

94

According to *Everyones*, release arrangements with Australasian Films and Union Theatres were "closed in the face of evidence given before the Royal Commission that neither firm would give the independent Australian producer a chance".[30] Nevertheless, before **The Romance of Runnibede** could be sold abroad, Phillips Film Productions was declared bankrupt, leaving Steele Rudd, who had invested in the company, and Eva Novak financially embarrassed. *Everyones* reported that Eva Novak's departure from Australia rang down the curtain on one act

of an eventful production enterprise; and Australia has now lost the entire contingent of American players and technicians who were working at full pressure twelve months ago.[31]

Nearly all the remaining releases of 1928-29 suffered from low budgets and a lack of inventiveness. Tropical exotica flowered (and withered) through **The Devil's Playground** and **The Kingdom of Twilight**; John F. Gavin returned to bush law-enforcement with **Trooper O'Brien** (using generous extracts from earlier bushranging films); and Phil K. Walsh threw together a rough, racist testimonial called **The Birth of White Australia**.

One of the exceptions was **The Exploits of the Emden** (1928), partly directed by Ken G. Hall. Its genesis was **Unsere Emden**, a German film directed by Louis Ralph and purchased for Australian release by First National Pictures. Feeling that the German portrayal of battle scenes and Australia's part in the *Emden–Sydney* conflict would be unacceptable to Australian audiences, First National assigned Ken Hall to produce, script, direct and edit replacement sequences. The resulting film enjoyed a profitable three-week run — three times the average — at Sydney's Prince Edward Theatre. In addition to finding critical favour, it was to be valuable training for Hall who was to become the country's most prolific director during the next decade.

Further evidence

In September 1927, only four months into the eight it took the Royal Commission to obtain evidence, *Everyones* observed:

The Royal Commission seems to be in the re-hash stage, where witnesses are covering ground already well-ploughed in every state of the Commonwealth.[32]

Press and parliamentary criticism emphasised the time and money already expended by the Commission. In October, the Melbourne *Age* leapt into the attack:

The facts in regard to the film industry in Australia are so well known that inquiry has been superfluous.[33]

Everyones in December related:

One story is that the Prime Minister more or less read the Riot Act when the cost of the enquiry was reckoned up; and unless some of the Christmas Spirit carries down into the New Year it won't be a very happy band of pilgrims that sits down to prepare the report.[34]

Whatever the criticism, the Commission became the first-ever forum for Australian film industry issues and added a rich cross-section of community attitudes to the known industrial facts. Trade and pressure groups were constantly at loggerheads over censorship requirements and procedure, and the question of on-screen morality recurred throughout the hearings. Women's groups and church groups were urging more vigilant censorship, with special emphasis on the protection of children. The censor's report, tabled at the same time as that of the Commission in 1928 commented:

There seems to be an impression abroad among most American producers that even a serious film is not complete unless one or more of the characters are shown without their nether garments.

The verdict of a British critic was quoted with approval that American films revealed "a whirl of surreptitious cocktail-drinking, graft, bad taste and vile manners". One witness from the Victorian Women's Citizens' Movement went so far as to catalogue the misdeeds witnessed by children during the screening of 250 films at Saturday afternoon matinees. The list included: "representations of 97 murders, 51 cases of marital misconduct, 22 abductions, 19 seductions, 42 suicides, 176 cases of thieving, 25 disreputable women and 35 drunkards". The witnesses did not actually state that all the films viewed were American but, given that at least 95 per cent of screenings in Australia during 1927 were American, the assumption can be safely made.

Many statements were made on the "unwholesome" effect imported American films were having on Australian national identity. Commenting on the evidence of this presented to the Commission, a *Sydney Morning Herald* editorial stated: "Without disparaging American culture, we would prefer to keep our own". William Gibson of AF–UT countered any such criticism with:

They [the Americans] carry on business on the right lines, and invariably they make money. That is what we are after.

Far sterner opinions included that of Raymond Longford:

I will not Americanise Australia in the pictures I produce . . . The only ideals that Australians have seen for years have been American ideals.

Another spokesman said:

It is deplorable that a country with such a regard should submit quietly to foreign exploitation, have its individualism undermined and its character and ideals practically shaped for it by a battering invasion of American films.

The reception of Australian films in America was also analysed. Gayne Dexter, Editor-in-chief of the magazine *Everyones*, stated that he had spent six years in America as the director of advertising and publicity for First National Pictures. **The Sentimental Bloke**, for which he had arranged the promotion in the USA, had failed, he said, not because of its slang, which was "cleared up slightly", but because it had been "hopelessly outclassed" by the sophistication of competing American and Continental films. The Snowy Baker films and **Silks and Saddles**, aimed directly at the American market, had been well-received, and it was up to Australian filmmakers to realise national limitations when it came to overseas competition. One reality to be faced, claimed Dexter, was that, "Nature made a wonderful job of this continent, but as human beings we [the Australians] are an ugly race". Naturally this provoked an uproar from the press.

Another consideration in the export of films to the USA was the time it took an Australian film to reach American screens, when the fashions of any contemporary subject would be out of date. Thus, advised Dexter:

The fields of our photoplay function are limited to our coast and sea, and to our outback. We must keep our heroines in the riding breeches of **The Romance of Runnibede** or the island costumes of **The Adorable Outcast**. There may be an occasional costume drama such as **For the Term of his Natural Life**, but the man who plays with period dress is doubling his own risk.

Gayne Dexter was to be one of the film industry's keenest observers during the 1920s and 1930s. His opinions on an industry which had little cultural identity are illuminating, especially when he stated:

Because a story is good enough for Australia, we consider it should be good enough for the world ... We are 10000 miles removed from the world's centres of culture and literature and yet we have the colossal impertinence to attempt to dictate.

Looking at the deficiencies more closely, he continued:

Fifty years hence we may have learned to see, think and feel internationally. But no less than that. Australia is passing through the phase of industrial development; until that is complete we shall have neither the money nor the leisure to spare for the cultivation of the arts ... You gentlemen may be making the mistake of regarding motion pictures as an industry instead of an art. We may produce two pictures annually that get into the world market; but it will take fifty years and entire mental and physical change in our race before we can compete successfully with the nations that are rich in literature, beauty and culture.[35]

Recommendations

In March 1928, the report of the Royal Commission into the Moving Picture Industry was tabled in Federal Parliament. It drew almost unanimous praise from politicians and the film industry, and even Raymond Longford shared the view of fellow producers that it was "a work of truly constructive merit".[36]

The Commissioners found no evidence to support the existence of an American film combine in Australia, although they did report that most of the Australian distributors were virtually branch offices of major companies in America. And while they conceded that block-booking militated constantly against the Australian producer (and was, in their opinion, the only factor that did), they could not accept that block-booking in the general sense was deleterious. Some of the major Royal Commission recommendations covered: the establishment of a Board of Censors and Censorship Board of Appeal; the re-classification of censorship categories; the limitation of distribution-exhibition contracts to twelve months; a five per cent rejection clause in all such contracts to make way for Australian productions; a three-year Empire quota; annual awards of merit for the best Australian production and best scenario; increased customs duty on foreign films; and an upgrading of the Commonwealth-produced series **Know Your Own Country** (including a recommendation that private producers be encouraged to contribute to the series). Altogether four out of the report's fifty recommendations were aimed directly at improving the lot of the Australian producer, if one counts the three covering the awards of merit and the one referring to the exhibitors' rejection clause.

Only nineteen recommendations of the fifty could be acted upon under the national constitution, and for this reason the Federal Government campaigned unsuccessfully for eighteen months to have the States cede their film powers to the Commonwealth. Some of the momentum of this campaign was lost by the death, in May 1928, of the industry's parliamentary ally, the Customs Minister, H. E. Pratten. In April 1928 the Commonwealth acted on two of the few recommendations which it did have power to implement by providing for censorship boards and the proposed production and scenario prizes, funded by the increased duty on imported films. It took until May 1929 for the announcement of the conditions for the prize competitions. In June *Everyones* reported that they had been drawn up without any consultation with the Commission's chairman, Walter Marks. The magazine commented:

It took the Film Commission a year's enquiry, and cost the Federal Taxpayer several thousand pounds, and the aims and objects of the report have been cast on the junk heap. Someone who, apparently, has no knowledge whatsoever of the industry, has drawn up the conditions, which are full of flaws and in a hopeless tangle.[37]

Thanks to the final refusal of the States to cede their film powers to the Commonwealth, the junk heap analogy extended to most of the remaining recommendations. But even if it had been possible to enact the quota clause, the fact that it covered Empire and not only Australian productions, had left the way open for exhibitors to concentrate on English films if they preferred. The long-awaited Australian quota was not only constitutionally out of reach, but would in any case have been secondary to the British Empire preferences championed by Prime Minister Bruce. By late 1929 it was clear that for over two years, the film industry had stalled, awaiting an effective blueprint from the Royal Commission. Those two years had seen a tighter grip by American films in Australia, the coming of sound and, from October 1929, an economic depression.

Everyones pointed out that investment in Australian feature production, which had stood at £100 000 at the start of the Royal Commission's inquiries in 1927, had dropped to £10 000 by late 1928.[38] By the end of 1929 it had virtually ceased altogether. In December 1929 the magazine stated bluntly:

For the first time in the history of the business since the late W. A. Gibson made **The Kelly Gang** in 1906, a year has passed in which not one Australian feature production has gone into general release . . .

Uncertainty following Government interference started the slump last year, and talkies this year delivered the *coup-de-grâce*.[39]

By March 1929, Raymond Longford had sailed for England to explore his chances of production in that country. Speaking of his own and other film-making careers that had been in decline by 1925 he claimed:

Today the position is so hopeless that the men in the game have had to get out. Not the combines but the Commonwealth Government has ruined us.[40]

To this could also be added Longford's observation at the Royal Commission that the combines had done only what they were allowed to do. The Government's attitude after the Commission had been not so much one of deliberate neglect but one hamstrung by constitutional impossibility.

Sound and Survival

PART TWO

Sound and Survival

5

The new pioneers
1930-35

By 1929, the permanence of sound was accepted by film industries throughout the world. The popularity of sound films had been firmly established after the New York premiere of Warner Brothers' feature-length **The Jazz Singer**, with its four "talkie" sequences presented through the Vitaphone sound-on-disc system, on 6 October 1927. For two years, the historical precedent and comparative simplicity of sound-on-disc vied with sound-on-film until the newer system outpaced its rival in clarity. Although the early constraints of sound technology would freeze the creative advancement of American cinema for almost three years, the very advent of sound at the same time confirmed Hollywood's world dominance.

As in other countries, Australia's introduction to the sound feature revolution was initially through part-talkies or silent features whose commercial life had been prolonged by the addition of synchronised music and effects. The age of sound films arrived in a big way on 29 December 1928 with the Sydney premiere of **The Jazz Singer** at Union Theatres' Lyceum, and on the same day **The Red Dance**, a silent production with sound-on-film musical accompaniment, at the Hoyts Regent. The theatres each grossed a record £4000 in their first six days of sound.

Within a few weeks, the Prince Edward became the next Sydney cinema to introduce talkies. In early February 1929 at the Athenaeum and the Auditorium, **The Jazz Singer** and **The Red Dance** introduced sound features to Melbourne. In May, installations were commenced in many suburban cinemas. The *Sydney Morning Herald* estimated that by 4 January 1929, 30 000 people had seen talkies at the Lyceum with 35 000 at the Regent. The newspaper asked:

Are the "talkies" just a craze, or have they come to stay? Judging by the
attitude of the audience inside the theatres, one is bound to admit that the
"talkies" will switch the motion picture industry on to an entirely new road.[1]

In the first three weeks of 1930, it was estimated that 200 000 people saw talkies in Sydney alone.

The spread of sound film was rapid and unremitting; the extent to which talkies were accepted can be gauged by the fact that in early 1936, the United States, the United Kingdom, Australia and New Zealand were the only countries where cinemas were fully converted to sound. Whereas a mere 350 of Australia's 1250 cinemas were wired for sound in June 1930, the figure more than doubled to 804 within five months. By March 1936, Australia had a total of 1334 cinemas, all of them wired. In the interim, many rural centres were serviced by touring sound projection units run by the major exhibition chains and independents; the latter continued to tour towns which had no cinemas until the war years.

Smaller exhibitors were disadvantaged by the cost of hiring sound equipment from the monopolistic Western Electric company, and by mid-1930 it was claimed that payments and hiring agreements had led the majority of suburban exhibitors to the point of bankruptcy. Because an outright purchase was not permitted, the standard contract imposed a £10 000 installation fee, together with a weekly service charge, that bound exhibitors to a minimum of ten years. To break the monopoly, Australian engineers began to develop their own sound projectors. The best-known of these was Ray Allsop's Raycophone, first publicly demonstrated on 10 June 1929. Later that month, when it was apparent that Western Electric was sharpening its tactics to block the growth of local projection equipment, *Everyones* reported:

According to Minister for Customs Gullett, assuming that Australian talkie equipment is up to the standard, the Federal Government will take steps to see that it is not ruthlessly stamped out by American picture interests.[2]

In early July, major distributors operating under licence to Western Electric, loosened their restrictions against Australian equipment and stated that, providing the sound was up to the best American standards, they were prepared to accept the installation of Australian Raycophone and Auditone equipment. Raycophone (which in the early 1930s merged with the theatre equipment suppliers Harringtons) proceeded to prosper; by mid-1937 the company had installed systems in 345 theatres and developed its own sound recording and mixing equipment.

Another exhibition-related enterprise that was to benefit from Federal Government action was film processing and printing. To minimise the effect of a federal tariff intended to protect Australia's projection equipment and processing industries, distributors began importing duplicate negatives to facilitate the bulk printing of films for local release.[3] In Sydney, the Commonwealth Film Laboratories (established in 1925 and privately run, despite its name) installed a continuous processor around 1932 and began the non-stop printing of features for Paramount, Fox and MGM. Cinesound Productions' laboratory, upgraded in late 1932, was capable of processing 300 000 feet of film weekly and as the decade progressed two more laboratory companies were formed in Sydney. In Sydney and Melbourne (where Cinesound and Herschell's were dominant), the printing of imported features had the effect of encouraging new technology and stabilising costs to the benefit of the local producers.

The effect of talkies on live theatre was catastrophic. Entire companies were disbanded, auditoriums either converted to film or were closed completely, and by February 1930 the Actors' Federation (predecessor to Actors' Equity) sought government assistance for 1300 unemployed members. J. C. Williamson Theatres for the first time in its history announced heavy losses in the financial years 1930-31 and 1931-32. JCW cited the main causes as the general economic depression, the talkies, and entertainment taxes imposed by the Federal and State Governments. The widespread dismissal of cinema musicians occurred soon after the arrival of talkies, to the extent that by May 1930, 3000 of them had been made redundant.

Some relief came with the revival of cinema stage shows. As distinct from the stage bands and the prologues (preparatory live routines linked to the theme of the film) which had helped create atmosphere in the 1920s, the new presentations brought back a much needed personal touch to a night's entertainment. Mel G. Lawton, the general manager of Sydney's Prince Edward Theatre, was a leading exponent of such events throughout the 1930s. He wrote in December 1931:

Spread over the past seven or eight months, we have experimented with different types of shows, and feel that we have now reached a recognition of the average public taste. I firmly believe that the most popular presentation is one that will run about fifteen minutes at most, consisting of a well-trained, youthful ballet, with speciality acts dovetailed in to balance.[4]

In January 1932, one of Lawton's more elaborate presentations, *Smile Through Smithy*, billed with the Marx Brothers' **Monkey Business,** was dedicated to the aviator Charles Kingsford Smith; while shortly afterwards, Orrie Perry as manager of the Sydney Capitol, combined MGM's **Mata Hari** with *The Empire Bridge Pageant*, a spectacular celebration of the Sydney Harbour Bridge opening. Union Theatres and Hoyts were able to ''double'' many of their features with vaudeville acts, but after 1932 the presentations diminished, leaving the ''star'' organists and several orchestras to play on in key cinemas.

Australian sound technology and newsreels

Two decades earlier — in fact, just prior to the First World War — Australia had first experienced synchronised sound film with the briefly popular Chronomegaphone and the Edison Kinetophone, both imported by Spencer's Pictures. The first known Australian experiments in synchronising sound with film were conducted in 1921 by the Sydney engineer Ray Allsop, who linked a sound-on-wax cylinder with film of a man reciting poetry. Throughout the 1920s, other local producers had brief commercial glory with films of musical routines synchronised with 78 rpm discs. Allsop himself in November 1928 made four such shorts in the course of developing his Raycophone projection equipment.

As mentioned previously, the activities of De Forest Phonofilms (Australia), were accorded surprisingly little significance after their demise, yet the company's pre-eminence in being the first to shoot with a sound-on-film recording process in Australia might have been recognised had it survived longer. Established in September 1925, De Forest made few synchronised items beyond various events surrounding the Duke of York's visits to Sydney and Canberra in early 1927, culminating in the Duke's opening of the first Federal Parliament in the national capital. Of greater impact was De Forest's importation from America and England of its sister companies' entertainment shorts. The first Australian demonstration of Phonofilm took place at the Piccadilly Theatre, Sydney, on 6 July 1925, and public screenings were held at the nearby Prince Edward Theatre throughout November and December of 1926. During the following two years, De Forest items were screened under contract in selected Union Theatres, but just when a surge of interest from the public and exhibitors seemed to assure the company of a good future, it wound down its activities, hampered by a lack of trained production personnel and a shortage of films.

More indicative of future Australian short film production was the increasing appearance in the late 1920s of brief newsreel segments with a disc-recorded commentary. Possibly spurred on by the arrival in Australia of Movietone newsreel production equipment in August 1929, a Melbourne company began in October several months' output of **The Australian Talkies Newsreel**. With sound recording by a leading contributor to the sound-on-disc period, Vocalion Records, one of the earliest items was a speech by the nation's new leader, J. H. Scullin. Sound-on-disc was also used by Stuart Doyle for Scullin's election campaign in early October 1929, when he had Australasian Films link up with Columbia Records in Sydney to produce a propaganda short opposing the Bruce-Page Government's proposed increase in entertainment tax and the introduction of a new film import tax.

The introduction of sound revolutionised the style and stature of the newsreel. From being just another part of a silent programme, it achieved a new capacity for realism and authority. A series of individual Movietone items were shown in the United States throughout 1927, but the first of the regular **Fox Movietone News** issues did not appear until the end of October, after **The Jazz Singer** had appeared. In the eight years since the first silent **Fox News**, the company had extended its coverage around the world. From 1919, Fox's Australian representative was Claude Carter, a freelance cameraman. In the mid-1920s, Carter established Filmcraft Laboratories with fellow cameraman Ray Vaughan, and processed Australian items for **Fox News** until the formation of Fox Movietone (Australia) in 1929. With the establishment of this branch, Ray Vaughan was sent across to the parent company for training as a sound newsreel cameraman. On 8 August 1929 he arrived back in Sydney together with Fox's Australian head, Stanley S. Crick, an American sound engineer, Paul Hance, and Australia's first Movietone truck. *Everyones* reported:

The welcome to Mr Crick started the moment the "Sierra" entered the heads. A squadron of planes flew overhead, ferry steamers whistled, and a contingent of reporters and camera-men swarmed up the ship's side to get at the Fox-Movietone sound unit, which was in action on the boat-deck, with Ray Vaughan and Paul Hance in charge of operations ... Coming up the harbour between 700 and 1000 feet were shot, and at the wharfside the first two to speak into the "mike" were Mr Crick and L. H. McNeill, assistant general manager of Vacuum Oil, who will lay down supplies for the truck wherever it moves throughout Australia.[5]

The arrival of the company's production vehicle added Australia as a Movietone centre to those in America, Great Britain, France and Germany. Nine days later, Vaughan and Hance began shooting further items for world distribution and on 2 November the first Australian issue featured a speech by Prime Minister Scullin. The first full-reel issue presented the 1929 Melbourne Cup, and was premiered on 6 November, the day after the race. By late September, the Australian Fox Movietone News Department had been formed under Claude Carter to organise regular production of Australian items for home and overseas, and after further consolidation of the unit, the first issue of a complete and regular Australian edition appeared in January 1931 under the editorship of Harry Lawrenson.[6]

Movietone's first Australian rival was the **Cinesound Review**, produced by Union Theatres and premiered on 7 November 1931. A fortnight later brought the debut of the Melbourne-based **Herald Newsreel**, produced by Herschell's Pty Ltd (who had been in Australian short film production since 1912) and the Melbourne *Herald*. The *Herald*'s proprietor, Keith Murdoch, was keen to link his newspaper with a sound newsreel following similar trends overseas. In March 1932, **Cinesound Review** scooped **Movietone News**, the **Herald Newsreel** and **Paramount News** with its coverage of Captain De Groot's slashing of the ribbon to prematurely open the Sydney Harbour Bridge. The other reels were to have their own exclusives, among them Movietone's coverage of Amy Johnson's arrival in Brisbane after her England-to-Australia flight in 1930, and the **Herald Newsreel**'s report on the sinking of the coastal steamer *Casino* at Apollo Bay, Victoria. In September 1932, the **Herald Newsreel** was absorbed by **Cinesound Review**, leaving Cinesound and Movietone as rivals until their merger as **Australian Movie Magazine**, in October 1970.[7]

The Depression

Prime Minister Bruce, quoted by *Everyones* on 3 July 1929, a few months before the collapse of Wall Street, had said:

We are facing more economic troubles now than ever before in Australia's history; tens of thousands of men and women are suffering through unemployment; and it is increasingly hard to obtain money for industry.

Surely, then, it is rather dreadful to see great queues of people waiting outside cinema palaces that have cost hundreds of thousands of pounds to build.

Australia had been economically depressed since halfway through World War I, but the Depression after 1929 brought a much higher rate of unemployment. While the percentage of the workforce unemployed in 1929 had been 11.1, by 1932, the peak year of the Depression, it had reached 28.1. Australia was proportionately worse affected than Germany. As the Depression deepened in 1931 the basic wage was cut by almost a third, the national debt soared to an alarmingly high level and export prices fell. As evictions increased and people roamed in search of work, unemployment camps sprang into existence around most Australian cities and large towns. Newspaper photographs showed the shanties, the cave homes, the relief and charity work, and confrontations with police. In providing entertainment that would allow their audiences a brief respite from these events, the Australian newsreels completely ignored them.[8]

After the boom that accompanied the coming of sound, the country's film exhibitors soon reflected the subsequent slump. By mid-1931, film returns across Australia were at their lowest for five years. After earning a profit of £80 000 in 1929-30, Hoyts Theatres Ltd lost £18 500 in the second half of 1930. Union Theatres Ltd and its associated companies suffered even more heavily. Early 1931 saw a £44 000 plunge in the profits of Amalgamated Pictures and J. D. Williams and in the first half of the year, Union Theatres and Australasian Films together lost £48 012. From May 1931, Union Theatres began to reduce salaries and retrench staff, the orchestras of the Sydney Capitol and Melbourne State were dismissed, and male ushers at the former were replaced by women on lower wages. Both Union Theatres and Hoyts claimed that their losses had been compounded by an increase in Federal and State entertainment taxes, introduced as a revenue measure by the Federal Government in 1916 and revised six times since.

In late 1929 a proposed increase in the Federal entertainment tax was enough to contribute to the downfall of the Bruce-Page Liberal-Country Party Government. The campaign against the tax, orchestrated by AF-UT's Stuart Doyle, was the most positive indication of the growing political influence of the Australian film trade. Bruce's August budget proposed a five per cent levy on all amusement admission receipts and "a tax of 12½ per cent upon the payments made to persons outside the Commonwealth by film importers for non-British films". The film import tax, Bruce explained in mid-September, was to obtain a proportion of budget-balancing revenue

from a section of the film industry, which is highly profitable and which, up to the present, has succeeded in escaping taxation by devices which have taken its profits beyond the reach of existing legislation.[9]

Following the budget, film industry shares plummeted on the stock exchanges, and trade representatives lobbied so intensively that the *Sydney Morning Herald* described the industry's tax fight as savouring of American politics. Under Doyle, AF–UT strenuously led the campaign. All the combine's shareholders and employees, and members of allied industries, were asked to wire or write expressions of protest to the Government, and most of them did. The campaign included the sound-on-disc short film produced by Australasian Films mentioned earlier which showed the prospect of closed theatres and further unemployment. Dissent and debate raged in the Federal Parliament. With the tax row as catalyst, a former Royal Commission chairman, Walter Marks, and the member for North Shore, William Morris Hughes, crossed the floor during a vote on another issue, forcing dissolution and a general election. It was hardly a coincidence that Walter Marks, federal member for Wentworth, was, as *Rydge's Business Journal* pointed out later, "a great personal friend of Mr S. F. Doyle":

Mr Marks voted against Mr Bruce because he did not agree with the amusement tax. And he did not agree with that tax because he has been impressed with the arguments of Mr Doyle, as well as his [own] knowledge as Chairman of the Royal Commission on Moving Pictures.[10]

Guided by Doyle, and under the direct supervision of Ken G. Hall, Union Theatres continued its publicity drive on the tax issue by supporting Marks and Hughes throughout the ensuing election campaign and in mid-October both were returned as independents, while a Labor Government was elected under James Scullin. After the election film shares rose once more.

Nevertheless, in early July 1930 the trade learned that it was to be deprived of £128 750 annually through the Federal Government's resolve to tax distributors on thirty per cent of their overseas remittances. In addition, film import duty was to be increased from 3d to 4d per foot, with a further levy of 2.5 per cent to be charged on each film. However, although the entertainment tax continued to be quoted by Australian exhibitors and live theatre companies as one of the main reasons for their losses, the restructuring of exhibition that began in late 1930 was caused more by a shortage of marketable films and a decline in audiences due to the Depression than by restrictions brought about by the taxes.

On 1 September 1930 the Fox Film Corporation became the first American distributor to enter Australian film exhibition when it purchased a controlling interest in Hoyts Theatres Ltd. Among those who sold virtually all their shares was F. W. Thring, who also resigned as managing director and announced he would embark on independent production. Thring told the press that he had taken the step

sincerely, feeling that the appreciation of a powerful production company such as the Fox Film Corporation with Hoyts Theatres is eminently desirable, and in the interests of the shareholders.

The sources from which quality film productions are procurable have become fewer each year, and, without an alliance such as is now brought about, we were in the position of not having any security of supply to present in the theatres.[11]

Thring stated that Fox and Hoyts had given him an assurance that they would distribute and exhibit the films he was to make as an independent producer. Fox also announced that it would embark as soon as possible on its own Australian features, and this was reaffirmed a year later by Hoyts' chairman of directors, Stanley Crick, who stated that local features would be the final result of Fox's expansion.[12]

The Fox takeover ended several years of speculation that Union Theatres and Hoyts would completely amalgamate their interests. A contemporary report that Paramount was interested in purchasing Union Theatres came to nothing, and Union Theatres' profits continued to sink. The bankers for both Union Theatres and Hoyts, the E S & A Bank, had halted the companies' elaborate theatre-building programmes in late 1929 (work on the Sydney Plaza, the last picture palace commenced for a number of years, started in September) and with the onset of the Depression, the large cinemas lost heavily. In early October 1931, after Union Theatres had reported a loss of £100 000, the E S & A Bank announced it would force the company's reconstruction. When it went into liquidation Stuart Doyle formed a new company, Greater Union Theatres Ltd, to purchase the assets for £400 000, the amount of the overdraft. Greater Union Theatres was to remain in a relatively precarious financial position until the early years of World War II; despite this Doyle, until his retirement, continued to look for new profit-making ventures. One of them was radio. In 1929 he had invested Union Theatres' money in the Australian Broadcasting Company, aiming to provide a national radio network. The company was taken over by the Federal Government and reconstituted as the Australian Broadcasting Commission in 1932. Doyle and his co-investors established the Commonwealth Broadcasting Corporation, which expanded swiftly after its initial acquisition of Sydney's station 2UW. Another, and far riskier, venture was a revival of Australasian Films' feature production programme. Doyle's first announcement of this, in December 1929, had preceded the production plans made public by Frank Thring and the Fox Film Corporation. In March 1931, eight months before Union Theatres' liquidation, Doyle repeated his announcement, stating that **On Our Selection** would be AF–UT's first Australian talkie feature.

Australian sound features begin

The first definite step towards talkie feature production in Australia had been the registration in August 1929 of Australian Talkies Ltd (no connection with the Melbourne company of the same name). The company was to be headed by Norman Dawn, the director of **For the Term of his Natural Life** and **The Adorable Outcast**.[13] The company's prospectus stated Dawn's intention to establish an Australian sound studio, train local staff and retire after ten years. Dawn himself returned to Australia in early October, commenting that the ideal form of Australian feature was a ''rugged outdoor narrative''.[14] By the time he started shooting from a script by Martin Keith in May 1930, his film was being described as a comedy-drama on ''the adventures of a motion picture troupe on location", incorporating "song-and-dance interpolations".[15]

It was eventually released as **Showgirl's Luck**, and dealt with the backstage rivalry of two tent-show leading ladies competing for the lead role in the first talkie to be made in Australia. Norman Dawn's wife Katherine (billed as Susan Dennis) played the actress selected for the role, and Sadie Bedford was the rival who masquerades as the rightful leading lady after intercepting her rival's telegram of notification. All that survives of the film is an energetic three-minute trailer consisting of musical, romantic and action scenes.

With bravura moments, like a chorus line tapping away on a cliff's edge, and Katherine Dawn's eyes grotesquely bulging — courtesy of her husband's optical effects — as she smokes a cigar, the trailer seems to promise more than reviews and recollections have indicated. With sound technology advancing rapidly between 1929 and 1932, **Showgirl's Luck** may have been considered stylistically crude even by the time of its first Sydney screening in November 1931. In the eighteen months after work began, the film was plagued by a vicious circle of sound problems and money shortages. After two months of retakes and few improvements Dawn abandoned his imported sound-on-disc recording plant and spent until December 1930 shooting the remainder of the film using the local, and still imperfectly developed, Standardtone sound-on-film process. By then, problems posed by sound editing had delayed the release even further. Unable to raise money for more Australian films he returned to America.

Norman Dawn had at least made the first Australian full talkie to enter production and achieve a release. This was more than could be said for the all-talkie **Out of the Shadows**, commenced by A. R. ("Dick") Harwood two months before the start of **Showgirl's Luck**, but which was never shown publicly because of similar problems with sound-on-disc. Two other Australian producers had meanwhile been adding sound sequences to silent films in order to improve their chances in the Commonwealth Government's 1930 production contest. In the early part of the year the McDonagh sisters with **The Cheaters**, and the team of Austin Fay and Arthur Higgins with **Fellers**, worked hard to meet the competition deadline. In view of the producers' enchantment with the concept of sound and the primitive technical resources available, the competition could not have been held at a worse time. The Appeal Board of the Commonwealth Censor's Department judged the competition and awarded only a third prize; £1500 went to **Fellers**, a wartime comedy-drama assessed by the *Sydney Mail* to be "a hotch-potch of absurd coincidences".[16] The fact that **The Cheaters**, a fine film in its silent form, was rated beneath **Fellers** indicates that in contemporary eyes at least the addition of sound had destroyed the impact of the original films as silents. Today **Fellers** is lost altogether and **The Cheaters** survives only as a silent.

The failure of the contest was resoundingly criticised by producers and press, and the accompanying scenario contest fared no better when first prize went to *Tutankhamen*, a Biblical spectacular well beyond the means of any Australian producer. Gayne Dexter, condemning both competitions as a fiasco, questioned the Appeal Board's "knowledge of the motion picture industry" and challenged

not only the Appeal Board, but the Government of Australia to have that scenario produced by any company in this world.[17]

There was no surprise when the Government announced the contests would be suspended indefinitely, but *Everyones* rightly asked what would happen to the remaining £21 500 the Commonwealth had so far collected in film duty with the object of aiding the Australian production industry.[18]

Ahead of anybody else in capitalising on the novelty of the Australian "all-talkies" was A. R. Harwood, who, undaunted by the disaster of **Out of the Shadows**, employed a radio engineer to perfect a sound-on-film process for two more low-budget features, **Isle of Intrigue** and **Spur of the Moment**. Filmed back-to-back in Melbourne between July and late August 1931, both were released on the same programme in late September. Compared with the static nature of Harwood's next feature, **Secret of the Skies** (1934), **Spur of the Moment**, a detective drama, is surprisingly fluid, with stagey performances counterbalanced by a mobile camera. Harwood was the first to present a programme of Australian talkies, beating F. W. Thring to the screen by two weeks.

Efftee established

By drawing on his knowledge of the film business and ability to judge the prevailing economic realities of the industry, Frank W. Thring became the first to inspire any real confidence in Australian sound feature production. Since the American film shortage had led to his resignation from Hoyts, Thring was now hoping to take advantage of the situation and invest his own money in nurturing the start of a full-scale production industry, even if that meant losing heavily at first. *Everyones* recounted in late 1931:

With the preliminary announcement that F. W. Thring would invest a large fortune in exploiting the possibilities of local production . . . it was realised immediately that at last, a determined effort had been made to place the home film industry on a solid foundation. From the outset it was realised further, that the handicap under which almost every Australian producing company in past years has laboured, was overcome. That factor alone inspired confidence.[19]

Thring moved swiftly after his resignation from Hoyts. In mid-September 1930, he announced the formation of Efftee Film Productions (the name derived from his own initials), and leased His Majesty's Theatre in Melbourne, from J. C. Williamson's as a studio. Norman Lindsay and C. J. Dennis were to be employed as literary advisers, and the first production was planned to be an adaptation of Lindsay's recently-published and banned novel, *Redheap*. In early October, Thring sent his general manager, Tom Holt, together with cameraman Arthur Higgins and sound engineer Alan Mill, to America to purchase equipment and employ a trained sound engineer to ease the studio into its first months of production. When an additional plan to engage two American directors was dropped because of high salary demands, Thring decided to direct most of the films himself.

Following the return of Higgins, Mill and Holt to Australia in January 1931, Thring sidestepped a heavy import duty on his £25 000-worth of RCA recording gear by persuading the Government to reduce it to several hundred pounds. Because of the time it was taking for the studio to be prepared, Norman Lindsay then impatiently withdrew *Redheap* and his own services, and another intended production, **Diggers**, was delayed to allow testing of facilities on a less ambitious project, the marital comedy **A Co-respondent's Course** (1931).

This film was to prove the least typical of all the Efftee output. Its young European director, E. A. Dietrich-Derrick and American sound engineer Dan Bloomberg respectively helped force the narrative pace and extensive use of locations, although there is no evidence of either attribute in their later collaboration, Efftee's comedy melodrama **The Haunted Barn** (1931). The visual mobility of **A Co-respondent's Course** was enhanced by the clever use of post-production dubbing over location shots, a rarity in local films of this period.

Diggers, started in May 1931, was Efftee's first major undertaking. The star, writer and co-director with Thring was Pat Hanna, whose First World War "Diggers" entertainment troupe had retained its popularity throughout the 1920s. Thring saw box-office potential in an adaptation of the troupe's three most popular sketches and the result, by today's standards, was to allow Hanna and cohorts the opportunity to stretch their routines well beyond the threshold of boredom. But there was enough public warmth for both Hanna and the Anzac mystique in the early 1930s to gross **Diggers** and its follow-up films, **Diggers in Blighty** and **Waltzing Matilda** (1933, both directed by Hanna), large returns. Given an improved production climate after 1933 and more filmically aware direction, Hanna might have been able to remain a considerable screen success. **Diggers'** linking narrative is a Returned Servicemen's League (RSL) dinner attended by Chic Williams (Hanna) and his soldier mate Joe (George Moon). The first flashback, "The Hospital", contains the most characteristic exchange in an emotional post-battle reunion between Chic and Joe. The "Rum" episode used a similar mixture of sentiment and slapstick in a comment on relations between formal British and easygoing Australian soldiers. The third, "Mademoiselle from Armentières", an illustrated song on the fragility of love in the face of war, is the most serious.

Frank Thring considered that every Efftee feature would stand its best chance as part of a "unit programme", each programme containing sufficient appeal to attract large audiences. Accordingly, in April 1931 he commenced an ambitious schedule of featurettes in the form of vaudeville interludes, stage recitations, documentaries and speeches by VIPs. The prodigious output of these shorts, numbering over eighty, becomes even more impressive when it is realised that all were produced in less than half the three-year period Efftee remained in feature filmmaking. Of the vaudeville items, the best are those showcasing the talents of comedian George Wallace, singer Kathleen Goodall, vocalist-composer Jack O'Hagan and the variety artist Athol Tier. Among the speeches was an official studio opening by the Federal Customs Minister, Frank Forde, on 2 June and a presentation speech for the first unit programme by Thring himself. In July the wildlife filmmaker Noel Monkman joined Thring to form Australian Educational Films, with the aim of producing a series of North Queensland wildlife documentaries. The first series, concentrating on the Great Barrier Reef (and featuring underwater photography for which Monkman became world famous), made these films an integral part of the unit programmes, and helped ensure the sale of the Efftee output to England in December 1932.

In October 1931 the first unit programme, featuring **Diggers**, was considered impressive enough for Fox and Hoyts to honour their earlier undertaking to acquire the studio's output for distribution and exhibition. Up to this date, Thring had invested £50 000 of his own money in Efftee films. Considering the £20 000 then being spent on his new version of **The Sentimental Bloke**, he must have felt greatly relieved when the **Diggers** programme, after an initially slack public reception, returned substantial box-office takings on its country tour and city re-run.

The Sentimental Bloke (1932) was the first Efftee feature to be released by the Australian branch of Universal Pictures, whose managing director, Herc McIntyre, proved to be the film trade's most consistent supporter of Australian production for almost three decades. **The Sentimental Bloke** was the most expensive of all the Efftee features, and the one most determined in its attempts to evoke what was considered to be the national spirit. Unlike the Longford version of thirteen years earlier, it had the advantages of a large budget, the participation of the author, C. J. Dennis, as screen writer and used the actual Melbourne locations of Dennis's verse narrative. Dennis also helped with casting and Cecil Scott, ''a middle-class and more romantic figure''[20] than Arthur Tauchert's 1918 incarnation, was cast as the Bloke. Ray Fisher was to play Doreen and Tal Ordell was cast as Ginger Mick, a role he had originally played on stage. Although the film was well-publicised and drew large audiences, the result in aesthetic and financial terms (relative to cost) was a failure.[21] Even if the freewheeling Longford version of 1919 had not existed to allow present-day comparison, Thring's **Sentimental Bloke** would still seem static and cloyingly moralistic. With the emphasis on sentiment, the two leads are given no opportunity to reveal vigour or depth, and the intended Australianism is undermined by a gangsterish subplot of crooks attempting to swindle the Bloke's adopted uncle out of a gold find. The film is occasionally redeemed by imaginative visual touches, notably the inclusion by in-the-camera matte shots (involving two different exposures) of Dennis's original verse to mirror states of mind; and finally comes to life with the Bloke and Doreen's move to the country. On

114

balance, it seems to be a fair indication of Thring's abilities as a director and is characterised by static camerawork and frequently stolid performances.

With **His Royal Highness** (1932), Thring struck a formula for box-office success. The vaudeville comedian George Wallace had been popular on the Australian stage since 1919 and early in 1932 made his first film appearances in two Efftee shorts, **George Wallace, Australia's Premier Comedian** and **Oh, What a Night!** Both contained the idiosyncratic stand-up comic routines that would be developed more fully through Wallace's three Efftee features: **His Royal Highness, Harmony Row** and **A Ticket in Tatts** (1934). Wallace was the comic larrikin whose stumble-footed antics allowed endearing glimpses of pathos. The limbs of a contortionist, unexpected grace and perfect timing allowed equal aptitude for tap-dancing and falls onto his left ear, while a good drinker's voice gargled hilarious double entendres of an early ocker strain. This was amply suited to the storyline of **His Royal Highness**, a fantasy operetta that has the stagehand Tommy Dodds (Wallace) involved in the palace intrigues of the Kingdom of Betonia after he has inherited its crown. His behaviour, horrifying to the court, includes a poker game with the footmen and a decree that geriatric staff wear roller skates. But despite a high degree of script inventiveness and the film's lavish scale (on a budget of £19 000), the final outcome was again shackled to a leaden visual style.

During the making of **His Royal Highness**, Thring announced that Efftee had postponed its plans for a move to outdoor subjects in order to satisfy the Australian public's renewed demand for musical comedy. But it was undoubtedly the appeal of Wallace himself, rarely off the screen, that ensured the financial success of **His Royal Highness**. It played to capacity houses throughout Australia and New Zealand; in England (where it was released as **His Loyal Highness**, in order not to offend Buckingham Palace) George Wallace was hailed by a trade paper as one of the greatest comedy finds in a decade.

Thring had already built up an impressive team by November 1931. In that month, experienced Efftee hands like writer C. J. Dennis (soon to co-write **His Royal Highness** with George Wallace), cameraman Arthur Higgins, sound engineer Alan Mill and set designer W. R. Coleman were joined by Raymond Longford who was, it was reported, to direct for the company.[22] But instead of an arrangement where Thring might have drawn the very best from his collaborators, his initial intentions were swept aside by benevolent autocracy and he remained very much the businessman-director in charge. Longford worked in an advisory capacity on **The Sentimental Bloke**, and remained as an uncredited "associate" on **His Royal Highness** and **Harmony Row**. It was ironic that remakes by Efftee and Australasian Films of Longford's earlier successes **The Sentimental Bloke** and **On Our Selection** had both been started in the same week of August 1931.

Cinesound

The entry of Australasian Films and Union Theatres into talkie features broadened the scope and competitiveness of the industry, while adding to its optimism. In December 1930, observers had seen Efftee as the only hope for local production for the next year[23], but only nine months later the enterprise of Australasian Films as a producer led *Everyones* to comment, "The future of film production has never been at a more promising stage".[24]

In one sense, the Australasian (soon to be Cinesound) revival was a logical flow-on from its late silent era schedule of feature production. But if it had not been for the precedent set by Thring's enterprise, Australasian's feature debut under Stuart Doyle might not have happened quite as soon as it did. The crippling losses made by Union Theatres had to be considered, as well as the high cost of importing sound production equipment. On the other hand Thring's initiative, coupled with the traditional Thring–Doyle rivalry and the success of sound-recording experiments at Australasian Films' Bondi Junction studio, seem to have pushed the venture forward.

The tests, clandestine at first, were started on the initiative of the laboratory superintendent Bert Cross, who was eager for Australasian to return to newsreel production after the arrival of imported talkie newsreels had spelt the demise of **Australasian Gazette**. From mid-1929, he encouraged first the *Wireless Weekly* editor Don Knock, then Tasmanian radio engineer Arthur Smith, to develop a sound-on-film recording system. Smith, joined in time by Cross's son Clive, was obtaining passable results by May 1930. In late July the team conducted their most successful work to date by adding effects and a dialogue sequence to coverage of the return to Sydney of the orchestra leader Henkell and the organist Scholl. The film was run for Stuart Doyle's assistant, Ken G. Hall, and soon afterwards for Doyle himself. After a fortnight of scepticism, Doyle agreed with Hall's opinion that the process was worth developing, and in late August he signed an agreement for Arthur Smith to develop a new studio recorder. Ken Hall was assigned to oversee and assist with the experiments, and to produce a series of shorts for theatrical release. Sound was added to the originally silent documentaries **Thar She Blows, The Wonderland of North-West Australia, Peeps at Darwin** and **Mysteries of Arnhem Land**. All were press previewed at Sydney's Prince Edward Theatre in mid-February 1931. For the next month the crew filmed "spot" items, such as a speech by Prime Minister Scullin on his return from overseas and tank exercises at Holsworthy Army Base. This period also saw the making of the first complete film by the team that would soon constitute the nucleus of Cinesound Productions: **That's Cricket**, directed by Ken Hall, was shot for the most part at the Sydney Cricket Ground, and featured speeches and demonstrations by members of the Australian Eleven.

In early March, Stuart Doyle decided to use the sound system on a feature to be directed by Hall. **On Our Selection** was chosen in response to the evergreen popularity of the stage production adapted by Bert Bailey and Edmund Duggan from the Steele Rudd stories. Most of the original stage cast were to be featured, headed by Bert Bailey, who was also the producer and assisted with dramatic direction. A small sound-proof studio was constructed in the middle of the Bondi Junction premises, otherwise un-soundproofed and used at night as a roller skating rink. The twelve-man crew was called on constantly for improvisation with converted or makeshift equipment, and Arthur Smith and Clive Cross developed a portable power supply only a matter of days before the unit left for location work. In the midst of shooting, Doyle asked Hall to start a Union Theatres newsreel, soon to be known as the **Cinesound Review** (a name which predated the formation of Cinesound Productions).

In August 1932, **On Our Selection** premiered to record-breaking audiences in Brisbane. It went on to screen continuously throughout Australia for the next three years[25], and by the end of 1934 had netted its backers a return of over £46 000 on their original modest investment of £6000. By 1937, the figure reached £50 000 and established a national record for any picture, domestic or foreign, released in Australia up to that time.[26]

Kenneth Wilkinson of the *Sydney Morning Herald* regarded the few flaws of **On Our Selection**

with a genial and affectionate eye, just as one looks on amiable weaknesses in the characters of one's friends. They never strike a jarring note, like the inept copies of Hollywood situations which used to be the bane of local silent films. The whole picture, from beginning to end, is typically Australian.[27]

Ken Hall, aware that Australian audiences had actually heard little of their country in local features, allowed the soundtrack to dwell on an introductory ''bush symphony'' of awakening birds, and the interlude of cattle fording a river, backed by the splash of water, shrill whistling of stockmen and cracking of whips. These scenes drew applause from early audiences, and another reviewer wrote: ''You hear the loveliness of the bushland, and hear its shy birds calling in the soft, clear dawn, and you know that here is the real Australia.''[28]

Viewed today, **On Our Selection** suffers discontinuity, lurching from broad farce to heavy melodrama and straight romantic interludes; but running as a lifeline throughout the film is a firm interaction between characters and location. Bucolic spontaneity abounds and the humour, frequently coarse, is generally funny. This and Bert Bailey's portrayal of Dad Rudd were central to the film's success. In the context of the Depression and early talkie stardom, Dad Rudd was even more the grass-roots folk hero than he had been on stage for the previous twenty years. His talk about battling floods, drought, fires and foreclosure had a new relevance to Australians thrown back on their own resources. In some respects Bailey was Australia's counterpart to the American film star Will Rogers, who at that time delivered home truths in the everyday language of his American audiences. Bailey, unmistakably Australian, was to be the industry's first and most bankable star of the 1930s.

In June 1932, even before the release of **On Our Selection**, Stuart Doyle was sufficiently heartened by its box office prospects to establish

Cinesound Productions Ltd to enter regular feature and documentary production, and continue making **Cinesound Review**.[29] Although nominally independent, Cinesound was part of the Greater Union Theatres company structure. Simultaneously Australasian Films went into liquidation and a new company, British Empire Films, was formed to facilitate the release of British films in Australia and the Cinesound films in Britain. The studio equipment and laboratory facilities at Bondi Junction were updated and, in early 1933, the old Rushcutters Bay studio was modernised in anticipation of extra demands being placed on available facilities by Cinesound and independent producers.

By the end of 1932, **On Our Selection** had played its part, with **The Sentimental Bloke** and **His Royal Highness**, in making that year one of the most encouraging in the history of Australian film production. *Everyones* commented:

It was the first year in which Australian pictures definitely established themselves as box-office mediums worth consideration; and the first occasion on which our producers gave promise of ever taking any serious part in the future of the world's film producing activities . . .

That 1933 will offer the producing companies of Australia their year of opportunity is clear.[30]

Ken Hall's second feature, **The Squatter's Daughter** (1933), again used a play by Bert Bailey and Edmund Duggan. It had already been filmed by Bailey and George Cross in 1910, but the new version disposed of most of the original plotline, bringing up to date a story which focused on the attempts of father-and-son villains to cheat their way into ownership of a wealthy grazing property. The cameraman was Frank Hurley, whose film of his recent Antarctic expeditions, **Southward-Ho with Mawson** (1930), had been the first feature-length film for which Arthur Smith's sound recording system was used.[31] In February 1932, Hurley signed a contract with Cinesound to produce a series of short documentaries for local and overseas exhibition. Additionally he was to be director of photography on all Cinesound features for the next three years.

On Our Selection evoked nationalism through mirth and sympathy for the underdog; the sentiments of **The Squatter's Daughter** were gauged with more subtlety to the pride of Australians in their wool industry, still dominant in spite of the Depression. The story's characters were upper middle-class and urbane — every inch the squattocracy of Australian popular novels like the "Billabong" series, and other films such as Pat Hanna's **Waltzing Matilda** (1933) and Beaumont Smith's **Splendid Fellows** (1934). Nearly three times the budget of **On Our Selection** was spent on **The Squatter's Daughter**, and the schedule was stretched to twelve weeks because of torrential rains during location work. The film begins with a eulogy to Australia's "health, optimism and progress" by Prime Minister Joseph Lyons, then backs its opening titles with a flock of sheep and a rousing rendition of "Land of Hope and Glory". Throughout **The Squatter's Daughter**, mustering, shearing and the importance of Australia's wool clip are exploited with wide-eyed wonder. The highlight is a huge bushfire, spectacularly staged with real peril to cast and crew who at one point took to their heels to escape the blaze. The reviewer of the Sydney *Sun* wrote:

Since the era of talkies, many pictures have depended all too little on the dramatic use of camera, but **The Squatter's Daughter** is not one of these. The photographs carry the action in a manner that is cinema at its best, so that the dialogue, which is not on the same high plane, falls into its proper place.

Within a few years, **The Squatter's Daughter** had grossed £35 000 and was released through MGM in the United Kingdom. For as long as Cinesound remained profitable, the company was now firmly committed to continuous production, but no subsequent film from the studio was able to match the returns of **On Our Selection** and **The Squatter's Daughter**.

The old guard fades

In August 1933, a rare public display of accord between independent producers, Cinesound and the Federal Government took place at the Rushcutters Bay studio. It was an event that might have temporarily soothed the career frustrations of Raymond Longford. In front of a gathering that included the Minister for Customs, T. W. White, Stuart F. Doyle and fellow filmmakers Ken G. Hall and Beaumont Smith, Longford directed a scene from Smith's new production, **The Hayseeds**. It was the first time he had worked as a director since completing **The Hills of Hate** for Australasian Films in 1926 and, fittingly, it took place at the studio in which he had made several of his greatest initial successes.

The occasion that brought these normally separate interests together was the opening of the studio, now converted to sound as Cinesound No 2. This studio and Cinesound No 3 at St Kilda in Melbourne were to be hired to independent producers in return for a release through Greater Union Theatres, provided that Cinesound considered the independent's film had "reasonable chances of success".[32] Cinesound had little reservation about **The Hayseeds**, which Beaumont Smith was making to cash in on the success of **On Our Selection**. But considerable doubts remained about Raymond Longford. Frustrated by what technicians recall as Longford's indecision and slowness, Smith was to take over and complete the direction of **The Hayseeds** himself. As he had at Efftee, Longford remained as associate director on this and Beaumont Smith's next production, **Splendid Fellows** (1934).

Although related thematically, **The Hayseeds** and **Splendid Fellows** are opposites in sophistication. Both are, as befits the period, heavily nationalistic, sometimes tongue-in-cheek and frequently effusive. At first glance, **The Hayseeds** is a rough evocation of earlier Beaumont Smith successes, and occasionally plagiarises moments from Hall's **On Our Selection**, among them shots lingering on the Australian bush, and determination-to-win speeches by Dad Hayseed (Cecil Kellaway). As the film progresses, the staginess of exchanges between members of city society are

119

bettered by a genuine, if naive, warmth for inland Australians as the country's most loyal and democratic citizens. With a cheeky tilt at the screen bushranging ban in New South Wales, Smith even has Dad and Joe (Tal Ordell) pose as bushrangers to protect a mate from the unjustified attentions of the law. The festive atmosphere is rendered particularly bizarre by the interpolation of bush hikers who sing and tap-dance in production numbers reminiscent of Busby Berkeley.

Despite being lashed by the critics, **The Hayseeds** returned a profit on top of its £4500 budget. Smith moved on immediately to **Splendid Fellows**; like **The Hayseeds** it was financed by J. C. Williamson Theatres and enjoyed the addition of separate technical and dialogue consultants whose contributions, together with that of cameraman George Malcolm, brought a new polish to Smith's work. The background to its story was the 1934 Melbourne Centenary Air Race, which was to attract twenty entries in an Empire-linking sweep from England to Australia. Intensifying the spirit of Empire that had been an ingredient of **The Hayseeds**, Smith's story leads up to the loyalty and self-sacrificing of an Australian entrant (Eric Coleman) leaving the race to search for a lost British friend and fellow entrant (Frank Leighton). **Splendid Fellows** begins well by injecting some originality into the tired cliché of a titled and monocled Englishman banished to a roughening-up in "the Colony". But after the first half-hour, Smith displays uncertainty by loading on enough further clichés to induce a credibility plunge long before the start of the race. The result was to reverse the experience of **The Hayseeds** — sympathetic reviews and box office failure. Beaumont Smith, whose work in sound film had begun more optimistically than that of any of his "old guard" contemporaries of the silent era, made no more features. He returned to the managing directorship of the J. C. Williamson Picture Corporation in New Zealand and, after his retirement and return to Australia, died in 1950.

Raymond Longford was given another chance, but it proved to be equally unhappy. In early 1934 he was employed by the producer J. A. Lipman to direct **The Man They Could Not Hang**, a property which had proved highly profitable in two Australian silent versions. Actors and technicians were to recall that Longford displayed little firm initiative as director of this film, although the result is not without its moments of visual and naturalistic invention. Despite the fact that the film made a small profit, Longford was given no further chance to direct. As the decade proceeded he made several attempts to re-embark on production, advancing no further than a factotum and bit player. With the decline of the industry in the early war years, Longford vanished from the film scene altogether. By 1950 he was working as a patrolman on the Sydney waterfront. "Rediscovered" by a *Sunday Telegraph* reporter in 1955, he enjoyed four years of renewed acclaim for his early achievements before his death in April 1959.

In addition to the final work of Beaumont Smith and Raymond Longford, 1934 also brought the release of the last feature by the McDonagh sisters. While Smith and Longford might have derived some consolation from looking back over several decades of achievement, the McDonaghs in the

120

early 1930s still had youth and creative potential on their side. A journalist who visited the set of **Two Minutes Silence** referred to Paulette McDonagh as "one of the few women picture directors in the world, and probably the most outstanding figure in the Australian motion picture industry today".[33] To this one might have added that with their current choice of subject, the McDonagh sisters were also the most daring.

Following the débâcle of **The Cheaters** disc sequences, the McDonaghs, in association with Standardtone Sound Recording Studios, produced a series of documentary shorts. In August 1930 they attended a Sydney performance of Leslie Haylen's anti-war play *Two Minutes Silence* and immediately bought the film rights. It depicted the World War I memories of four people in the household of an army general. *Smith's Weekly*, who rated it "the best Australian play of the year", stated that *Two Minutes Silence*, in a deliberately abstract style, was "a piece of biting satire, with no hero, with no centrality of interest, indeed, but with a gallery of human portraits linked only by their respective reactions to the anniversary of the Armistice".[34]

The film was to be as far from the McDonaghs' earlier work as the play itself was from prevailing trends in Australian theatre, although Paulette McDonagh tried to retain the play's spirit and outward simplicity. Voluminous publicity boosted the film's theme, its world-wide relevance, and the maturity it was expected to bring to the Australian cinema and stage. Public praise included a testimonial from the former Prime Minister, W. M. Hughes, who found its starkness laced with vitality and inspired humour. Kenneth Slessor, reviewing the film for *Smith's Weekly*, found

the whole effect [to be] one of beauty and strength. There is nothing cheap about the theme, nothing rubbed or shop-soiled; and the treatment is surprisingly free from banality.[35]

The bulk of critical and public opinion, however, was far from favourable. As **Two Minutes Silence** is now lost, there is no way of knowing whether today's standards would find it, as the *Sydney Mail* stated, "slow and laboured"[36], or, in the words of the *Sydney Morning Herald*'s critic, "flat and devoid of real dramatic content".[37] Paulette McDonagh, who considered the film to be the sisters' best, thought it was generally misunderstood. In retrospect, its significance derives from being the first Australian sound feature to tackle a theme of social concern, and to do so in a way felt at the time to be adventurous, perhaps even avant-garde. But this was no compensation for the financial losses on **Two Minutes Silence** in the early 1930s. Although Paulette McDonagh strove to set up another feature, the sisters dissolved their filmmaking partnership, and as a lone independent Paulette found the odds too great.

Efftee suspends

Just as Stuart Doyle had diversified Greater Union's investments into radio, mini-golf and ballroom dancing syndicates, Frank Thring extended Efftee's activities into radio and live theatre. From August 1933 until Easter 1935, he promoted theatre in Sydney and Melbourne with a series of Australian and imported plays. In March 1935, he purchased the operating rights to Melbourne's radio station 3XY, and began broadcasting on 8 September. Both activities supported Thring's aim of fostering Australian talent. He intended the lessons learned from each of the film, radio and theatre enterprises to flow through to the others; his initial aim in theatre was to try out "plays with motion picture possibilities", and to provide "a training ground for players deemed to have screen personality".[38] **Clara Gibbings** and **The Streets of London** (1934) were both films of plays thought to have world potential; later, in Sydney, Thring intended to produce *Collitt's Inn* as a screen adaptation of the first, and hugely successful, Australian play staged by him in 1933.

The more identifiably Australian content of the Efftee production schedule continued into the second and third George Wallace features and an adaptation of William Hatfield's well-known semi-autobiographical novel *Sheepmates*. **A Ticket in Tatts**, the final feature Efftee would make at its Melbourne studio before transferring to a renovated dance hall at St Kilda, featured more location footage than any Efftee feature since **The Sentimental Bloke**. But it was with **Sheepmates** that Thring intended to upgrade the scale and prestige of the company's output.

As the Australian "epic that never was", **Sheepmates** provided Thring with conclusive evidence of the inadequacies of the Efftee scripts and of his own work as a director. Following his purchase of the Hatfield novel — another tale of an Englishman proving himself against the rigorous inland — Thring filmed several studio interiors before departing with a crew in late September 1933 for six weeks' filming of cattle station scenes around the Queensland–South Australian border. Disasters befell them at every turn; dressed formally and chauffeur-driven in a luxury Packard, Thring suffered exhaustion; crew members narrowly escaped death in a tent fire; communication difficulties delayed cattle mustering scenes. On the unit's return to Melbourne, **Sheepmates** was abandoned. Thring stated that he intended to have the film's script and direction revised by experts he would employ on his next trip abroad.

The same intention seems to have played a part in Efftee's total suspension of production in April 1934, after the making of **Clara Gibbings** and **Streets of London**. But the stated reason was far more dramatic, connected as it was with the industry's threatened extinction no more than sixteen months after the early Efftee and Cinesound productions had made it appear so promising.

Film war and inquiry

On his return to Australia after a successful sales trip to England, Frank Thring observed that an event had occurred in his absence that made the position of the Australian independent producer far less secure. In January 1933 a new company, the General Theatres Corporation, had begun trading to operate and buy film for all theatres run by Hoyts and Greater Union, with the exception of Hoyts' suburban theatres. Prompted by the E S & A Bank, who wanted to curb the rivalry, expenditure and losses of both chains, the merger intensified divisions already in existence between American-backed distributors and local distributors. To fight this, American distributors increased their determination to move into the exhibition business throughout the country. The American plan presented even more of a threat to Australian producers; by the end of December 1933, five long-completed Australian features already awaited release in Sydney, while the conflict over contractual conditions between exhibitors and distributors had reached the level of a ''film war''. With Australian producers renewing their call for a domestic quota and the film trade at a stalemate, the New South Wales Government in late December announced a new industry inquiry under the Sydney consulting accountant F. W. Marks. All sections of the film community welcomed the news, for each expected their interests to be better served by the State inquiry than the 1927 Federal Royal Commission.

The campaign for an Australian film quota was led by Thring who individually had more invested in the film industry than any other producer. The release of Efftee output in States other than Victoria had always been uncertain, but the formation of the General Theatres Corporation now eliminated Thring's bargaining power and reduced his terms with Hoyts. Where he and other producers formerly had the choice of two outlets for exhibition, they now had only GTC. At the New South Wales Inquiry in January 1934, Thring lashed out at the Fox Film Corporation, who, through Hoyts and GTC, he claimed, had the power

to say whether an Australian production, no matter how worthy, shall or shall not be shown in the principal theatres of the Commonwealth. This is an intolerable situation and must be rectified.

Thring added that Stuart Doyle, in his opposition to an Australian quota, had nothing to gain but much to lose from such a device. ''Mr Doyle is not only the head of a producing company [Cinesound], but is also a director of General Theatres Ltd''.[39]

In August 1932, Thring, in a detailed submission to the New South Wales and Victorian Governments, had explained the advantages of the quota system in other countries, then went on to define the cultural and economic importance of the Australian film industry, and emphasise the necessity of overseas markets. He and others felt that these markets could be secured by means of a ''contingent'' system whereby (as in Germany) the number of foreign films imported or exhibited was controlled by the number of domestic films exported or screened overseas. Thring claimed that Efftee was aware of the need for an export market when it commenced production,

but the introduction of the Quota and Contingent systems in Australia could not be considered by the Government until it had been shown — and we claim this has now been done — that pictures of the highest standard could be produced in Australia.

The quota issue had been the subject of buck-passing between the Commonwealth and the States since the time of the Royal Commission. At first the poor track record of the 1927 Victorian quota served as a deterrent to the New South Wales Government, but after the New South Wales Inquiry had heard a mass of evidence in support of quotas, legislation for a quota appeared to be the only remedial action to take. Such a system was advocated in the evidence of Thring, Raymond Longford, Charles Chauvel, A. R. Harwood and Pat Hanna. Longford claimed that, "Here in this country we have a home market to which the local film is denied full access", and Harwood saw the Australian producer "in a very precarious position and . . . virtually in the grip of Mr Doyle". Longford further observed that blind-booking and block-booking "is the keystone of the domination of the country by foreign film interests. It has been eliminated in England by the Films Act and should be embodied in the suggested State Quota". But the statement which summed up the producers' attitudes came from Thring:

The people who oppose the Quota are, I believe, anxious that picture production in Australia should not progress beyond its present limits. They know that with a number of small producers working in a spasmodic fashion with small capital, that Australian production will never be formidable to the interests they represent.

It was a comment that not only emphasised the fragility of the local industry but also proved to be a grim prophecy. In mid-February 1934, just over a quarter of the way into the hearings, Thring dramatised the precariousness of his own position by announcing the suspension of production at Efftee. When it became effective two weeks before the end of the inquiry, he stated that a resumption would depend entirely on the willingness of his home State, Victoria, to introduce a revised quota for Australian films.

From 2 January to 20 April, the Inquiry into the Film Industry in New South Wales conducted fifty-four public sittings and heard evidence from eighty-four witnesses. The evidence ran to nearly four thousand pages. Besides the coming of sound and the now bitter divisions between distributors and exhibitors, the evidence showed that the industry had changed little since the 1927 Royal Commission. Once the novelty and boom of early sound had subsided, Australian producers faced exactly the same desperate battle for a release as they had before. In contrast to the pre-Royal Commission hearings by the Select Committee, F. W. Marks found every witness willing to be frank, tabling their accounts whenever necessary.

Between late June and early July, Marks' report was released in four parts. It recommended no government restriction of theatre licences, and no interference in such sensitive areas as film hire rates, blind and block booking, and rejection rights. The action Marks did urge was the introduction of a five-year quota for Australian films, beginning with a four per cent quota for exhibitors and five per cent for distributors. Having said that protection of existing theatres by restriction of theatre licences would set a harmful precedent for other industries, Marks similarly justified quota protection for Australian films as "a commonsense business procedure". Producers were jubilant and distributors, with Stuart Doyle as their spokesman, were predictably pessimistic. Ignoring their prophecies that the proposal would lead to the formation of harmful fly-by-night companies, the State Cabinet instructed the Chief Secretary to draft the required legislation, and in early December the Cinematograph Films (Australian Quota) Bill was tabled in the Legislative Assembly. The Government's argument, stressing the nationalistic and trade advantages of an Australian film industry which would surely die in the absence of the measure proposed, was accepted and the Bill passed both Houses. The Act was proclaimed law on 17 September 1935. As the fifth year of the quota period demanded the screening of at least sixty features every year, eleven new production companies were formed within months of the proclamation.

The demise of Efftee

Relations between Frank Thring and the Victorian Government continued to deteriorate. Throughout 1935 he threatened to move his operations to Sydney unless Victoria introduced quota legislation similar to that of New South Wales. On 7 January 1936, Thring announced that his intention to re-establish production in Sydney would be carried out, explaining that the Victorian Quota Bill passed in November 1935 was rendered valueless by a proviso that the Act would not operate until it was justified by a sufficient number of films.

Thring was determined to start Efftee's Sydney enterprise on a sound basis by realising his long-held plans to import overseas talent. In March he sailed for America, announcing that he would employ scriptwriters, directors and actors, and negotiate advance sales of the output of Efftee and a Sydney production company in which he was involved.[40] Three months later he began the return journey, bringing with him news of having secured an option on five American stars and two directors. After returning to Sydney in mid-June, he proceeded immediately to Melbourne. By the end of the month newspapers carried the announcement that F. W. Thring had died of cancer in a Melbourne private hospital at the age of fifty-three.

It was a severe shock to the industry, and his sudden and untimely death was to have long-lasting effects. The Australian cinema had lost its most persuasive advocate of the quota system, and one whose political and business abilities might have made it work. Although his talent as a director was limited, his ability as an executive could have boosted the careers of other filmmakers, and ultimately brought unity and bargaining strength to independents who had pinned their hopes on the quota system. Thring had gambled a private fortune an achieving this aim, producing nine feature films and around eighty shorts. *Film Weekly* estimated that in film production and live theatre, he had lost a total of £75 000.[41]

A national outlook: Charles Chauvel

As in every period of resurgence in Australian cinema, the first wave of the early 1930s production boom carried its share of concern about the lack of freshness in national outlook. Industry observers like Gayne Dexter of *Everyones* and Kenneth Wilkinson of the *Sydney Morning Herald* constantly noted the lack of recent and filmable Australian novels and plays that could be regarded as "box office" while still reflecting Australian attitudes. In December 1931, Dexter asked where the industry would turn after its secure bets with **The Sentimental Bloke, On Our Selection, The Squatter's Daughter** and **The Silence of Dean Maitland**. On the question of international viability, he wrote:

If we are to derive motion picture revenue from abroad we must see ourselves as the world imagines us, and conform with international ideas.[42]

Four years later, Kenneth Wilkinson was to ask, if Australian producers were aiming more and more for a world market:

How can they best appeal to that vast babel of a public? By stressing Australian national characteristics? Or by adopting a cosmopolitan style?[43]

A year earlier, the *Bulletin*, chauvinistic as ever, had said of Australian producers: "Let them put down the life around them and not bother a damn about international appeal".[44]

The British film trade, which by now had seen the first products of Efftee and Cinesound, was inclined to hold a low view of Australian films. In May 1933, for instance, the *Era* regarded the approach of Australian filmmakers to be condescending and second rate, and stressed that they should seize the many untapped "exciting themes and backgrounds" and treat them with "sufficient vision, sincerity and cleverness to give them an immediate appeal in whatever country they are shown".[45] In advocating Anglo-Australian and bushranging stories, the magazine suggested nothing new.[46]

The Australian filmmaker of the 1930s who was to be the most conscientious about evoking a national outlook on screen was Charles Chauvel. If Ken Hall's **On Our Selection** dominated the first half of the decade by exciting the industry's optimism, Chauvel's **Forty Thousand Horsemen** (1940) closed it on a high note of creative as well as industrial promise. And while Hall sought to refine a series of formulas, Chauvel spent the rest of his career exploring a personal vision of Australia by examining the dominant themes of pioneering zeal and mateship, often testing these in conflict with the land or in battle. The vision was always an epic one, pitting individuals against apparently insurmountable forces. Most of the heroes had direct links with the soil, for Chauvel believed that the true spirit of the nation was constantly regenerated in its rural heartlands. At its most parochial, such screen nationalism seems dated today, but it does convey much of the attitude of the "ordinary Australian" with whom Chauvel was anxious to identify. Although he learned that to ignore Hollywood ingredients could deprive him of an income, these were generally held at arm's length and only included as a token box office gesture. To the nationalistic and Hollywood components was added Chauvel's admiration for European filmmakers, among them Abel Gance, whose guiding belief "Enthusiasm is everything" he shared.

The 1930s provided an apprenticeship for Chauvel. During the decade he refined not only his skills as a filmmaker but as a businessman and publicist, skills essential to his viability and success. Like most Australian producers, Chauvel was forced into a far greater range of activities than would have been required in England or America. He raised money, worked on scripts, searched for locations, supervised casting — and finally directed. His name became well known despite his small output. In business dealings his idealism was infectious and he retained credibility in the eyes of the film trade despite his box-office failure until **Forty Thousand Horsemen**. His films were promoted by educational authorities and in Herc McIntyre, managing director of Universal Pictures' Australian branch, he found a loyal and energetic distributor. At various times he was the subject of public eulogies by Stuart Doyle and the New South Wales Premier, B. S. B. Stevens; in 1934 Chauvel, with three films to his credit, was referred to by Doyle as a "pioneer of great knowledge and courageous enterprise".[47]

Returning to Australia from Hollywood in March 1929, Chauvel emphasised the importance of the American market, stating that Australian producers with an eye in that direction "must make typical, local colour films, with character, background and new dramatic angles".[48] While thinking about the subject of his first sound feature, he ran a small travel agency and worked briefly as a house manager for Hoyts. Then, in January 1932, with backing fom Sydney businessmen, Chauvel formed Expeditionary Films, "to film stories off the beaten track". The production he planned was **In the Wake of the Bounty** (1933), conceived as the first of a series of travel films. Combining dramatic reconstruction with contemporary documentary, it was to elaborate the story of the **Bounty** mutineers and include coverage of life on Pitcairn Island. From March 1932 Charles and Elsa Chauvel with the cameraman Tasman Higgins, spent three months on Pitcairn Island and a further period in Tahiti. On their return to Australia, Chauvel had the first of his well-publicised brushes with officers of the Customs Department, who demanded cuts in scenes of bare-breasted dancers; a compromise was eventually reached in time for the film's release. While Chauvel was preparing to shoot dramatised interiors at Cinesound's Bondi studio the assistant director, John Warwick, drew his attention to a newspaper photograph of a young adventurer whose yacht had run aground in New Guinea. Warwick suggested that the young man might be tested for the role of Fletcher Christian and soon after this Errol Flynn was being rehearsed by Chauvel for his first acting appearance. He was paid £10 per week for three weeks work.[49] Amid **Bounty**'s rather laboured interior scenes, Flynn's wooden performance allows no more than a hint of the charisma that three years later brought him prominence in Hollywood. **Bounty**'s mainstay was its unique documentary ingredient. This led to the film being the first

Australian sound feature to obtain an American release, albeit in fragmented form, when it was screened as two separate shorts to promote MGM's **Mutiny on the Bounty** (1935).

In July 1933, five months after the premiere of **In the Wake of the Bounty**, Chauvel announced that his next production would be an ambitious "panorama of Australian history and the story of an Australian family through successive generations". He had to do some fast talking to justify a project of this magnitude to the board of Expeditionary Films, but was aided in September by the Commonwealth Government's announcement that it would revive its awards of merit for best production and scenario. The budget for **Heritage** (1935) was £24 000, less than half that spent by Australasian Films on **For the Term of his Natural Life**. **Heritage** was in production for six months of 1934, utilising carefully chosen locations between Sydney and southern Queensland and interiors at Efftee's Wattle Path studio. Lavish publicity, bigger than for any Australian film since **For the Term of his Natural Life**, included daily radio talks, newspaper spreads, a variety of posters, a book by Chauvel and testimonials from public figures. In Sydney squads of colonial soldiers marched the streets and collected the Harbour Bridge toll. "I hope this proves something worthwhile", Norman Lindsay was quoted as saying as he arrived for a preview of the film.[50]

The result was uneven confrontation between grand and intimate events, some impressive in spectacle and richness of detail, others bearing out Elsa Chauvel's recollection that the experience was like "trying to furnish a million-dollar home with only an account at Woolworth's". **Heritage** presented Australian history as a series of tableaux not as an interpretation; but it was to be the prototype for a nation-building statement that Chauvel refined fourteen years later, with considerably more money and maturity, in **Sons of Matthew**. However, Chauvel's use of an amateur actor, Franklyn Bennett, as a colonial pioneer and his successful modern-day parliamentary descendant added neither conviction nor consistency to the proceedings.

Additional publicity was generated when, ahead of Cinesound's **The Silence of Dean Maitland** and Efftee's **Clara Gibbings**, **Heritage** won the first prize of £2500 in the Commonwealth production contest. Despite this, the film was unprofitable and Chauvel realised that more than an emphasis on straight nationalism was needed to advance his career and the status of Australian film. For **Heritage**, it was too late to heed Kenneth Wilkinson's prediction of December 1935 that for a while longer, in Australian films,

the background will be emphasised at the expense of the foreground — the scenery at the expense of the actors and the play.

Later there will come a strong reaction. Local colour, having failed to ensure the success of every flimsy story on which it is imposed, will fall under suspicion. That will be the real critical period for Australian films — the period in which wise guidance will most of all be necessary.[51]

Actuality film in the 1930s

One aspect of production that did not change much throughout the 1930s was actuality film — both in the form of newsreels and the output of documentaries by commercial and government organisations. After the coming of sound, no great changes occurred until the early war years. But actuality did have its achievements as well as richly deserved prominence.

Newsreel was the most regularly shown and popular form of actuality. The crews of the rival **Cinesound Review** and **Movietone News** worked hard for their stories, ingeniously coping with subjects that were often difficult to film and bringing zest to even the most routine. A newsreel was normally divided into "news" and "magazine" items, the former ranging from the annual Melbourne Cup to grand events like the Duke of Gloucester's visit in 1934, the latter frequently embracing such novelties as performing pets. The greater appeal of **Cinesound Review** was for the most part due to the colloquial gags of the commentator Charles Lawrence, but from 1935 he had spirited competition from Movietone's Jack Davey.

The most characteristic and best-known documentaries were those of Frank Hurley, who was employed by Cinesound for most of the decade to make films on commission to industry and government departments. Nearly all of them displayed his love of exoticism and visual perfection and several, like **Fire Guardians** (1931) and **Treasures of Katoomba** (1936), give intriguing glimpses into the period's parochialism. Hurley's output for most of the decade consisted largely of travelogues (e.g. **Jewel of the Pacific, Oasis, Here is Paradise**) and industrials (**Pageant of Power, Brown Coal to Briquettes**) while two films that drew a good deal of public attention were the grand-scale **Symphony in Steel** (1932), which documented the construction of the Sydney Harbour Bridge, and **A Nation is Built** (1938), produced for the New South Wales sesquicentenary.

While Hurley and his films retained a public profile, comparatively little notice was taken of the prolific work of the Commonwealth Government's Cinema and Photographic Branch, based in Melbourne. The Cinema Branch had come into existence during 1921, when the Commonwealth cinematographer Bert Ive was transferred from the Department of Home and Territories to the Department of Immigration, then commencing a new immigration drive. For most of the 1920s, and especially after 1924 when facilities and staff were expanded, the Branch concentrated on films that would promote immigration and generally publicise Australia at home and abroad. The films were intended primarily for screening through Australian embassy outlets but many, including the long-running series **Know Your Own Country** and **Australia Day by Day**, also obtained a domestic commercial release. Ernest Turnbull, the first Officer-in-Charge (from 1924) and his successor (from mid-1926) Lyn T. Maplestone, wrote, edited and frequently directed the films, shot for the most part by Bert Ive. The Branch itself moved swiftly into sound production after its transfer in 1930 to the Department of Markets (which became the Department of Commerce in

1932). After the onset of the Depression, however, immigration was dropped in favour of the promotion of Australia's industries and tourist attractions.

As Officer-in-Charge, Lyn Maplestone was determined to encourage as many new initiatives within the Branch as gross under-funding and under-staffing would allow. In the early sound period, he persuaded the Federal Government to finance the installation of an up-to-date film processing machine, defraying the costs by hiring it out to Efftee and Movietone among others.[52] In the late 1930s, the organisation moved into 16 mm production for educational and trade use and was also experimenting with a bi-pack colour system. From its somewhat unexciting regular production schedule, an occasional gem like **Among the Hardwoods** (1936) emerged. Without commentary, and making effective use of natural sound and inter-titles, **Among the Hardwoods** is a lyrical account of timber-getting in the south-west of Western Australia. Other out-of-the-ordinary moments of visual and editorial sophistication occur in films like **Mineral Wealth** (c. 1934), **The Growing Child** (1937), and **The Triumph of the Telegraph** (1939), but these are rare. More typical of the Branch's films are **Conquest of the Prickly Pear** and **Australian Eggs**, complete with drowsy organ music and non-stop commentary.

16 millimetre gains acceptance

From the time of its introduction by Kodak in 1923, the use of 16 mm film had rapidly diversified, even though its popularity for home movie-making had tended to typecast it as an "amateur" gauge. In Australia as elsewhere, only the affluent could generally afford a 16 mm record of their home life, picnics and holidays. Some amateurs filmed widely and proficiently, taking pride in their expertise and winning prizes at amateur ciné societies. In time, of course, home movies would provide a rich store of sociological and historical detail through their unique coverage of customs, pastimes and values long since vanished.

The increased use of 16 mm film on a professional basis derived largely from its portability and comparative cheapness. Almost from the time of its introduction, 16 mm film was used for commercials and sponsored shorts that would be screened anywhere from department store windows to lecture halls. Albert J. Perier and Frederick Daniell were two Sydney filmmakers who made early use of the gauge for these purposes, and in the late 1930s Perier's son Reg built up a 16 mm production division at the Russell Roberts photographic studio. A less typical example of the professional use of 16 mm occurred in the early 1930s, when members of the University of Adelaide's Board of Anthropological Research shot coverage of various expeditions they made among the Aboriginal tribes of South Australia. The resulting long series of films became world-renowned as ethnographic records. From 1936 until the early 1940s, a Melbourne balletomane, Dr Ringland Anderson, documented on 16 mm film almost the entire repertoire of the visits of Colonel de Basil's touring companies. His colour footage (on Agfa stock) of some of the world's leading dancers of the time was also to stand as a unique record and is now lodged in the archives of the Australian Ballet.

Education was one area where the professional value of 16 mm was recognised in the 1920s and 1930s. By 1927 a number of schools in NSW screened films regularly as part of their curricula, and film was also in regular use in Victorian schools by the early 1930s. The 1927 Royal Commission had recommended that the Commonwealth help the States "in every possible way" with their use of film in education, and during 1936 the Commonwealth Cinema Branch was involved in "plans for the setting up of a Visual Education Bureau to function as a Commonwealth clearing house and to secure suitable films".[53]

6

The quota question
1936-40

National goes British

The New South Wales Premier Bertram Stevens was the film production industry's foremost political ally during the 1930s. Stevens, representing the United Australia Party, had come to power following the dismissal of Jack Lang in 1932. His public eulogies at studio openings and a production company launching, made consistent reference to his Government's determination to foster the industry, beginning in December 1933 with its decision to conduct the State Film Inquiry. Three Acts of Parliament over five years attempted to put this into practice, with the first Act preceded by the most optimistic flurry of planning the industry had seen in two decades.

Stevens's support for local film production appears to have dated from the time of his election. The supervisor of the radio broadcast of his campaign speech was Frederick Daniell. A sales promotion manager for Associated Newspapers, which owned the radio station 2UE along with the Sydney *Sun*, *Telegraph* and *Sunday Sun and Guardian*, Daniell had persuaded Stevens that a series of five-minute talks broadcast every night for a fortnight would have more impact than the single half-hour speech planned by the candidate. The new series, written by Daniell, was broadcast by almost every Sydney radio station. Daniell recalled years later:

As far as I know this was the first time a politician had consented to challenge an election with short policy speeches. When he won the election, he presented me with a gold cigarette case, and I was his friend for life.[1]

Two weeks before the New South Wales Film Inquiry completed its hearings in late April 1934, National Studios was formed with a capital of £50 000. Its principal backer was Sir Hugh Denison, chairman of Associated Newspapers; a directorate of distinguished business names comprised Sir John Butters, Sir Samuel Walder, Sir John Harrison KBE, C. M. C. Shannon, Colonel Alfred Spain, and Sir James Murdoch KBE, CMG. As well as being an important figure in the commercial world, Sir Samuel Walder was a member of the State

Legislative Council and a former Lord Mayor of Sydney. Denison's entry into the film field was in line with suggestions made by Frederick Daniell, who, in addition to his sales promotion position, had been appointed as Denison's adviser on the use of radio and film.

National Studios was established with the aim of providing facilities for the independent producers expected to become active with the passing of the quota legislation. The use of the word "National" reflected the hopes for industry solidarity expressed among independents since at least the mid-1920s. At the 1927 Royal Commission, calls for the setting up of a government-run "national" studio had been frequent but without effect, but the pressing priorities of the Depression soon afterwards had allowed the federal authorities to turn a deaf ear to any such suggestion.

After the formation of National Studios, Frederick Davies, the company's general manager, left to inspect studios and equipment in England, as National aimed to import experienced crew members who would train local staff. On Davies' return, the company acquired a State Government lease on twenty-five acres of land for the construction of a studio complex at Pagewood, then a market garden suburb near the northern shoreline of Botany Bay.

The establishment of National Studios' sister company, National Productions, occurred in late September 1935, just over a week after the proclamation of the Quota Act. Under Sir Hugh Denison as chairman, the new concern's directorate included a trio of business knights — Sir John Butters, Sir Samuel Walder and Sir James Murdoch — shared with National Studios. The joint aim of the two companies was to establish a large-scale independent film industry producing features for a world market and provide advanced studio facilities for the benefit of independents. Amid stirring speeches at a dinner at the Hotel Australia in Sydney, held to announce the new concern, Sir Hugh Denison stated:

I may say on behalf of my colleagues that we are actuated not solely by any spirit of commercial enterprise ... We are hopeful and confident that we shall be able to help along those who have pioneered [the industry].[2]

The Premier, Bertram Stevens, replying to a toast to the Government, said that with the aid of the Quota Act local filmmaking would become a "great industry". He claimed that in providing the quota, the Government could "go no further than to remove what appeared to it to be a natural barrier". It was, he said, now up to "our Australian entrepreneurs and for you gentlemen who have interested yourselves in the advancement of the industry to do the rest".[3]

Much of the optimism voiced during the dinner stemmed from the National companies' involvement with the Gaumont-British Picture Corporation. As part of the local film industry's first co-production agreement, Gaumont-British was to provide assistance for the design and construction of National Studios, to provide key staff to train Australian technicians, and to supply an almost entire production crew, including writer and director, to make their first feature, **The Flying Doctor** (1936). Local release of the completed film was to be through the Twentieth Century-Fox company which from the early 1930s had owned a controlling interest in Gaumont-British and from mid-1933 handled Australian distribution of its films. Gaumont itself was expected to release **The Flying Doctor** in England.

Partly because of the Fox ownership, Gaumont-British had been the focus of an attack published by Frank Thring in December 1933 against British film interests in Australia. The fact that the company was owned by Fox meant, in Thring's opinion, that any Australian quota legislation catering for British films would only increase the stranglehold that both American and British interests already exerted on the Australian market.[4] Early the next year Thring and Raymond Longford proceeded to tell the New South Wales Film Inquiry that Britain's opposition to the local quota was determined by its own monopolistic aims, and that it required no quota protection.

Since the passing of the Cinematograph Films Act of 1927, which provided a domestic quota for British (including its Dominions') films, the United Kingdom's feature output had soared in quantity, if not at first in quality. As American and British distributors rushed to invest in productions to meet the quota's terms at the cheapest possible price, the term ''quota quickie'' was soon applied to much of the output. Hollywood's pre-eminence diminished: supplying an estimated ninety-five per cent of the world's films by the end of the silent era, Hollywood's dominance slipped as quotas and language barriers reshaped the industries of Britain and Europe. In 1932 British films represented a quarter of all those screened in Australia and after that year the quality and reputation of British cinema improved significantly through the output of filmmakers like Alexander Korda, Alfred Hitchcock and Victor Saville.

By 1929 Gaumont-British, which owned combined interests in production, distribution and exhibition, was one of the major forces in Britain's film industry. Two years later its products and that of a subsidiary, Gainsborough Pictures, were linked under the supervision of Gaumont's production head, Michael Balcon. By the time Gaumont sent a special representative to Australia in 1932, it had £25 000 000 invested in all its motion picture enterprises and was making forty feature films a year. The Australian representative was Alan J. Williamson who, after his local work for Cozens Spencer between 1910 and 1913, had returned to England to work as a film buyer, war photographer and managing director of a London film laboratory. However, Williamson was not the first to offer sustained representation of British film interests in Australia; Ernest Turnbull had supplied the Australian and New Zealand markets with product through British Dominion Films since June 1928. In early 1932 Turnbull instigated a policy of ''all British'' cinemas in Australian capital cities — theatres devoted specifically to the screening of British films.[5] By then BDF was one of Gaumont's main Australian customers, and Williamson's arrival forged further links with Australian distributors as well as allowing him to serve as unofficial spokesman for British film interests at large.

At the 1934 Film Inquiry Williamson was kept busy answering the charges levelled by Frank Thring and Raymond Longford of British discrimination against Australian production. Longford felt that English distributors in Australia resembled their American counterparts in many respects:

They take full advantage of blind and block booking but do not take the interest in the local film that Australia takes in the British film. They consider Australia as a ground for exploitation without suggesting the slightest degree of reciprocity.[6]

Williamson told the Inquiry that he was opposed to an Australian quota because the extent of American domination which had led to Britain's Cinematograph Films Act did not exist in Australia. Like other witnesses, however, he suggested that if a quota were to be enacted it should provide a clause to guarantee the quality of the productions that sought its benefits. Realistically, he saw no need for the quota protection of British films in Australia because any such measure "might react against normal progress". He added that in the two years since his arrival he had repeatedly urged Gaumont-British to send a production unit to Australia

for the purpose of making a film, putting Australian technicians into the unit, and thus pass on the technical knowledge we have acquired over years and by vast experience.[7]

Neither the Film Inquiry report nor the ensuing legislation was to stipulate a British film quota in addition to the Australian and many leading British producers reacted angrily to the news. Premier Stevens, during a visit to London in July 1936, was met by the Federation of British Industries Film Group who urged that the Quota Act be amended to include provision for their films. Also, the dominant view of witnesses before the Moyne Committee, which had that year investigated the renewal of the British quota, was that the new Act should not continue to provide for the guaranteed release of Australian films in Britain.

The announcement that Gaumont-British would produce films in Australia was made the same week that Alan Williamson appeared before the New South Wales Inquiry. Although the timing was politically opportune the company had, as Williamson intimated, been interested in foreign production since the expansion of its overseas sales operations early in 1932. The February 1934 announcement promised work by a major filmmaker, and one whose expertise might have a radical effect on Australian film conventions. Robert Flaherty, the internationally-acclaimed director of the feature-length documentaries **Nanook of the North** (1922) and **Man of Aran** (1934), was to be sent by Gaumont-British to Australia to shoot a film of his own choice. As Harry Watt was to do with **The Overlanders** a decade later, Flaherty would, it was claimed, spend three months researching his project, "getting local colour, [and] acquainting himself with the people and their customs".[8]

Two months later, the newly-registered National Studios was reported to be offering Gaumont the hire of its facilities, but after the signing of a different agreement between Gaumont and National in July the Flaherty plans evaporated.

What emerged from the negotiations set in motion by Alan Williamson was assistance from Gaumont with the design and construction of National Studios and the involvement of a Gaumont production crew in **The Flying Doctor**. These results were less radical than a visit by Robert Flaherty might have been, but promised a great deal for the advancement of an industry. Although National Studios were to spend £75 000 on building studio facilities and the purchase of equipment, Gaumont's advice was free and its no-charge supply of a crew for **The Flying Doctor** was, in effect, co-production. The National companies made much of the importance of using imported technicians to train Australian counterparts. An awareness of this was conveyed in the earliest press announcements concerning the studio and was confirmed when Sir Hugh Denison and Frederick Davies observed production at the Gaumont-British Shepherd's Bush studio in London and talked to executives. On his return Davies announced National Studios' intention ''to obtain the same perfect routine as in the Gaumont-British studios'',[9] while Sir Samuel Walder, speaking on behalf of National Productions, stated: ''By depending on the English producing unit we will endeavour to put local pictures on the map''.[10] Behind this, and beyond the bustle observed at Gaumont, can be sensed the influence of diehard imperial loyalties because Sir Hugh Denison was a senior Australian member of the Royal Empire Society. Stuart Doyle was to allude, with slight mockery, to the group's British orientation while stating Cinesound's intentions in the same week that National Productions announced its policy:

America taught England how to make modern pictures, and has sent them the directors, cameramen and equipment with which to do it. If we are to aspire for world exhibition, and that, I take it, is the suggestion of the Film Quota Act, then we must get from the teacher, not from the pupil, the ideas and equipment designed to make the classics of the future.[11]

With advice from Gaumont's architects, construction of the National studio — Australia's first to be built completely for this purpose since 1912 — provided a spacious soundstage with a catwalk and aerial crane system, workshop, property and make-up areas. Under the supervision of Charles Fry, the first British technician to arrive under the agreement, installation of equipment was begun in May 1935 and the studios were completed by September. The first films to be made were several sponsored documentaries produced by Pacific Productions, a subsidiary of National Studios. Early November brought the arrival of the director Miles Mander and the remaining Gaumont-British crew members (a writer, two cameramen, a unit manager and sound recordist) who immediately commenced preproduction on **The Flying Doctor**. That same week a Pacific Productions crew under the Australian director Claude Flemming began work on the first dramatised film to use the complex.

This was **The Magic Shoes**, a "pantomime fantasy" adapted by staff writer Peggy Graham from the Cinderella story. Produced over eight days in the secondary studio as a trial run for the facilities, it featured Gloria Gotch, Helen Hughes (daughter of the former Prime Minister), Norman French and, from Flemming's own casting agency, a newcomer to the screen named Peter Finch. Cameraman Mel Nichols heightened the air of fantasy with the use of diffusion filters and those who saw the completed film were to recall that camerawork and settings brought imaginative visual richness of a calibre rare in Australian films of the period. Otherwise, **The Magic Shoes** was not regarded as a creative success and failed to find a distributor. But there was to be no such obscurity for the first feature to use Pagewood's main studio. In December 1935 Premier Stevens watched dances and spear-throwing by Palm Island Aboriginals, and then turned on the lights for the first interior set of the film in which they were appearing, Charles Chauvel's **Uncivilised**.

The production and lead casting of **The Flying Doctor** seemed a logical extension of Gaumont's production rationale and at one point it was mentioned as one of a number of "Empire" productions in which they had an interest.[12] In their own film programme's bid for the American market, Gaumont-British had taken to Britain a number of Hollywood stars such as Constance Bennett, Richard Dix, Paul Robeson and Charles Farrell. During one of his frequent trips to Hollywood Michael Balcon signed a new contract with Farrell, this time to head the **Flying Doctor** cast. His career had peaked and declined in the early sound era but he retained enough of a name for British and Australian publicists. Miles Mander, the director, was a veteran character actor and stage director with some film experience, while the writer, J. O. C. Orton, was yet to achieve fame with several of the English comedian Will Hay's best film comedies. Although the overseas talent helped make **The Flying Doctor** one of the most stylistically advanced Australian films of the decade, scripting and directorial control rambled through a process of aimless confusion. Disparate plot elements tended to obscure a weak storyline and it is said that a large proportion of unused narrative survived in the Pagewood film vaults for many years afterwards. The Flying Doctor himself, played by James Raglan, was too seldom on screen to justify the prominence given him by the title.

The principal ingredients, recalling the something-for-everyone formulas of Beaumont Smith, were Western appeal, sporting excitement (with a well-publicised appearance by Don Bradman), society melodrama and an emergency medical mission, all linked by the increasingly tragic wanderings of a drifter, played by Charles Farrell. The drifter is eventually blinded and is adopted by the Flying Doctor who, it transpires in an "Enoch Arden" denouement, has married the drifter's own estranged wife. The British magazine *Today's Cinema* found the narrative to be "a medley of proven and popular ideas"[13], while the Sydney *Daily Telegraph* noted the "unequal sympathy of the characters" and the "unnecessary presence of sequences which have purely scenic or newsreel value".[14] The ABC's film critic felt that after due praise for "slickness of technique", there remained "little for eulogy".[15]

Initial box office returns for **The Flying Doctor** augured well. The Australian branch of Twentieth Century-Fox undertook to distribute the film free of charge, its opening night at the Sydney Lyceum earned that theatre its best gross in five years, and it proceeded to do record business in all Australian capitals. It still needed an international market to return the cost of the budget which had climbed to over £40 000 (twice the amount averaged by Cinesound in the late 1930s), but its shortcomings and unfortunately-timed events in the British film industry made profits impossible.

In 1937 Britain's film boom collapsed. Not only had the 1927 quota led to an over-production of damaging quota quickies, but many of the more elaborate films had failed to penetrate the American market. Throughout 1936 the industry was reported to have lost two million pounds and at the end of the year Gaumont-British closed one of its three studios. Soon it withdrew from direct involvement in distribution, cancelling among other things the distribution agreement for **The Flying Doctor**. Gaumont had already reconstructed the film extensively and as it transpired, National Productions' general manager Frederick Daniell (who had worked as associate producer) was only able to obtain a small outright sale to Britain in late 1937. As Gaumont had found with its other films, the American market was unresponsive. In September 1937 **The Flying Doctor** was awarded a special certificate at the prestigious Venice Film Festival. The citation noted ''the considerable progress realised in film production by certain countries enjoying only a limited market''.

Although National Productions was to make no more features, the sister company, National Studios, raised further capital after the production of **The Flying Doctor** and announced its own schedule of at least two films, beginning with the co-production **Rangle River**. Their partner was Columbia Pictures, the only American distributor to comply with the production investment requirements specified by the New South Wales Quota Act. Director and star were again to be imported in an attempt to capture international sales. In June 1936 Cecil Mason, general manager of Columbia's Australian branch, announced that the veteran American director Clarence Badger and the actor Victor Jory would work on the film. The story had been written by Zane Grey, the prolific author of Westerns. What actually emerged was a very lightweight few pages which then had to be expanded by Charles and Elsa Chauvel. Clarence Badger and Victor Jory worked on the final draft adding such ''local'' touches as an Aboriginal gumleaf band and a bizarre stockwhip fight. Camerawork was by Errol Hinds, a British cameraman under contract to National Studios, and he was assisted by Damien Parer, a young Australian who with Hinds had also contributed to **The Flying Doctor**.

Rangle River is a range-war Western with key elements in common with Chauvel's earlier **Greenhide**. It begins with Dick Drake (Jory), a tough property overseer, persuading Marion (Margaret Dare), the daughter of his employer, to give up extravagant living and return to help her father who faces financial ruin. As an uneasy alliance grows between overseer and daughter the source of the impending ruin is revealed — the river-damming tactics of a neighbour who wishes to obtain valuable meat contracts. Badger's direction breathes life into these stock elements and even such a cliché figure as the silly-ass Englishman is made plausible by the perfect timing of Robert Coote whose debonair lunacy threatens to steal scene after scene. The *Sydney Morning Herald* found the script "intelligent and intelligible", and the film,

in its quiet way, ... full of interest and of picturesque romance. The scenery alone should persuade American producers that this country offers them something new in the way of backgrounds.[16]

Rangle River, like **The Flying Doctor**, enjoyed Australian success, but beat its predecessor onto British screens. Unlike **The Flying Doctor** it also obtained an American release — but not quickly enough to return the money required to National Studios. Although several of the company's directors served on the boards of other film companies, neither of the National concerns was able to raise sufficient capital for a second feature. The studio was used only sporadically for the next four years and the only continued activity by National Productions was their handling of further foreign sales of **The Flying Doctor**.

It is easy to see the failure of the National companies as an isolated venture hampered by inexperience. In the case of **The Flying Doctor**, a poorly developed story was filmed with disproportionately lavish production methods and only a hazy notion of overseas market acceptance. Disregarding Cinesound's aim of producing predominantly for the local market, National Productions preferred to follow the example of Gaumont and other British companies, unaware that Gaumont's own bid for a world market was to remain unfulfilled.

New trends in exhibition

The second half of 1935 not only brought hope to producers with the proclamation of the New South Wales Quota Act; it also brought signs that the prolonged effect of the Depression on the distribution and exhibition trade had run its course. In Australia, as in America, the entertainment industry had continued to struggle for some time after other industries had stabilised. Between 1930 and 1934, annual gross film rentals and remittances overseas had almost been halved, and box office takings were reduced by one third.[17] By 7 August 1935, however, Norman B. Rydge could write in his *Business Journal*, "The time to buy picture shares has arrived".[18]

During 1936, an increase of 25 per cent in the gross receipts of exhibitors around the world brought box office returns to their highest level since 1931. The trend flowed through to Australia, and the new confidence was manifested in a boom of theatre building and reconstruction. By the start of 1935, Hoyts had already announced that they would extensively alter many existing theatres and expand their Sydney and Melbourne circuits. Early the following year, modernisation of the Greater Union circuit was begun. In June 1935, Hoyts had allocated £63 700 to streamline their Melbourne suburban theatres, and by the end of the month, *Everyones* reported that in suburban Sydney the reconstruction of established houses was taking place "in an exceptionally large number of centres".[19]

The rise of the suburban cinema was a by-product of Australia's massive suburban growth during the 1920s. For most patrons, the local cinema was easy to get to and cheap to enter and by 1934 Sydney's suburban cinemas outnumbered those in the city by more than five to one. Although some major suburban cinemas, like the Roxy at Parramatta (opened 1930) and the Cremorne Orpheum (1935), were almost as lavish as the best city theatres, the majority exercised a clever economy in construction and decoration. In its article on the opening of the Kings Theatre, Clovelly, in June 1939, the *Australasian Exhibitor* reported that its architects, Guy Crick and Bruce Furse, were expert at eliminating

all wasteful ideas caused by precedent in theatre building . . . For instance, with the use of modern lighting and the color effects gained therefrom, it has been noticed that this is a form of decoration sufficient in itself.[20]

By this time, Crick and Furse were Australia's leading cinema architects and had built, remodelled or modernised more than a hundred cinemas. Central to their work was the "moderne" motif, which in 1936 alone they applied to their design of ten new and ten remodelled cinemas within New South Wales. The trend at this time was increasingly towards the "intimate" theatre seating 800 to 900 patrons. In Sydney, this was most evident in the rapidly spreading Kings suburban cinemas which Crick and Furse had designed. *Everyones* wrote of the Kings theatres:

At each house there is an atmosphere of intimacy and congenial comfort which must please, while the attractive features of the exterior, invariably futuristic, are highlighted by the architect's guidance on an expertly balanced use of tube lighting in suitable colours.[21]

Suburban managements frequently vied for custom with street publicity stunts, free tickets and give-away prizes. Occasionally these gimmicks fell foul of the law. In July 1931, police arrested some of the 150 couples who entered a prize competition to dance along roads from various suburban cinemas to the Sydney Plaza in a promotion of MGM's **Dance, Fools, Dance**. As part of a free gift "war" among exhibitors in late 1935, showmen were spending as much as £750 per week on items that ranged from kitchen utensils to suites of furniture in bids to increase attendances. Managements even billed the gifts above films in advertising. When the war reached its height between three North Sydney exhibitors, the owner of the Orpheum Theatre was fined for contravening State lottery laws. Other exhibitors used a coupon give-away system to avoid legal action, but the popularity of the stunt had waned by late 1937 when distributors moved to halt it with a clause in film hire contracts.

Film and society

Film censorship was a more constant form of official intervention, and in this decade it began to face new political challenges on top of the old and vexatious issues of morality. But at first it was the moral question that kept the censor's work foremost in the public eye.

The coming of sound had brought unprecedented social and sexual frankness to many American and British films. Women's groups who deplored cinema's moral standards at the time of the 1927 Royal Commission increased their efforts to suppress films they considered would promote moral depravity, corrupt family and community life, or destroy Australian and British sentiment. American and British early talkies came in for an equal measure of attack. But while some members of the public resented the invasion of all-too-audible American speech, the Commonwealth Chief Censor's annual report for 1929 revealed that more British films warranted censorship than American. By 1934, the improved quality of British productions seems to have left the Chief Censor, Cresswell O'Reilly, less aghast at their content, but he continued to champion the popular belief that the majority of imported films were unsuitable for children. The imports were not the only ones to draw O'Reilly's fire: in his reports covering the years 1932-33, he criticised local rural comedies for

showing Australians as ultra simple-minded and mentally childish ... Such films are doing much harm to the prestige of Australians abroad, and if any more are presented to this Censorship for export, it will be necessary to take drastic action.[22]

After 1934 a more stringent morality was enforced in Hollywood and community groups and censors around the world were able to relax their vigilance a little. According to Will Hays, president of the Motion Picture Producers and Distributors' Association of America, even the Pope approved the new trend in American-made films. Cresswell O'Reilly shared this lofty view in his report for 1936, but not all Australians could agree. In May of that year, the Bishop of Maitland (New South Wales) sent a circular letter to the clergy of his diocese requesting prayers for the purification of the cinema, and in November a speaker at the Sydney national conference of the Band of Hope accused the screen and radio of "encouraging the drink at dances evil".[23]

The political use of cinema and its repression became evident just as sensitivity over sexual content was subsiding. Communist cultural organisations were formed in Australia during the Depression, and the books, magazines and visual materials they imported were subjected constantly to Commonwealth and State censorship.[24] An instance of how one conservative establishment counterposed its own propaganda against Communism occurred in May 1932 when the minister at the Congregational Church, Croydon (Sydney), screened **Frankenstein** to his flock to draw an analogy between Frankenstein's "atheistic monster stalking the country as a man" and Communism as "an atheistic system ravaging civilisation".[25] In that same year the Chancellor of Melbourne University banned the on-campus screening of **Russia To-Day** and Cresswell O'Reilly, amid considerable furore, suppressed another Soviet film, **The Five Year Plan**, on the grounds that it was considered not "in the public interest". In 1936 further public outcry followed the Chief Censor's banning of Eisenstein's **Ten Days that Shook the World** before its release was allowed by the Appeal Censor, while deletions and reconstructions of films dealing with the Spanish Civil and Chinese wars were made to placate the Spanish and Chinese Governments and protect the local public against horrific sights. Public pressure to release such films was generated by a number of organisations such as the Movement against War and Fascism and the Spanish Relief Committee, who imported prints (usually on 16 mm) to finance and publicise their activities.[26]

The commercial film trade also had a lobby group to define and protect the validity of its claims. This was the Motion Picture Distributors' Association (MPDA), established in September 1926 with the former South Australian senator, Sir Victor Wilson, as its president. Its principal aim, based on that of the Motion Picture Producers and Distributors' Association of America, was to combat criticism of distributors in Australia and the films they released. As the Sydney *Sun* put it, Sir Victor Wilson's chief duties were

to reply to attacks on motion pictures and artists, and to take such action as may be deemed necessary to safeguard the political, commercial and moral phases of the picture industry.[27]

Although initial hopes were raised that Wilson's work would include the active development of the Australian production industry, his alliance with the established film trade left him with little inclination other than to pay lip service to the concept. A typical example of his work was to persuade the South Australian censors to lift a ban on the American film **Strictly Dishonorable** (1931), although he failed in a similar attempt to have **Frankenstein** released in that State.[28]

The protest against the banning of the Russian, Spanish and Chinese films indicates that many members of the public now decried the monotony of mainstream film diet. Raymond Longford pointed out at the 1934 Film Inquiry that the block and blind booking imposed by major distributors left no room for the screening of Continental films, prompting

intellectuals to speak of this country as a cultural desert. If the art of other lands were to be shut off from Australia it would be most unfortunate for the welfare of local artists. And so it is with local producers. Local technique depends for improvement upon intellectual criticism by critics who comprehend the meaning of cinema art; and access to the technique of other countries than England and America.

Turning more directly to the need for films that would generate an alternative film movement in Australia, Longford continued:

We still lack a Little Theatre Movement in the film business, and it is of interest to note that the technique of the Continental film is sometimes high enough to permit the screening for some weeks in a London theatre of a Swedish film in the Swedish language and explained only by silent superimposed titles.[29]

The Film Society of Australia (a breakaway group from the heavily moralist Better Films League) could not have agreed more, for two years earlier it had championed British and Continental films which it claimed were "of higher artistic standard than any other", and supported any foreign film that upheld "the cause of art, whatever its moral aspects".[30] But anything like Longford's ideal of an ongoing "Little Theatre Movement in the film business" was not to appear until the growth of film cooperatives in the late 1960s and 1970s.

Cinesound: 1934-1937

Visiting the set of **The Silence of Dean Maitland** (1934), being shot from late 1933 under the direction of Ken G. Hall at Cinesound, the journalist Lin Endean reported how different work on this film was to his recollection of interior shooting on Hall's first feature for the company, **On Our Selection**: "a vision of a cramped, hellishly hot studio, a worried young man hoping for the best, a small but capable band of helpers". From the cramped box used as **Selection**'s soundstage, the studio space had now been increased five-fold with the complete insulation of the old Australasian Films studio. To Endean, the approach of director and crew was now much more businesslike, testifying to the value of new equipment and the experience of a crew that had been enlarged before the production of the intervening film, **The Squatter's Daughter**. He wrote of Ken Hall:

Frankly admitting to mistakes in previous efforts, it is easily sensed how valuable he has made them ... One analyses Ken as an ambitious enthusiast, but one who has the essential possession of balance and clear reasoning. He is not the man likely to be overwhelmed by the bright flash of achievement. His knowledge of audiences, their desires and reactions, is remarkably extensive.[31]

At the end of 1936 Hall himself wrote:

An ordinary Australian-made programme picture can have little or no chance either outside or inside Australia ... Unless the pictures we make have that "something" about them which puts them in the special class — in this country anyway — then the cause is lost. So we are faced with making pictures which hit the special class in Australia and the good programme class overseas at a very low cost.[32]

By this time Cinesound was calculating that 60 per cent of the initial cost of each of its feature films would be returned from the Australian and New Zealand markets with the rest coming from Britain.[33] Unlike the National group, Cinesound's aim was to keep its budgets modestly in line with these known markets and to regard America as entirely uninterested. This proved to be no impediment to Hall at Cinesound who came closer than any other Australian producer to Hollywood-style backing, facilities and continuity of output. With ongoing production and release of the company's films assured for as long as they continued to make money, Hall worked progressively to refine the formulas he sensed would attract audiences. The enthusiasm that Lin Endean observed was applied to every aspect of film production, from the choice of subject right through to the process of marketing. Hall's constant viewing of other filmmakers' work (mostly American) allowed him to develop a keen appreciation of the titles, plotlines and special ingredients that appealed to audiences and he deployed his own resources to match and, wherever possible, better them. His strategy for competing with American and British films was summed up in the concept of "showmanship", its fundamental rule was: "Never let an audience down."

"Showmanship" was first applied to Hall's choice of a story, which wherever possible was taken from an established novel or well-tried stage or film formula. The publicity accompanied a production from the outset and ended with news of its reception at the box office. In scripting, Hall and his collaborators aimed at combining ingredients of known appeal with newly-exploitable angles. Such an angle was frequently the climactic set-piece of each film — for instance, the timber drive of **Tall Timbers** and dam-burst of **Dad Rudd, M.P.**

Although expectations served by the publicity and achievements of one film paved the way for the next, Hall rarely used this conditioning to create new myths or to offer a more penetrating look at social mores. In his own defence he claims he was striving "to entertain the people who were creating the Australian way of life", not to interpret that in new ways.[34] Such interpretations, if they did occur, were always incidental to the broader scheme of keeping the production company afloat. By this means Hall was able to become the most consistent film craftsman among his contemporaries. Backed up by the sustaining loyalty for most of the decade of Stuart Doyle as Cinesound's managing director, he had the ability that no other producer did of refining the essential ingredients of filmmaking with a regular team of technicians, actors and script collaborators.

Lin Endean continued his account of **The Silence of Dean Maitland:**

Hall can be credited with having imbued his people with a spirit of confidence
and assurance that leads a long way toward success. You watch him calmly move
in supervision of all details incidental to the particular job in hand. Encouraging
technicians and and actors alike, . . . Hall does not act the Big Chief. He aims at
team work and he certainly gets it from a gang which enjoys every ounce of its
work.[35]

The ability to inspire the loyalty and excite the aspirations of his regular studio team was, next to Hall's box office sense, the most important factor in the continued success of production at Cinesound. This success testified to his ability both as general manager of the studio and director of its films. The company's continued success, its public attention and security of employment

144

obviously contributed to the loyalty, and this in turn both fed and was nurtured by the increasing expertise that the permanent staff of around thirty brought to their achievements.

By the time of **Orphan of the Wilderness** (1936), the crew that would work through the studio's increasingly busy next four years' production was virtually complete. George Heath, the cameraman, had begun his career in newsreel and laboratory work and developed his skills as an associate cameraman to Frank Hurley on **Strike Me Lucky** (1934), and **Grandad Rudd** (1935) before receiving credit as lighting cameraman on **Thoroughbred** (1936). The sound recording on most of the Cinesound features was done by Clive Cross and credit for film editing, after collaboration on **The Squatter's Daughter**, went to Bill Shepherd. From **Tall Timbers** (1937) onwards, studio settings were either the domain of Hollywood-trained Eric Thompson or of J. Alan Kenyon, who also achieved some of Cinesound's most spectacular special effects; the same film saw the first of a series of key contributions by Frank Harvey as dialogue director and collaborator with Hall on scripts. Publicity and marketing (until mid-1937) was coordinated by Herbert Hayward.[36]

Cinesound had intended to produce **The Silence of Dean Maitland** after **On Our Selection**, but delayed its plans due to the impossibility of finding a suitable lead. In mid-1933 John Longden, an English stage and screen actor touring Australia with the Nicholas Hannan—Athene Seyler company, was cast as the Dean and production began in November. The play by Maxwell Gray, although originally English, had no specific national setting. After the wholehearted Australiana of the first two Cinesound films met with poor critical response in England, Hall had decided to feature a "reasonably glossy" look that incorporated settings and characters acceptable as either English or Australian.[37] **The Silence of Dean Maitland** told of a clergyman who, having been seduced by the daughter of a fisherman, kills him and sees his best friend, falsely accused of the crime, languish in prison for twenty years. After the friend's release and an embittered confrontation, the Dean confesses from his church pulpit and promptly dies. Hall and Stuart Doyle saw the original stage play performed by a suburban theatre company and had to leave the theatre "in a fit of uncontrollable laughter". Nevertheless, Hall recognised it as "good melodrama"[38] and after considerable work on the script with the writers Edmund Barclay and Gayne Dexter, achieved a balance between emotion and dramatic economy. A sense of urgency and doom effectively pervades the film, reinforced by the camerawork of Frank Hurley, which alternates stark luminosity with brooding shadows. John Longden is initially plausible as the young and tempted Dean, but becomes less so as the character ages. Charlotte Francis strikes an appropriate key of sexy mesmerism as Alma, the fisherman's daughter, and a stock gallery of villagers includes George Lloyd, Leal Douglas, Fred McDonald and Claude Turton.

The Silence of Dean Maitland grossed £33 000 in Australia, an amount higher than that earned by most imported features of the period. It was sold outright to RKO for its British release and was reputed to have made £40 000 there by 1937. Presumably because of the poor reputation of Australian films, all references to its Australian origin were omitted. One critic wrote:

The truth is that England will accept good stories and good productions, whether their stories are laid in Manitoba, Singapore, Johannesburg or Perth. Australian films have failed in London for the simple reason that, up until now, their dramatic material has fallen below the requisite standard.[39]

Taking into account its British success, Ken Hall considered that **The Silence of Dean Maitland** established Cinesound's name more than any other film. It was certainly with a new confidence that he embarked on his next production, **Strike Me Lucky** (1934), which was intended to showcase the popular vaudeville comedian Roy "Mo" Rene. It was another radical departure from Cinesound's first two features and was the first project of Hall's own choosing. The primarily city-based story covered Mo's befriending a small girl who, although claiming to be an orphan, is a runaway from a wealthy family. A gang of crooks attempt to kidnap her and, taking flight, Mo is pursued by infuriated Aboriginals and in the process stumbles across a lost gold mine.

Recognising that Mo's following for his often "blue" stage material was confined principally to Sydney and Melbourne, Hall and his co-writers tried to tone down the bawdry and surround their star with enough gimmicks to attract a wider audience. The result is a bizarre mixture of laboured stage routines and exaggerated attempts at cinematic invention, sometimes funny in isolation but ponderous as a whole. The moments of inspired lunacy show that with a stronger script Hall might have made **Strike Me Lucky**, in many ways his most experimental and daring work, the basis for future innovation. He said later:

This film scared the daylights out of me, and it frightened me off, back to a treadmill. On this one I was easily scared, because I had such a thin edge between success and failure.[40]

In its first four days of release, **Strike Me Lucky** took more money than **On Our Selection** in the same period but public interest waned as the word-of-mouth reputation and reviews revealed its quality. The film came closest of all the Cinesound films to financial failure but eventually broke even.

Grandad Rudd (1935), with Bert Bailey, returned to safer ground. It was an adaptation of a sequel, written by Steele Rudd himself, to the play *On Our Selection* which had been first staged in 1912. What the film lacks in terms of the broad sweep of the 1932 screen version, is nearly made up by being the first Cinesound film to show Ken Hall's full confidence as a director. Structurally almost as episodic as **Strike Me Lucky**, its comedy is more inventive: a quick and clever montage covering the bedlam of a runaway tractor and a scene of animals accompanying humans in an angry delegation to complain about Dad's mean-heartedness, are executed with a well-judged wit only exceeded by the country cricket match that serves as the film's climax. Part of the humour derives from a questioning of popular nationalism. At one point Dad scoffingly refers to running across the plains barefoot, picking gums; he also has a harsh word for the growing dominance of motor cars and "halfway pubs every mile". His kindest comments are reserved for the pioneers of his early days: "men who could run all day and night".

Grandad Rudd was a transitional work in other respects. Following adverse criticism overseas for the broad caricature of the **On Our Selection** characters, it began a process of gradual change for the Rudd family. Although their manners became more refined and the backgrounds more prosperous, the portrayal of Grandad Rudd as a skinflint drew criticism which brought about modification of the character for the next Rudd family film, **Dad and Dave Come to Town** (1938). **Grandad Rudd** was made in the shortest time of any Cinesound film to date, and was the last of the early Cinesound features completed prior to Ken Hall's departure for Hollywood in December 1934.

Hall's visit to the USA had been planned since 1932 and his aim was to purchase equipment and study production techniques. In the four months in which he was based at the Fox studios Hall was able to observe some aspects of organisation that he incorporated into the established routine back at Cinesound. He also watched work using new back-projection and sound playback facilities — for which he placed orders together with a mobile De Brie camera, three additional Bell and Howell cameras, a sound oscillator, the unique Davidge negative developer and a battery-pack for emergency power supplies. In addition to observing features in production at several studios, he studied budgeting, distribution and exhibition trends and spoke to various writers and actors about the possibility of working for Cinesound. On the question of overseas market prospects, Hall said on his return in April 1935 that the world was "starving for the unusual", and the best way into the American market was to make features "of international character and appeal, but with Australian background".[41]

Hall's consideration of the American market at this point was part of Cinesound's reaction to the prospect of expanded activity under the New South Wales Quota Act. At no other time during the decade did the company seriously consider the likelihood of reaching an American market. The newly raised hopes of 1935 and early 1936 were based on the belief that co-productions with several American distributors would guarantee the release of these and Cinesound's own films in the United States. However, due to doubts that were soon raised over the compulsion distributors faced in having to produce under the Quota Act, none of the Cinesound co-production plans (which had included at least one film with United Artists) ever eventuated. Instead, Cinesound went ahead with its plans to import American equipment, a lead actor and a writer for **Thoroughbred** (1936), its first film of genuine international standard.

The principal drawcard, and the one around whom considerable publicity was built, was another American star of the late silent and early talkies periods, Helen Twelvetrees. In **Thoroughbred**, she gives the film's most consistent performance as part-owner of a racecourse who is under threat of death from a Paris-based gambling syndicate. Although the plot is at best erratic, the film benefits from sophisticated dialogue and the interpolation of subplots of a kind absent from earlier Cinesound features. The horse race climax, a technical tour de force, is excitingly constructed and includes close-ups of flying hooves, stunt doubling and the studio's first use of its newly acquired back-projection equipment.

Thoroughbred returned its £20 000 outlay in Australia but failed to penetrate the American market. In Britain its scenes showing apparent cruelty to animals were heavily censored. The next Cinesound production, **Orphan of the Wilderness**, was completely banned in Britain for much the same reason although ironically, in the light of **Thoroughbred**'s intentions, it was the first Cinesound feature to obtain an American release and receive good notices from New York critics. Although initially planned as a low-budget feature, **Orphan of the Wilderness** was upgraded before it began production in May 1936 and its running time extended from fifty to eighty-five minutes. The original story, by Dorothy Cotterill, told of the orphaning and adoption of Chut, a baby kangaroo, and his later humiliation as part of a circus boxing act. As in the climax of the previous film, the opening of **Orphan of the Wilderness** showed evidence of the studio's experienced team and new technical resources. On the Bondi soundstage, art director J. Alan Kenyon had designed and supervised the construction of a massive bushland setting. The filming, which took several weeks, allowed the scrupulous observation of a collection of marsupials, reptiles and birds accustomed to the simulated natural conditions and to the patient technicians and their equipment. When these shots were integrated with the rest of the film, the result was regarded by the critic of the *Sydney Morning Herald* as

extraordinarily beautiful ... the tender, lyrical images flow across the screen, graced by exquisite photography and pleasant music, in a way which recalls the soothing beauty of the silent screen.[42]

Between 1937 and 1940 Hall worked at refining the conventions which he had developed in Cinesound studio's first five years of production. Regardless of the setting, each film became further tailored to the expectations of available markets abroad, and the period saw the final abandonment of pronounced national sentiment. In response to the Hollywood-conditioned requirements of the local market, the later films placed greater emphasis on story and "star" value and to this end several new initiatives were taken with and following the making of **It Isn't Done** (1937). First came the creation of the studio's "story board", a pre-production advisory committee representing the views of publicists, distributors and exhibitors, which was used by Hall to test reaction to stories and script content. Second, in the wake of **It Isn't Done** came the signing of one of its leading players, Shirley Ann Richards (who had made her debut in this film), to a long-term contract. Given the benefit of training and publicity also calculated to bring prestige to the studio, Shirley Ann Richards appeared in four more Cinesound features before embarking on a successful Hollywood career — billed as Ann Richards — in the early 1940s.

Despite the predominance of literary and stage adaptations prevalent in the early 1930s, most Australian screenplays of the decade were to be derived from original ideas based on tried-and-true formulas. Screenplay work at Cinesound from 1937 was often a collaboration between the actor-writer Frank Harvey and a leading actor like Bert Bailey. Hall took part in all scripting but he never credited himself as such, only by pseudonym. Harvey had written and appeared in several successful plays in London's West End and his name was prominent in theatrical billings both in England and Australia. Most of his film experience prior to Cinesound had been as an actor-writer with Efftee. **It Isn't Done**, drawn from an idea by Cecil Kellaway, was Harvey's first Cinesound screenplay — a comedy of Anglo-Australian manners, and the most rewarding of a long line of films on that subject. The critic of the *Sydney Morning Herald* found:

By looking toward England frankly, and sometimes a trifle crudely, from the Australian point of view, the film is doing something really significant in the development of a national consciousness.[43]

The story features Cecil Kellaway as a cheerful Australian grazier who travels to England when he inherits an English title. Finding himself and his wife regarded as social misfits he ultimately renounces the title and, before returning home, tells his daughter, "It's all a matter of soil . . . Mother and I know where ours is, and we're going back to it". A convincing impression of English backgrounds is sustained by the second-unit work in Britain, opulent interiors designed by the Hollywood-trained Eric Thompson and special effects in the form of back projection and glass shots.

Special effects, this time by J. Alan Kenyon, were again featured in the next two Cinesound films, the adventure melodramas **Tall Timbers** and **Lovers and Luggers** (1937). The highlight of the first of these was a spectacular timber drive, constructed by intercutting shots of falling trees with a model representing an entire mountain forest progressively crashing earthwards. The well-constructed climax of **Lovers and Luggers** took the form of a seabed fight to the finish which was filmed — after an unsuccessful attempt at the studio — in North Sydney's Olympic pool. Its star was Lloyd Hughes, another Hollywood import past his prime but again fully justifying the studio's publicity efforts. The film was to become Hall's favourite but it is by no means his best, although on release it drew a warm response from both the public and the critics and was shown in England and the United States.

Before the production of **Lovers and Luggers**, events within Greater Union Theatres were to cast a shadow of doubt over Cinesound's continued production of features. Despite Stuart Doyle's attempt to preserve the liquidated Union Theatres' interests by the formation of Greater Union

Theatres in late 1931, the organisation's overdraft had climbed to £50 000 by 1936. Between March and September of that year, under continued pressure from the Greater Union board and the E S & A Bank, Doyle travelled abroad in his capacity as Greater Union's managing director in order to seek new capital. In July, the J. D. Williams Amusement Company, one of the four companies which owned and controlled Greater Union (the others were Amalgamated, Spencer's and West's Pictures), appointed the Sydney chartered accountant Norman B. Rydge to its board. Soon afterwards Rydge became Greater Union's chairman and on Doyle's return the two men settled down to work, apparently in harmony. But in May 1937 Doyle suddenly issued Rydge with a £25 000 writ on grounds that were never revealed. Then, just as abruptly, he withdrew it. In June Doyle resigned from Greater Union, leaving the combine to reorganise itself under Rydge as chairman and managing director. It was a sudden severance for Doyle, who had worked tirelessly for almost three decades to build up the film trade. It occurred exactly a year after the death of his former rival Frank Thring. Doyle had been the Australian film industry's most influential and colourful entrepreneur and his long-term gambles in exhibition and production had laid foundations for developments that might not otherwise have occurred. Cinesound now awaited new orders.

Quota incentives

Within months of the passing of the Quota Act in September 1935, among the producers who announced plans for films that would contribute to the minimum of twenty-five features required for 1936, were (besides National and Cinesound): Charles Chauvel, Mastercraft Film Corporation, Film Players Corporation, and the theatrical interests of J. C. Williamson and Ernest C. Rolls. Of these, only Chauvel and Film Players Corporation actually entered production. Others, whose announcements came later, were to make one film, or at the most two, before vanishing from the industry. The reason for this fall-off was made apparent by early 1936, but the widely-assorted independents who entered production during the next two years seem to have been temporarily sustained by the promised benefits of the quota as well as the example of Cinesound's continued success. In order to sort the genuine from the dubious and avoid a quota quickie glut, the Act had required that local films eligible for its benefits should measure up to a standard of quality and entertainment which would be judged by a Film Advisory Board.[44] Ominously, the film advertised as "The First Australian Quota Picture!" was also the first to be refused registration.

The Burgomeister (1935), directed by Harry Southwell for Film Players Corporation, was the first independent production to make use of Cinesound's Bondi studio during Ken Hall's absence on his trip to Hollywood. Backed to £10 000 by a syndicate of prominent business and society people, **The Burgomeister** was a twice-removed adaptation from the Erckmann-Chatrian play *Le Juif Polonais*. The play had formed the basis for an in-between adaptation, **The Bells**, staged in England by Sir Henry Irving and first filmed in Australia in 1910. Despite the construction of the most elaborate set built at Cinesound in five years, the participation of key Cinesound personnel and musical direction by Isadore Goodman, **The Burgomeister** suffered an even worse fate than Southwell's three low-grade and much-banned Ned Kelly features made between 1921 and 1934. Rupert Kathner, who collaborated with James Coleman on the art direction, later wrote:

The locale of this harrowing ''drama'' was set in Alsace-Lorraine. I know, because ten tons of salt, plus five hundred packets of a well-known brand of cornflakes were used for the snow, and every employee of the studio ate cornflakes for breakfast for at least six months after the completion of the picture. . . . After the exclusive and toney Sunday night Preview . . . there was an unearthly silence. . . . The audience rose, and like a crowd who had just attended a cremation, quietly moved toward the drinks.[45]

The first two features directed by Kathner himself were also refused quota registration. **Phantom Gold** (1937), a partly dramatised documentary investigation of the disappearance of the gold prospector Harry Lasseter, had only a limited release before threatened legal action forced its withdrawal; **Below the Surface** (1938), a coal-mining drama, failed to obtain release. Kathner possessed talent, as was later to be shown by **Racing Luck** (1941), but the fact that he often spread it too thinly on meagre resources was apparent in all his other features. As a keen and somewhat sardonic observer of the Australian film industry he was to encapsulate his feelings in the book *Let's Make a Movie*, published in Sydney in 1945.

A. R. Harwood, having returned to direction with the low-budget **Secret of the Skies** in 1934, shot two productions, **The Avenger** (1937) and **Show Business** (1938) virtually back-to-back. **Show Business**, the most elaborate of all his films, no longer survives but **The Avenger** shows flashes of directorial skill amidst a plot that alternately slumbered and raged. Greater visual sophistication than on Harwood's earlier films was provided by the cameramen Arthur and Tasman Higgins, while Raymond Longford appeared in one of his better supporting roles as a kindly judge.

The sound on this and many other independent films of the period was recorded by Mervyn Murphy, a Sydney technician who had established the Supreme Sound System company in 1935 after developing his own recording process. In addition to features, Murphy worked on sponsored documentaries and cinema advertising films. One of his earliest documentaries was **Conquest** (1935), sponsored by the Rural Bank, directed by Harold Gray and photographed by another leading technician from the 1930s onward, George Malcolm. Both Murphy and Malcolm also contributed to the short film **Eaglets** (1935) produced by Commonwealth Film Laboratories and for the same company next year travelled to one of the Admiralty Islets near Lord Howe Island to work on the feature **Mystery Island**, directed by J. A. Lipman.

151

Beyond evocative visuals and hilariously hoary performances, **Mystery Island** was unremarkable; but in June 1937 Commonwealth Film Laboratories commenced a project of far greater quality. The managing director of the company, Jack Bruce, had several months earlier announced a continuing feature schedule:

We propose to concentrate on features of appeal directly to local audiences, and at this stage have no ideas of world-marketing our product.[46]

A co-founder of the laboratory, Bruce had built up the company's production resources with the coming of sound, and continued to supply technicians and facilities for local films until the mid-1950s. Although the company was to later co-invest in production ventures, **Typhoon Treasure** (1938) was the final feature it made alone. Noel Monkman, the film's director, had followed up the production of his two wildlife series for Australian Educational Films in the early 1930s with work as a strenuous advocate for the New South Wales film quota. With money borrowed from friends, he and his wife Kitty (who worked on all Monkman's films) returned to the production of nature shorts.

Typhoon Treasure was first proposed as a co-production by Monkman and Frank Thring but the link with Commonwealth Film Laboratories came about almost a year after Thring's dealth. Monkman had to work without a salary. The story is about a pearler, played by Campbell Copelin, who is forced to trek overland to lay claim to pearls lost in his wrecked lugger. During the journey he and his sidekick (played by Joe Valli) encounter bloodthirsty natives, are forced to scale a treacherous rock-face, and wade through crocodile-infested mangrove swamps. Opium smuggling is also thrown into the plot and, casually intermingled with the mayhem, are some authentic observations of wildlife. Monkman's adventurous, wide-ranging use of exotic mountain and coastal inlet settings contributes greatly to the atmosphere.

Despite many merits **Typhoon Treasure** attracted little attention on its release and Monkman waited more than two years before starting his next feature, **The Power and the Glory** (1941). He later recalled:

I wrote **The Power and the Glory** in 1940 for a young actor who would, I thought, if given the chance make the finest film actor in Australia — Peter Finch. We used to get together in the Metropole Hotel bar in Sydney and bemoan the lack of an Australian film production industry. I told Peter that I was writing a film story and scenario that would give him his chance in films if ever I had the opportunity to produce and direct the picture.[47]

Finch had already appeared in two features, but **The Power and the Glory**, in which he played a German fifth columnist in wartime Australia, gave him his most demanding role to date. The film also shows Monkman in tight control of visual and narrative structure, and he was able to gain the utmost production value from a limited budget. To judge from the chase and aerial dogfight scenes, Monkman might have gone on to rival Charles Chauvel as an action director; his portrayal of character relationships had already matured. The *Sydney Morning Herald* found **The Power and the Glory** to be "on a better-than-average scale", and felt that "it must give an impetus to the Australian film-producing industry".[48] Nonetheless, the vagaries of the industry made sure that it would be the last feature Monkman ever made. Until his death in 1969 he remained with the production of documentary shorts.

The funding of **The Power and the Glory** was complex and frustrating. Despite the number of new companies announcing production plans in late 1935, private investment was not forthcoming; only three features — **Uncivilised**, **The Flying Doctor** and **Rangle River** — were made and released directly in response to the proclamation of the Quota Act in September. Columbia was to be the only American film distributor to invest in Australian production before the war, and of the thirteen distributors registered under the Act, only seven had handled Australian films by the end of 1936. All were aware that although they were bound by the quota system to produce films if an insufficient number was available, they could be exempted from their obligations if compliance was "not commercially practicable". Exemptions were granted for 1936 and the following March various member companies of the Motion Picture Distributors' Association (including American film exchanges) indicated they would withdraw all film supplies from New South Wales if forced to comply with 1937 requirements. Phil Reisman, then visiting Australia as vice-president and export manager of RKO Radio Pictures, explained that American producer-distributors had lost a total of £700 000 by investing in British production during 1936, and estimated that by 1939 they would lose another £600 000 if forced to meet Australian quota requirements. He continued:

The total profits which go to America from the operations of American companies here amount to only £750 000 a year. It seems fairly obvious that we cannot afford such a slice out of our earnings.[49]

Frederick Daniell, now general manager of Argosy Films (formed in 1937 and related to the National companies), replied:

Except to make a gesture, which they would find it unprofitable to maintain, the American companies are not likely to cease operations in New South Wales, or in any part of Australia. It is imperative, therefore, that the State Government stand firm.[50]

Indeed, following Reisman's statement, Premier Bertram Stevens emphasised that the State Government would not abandon its determination to encourage local filmmaking. But in December 1937 it passed the Films and Theatres Act which made provision for a scaling down of quota percentages and required only eight Australian films to be released in both 1938 and 1939. The *Sydney Morning Herald* saw it as:

a strategic retreat — the covering up of a temporary failure ... The principle of the quota is upheld; but there are no longer any illusions about making Sydney a little Hollywood.[51]

Even less hope remained after February 1938. In that month, Britain renewed its quota under the Cinematograph Films Bill but it no longer provided for the guaranteed domestic release of films from the Dominions. There were reactions of alarm from almost every Australian producer because the British market had become vital to the recouping of production costs. Although the new measure was intended to stop American producers having features made in Canada to qualify for the Dominion quota, Australians also considered the Act a reprimand for not giving quota privileges to British films under the 1935 legislation in New South Wales. With the British market no longer assured, the backers of at least one producer-director, A. R. Harwood, withdrew entirely from production. Ken Hall announced that without the guaranteed sale to Britain of three recent Cinesound films, his company would have been "in the soup"[52], and in November 1938 Norman Rydge stated that unless a government subsidy were granted, Cinesound could be forced to close within a month. He added: "If something is not done immediately, I can conceive the break-up of the whole Australian film-producing industry".[53]

The crisis had been fully evident by October 1938 when Cinesound and National Productions, along with Figtree Studios, sent a joint memorandum to Bertram Stevens advocating legislation to protect Australian production and exhibition from the further trade incursions of foreign film interests. They also argued for a local quota for British films.[54] In the light of the continued failure of the domestic quota legislation, the request included direct financial assistance for producers. On 22 December the Government introduced the Theatres, Public Halls and Cinematograph Films Bill. It provided a fifteen per cent quota for Australian films (set at a meagre 2.5 per cent for the first year), and guarantees for bank overdrafts providing sixty per cent of the budget of four features to be produced over a year's trial period. The conditions of the Act were to be administered by a newly formed body, the New South Wales Theatres and Films Commission. Its responsibilities were to include, when necessary, the enforcement and review of the quota; to prescribe and oversee contractual relations between distributors and exhibitors; grant licences for the building or alteration of theatres; to review and make recommendations on applications for government assistance; and to approve the quality of films for registration under the quota. To conduct any inquiry, the Commission was given the powers and immunities of a Royal Commission.

Although the four features receiving State Government assistance were to have been produced by the end of December 1939, the State Treasury's guarantee was not made available until January 1940 — and only after a special agreement to extend the plan beyond its trial period. In the meantime, two of the applicant companies, Argosy and Cinesound, had kept their studios open for longer than they would otherwise have done in the absence of the

Government's undertaking. Frederick Daniell wrote to the State Treasurer on 26 October 1939:

We cannot emphasise too strongly that the delay in giving effect to the Act ... has resulted in this company becoming heavily involved through no fault of its own, in a considerable loss to many individuals associated with us, in a great amount of unavoidable distress, and an industry already in a state of extremis has been saddled with a further load of overburdening expense and debt.[55]

The reason for the delay was more than twelve months' haggling over such minutiae as the guarantee's interest rates; interpretation and amendment of clauses; differences of opinion between State and Federal officials; and, after the outbreak of war in September 1939, the consent of the Federal Treasurer becoming essential under new National Security (Capital Issues) regulations. As one complication succeeded another, the Theatres and Films Commission rejected applications and called for new ones, sent out questionnaires and conducted a series of lengthy and tangled meetings with producers and their representatives. The meetings can hardly have impressed Norman Rydge who attended on behalf of Cinesound and, like Sir Hugh Denison, had been persuaded by assurances from the Treasurer in April 1939 not to shut down his company's production activities altogether.[56]

With the funds eventually made available, Cinesound was to receive £15 000 for **Dad Rudd, M.P.**, Argosy a total of £25 000 for **That Certain Something** and **The Power and the Glory**, and Expeditionary Films (Charles Chauvel) £15 000 for the completion of **Forty Thousand Horsemen**. Although conceived during peacetime, all were substantially filmed after the outbreak of war (initial footage for **Forty Thousand Horsemen** had been shot in 1938), and all but one showed the influence of the war itself.

The exception, **That Certain Something** — significantly in the light of the industry's earlier quota aspirations — presents a fantasy of the local production industry as a small-scale Hollywood. The story, of a visiting Hollywood director whose mission is to glorify the Australian girl, satirises the experiences of writer-director Clarence Badger, who four years earlier had made **Rangle River** under the tight control of a production committee. Badger's presentation of the industry is as nebulous as the film's title, and both the pace and the performances are lethargic.

Despite high hopes that a reciprocal British quota measure would be introduced in the wake of the New South Wales Act introduced in 1937, none was forthcoming. However, prominent Australian films continued to obtain their release in Britain. The Act's local production guarantee scheme, initially valid for a twelve-month period only, depended for its renewal on a recommendation by the Theatres and Films Commission and a decision by the Government. Before the recommendation was made Stevens was replaced as Premier by the former State Treasurer Alexander Mair in early 1939 and after Stevens's departure the industry found itself without a champion. At the request of the Theatres and Films Commission at least one company, Argosy, supplied information on the films it would make during 1941 if the guarantee scheme were continued. However, the scheme was not renewed and the quota provisions were not seriously considered again until the late 1960s.

Cinesound: 1938-1940

To Greater Union Theatres, struggling to solve financial problems between 1938 and 1940, the existence of Cinesound presented a dilemma. After the decline in British production in the mid-1930s, Greater Union's film supplies, through its distribution offshoot British Empire Films, shrank almost to the point where their only reliable source was Universal (whose quality could vary radically) and Cinesound. But, although Cinesound films continued to return their capital outlay, a general downturn in exhibition in the two years from 1938 meant that, from **Lovers and Luggers** onward, the productions were taking longer to recover profits. The position was hardly helped when British Empire Films, Cinesound's distributor under their parent company, Greater Union, charged an above-average distribution fee of thirty-five per cent for each Cinesound feature, and then Greater Union itself charged exhibitors' rates which Ken Hall claimed that no American producer-distributor ''would have even looked at''. Hall continued:

As the new regime saw it, financial faith had to be restored in the theatres, by far the major part of the company's overall operation. You could not argue with that, because without its theatre outlets there would be no company.[57]

In the appointment of Norman Rydge, Greater Union had chosen first and foremost a businessman. In contrast to Stuart Doyle whose principal investment decisions — theatre expansion and film production — were entrepreneurial gambles calculated on his own assessment of returns, Rydge demanded indisputable evidence that any investment could earn a consistent profit of at least 10 per cent.[58] His outlook on Cinesound feature filmmaking was initially bright, buoyed by the company's apparent viability and the resulting goodwill throughout the trade and the community at large. Towards the end of his first month as chairman and managing director of Greater Union, Rydge told a group of suburban and country exhibitors visiting the Cinesound studio:

You gentlemen are in business for one reason — to make money at the theatre box office, and I am confident that this company will continue to make pictures which will allow you to achieve this purpose.[59]

After the widespread success of **It Isn't Done** and an encouraging premiere season for **Tall Timbers**, Cinesound's company directors approved a five-feature schedule with a total budget of £100 000. However, with the release of **Lovers and Luggers** in December, the opinion of the hierarchy changed. Ken Hall remembered:

It went into the State [Theatre, Sydney], and it didn't do well there, and Rydge got cold feet right off the bat. He now thought film production was risky — not knowing that it goes up and down, all over the place. I knew then — when **Lovers and Luggers** didn't do the bonanza business that he'd been led to believe all the other films had done — that he wanted out.[60]

Rydge had advocated government aid for the industry, especially for Greater Union, months before the release of **Lovers and Luggers** and the announcements of early April and November 1938 which stated that Cinesound would cease production unless aid was quickly forthcoming.[61] However, in view of the apparent imminence of government aid and Greater Union's continuing problems with new film supplies, feature filmmaking at Cinesound continued. In order to cut down the studio's increasingly heavy overhead, Ken Hall announced that the schedule of five features, beginning with **The Broken Melody**, would allow only two weeks between the end of one film and the start of the next, in which the studio lay idle.[62]

The Broken Melody (1938) saw a return to high quality melodrama, first made by Cinesound with **The Silence of Dean Maitland**. A major innovation was its operatic finale which made full use of the sound playback system and presented Hall with "a shocking risk . . . If the musical section did not work, we had no film".[63] **The Broken Melody** was also the only local feature of the decade to directly portray the Depression. But, despite this potential for realism, Hall chose a romanticised approach, incorporating dramatic and comic devices then common in American film. Stylistically slick and emulating the look and pace of many Hollywood "big city" films of the period, **The Broken Melody** was yet more evidence of the intention that Cinesound films should be as exportable as possible.

Local critics disagreed over the value of the cosmopolitan content. The Melbourne *Herald* thought that one of the "most pleasant surprises . . . is the total omission of a 'real Australian type' so popular in earlier film efforts, trashy novels and radio plays".[64] Conversely, the *Sunday Sun* reviewer expressed a general preference for Hall's earlier action films and wrote: "Our belief is simply to be individual in our films, we should be national".[65] Most critics, however, agreed on the success of its concluding seven-minute operatic sequence, composed in personable Italian style by the doyen of Australian classical composers, Alfred Hill, and sung by his daughter and the tenor Lionello Cecil. The recording of the music playback involved the simultaneous mixing of a forty-voice choir, soloists, and over fifty members of the Sydney Symphony Orchestra.[66]

Comedy to the end

Nationalism re-emerged in the Cinesound films of the late 1930s, as it had in Australian society at large. The year 1938 brought a much-publicised certification of national pride with the New South Wales sesquicentenary celebrations. Newsreels recorded the firework displays and the re-enactments of the arrival of the first European settlers 150 years before — which somehow managed to include thousands of children choreographed on the

Sydney Showground to form a "living symbol of nationhood — the Southern Cross". In the Sydney Domain, Anglican Archbishop Mowll delivered thanksgiving for "divine aid in the building of a nation"; at Vaucluse House, socialites and actors paraded in the costumes of William Charles Wentworth's pioneering days. The ties with Britain were emphasised when robes from the coronation of the previous year went on display in the National Art Gallery. The visiting American General James G. Hubbard spoke of America and Australia as allies in peace and war. Frank Hurley's documentary **A Nation is Built**, produced by Cinesound for the New South Wales Government, focused with a proud parochialism on Australia's assorted industries and re-enacted moments from the lives of the rural pioneers John Macarthur and William Farrer. In the same year Qantas started an Australia to Europe flying-boat service when a Short Sunderland "Empire" class craft named "Cooee" lifted off from Sydney's Rose Bay on its long, nine-and-a-half day journey to Southampton.

In a darkening outside world, Hitler annexed Austria and assumed control of the German Army; Britain and France resisted the Führer's demands during the first Czechoslovak crisis. Further intimations of a world war were temporarily postponed, but Germany now stood as the dominant European power and Australia's reaction to the events was the introduction of a new defence programme and an expansion of its Citizen's Military Force. A tangible reminder of what was happening on the far side of the world arrived in the form of several thousand Jewish refugees who settled in Sydney and Melbourne. According to Ken Hall, as Australia reacted to the world situation:

There was a great disquiet among people able to think. The economy fell into low gear and the theatres were once again battling for survival against pretty heavy odds. But they were to get heavier still.

We had proved something in 1932: when times are tough — make comedy.[67]

Let George Do It (1938), begun at the start of 1938, was the first of a series of six comedies produced by Cinesound over the next two years. It was also one of two films featuring George Wallace, and employing Jim Bancks, Hal Carleton and Bill Maloney as a "comedy creative" — or gag — team to provide humorous ideas and dialogue for Hall to extend visually. Care was taken with **Let George Do It** to provide a more suitably filmic screenplay than Cinesound had prepared for Roy Rene, or Efftee had given Wallace in the early 1930s, and the result is by far the best of Wallace's features. The slim plot involves Wallace as an unemployed stagehand on the run from gangsters who discover that he is the heir to a fortune. Traces of Wallace's stage origins remain, especially in an extended sequence in which he foils Alec Kellaway's efforts as a conjuror. But a good deal of cinematic inventiveness is climaxed by a speedboat chase around Sydney Harbour making use of rear projection, stunt doubling and swift comic cameos.

Dad and Dave Come to Town (1938), the third of the Selection series, continued the "cosmopolitanisation" of the original Bert Bailey stage characters by removing the family from the backblocks, by way of a lucky inheritance, and depositing them as the awkward owners of a city dress salon. This device allows a more deliberate articulation of national sentiment than is present in the earlier Dad and Dave films as Dad's bush honesty is severely tested by the crookedness of city business rivals. Bert Bailey's portrayal of Dad shows greater warmth and stature than in the earlier films, and his key speeches are delivered with an appropriate epic sincerity. By 1939 the Rudds' reputation was such as to inspire the London *Sunday Despatch* to compare Australia's most famous film family with the American industry's Hardy family, whose latest film had opened in England at the same time.[68] Re-titled for the UK as **The Rudd Family Goes to Town**, this third of the Dad and Dave series was the first full-length Australian film to be shown in London's West End and with two subsequent releases on the Odeon circuit it earned £40 000.

Mr Chedworth Steps Out (1939), a comedy-drama set almost entirely in an Australian city and suburbs, is perhaps the best of all the Cinesound films. Cecil Kellaway (brought back from Hollywood where he had signed a contract with RKO following **It Isn't Done**) plays George Chedworth, a suburban "little man" who is much put-upon by his family and society in general. Demoted from clerk to warehouse caretaker, he stumbles across a cache of money which he proceeds to spend before being tracked down by a treasury official and a gang of counterfeiters. A mixture of bad luck and happy coincidence eventually enable him to make a stand and take gentle revenge against his hen-pecking, nouveau riche wife (Rita Pauncefort). He also sorts out the problems of his children, including a Deanna Durbin-style trilling daughter (Jean Hatton) and a gambling son (Peter Finch). Although not without its melodramatic jolts, the story comes closest of all the films of the decade to portraying a way of life common to the majority of Australians. The rituals of an early morning household, a dinner table conversation and higher suburban aspirations progressively take the mood from quiet despair to a final cheeky achievement of the Australian Dream in the form of Chedworth's greater wealth and larger house. While Chedworth wins in his own terms, most of the comedy derives from opposition to his wife's social-climbing and spendthrift habits. Many of the moments of drama, like the comedy, are directed with finely judged subtlety. The early scene of Chedworth's demotion is played just on the right side of pathos, while his son's interrogation and torture by the crooks is made all the more sinister by being understated.

The last three of the Cinesound features showed evidence of the increased assurance with which Hall integrated the elements he knew would appeal to his audiences. Partly reflecting the production pressures, all returned to safe ground and, more than any other sequence of Cinesound films, followed the Hollywood studio pattern of safe formulas styled for a family audience. All carried on the line of comedic or semi-comedic "little men", opposed to powerful individual or corporate forces, finally triumphant with the aid of sympathetic friends. According to Ken Hall, two of the three films followed his favourite comic formula of "a comedian in jeopardy".[69] The events they contained, however coincidentally, bore some relation to the threatened world conflict; and the third film, **Dad Rudd, M.P.** (1940), was intended as a loose allegory of the war then in progress.

Gone to the Dogs (1939), starring George Wallace, is more consistently cinematic but less spontaneous than **Let George Do It**, and its best moments feature Wallace as a zoo-keeper at the beginning of the film. The other highlights include song-and-dance routines and a haunted house, complete with headless ghost, ghoulish faces and an ingenious upside-down room. **Come Up Smiling** (1939), scripted and directed by the English actor William Freshman under the supervision of Hall, displayed a far better sense of the ridiculous. Will Mahoney plays Barney O'Hara, a sideshow entertainer who undertakes to fight a villainous boxer to pay for his daughter's throat operation. Amid a pleasant blend of music and Chaplinesque pathos, the funniest moments are provided by O'Hara's preliminary accidental bouts with the boxer (a wonderfully punch-drunk Alec Kellaway), and the final match which has O'Hara walking the ropes in fright then trouncing "The Killer" with the aid of bagpipe music, a known spur to his anger. Jean Hatton again plays the Durbin-style daughter and, like **Gone to the Dogs**, the film concludes with hero and friends restoring optimism with a spirited delivery of the title song.

Dad Rudd, M.P. took the Rudd family characters closest to sophistication, but was still similar to the overall approach taken by **Dad and Dave Come to Town**. As the characters from the 1938 film spill back across the screen the impression is given of a series of films settling down into an unvaried pattern that might have continued — but for the intervention of war and a change in corporate policy — for another decade at least. Having cast aside their original earthiness, the Rudds could have developed further into a Hardy Family, or perhaps an early equivalent of the American rural series featuring "Ma and Pa Kettle". **Dad Rudd, M.P.** is the most carefully structured and most surely directed of all the Cinesound films, although it comes nowhere near the acute perception of **Mr Chedworth Steps Out**. In leading the fight by small farmers for the completion of a dam according to its original plans, Dad Rudd is a staunch political advocate for the interests of "the plain people who are the heart, soul and backbone of this country". Dad's opponent in a district election is a wealthy landowner whose interests will be served if the dam is not built to its full height. This issue introduced a greater degree of drama into **Dad Rudd, M.P.** than any of its predecessors and the allegorical impact of small and democratic interests opposing powerful enemies doubtless helped to put it among the most popular Australian features screened in wartime Britain. After the major set-piece of the dam's collapse, the film ends on a patriotic note with Dad's maiden parliamentary speech turning to a call to the flag with the "drums of war" sounding in Europe and "Land of Hope and Glory" playing in the background.

Dad Rudd, M.P. was followed almost immediately into the studio by one of its fellow recipients of the government guarantee, Charles Chauvel's **Forty Thousand Horsemen**. Not long after the June 1940 release of **Dad Rudd, M.P.**, Norman Rydge announced that Cinesound's feature production would have to be suspended for the duration of the war. By November 1940, the principal work on **Forty Thousand Horsemen** was complete. After most of Cinesound's staff had left for war service, only a handful remained to work on newsreels and official war films. Ken Hall himself turned his energies to these new projects, reasonably confident that features would resume when the war was over.

Charles Chauvel: 1936-1940

With **Uncivilised** (1936) and **Forty Thousand Horsemen** (1940), Charles Chauvel was the only filmmaker to manage the production of a feature at either end of the New South Wales Government's 1935-1938 legislative attempts to aid the industry. One might argue that Chauvel, more persistent than any other independent, would have made films regardless of the quota and guarantee legislation; but **Uncivilised** was prompted directly by the 1935 Quota Act, and almost half the budget of **Forty Thousand Horsemen** was supplied by the guarantee award in January 1940.

In view of the financial failure of the nationalistic **Heritage**, **Uncivilised** was to mark the furthest swing Chauvel would make in an attempt to reach the American market. Containing aspects of **Tarzan** and **Sanders of the River**, the script, by Chauvel and E. V. Timms, charts the adventures of a sophisticated girl reporter (Margot Rhys) who ventures into remotest northwestern Australia in pursuit of the story of a wild white man who leads an Aboriginal tribe. Kidnapped en route by an Afghan trader, she is sold to the white king (Dennis Hoey) who manages to take time off from his involvement in tribal conflict and opium trading to gain her love. In the battle scenes, Chauvel gives the first indication of his talent as an action director. Unlike the rudimentary coverage of a native attack in **Heritage**, the set-ups are precise and crisply cut. The feeling for landscape is also more vivid, best realised in the Afghan party's opening canoe trip up river through twisting mangroves and jungle to mist-shrouded mountains. The *Sydney Morning Herald* regarded the backgrounds as "curiously primaeval and intense", but shared other critics' reservations about plotline and dialogue.[70]

In principle, Chauvel's marketing bid with **Uncivilised** was a success. But after extensive screenings in Australia and across America, it failed to yield his production company, Expeditionary Films, more than a minimal return. In the meantime, Charles and Elsa Chauvel had departed in November 1936 to study production at Hollywood's Universal studios. During their stay, organised by Herc McIntyre, the managing director of the company's Australian branch, Chauvel was offered a position as an assistant director with the possibility of soon directing his own feature. Elsa Chauvel recalled: " 'In the end', he said to me, 'I'm not in the game just to make

161

pictures. I want to make pictures about Australia. I want my own country'.''[71] For several months back in Sydney, the Chauvels produced a variety programme for the radio station 2GB. Although they were contracted for a year, Chauvel became even more restless to be back in filmmaking, and both resigned to concentrate on his next feature.

Since the beginning of the decade, Chauvel had been trying to raise backing for a project that would relate the exploits of the Australian Light Horse brigade in Palestine during World War I. The brigade had been commanded by Chauvel's uncle, General Sir Harry Chauvel, and their original nucleus, known as the Upper Clarence River Lancers, had been formed by Chauvel's grandfather. Chauvel's plans for the film began to crystallise in Hollywood during early 1937, when he discussed the idea with an old friend, Frank Baker (the brother of Snowy), who supplied a story outline.[72] On his return to Australia, he worked on the story with E. V. Timms, then developed a script with Elsa Chauvel.[73] As the board of Expeditionary Films had been discouraged by the poor returns from **Uncivilised** and did not wish to embark on a project of the magnitude of the proposed **Forty Thousand Horsemen**, they agreed in late 1937 to sell the company's shares to Herc McIntyre of Universal Pictures.[74] He tried to persuade his parent company in America to invest in the film, but meeting no enthusiasm personally gave Chauvel £5000 to shoot a ''shop window'' sequence to attract funds from other sources. One day in February 1938, Chauvel directed a section of the film's climax, the Light Horse charge, using four cameras and a cavalry division of five hundred horsemen — in Sydney for the sesquicentenary celebrations. With this sequence, filmed on the extensive sandhills of Kurnell, south of Sydney, McIntyre gained the interest of Charles Munro, the managing director of Hoyts Theatres, who had his company invest £10 000 in the film.[75] This amount, added to McIntyre's money and the State Government guarantee, helped bring the budget to its eventual £32 000.

The four-month schedule began in May 1940, making substantial use of the Cinesound crew and some of the largest interior sets the studio had seen. During the production of final interiors, a team of carpenters constructed an Arab village on the Kurnell sandhills, and its streets were soon packed with hundreds of extras, camel teams, donkeys and geese. Filming of further action scenes required a full-time contingent of a hundred expert horsemen, with the most spectacular of the falls being executed by two stunt riders.[76]

Working from a shooting script prepared by his wife, Charles Chauvel proceeded to develop his shooting pattern on set. A perfectionist very much in control of all areas, he used the script as a starting point only; from this base dialogue could be modified and new scenes added to enable later flexibility of construction on the editing bench. Working with virtually untried leading actors (Grant Taylor had played a supporting lead in **Dad Rudd, M.P.** and Chips Rafferty was an extra in the same film), Chauvel sought on set to draw out aspects of the players' own personalities to enhance their roles. In the case of Chips Rafferty, director and actor worked to create a performance that was partly Rafferty himself, partly derived from Pat Hanna's earlier "Digger" performances, and substantially Chauvel's interpretation of the World War I Anzac as a national legend. The Grant Taylor role represented a more heroic aspect of the legend while Pat Twohill, quieter than the others, brought balance of a more conventional kind.

The story follows the exploits of three of the horsemen, Red (Grant Taylor), Jim (Chips Rafferty) and Larry (Pat Twohill), in several extensive Middle East campaigns, culminating in the charge at Beersheba. The romance between Red and Juliet (Betty Bryant), a French woman spying against the Germans, is interwoven with the main story. The completed film, released in December 1940,[77] was to be Chauvel's best work, memorable for its exuberantly-mounting pace, grand and precisely-controlled action, and for its fresh perspectives on national character. The principal sequence, the Beersheba battle and charge, is edited from numerous intimately detailed and panoramic shots — tracking swiftly, intercutting explosions with the defence of trenches, thundering hooves and flying bodies, and a confusion of falling horses. Comparable with the climax of Michael Curtiz's **The Charge of the Light Brigade** (USA, 1936), this sequence went a long way towards making **Forty Thousand Horsemen** the first Australian film of genuine international stature. It quickly returned its money, the government guarantee being repaid in a few months. After great success in Australia, it played on every continent, gaining lavish attention in London and New York and serving as a wartime morale-booster. At the very time that grave fears were held for the continued existence of a local film industry **Forty Thousand Horsemen** seemed to offer as much, if not more, encouragement as **On Our Selection** had eight years earlier.

7

Renewed hopes
1941 - 50

From the outbreak of World War II, the film trade supported the country's stance with special newsreels on national defence and the active promotion of war bonds, recruiting drives, austerity loans and penny-a-plane schemes, in which children contributed to the war effort. From June 1942 distribution exchanges provided mobile cinema units and prints without charge to troops based in remote areas of Australia and New Guinea. Free distribution was given to propaganda film from government sources, and from late 1940 onwards Australian commercial producers made a growing number of these films for the Department of Information (DOI).

By the end of the war, Cinesound's editing and presentation of New Guinea footage by the DOI cameraman Damien Parer had gained Australia's first American Academy Award, and Australian war newsreels and selected DOI featurettes had been screened regularly and with frequent praise in all the Allied countries. But this contribution could in no way compare with the best of the patriotic features and documentaries from Britain, Canada, the USA, Germany and the Soviet Union. The Australian Government, lacking strong propaganda policy, failed to promote filmmaking in the way familiar to other countries long before the outbreak of the war. While the assumption may have been that production (especially in the form of newsreels) was adequate, only after the war did Australia begin to produce documentaries of a kind popularised by the John Grierson movement in Britain since the early 1930s.

Coming into the film world in the mid-1920s as a critic, Grierson defined "documentary" (derived from the French word *documentaire*) as "the creative interpretation of actuality". As a theorist and filmmaker, he helped to shape the medium in such a way that it could directly serve society. His films, as much as his writings, set out to communicate universal issues, ways of life, occupations and attitudes. As a public service, documentary could be educational and could also seek to reform society. Sponsorship, whether from government departments, institutions or private industry, removed conformist pressures and often permitted experimentation or reformist propaganda. Another member of the Grierson group, Basil Wright, has written

documentary built up a true conception of practical internationalism in which national characteristics and national achievements were seen to form the best basis for interchange of ideas and the promotion of mutual understanding between peoples.[1]

The achievements of the Grierson movement were eventually to influence the documentary production of no less than ten nations.

Between 1938 and 1940, John Grierson visited Canada, New Zealand and Australia on behalf of the Imperial Relations Trust to compile a report on the state of official documentary work in each country and make suggestions about future activity. In Canada and New Zealand sympathetic community attitudes allowed the early implementation of his recommendations. Both countries had, like Australia, employed full-time official cinematographers since at least the 1910s, and now moved to improve the old-style government film units by allowing the introduction of the new philosophies urged by Grierson. In Australia where, according to Stanley Hawes, Grierson's political nous met its match "when confronted with the indifference of [Prime Minister] Robert Menzies"[2], Grierson's recommendations for non-theatrical documentary production and distribution were not implemented until 1945 — and then only in a modified form. Not until public and political priorities eventually allowed the formation of a National Film Board was Australia's war effort on film taken from the hands of the commercial producers.

Wartime features and actuality

The number of independent features made and released during the war years totalled five. (This does not include another five conceived before the outbreak of war and released in 1940-41.) An awareness of the hostilities ran through nearly all of them, although only Chauvel's **The Rats of Tobruk** (1944) dealt directly with Australians in battle. Rupert Kathner revived mateship among old diggers for his best feature, **Racing Luck** (1941). The film contains sincere, naturalistic performances from Joe Valli and George Lloyd and its significance lies in the fact that it is one of the few early sound features to present working-class Australians with credibility instead of caricature. It was a virtue shared and heightened by Mervyn Murphy's only feature, **Harvest Gold** (1945, sponsored by Caltex) which, blending fiction with semi-documentary, showed another Joe Valli character stubbornly at odds with mechanised farming. In 1942 and 1944 the theatrical entrepreneurs Austral-American Productions produced two short and stage-bound features, **A Yank in Australia** and **Red Sky at Morning**. The latter, based on a play by Dymphna Cusack, was noteworthy for the appearance of Peter Finch as an Irish political prisoner in colonial New South Wales. The film was released twice in England — the second time to cash in on Finch's name — but does not seem to have had a release in its home territory.

Apart from obvious wartime financial constraints, two factors limited the ability of producers to make features: shortages of manpower and film stock. A number of film personnel had enlisted at the outbreak of war, but the problems became acute after the level of recruitment rose from early 1941. Experienced production and laboratory technicians as well as actors were suddenly lost to the industry, although by April 1942 a measure of protection was introduced for Cinesound and Movietone newsreel employees; and at times, after 1942, newsreels were the only form of production able to obtain raw film stock. Government controls and international shortages meant that even the number of imported theatrical features was reduced and all available stock was pooled under the jurisdiction of the Departments of Import Procurement and Information. Stock priorities also played a part in decisions by the DOI on what films would be made and released in Australia and abroad.

The purpose of the Department of Information, which had been formed five days after the outbreak of war, was to coordinate and censor all media information released in Australia dealing with the war. The function of its National Films Council (formed in June 1940) was to advise and help the DOI in its film production, distribution and exhibition activities, and the DOI's Film Division (formed on 9 August) was intended to coordinate government and commercial film activity "and to mobilise the film medium for national ends".

Although it had no production base beyond that of the old Cinema Branch, the Division controlled a small film unit of accredited war correspondents. Damien Parer, the DOI's first war cameraman, was despatched to Palestine in February 1940. In September, the Film Division sent a complete unit to the Middle East under Frank Hurley. Besides Hurley and Parer, the unit consisted of Maslyn Williams as scriptwriter-producer-director, Alan Anderson as sound engineer, and George Silk as stills photographer. Although the DOI was the first department to employ Australian cinematographers as war correspondents, the Army and the Royal Australian Air Force were soon to appoint their own film staff under the auspices of Military History and RAAF Public Relations.

The DOI's war footage was made available to Cinesound and Movietone, whose handling of the material was often markedly different. Where Cinesound reels emphasised only the Australian war effort, Movietone's tended to place it in an international context, interspersing Australian footage with material available from its branches overseas. Both reels emphasised the human side of war, and the cameramen, including Damien Parer, aimed increasingly at recording the effect on the front-line soldier. Parer's images and his own commentary for the special **Cinesound Review: Kokoda Front Line**, helped it share (with John Ford's **Battle of Midway**) the American film industry's 1942 Academy Award for Short Documentary. The most famous wartime documentary completed at Movietone was **Jungle Patrol** (1944), with footage by Bill Carty and J. W. Tresise. *Smith's Weekly*

17
Norman Dawn directs the
chorus line in *Showgirl's Luck*
(1931). At left are Arthur
Tauchert and Arthur Clarke.

18
Publicity for *Diggers* (1931). (The
Sentimental Bloke referred to
was clearly not the Efftee
version of the following year.)

19
In March 1932 Movietone and
Filmcraft Laboratories staff
gathered at Camperdown after
the opening of the Sydney
Harbour Bridge. Standing on
trucks: Bill Trerise, Stan
Pentreath and Eric Bierre.
Ground level: Kel Vaughan,
Denis Box, Sid Wood (obscured),
Walter Sully, Bill Thorpe, Fred
Batten, Merv Callow, Reg
Edwards, Wally Bird, Ted
Marden, Colin Hall and Hugh
McInnes. The vehicle at right is

20
The Sentimental Bloke (1932).
Doreen (Rae Fisher) and the
Bloke (Cecil Scott) enjoy their
rural idyll.

21
Three cameras and a live orchestra cover a musical number for *His Royal Highness* (1932). George Wallace, in the checked shirt, croons at left in the background. Raymond Longford is at far right.

22
On Our Selection (1932). Kate and Dad Rudd (Mollie Raynor and Bert Bailey) confront a villainous creditor (Len Budrick).

23

24

23
Diggers in Blighty (1933). Joe Valli and Pat Hanna encounter a German spy (Raymond Longford).

24
Strike Me Lucky (1934). An unemployed Mo (Roy Rene) befriends two wealthy sisters (Pamela Bevan and Lorraine Smith).

25
26

25
A break in the filming of *The Flying Doctor* (1936) at Pagewood — Alan J. Williamson, Mary Maguire, Miles Mander and Fred Daniell.

26
Thoroughbred (1936). Frank Leighton with Hollywood import Helen Twelvetrees.

27

27
Let George Do It (1938). Bar room cronies Joe Valli and George Wallace plan Wallace's suicide before learning of the latter's inheritance.

28

28
The central heroes of *Forty Thousand Horsemen* (1940) — Chips Rafferty, Grant Taylor and Pat Twohill.

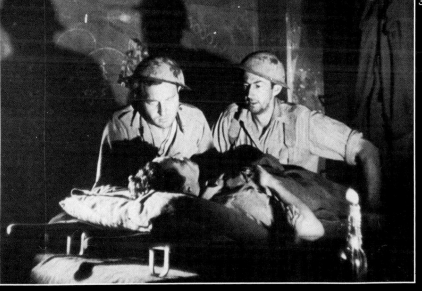

29

30

29
The Power and the Glory (1941).
Behind the scenes at Pagewood
— Eric Bush and Peter Finch.

30
The Rats of Tobruk (1944).
Watched by his Australian mates
(Grant Taylor and Chips
Rafferty), an Englishman (Peter
Finch) dies during the defence
of Tobruk. A frame enlargement.

31

Chips Rafferty in *The Overlanders* (1946), a film whose international success attracted a spate of overseas producers to Australia.

32

Location filming in South Australia for *Bitter Springs* (1950). The group includes Gordon Jackson, Ralph Smart, Ross Wood, Chips Rafferty, Hans Wetzel and Bill Grimmond.

wrote that the film ranked "with anything the war has produced", and

makes you sit on the edge of your seat. Written and directed by Tom Gurr, this is the Australian soldier at work, and how quietly and with what deadly precision he goes into the business.

[The] whole picture has a curious quietness which makes for the last word in intensity. Peter Finch is the commentator for these men who are doing such hair-raising things. Here again, there is no attempt at dramatisation, the story being told with absolute simplicity.[3]

Among the overseas items included in Movietone newsreels at the time were Canadian National Film Board documentaries with episodes from the **Canada Carries On** series. Although they were sometimes re-edited to conform to standard newsreel length, their techniques were admired and to a small, but notable degree, imitated.[4]

The war and its exigencies changed the style of newsreels. The emphasis on propaganda led to stronger statements in the stories and an increasing number of newsreels took the form of full-reel "specials".[5] As newsreels turned from novelty to necessity, newsreel theatres flourished, especially after 1941 when Australians at home became more conscious of their own vulnerability. By mid-1942 both reels averaged ninety per cent war content and were seen by ninety-seven per cent of patrons. In the early part of the war, the employees demonstrated their versatility when Cinesound gave post-production aid to the US Signal Corps' weekly **SWPA News** (South-West Pacific Area) and several Movietone staff were recruited through the DOI to make propaganda shorts for the British Ministry of Information's Far Eastern Bureau.[6]

As no clear policy had been spelt out by the Department, commercial filmmakers were able largely to take their own initiative and during the war a total of ninety-four films were made under the DOI's auspices. Dramatised shorts were commissioned from producers like Cinesound, Chauvel and Argosy, who had the experience to handle this type of work, while films of a more directly factual nature were made by Movietone, Herschell's, Commonwealth Laboratories, Mervyn Murphy, George Malcolm, John Heyer, and the Arthur Higgins–Neville Bletcher team. From Chauvel, who made four semi-dramatised DOI shorts in 1942-43, and Ken G. Hall at Cinesound, who made many more (both of a semi-dramatised and exclusively factual nature), several of the featurettes received creative input of a level to compare with the best of their feature work. Although Hall's **South-West Pacific** (1943) stretches its war message too thinly, his **100 000 Cobbers** (1942) adroitly combines the sophistication of the late Cinesound features with a keen eye for actuality detail. Grant Taylor, John Fleeting, Joe Valli and Shirley Ann Richards play characters whose reactions to recruitment and training are closely observed, and it echoes the wartime patriotism and democracy stressed at the end of **Dad Rudd, M.P.**[7]

After his DOI work, Charles Chauvel persuaded Hoyts Theatres, RKO-Radio Pictures and the Commonwealth Film Laboratories to back his second war feature, **The Rats of Tobruk** (1944). Concerned at the absence of the Australian soldier from feature films, Chauvel intended to pay tribute to the heroes of desert and jungle warfare, who provided the closest parallel to the First World War exploits depicted in **Forty Thousand Horsemen**. Whereas the earlier film had been influenced by Hollywood-style myth-making of the late 1930s, **The Rats of Tobruk** took a less romantic view, occasioned as much by general war fatigue as by Chauvel's documentary experience of the previous two years. By late 1943, when the film entered production, enlisted Australians totalled 790 000 and Darwin had been bombed fifty-nine times by the Japanese. To stress the contribution that Australians had made on two fronts, Chauvel spread his action through the long defences of Tobruk and New Guinea. Two of the three heroes are killed near the end of each campaign, while Grant Taylor is the survivor who, as in **Forty Thousand Horsemen**, avenges the loss of his mates (Chips Rafferty and a Shakespeare-quoting Peter Finch) with renewed zeal against the enemy. The loyalties of mateship are again central to the fighting spirit, although Chauvel's aim to explore freshly battlefield relationships is deflected by overextended action footage and the addition — at Hoyts' insistence — of a love interest in the prologue and epilogue. Character development is uneven, with Taylor allowed to show little of the easy charm displayed in **Forty Thousand Horsemen**, and the comic moments so well integrated in the earlier film appear in **The Rats of Tobruk** to be tacked on.

The Rats of Tobruk was the only major Australian-produced feature to be made in its entirety and released during the war years. Plans by other producers, including Ken Hall and Frederick Daniell, were curtailed by financial restrictions, although story ideas were abundant. In February 1941 an attempt by Daniell to refloat Argosy Productions to make features from American distributors' frozen remittances met with no success; and further efforts by both Hall and Daniell to become involved in patriotic production with the cooperation of the armed services were smothered by the caution of private investors. Charles Chauvel's achievement aside, the only tangible hope seemed to lie with initiative from abroad.

The Overlanders

While **The Rats of Tobruk** was still in production, Harry Watt came to Sydney to search for a story idea. His visit was to become, in retrospect, a landmark because the feature he made was **The Overlanders** (1946), a major international success which persuaded Ealing Studios to become the first overseas company to produce films in Australia on a regular basis. This venture was to attract more outside producers over the next fourteen years.

By the provision of equipment, transport and personnel, the Australian Government was to do more for Ealing with this and its subsequent Australian films than it had for any local producer. The original stimulus for **The Overlanders** came from the Government's complaint to the British Ministry of Information that the Australian war effort was not being sufficiently publicised in British propaganda. The grievance — revealing Australia's continued dependence on Britain and the lack of its own propaganda — led to the BMI discussing the matter with Michael Balcon. As Harry Watt had already expressed his interest in Australia, he was assigned to travel, in Balcon's words, "not with a film to make but to find a theme for a film which would in some way deal with the problem".[8]

Watt had been the first of the British documentarists after Robert Flaherty to effectively incorporate dramatic episodes and, also like Flaherty, was prepared to spend months familiarising himself with actual locations and people before the development of a storyline. Out of five months and 25 000 miles travel in Australia from February 1944, Watt had "five ideas and scrapped the lot".[9] Any thought of dramatising battles in the Middle East or New Guinea was dropped so as not to compete with **The Rats of Tobruk,** and Watt was aware that any such film would be useless if the war ended before its release. After one month more, he found his subject during a conversation with the Commonwealth Food Controller — the overland drive in 1942 of 100 000 head of cattle from the Northern Territory to the Queensland coast when a Japanese invasion seemed imminent.

For five months from April 1945 **The Overlanders** unit, accompanied by a thousand head of cattle, filmed in locations around the Northern Territory's Alice Springs and the Roper River. Watt wrote:

Much of it was such a nightmare that it is best forgotten. But when I say that every road, every track, every cattle-yard and most of the close bush in which the cattle appeared on the screen was built by the unit, it will give some idea of the work we put in. And built by the unit means built by the technicians, the actors, the drivers, the cooks and the secretaries.[10]

The narrative begins with the enforced evacuation of a farm under a scorched earth policy. Those displaced join with a stockman, Dan McAlpine (Chips Rafferty), who has chosen to drive a massive herd of cattle overland rather than see them shot. Their venture is threatened en route by a water shortage, two stampedes and the herd jamming on a precipitous cliffside path. Horses are poisoned, one of the party is trampled, but once safely in Rockhampton, Queensland, almost the entire group are prepared to return across the vast continent for more cattle.

Watt's main achievement was the way in which he incorporated factual information learnt from his own inland research and from government files. This approach is soon evident when a commentary by Rafferty's Dan McAlpine character establishes the background with an explanation of routines such as the waking of cattle and the positioning of riders for the drive. Helped by the astringent harmonies of John Ireland's music score, the documentary style builds the impact of action sequences — especially the stampedes and the trapping of wild horses — and reinforces such suspense ingredients as the droving team's fears of Japanese invasion. The team's feelings of strategic insecurity come to represent that of most Australians at home during the war, for the team as portrayed by Watt becomes a

169

distillation of the Australian national character. At its centre is Chips Rafferty's interpretation of the typical bushman — a role central to this actor's work over the next two decades.

The 1940s revival

With the surrender of Japan on 14 August 1945, World War II was at an end. Two new Australian features were in production, and at least three more planned. Australian filmmakers were feeling optimistic because, besides the coming of peace and the expected release of manpower, there was a box-office boom to be considered. In 1942 Greater Union Theatres had earned its first substantial profit in more than a decade as Australians turned increasingly to cinema for escapism. Between 1942-43 and 1944-45, the number of cinema admissions rose from under 102 million to over 151 million, although once the war was over there was a small decline.

One early effect of the war had been the Government's restrictions on the earnings distributors could remit to their home offices in America. In 1943 Columbia Pictures was persuaded by the managing director of its Australian branch, N. P. Pery, to spend some of their accumulating capital on the production of an Australian feature. Pery chose Ken Hall to make the film and gave as his brief a subject that would portray the life of a world-famous Australian. For various reasons, the lives of Ned Kelly, Don Bradman and Nellie Melba were rejected, leaving Sir Charles Kingsford Smith as the leading contender. Not only was his Pacific flight of 1928 relevant to both America and Australia, but much of it could be filmed against the Cinesound studio's back-projection screen. The final budget, at £53 000, was more than twice that of the costliest Cinesound feature of the 1930s. Hall later remembered:

For the first time in my life I would have money to spend, real money. For the first time in my life I could let my head, and my imagination go a bit. There would be no restricting the story line because we could not afford it.[11]

Extensive screen testing for the title role of **Smithy** (1946) included Peter Finch and Dick Bentley, but at Pery's insistence Ron Randell was chosen as the one most likely to conform to the Hollywood ideal of good looks. The Cinesound team faced great difficulty in having to use worn-out equipment not renewed since the mid-1930s, but the result is remarkably fluid, combining patriotic sentiment and spectacle with Hollywood biographic practice. In preparing the script, Ken Hall realised that Kingsford Smith's disappearance at the film's end would have to be an anti-climax and the Pacific flight as the actual climax of his career would occur halfway through the story. To an extent this succeeds, with sentiment rising to a final pitch as a fleet of aircraft follow Smithy's self-sacrificing disappearance into a symbolic sunrise. In between, the pace drags by fixing on Smithy's personal doubts and domestic traumas. The excitement of the events that lead up to the Pacific challenge and the flight itself far more satisfactorily explain the hero's all-consuming perfectionism. The authenticity and enthusiasm with which they are rendered shows the Cinesound team at the peak of its abilities.

Hall worked hard to shape **Smithy** for an American market and the film contains more than the usual quota of Cinesound efforts to link Australian and American conventions. "Australia" is carefully distinguished from "Austria" and the Pacific flight means "as much to Uncle Sam as it does to Australia". Ironically almost all references to **Smithy**'s country of origin were deleted for its American release under the title **Pacific Adventure**. This order was said to come from Columbia's head, the impulsive Harry Cohn, who, despite good returns from **Smithy**, announced to Ken Hall in 1947 that Columbia did not intend to proceed with further Australian production.

Eric Porter's **A Son is Born** (1946) was completed before **Smithy**, shared its leading actors (Ron Randell and Muriel Steinbeck), but had a delayed release in order to capitalise on the later film's publicity. Porter, who had begun his film career as a camera assistant with Cinesound, had become a successful independent animator by the late 1930s. In spite of a drawn-out and frequently humourless plot, **A Son is Born** is a first feature of some stature. Against the inter-war period, the story features Randell and Steinbeck as an ungrateful son and his long-suffering mother, both of whose lives — despite the reformist intentions of second husband John McCallum — are influenced for the worse by the first husband, played by Peter Finch. The film shows a fundamental respect for the Hollywood conventions of the period, cushioning its melodrama in opulent surroundings which are nothing short of miraculous within a budget of £10 000. The visual impact of the film benefited from the close collaboration of Porter with the veteran cameraman Arthur Higgins who devised a special camera boom to swoop and soar, creating greater depth for the interiors. In the climax, set in wartime New Guinea, spectacular footage of an enemy attack shot by Damien Parer was intercut with the gunning-down of Randell and his final reconciliation with his estranged wife.

With **Always Another Dawn, Into the Straight** and **The Kangaroo Kid**, the Australian producers closest to achieving feature continuity during the 1940s were T. O. (Tom) and A. K. (Alec) McCreadie, theatre proprietors from Double Bay in Sydney. These two brothers injected cosmopolitan elements into Australian subjects for their first two features, and reversed the trend for the third, a co-production.

Always Another Dawn (1948), is a story of naval heroics which, although lethargically paced, is redeemed by an engagingly sentimental view of the Australian countryside that recalls the painterly nationalism in the surviving films of Franklyn Barrett. Throughout the McCreadies' next two films this feeling is replaced by strictly commercial priorities. In this regard, **Into the Straight** (1949) is a transitional work, both for the McCreadies and for the entire production industry between the late 1940s and the early 1950s. Its pot-pourri of past formulas includes English new chums, horseracing, an underhand spendthrift son of a wealthy squatting family and a musical climax. The spirited direction of Tom McCreadie almost makes the mixture work, but the central tale of the crippled heroine's miracle recovery too often has an air of desperation.

It was hardly surprising that **The Kangaroo Kid** (1950) returned more single-mindedly to proven ground — in this case the heroics and dastardly villainy reminiscent of **The Man from Kangaroo** (1920). Further similarity lay in the importation of an American director, Lesley Selander, and American leads Jock O'Mahoney and Martha Hyer. In the Western genre, **The Kangaroo Kid** is barely Australian, although its bizarre range of backgrounds, including the Aboriginals and fauna, places it in the comic-strip class. Perhaps the film's only achievement was the expertise passed on by American technicians to the employees at the McCreadies' usual base, the studio of Commonwealth Film Laboratories in Sydney. Any promise of further production continuity by the McCreadies came to an end; personal and financial difficulties forced them apart and both vanished from the field leaving further co-production plans in the air.

The McCreadies' ultimate move to a subject set in Australia's past added yet another to the list of Australian features of the late 1940s and early 1950s which tackled historical themes. Just as many novels of the time employed backgrounds of the distant past, the films **Strong is the Seed**, **Sons of Matthew**, **Eureka Stockade**, **The Glenrowan Affair**, **Bitter Springs**, **Kangaroo** and **Captain Thunderbolt** endeavoured to find their market through familiar pageantry. Several, like **Strong is the Seed** and **Kangaroo**, were strictly commercial exercises; but others served their makers as parables for the period's nationalistic and political preoccupations. In the former category, the most successful was Charles Chauvel's pioneering saga, **Sons of Matthew**.

This production was prompted by two books by the Queensland author, Bernard O'Reilly — *Green Mountains* and *Cullenbenbong*. Drawing inspiration from these and memories of his own boyhood Chauvel, in collaboration with his wife Elsa and Maxwell Dunn, developed the story of rural pioneering by the large O'Riordan family in New South Wales and southern Queensland. As interpreted by Chauvel, the trailblazing family unit was to represent the best qualities of nation building.

With backing from Universal Pictures and Greater Union, **Sons of Matthew** was filmed during Queensland's wettest season for eighty years. The delays were frequent. After months of scant progress Universal's Herc McIntyre and Greater Union's Norman Rydge visited the location to order Chauvel to finish the film closer to Sydney or abandon it altogether. Chauvel somehow persuaded his visitors of the absolute need to complete **Sons of Matthew** on the Queensland location and, taking a second expedition into account, was to film there for a total of eleven months. The result of this and further bad weather boosted the budget to £120 000.

The production logistics were formidable. A large contingent including actors, child actors and technicians had to be accommodated at remote hotels and boarding houses. Incessant rain delayed the start of filming by six weeks.

After an initial six months on the Lamington Plateau, followed by a spell in the studio, Chauvel returned to the Plateau and then shot additional scenes in the Blue Mountains, west of Sydney. The production was completed in mid-1948. Key members of crew and cast worked for eighteen months on the film by which time nearly all of the original script had been radically revised.

Chauvel's perfectionism, given virtual free rein for the first time, resulted in a cleverly-constructed and stirring saga. The land-clearing and farm-building scenes on the Lamington Plateau have particular exuberance and documentary impact, and the catastrophes — a bushfire and a cyclone — are believably harrowing. Although the broad symbolic implications of national achievement, coupled with Chauvel's tendency to showcase the landscape, sometimes makes the main conflict between the two brothers stand out in melodramatic separation, the portrayal of family relationships is for the most part tight and convincing.

Despite good reactions in Australia the film did not return its budget from the local market. The response from Britain and America was poor at first but after concentrated publicity **Sons of Matthew** moved into profit from its UK takings. With **Forty Thousand Horsemen** and **Smithy**, it was one of the film industry's major successes of the 1940s.

Cinesound's eclipse

After the release of **Smithy**, Cinesound had every reason to be optimistic about the revival of its own feature production. The studio maintained its stature throughout the war years and in early 1946 there was talk of co-production with the British Rank Organisation. But the event that initially made this likely — the purchase by Rank of half the shares in Cinesound's parent company, the exhibitor-distributor Greater Union Theatres — ultimately proved to be as threatening to local production as the Fox purchase of Hoyts had been in 1930.

At first the intended co-production programme had the approval of J. Arthur Rank himself who was impressed by the success of **The Over-landers** and, like Hall, was eager to film a sizeable adaptation of *Robbery Under Arms*. In November 1946 Hall visited England to discuss with the Rank production head Earl St John the preparations for what promised to be the Australian industry's most ambitious enterprise to date. In addition to production work and guaranteed release of the output, the agreement was to involve Rank's aid in the refurbishing and expansion of the Pagewood studios in Sydney. The *Australasian Exhibitor* predicted that if the Cinesound-Rank plans were ''actually only bally-hoo, then it will be bad luck for Ken [Hall]. He'll never get such a chance again!''.[12]

For Norman Rydge the seeds of doubt were sown early. During his trip to England in 1945 to negotiate the Rank purchase, Rydge had been persuaded by Herc McIntyre to invest £10 000 of Greater Union's money in **Sons of Matthew**. By the time Hall returned to Australia Rydge was openly expressing alarm at the film's lengthening schedule and rising budget. Added to this was the Greater Union Board's growing timidity at the prospect of co-production with Rank and Ealing, an enterprise which they feared would lead their company beyond its financial capacity.[13]

In April 1947 an event occurred that exacerbated these doubts. In an attempt to combat the domination in the UK of American film interests, the British Labour Government proposed to tax seventy-five per cent of the earnings from all imported films. In Australia, news of the proposal (which never became truly effective) was sufficient for Greater Union to conveniently terminate the co-production plans. Norman Rydge told the *Sunday Sun* of 31 August: "Until the opportunity of obtaining revenue again becomes possible there can be little hope for the Australian film industry." When the British tax was lifted, the Rank Organisation — which had produced films prolifically in order to replace an anticipated downturn in the supply of American films — was in no financial position to reconsider Australian production. Rank's priority was to recoup as much as possible from the films already made — a priority which Greater Union was fully prepared to accept. Greater Union suffered a decline in postwar box-office receipts; the link with Rank had at least enabled a strengthening of its position with the purchase of more theatres. The screening of a guaranteed supply of imported films in its own theatres, rather than entertaining any thought of its own feature production, was to be company policy within Greater Union for the next twenty-five years.

Cinesound, which had not been given the opportunity to make a self-sufficient feature film since 1940, found itself in no position to argue. Greater Union discouraged any replacement of the company's obsolete production facilities by closing down the Cinesound laboratory in July 1948 and selling the Bondi studio in 1950. In early 1951 the remainder of the staff and equipment was moved to the former Amusu cinema in Balmain. Ken Hall and his staff were "banished to years of utter frustration"[14], with only newsreel and documentary output to justify the company's continued existence.

Cinesound's disappearance from feature film production was a severe blow to the optimism of postwar Australian producers. From **On Our Selection** to **Smithy**, Hall's studio team had proved its ability to make well-crafted films that could compete on both home and overseas markets. That Cinesound was not permitted to continue proved that financial conservatism was becoming the accepted thinking, and that the industry's momentum was already on the wane. In a postwar social climate that placed emphasis on national growth and international prominence, community support for a local film industry was to diminish more than at any time previously.

Documentary hopes

Since the early war years, sweeping changes had taken place within Australian society. The war had brought an end to the Depression which had crippled and demoralised the country. A new sense of national unity, born of wartime solidarity and expanded industrial growth, together with the experience earned by servicemen abroad, sharpened responses to the wider world. Interest in the arts increased. Literary journals promoted the importance of defending Australian culture in the face of outside threat, and in painting and poetry the modest radical developments begun in the late 1930s were continued. The questioning of past attitudes and allegiances was again revised together with hopes for a new kind of postwar world.

Discontent with the political past and a prevailing intellectual vacuum manifested itself in new dissident groups. With Russia an ally during the war years, Communism moved openly into the foreground of intellectual concern. The New Theatre movements of Sydney and Melbourne staged socialist plays by Clifford Odets and Sean O'Casey and encouraged new left-wing writers to contribute Australian works. From 1945, the Realist Film Association of Victoria began the nationwide distribution and screening of socialist films, and the following year the Association itself embarked on five years' production of short documentaries, newsreels and compilation films.

The postwar introduction of large-scale European immigration (the greatest influx since the 1850s gold rushes) brought new life styles and consumer needs. Along with the outward signs such as delicatessens and coffee lounges came an increasing acceptance of imported culture, including Continental films.

Federal Government administration had become more complex in the course of the war and when the war was over many of the businessmen and young academics who had been recruited into government remained to initiate plans for the future. Under the guidance of Dr H. C. Coombs, the Department of Post-War Reconstruction added to the more obvious objectives (such as immigration and full employment) some new initiatives which included government support for the arts and higher education. This new recognition for the arts was to include a Commonwealth Cultural Council and a National Film Board.[15]

Film societies were an important part of the new cultural diversification, both in the way they served adult education and the way they helped to develop an intellectual appreciation of cinema. A recommendation by John Grierson on the promotion of 16 mm non-theatrical film in Australia had been adopted by the New South Wales State Cabinet, which created the Documentary Films Committee of New South Wales in June 1940. The Committee's first president was the State Education Minister, David Henry Drummond, who had urged the use of film in schools during the 1930s and, like others who met Grierson during his tour, was convinced of the need to develop a national documentary movement. The Committee's principal role was to acquire and distribute non-theatrical films throughout the State, and with the aid of a grant from the Department of Education, it gradually built up a large 16 mm informational film-lending collection. By 1946 the Premiers of the other States agreed to set up advisory committees to represent all those who wanted to use film ''for such purposes as education, social development and trade expansion'', and who would ''advise the [National

Film] Board of State needs and organise distribution within each State".[16]

By 1950 prominent film societies in Sydney included the Sydney Film Society, the University Film Group, the Independent Film Group, and the WEA Film Study Group. By 1951 Sydney joined Melbourne in starting a Realist Film Association. The Sydney Film Society had among its members filmmakers from the DOI's Film Division. It published its own journal, *Film*. Other publications of the period, which contributed in various ways to quality film criticism, included *Realist Film News*, published by the Realist Film Association of Victoria, and the more conservative *Film Guide*.

As the war had progressed Australians became conscious of documentary in a variety of forms. As well as official Australian newsreels, theatre screens presented the immediacy of war through British Ministry of Information films and the documentaries of the National Film Board of Canada. Imported training and educational documentaries were screened outside the theatre circuits to the armed services and in the last year of the war the presence in Australia of the internationally-renowned documentarists Harry Watt and Joris Ivens helped to bring the documentary greater recognition.

With the decline of feature production in the 1940s, documentary filmmaking in privately-sponsored as well as government contexts brought opportunities to both established and up-and-coming filmmakers. Independents like John Kingsford Smith, Mervyn Murphy, James Pearson and Mervyn Scales, who each made a variety of sponsored films, had all entered the film industry by the mid-1930s and worked on other people's films before establishing their own companies. But for almost a decade after the war the greatest concentration of postwar film talent was to be employed by the newly-formed Film Division of the Australian National Film Board.

The first solid progress towards the formation of the Board was a proposal made at a meeting convened by the Commonwealth Government in June 1944. In September a specific recommendation toward this end was made by a conference organised by the Ministers for Information and Post-War Reconstruction. The departments subsequently organised an inter-departmental committee to study the feasibility of establishing a Film Board similar to those of Canada and New Zealand; on the committee's recommendation, the Australian National Film Board was established by Cabinet on 26 April 1945. The Board's principal purpose was to produce and screen documentary films about Australia and to arrange the screening of imported documentaries, in conjunction with the State Governments. The Board was to be linked with the Department of Information for administrative purposes and the DOI's reconstituted Film Division became the Board's production arm. The National Library was to fulfil the Board's film acquisition and distribution scheme, collaborating with State advisory committees.[17]

The Board was intended to parallel its Grierson-inspired British and Canadian counterparts. In mid-1946, Professor Alan Stout, a foundation member (as well as chairman of the New South Wales Documentary Films Committee), stated that the Board is not just a Government propaganda machine ... In their own productions, they seek to give a true and objective picture of Australian life and Australian problems, to encourage self-criticism rather than complacency, to inform rather than to sell a policy.[18]

In September 1945, Ralph Foster, who had visited Australia on behalf of the National Film Board of Canada, was appointed the Australian National Film Board's Film Commissioner, a title which Grierson himself had held as head of the Canadian body. But very quickly Foster learned that his position was in no way equivalent to that held by Grierson in Canada and the Australian organisation would have none of the autonomy which had made the progressive NFBC relatively immune from direct government control. The restricting factor was the Board's connection with the Department of Information. While the original seven members, chaired by Arthur Calwell as Minister for Information, ostensibly represented a wide spectrum of government and community film needs, the Department clearly saw the Board as little more than an instrument for its own publicity needs. After several months of meetings, Calwell directed E. G. Bonney, Director-General of the DOI, to take over as chairman. Bonney, a former journalist and a wartime Chief Publicity Censor, was opposed to Film Board autonomy. Alan Stout, the only non-Public Service member, later wrote:

I soon found myself at odds with Mr Bonney's film policy. It seemed that he wanted the Board to be primarily an instrument of the DOI and its films to be propaganda.

Stout stood his ground in pressing for the kind of films that he and other followers of Grierson had advocated:

There were other Board members (not to mention the people who actually made the films) who shared my view, but as a private citizen I was in a stronger position to express it.

However, I didn't last long. I was unceremoniously removed from the Board in December 1946 with what were palpably specious excuses.[19]

Stout's departure signalled a reorganisation within the bureaucratic ranks. The new Board consisted entirely of government department heads, and through its chairmanship (with E. G. Bonney being replaced by Kevin Murphy, the new DOI Director-General, in 1948), the DOI aimed increasingly at controlling the production policy and operations. Ulrich Ellis, another former member, wrote to the *Sydney Morning Herald* stating that the Board had been "knocked on the head" because "certain members exhibited an imaginative approach" ...

The members of the film organisations established as a result of Grierson's visit in 1940, or formed subsequently, will be dismayed at the retrograde step now taken ... Film societies and other organisations which pinned their faith to the National Film Board are entitled to some ministerial explanation of the Government's action in replacing the original board by an inter-departmental committee controlled by the Department of Information.

We feel that something more than an explanation is required.[20]

Writing also to the *Herald*, Harry Watt urged creative freedom for government filmmaking: "If you want a good film made, get a sincere filmmaker and leave him alone".[21]

In spite of these manoeuvres, the Division's early years were creatively strong. Under Ralph Foster the staff nucleus comprised former war correspondents, Cinema Branch employees, and others who had minimal film experience but did have fresh ideas. The most impressive director of the period was John Heyer, a freelance technician who had moved into documentary filmmaking during the war and was a stalwart of the postwar film society movement. His **Journey of a Nation** (1947), pressing for standardisation of Australia's railway gauges, and **The Valley is Ours** (1948), showing the work of soldier-settlers along the Murray River, display a conscious national style. Mixing sympathetic observation of ordinary individuals with imaginative interpretation of the life that surrounds them, Heyer utilises personal commentary, dramatised cameos, point-of-view shots, swooping aerials and, in the earlier film, stylised model shots that ridicule the national rail disunity. Through its objective and execution, **Journey of a Nation** (scripted by Catherine Duncan) is one of the most persuasive of the many DOI films of the time which close with an optimistic affirmation of the country's faith in reaching goals of postwar reconstruction.

Ralph Foster, in his capacity as Film Commissioner and Director of the Film Division, took an active role in directing several films, among them the quietly assertive **Namatjira the Painter** (1947), and supervising the production of films like Heyer's **Men and Mobs** (1947), before his return to Canada at the end of his twelve months stay. His place in the new position of Producer-in-Chief was taken by a fellow disciple of Grierson, Stanley Hawes. Hawes was to remain until his retirement in 1970, doing more than any other individual to train, build and sustain the Division in the face of bureaucratic antipathy.

As Grierson had done in the 1930s, Hawes set about seeking industrial as well as government cooperation for the sponsored part of the Division's production programme, gaining commissions from a number of government departments willing to sponsor films. The second part of the Division's programme was, and has continued to be, films made on the Division's own funding and initiative. Hawes ultimately was to participate in or oversee the production of more than 500 films at the Division, which in 1956 became known as the Commonwealth Film Unit. His own **School in the Mailbox** (1946), an ambitious and engaging account of the New South Wales correspondence school system, was recognised by an American Academy Award nomination in 1947.

Early in 1948 the Division moved from its three rooms in King Street in Sydney to larger accommodation in buildings lent by the Department of Education in the suburb of Burwood. Its King Street premises had adjoined those of Mervyn Murphy of Supreme Sound System, who hired equipment and staff to the Division until it had built up its own resources. This work helped Murphy expand Supreme Sound, which was also to be one of the earliest companies sub-contracted to make films on behalf of the new Division.

Contributing visitors

Two overseas filmmakers who visited Australia in the late 1940s were to make vastly different contributions to Australian cinema. Unlike other visitors of the next decade who dropped in to use the countryside as the background for one film's exotic locale and left as soon as possible, both Joris Ivens and Ralph Smart had worked in Australia for several years before embarking on their noteworthy projects.

Joris Ivens, the internationally-famed maker of documentaries including **Rain** (1929), **New Earth** (1934) and **Spanish Earth** (1937), had been appointed Film Commissioner for the Netherlands East Indies Government in October 1944. With a staff of 185 at his disposal and operating from Australia, he was placed in charge of films made by the NEI Film and Photographic Unit to report the Netherlands' Pacific war effort, along with propaganda items to boost the morale of Dutch Indonesians in their territorial fight against the Japanese.[22] Following the defeat of Japan, Ivens, in league with Edmund Allison, Marion Michelle, Catherine Duncan and occasional helpers like Harry Watt and Peter Finch, began secretly to make **Indonesia Calling** in support of the new Indonesian republic. The film, shot for the most part around Sydney Harbour, showed the refusal of seamen and waterside workers to man Dutch ships containing arms and ammunition for attacks on Indonesia. **Indonesia Calling** employs strong, emotive images and montage reminiscent of Russian propaganda classics. Its strengths are the commentary, spoken with quiet conviction by Peter Finch, and scenes of the inexorable build-up of support by unionists climaxed by the dramatised pursuit and halting in mid-harbour of one of the Dutch ships. It was a type of film not previously made in Australia and it was to influence the formation of the Waterside Workers' Federation Film Unit in 1951. Despite attempts at suppression, **Indonesia Calling** was screened the world over. After official investigations and newspaper exposure had revealed his hand in the project, Ivens resigned from the NEI unit and returned to Europe.

In early 1947 Ralph Smart produced and directed a film with vastly different motives. Smart, of Australian parentage and with British film experience, had made wartime films for the RAAF and worked as associate producer and uncredited writer on **The Overlanders**. **Bush Christmas** was to be the first of a series of feature-length productions made by the Children's Entertainment Film division (later Children's Film Foundation) of Gaumont-British Instructional. The division had been formed under the initiative of J. Arthur Rank who required children's films for the Saturday morning cinema clubs of his Odeon and Gaumont circuits. Contracted by the division's director, Mary Field (for whom he had written documentaries in the 1930s), Smart developed a story for children between the ages of seven and twelve. He subsequently wrote:

There was no tradition or established technique to follow. It seemed important that the film should have as much action and as little dialogue as possible; our plot should be extremely simple. Above all we had to be careful not to patronise or play down to our audience.[23]

Smart's script was written with Chips Rafferty in mind as one of three villainous horse thieves pursued into mountain country and trapped by six holidaying children. As the children keep out of sight and start to build up a war of nerves, the pursued begin to believe they are being trailed by a large-scale posse.

Alan J. Williamson, who had worked with Cozens Spencer in the 1910s and helped engineer the **Flying Doctor** co-production deal in 1936, served as unofficial executive producer on behalf of the Rank Organisation. George Heath was chosen by Smart as cameraman for his ability to ''capture the sharp, brilliant out-door qualities of the bush country'',[24] and as casting director, Chips Rafferty selected four white children (Helen Grieve, Michael Yardley, Maurice Unicomb, Nicky Yardley) who had acting experience, together with an Aboriginal boy (Ebenezer Saunders) he had found on a Queensland reserve. The four months Blue Mountains shoot was a happy affair that contrasted with the rigours of the **Sons of Matthew** unit which was filming concurrently. This is evident in the relaxed naturalism of the children's performances and the relish of the thieves played by Rafferty, John Fernside and Stan Tolhurst. The bright adaptability of the children opposed to the tangle-footed villains is a source of constant delight and eventually ensured the film's fame and continuing popularity. Like **The Overlanders**, **Bush Christmas** combines a crisp documentary feeling for locations with events that flow naturally from their moods and challenges. The scene of the children's Christmas dinner is a mixture of comedy and desperation as the white children pick with polite repulsion at their cooked snake, and the youngest hurls a billycan at a mocking kookaburra. The highlight has the crooks trying to emerge from a valley only to be blocked by a succession of falling boulders aimed too accurately to be accidental. ''It's a put-up job, all right'', declares Rafferty after the third rock has hurtled by him.

Ealing comes to stay

Sons of Matthew and **Eureka Stockade**, the two biggest films to enter production in Australia during the 1940s, were begun in 1947. Both were embarked upon with high hopes for the prestige of the industry; each was delayed at the outset by unprecedented rain; and the growth of their scale and budgets fuelled doubts about a permanent postwar Australian production industry.

Following the huge commercial and critical success of **The Overlanders**

Harry Watt was able to persuade Ealing that his next suggestion was equally viable — **Eureka Stockade** (1949). He wrote:

This was one of the subjects I'd found when investigating the Australian scene. We documentary people had never tackled history, and here was an important historical moment that fell so perfectly into film shape that there was no need to distort events or create false situations. It could be treated completely realistically.[25]

Again Watt immersed himself in six months of concentrated research. All the written accounts of the Eureka Stockade miners' rebellion of 1854 were compared; Watt visited Ballarat in Victoria, the scene of the conflict, to talk to locals and search through libraries and museums while a further team of researchers conducted a detailed study of goldfields life, work, and personal possessions. A mining town and its gold diggings were created on a vast scale near Singleton (NSW), and the Federal Government lent hundreds of Army personnel to work as extras and production assistants. However, **Eureka Stockade** came close to being abandoned just weeks before production was due to start when the British Government announced its tax on foreign film imports. After a frustrating delay, production began with the assurance that it could count as a British film if it was imported and employed a greater proportion of English artists and technicians. Watt recalls that the initial setback of the proposed film tax "started a run of bad luck from which we never quite recovered".[26] In the first five weeks of the schedule, the heavy rain permitted only five days of filming; roads turned into quagmires, the miners' tent city was twice blown to the ground, and Chips Rafferty broke two ribs in fight scenes, then burnt his hands in a fire rescue. With the return of good weather, two units — the second under the direction of Leslie Norman — sometimes filmed around the clock. Eighty per cent of the production was shot on location, with Watt packing in every possible background with his hundreds of extras. Since the tax plans had terminated an order for new equipment, most of the filming was done with a camera George Heath built himself.

For the elaborate interiors, Ealing re-equipped the Pagewood studio, which had badly deteriorated since the early 1940s. By now, **Eureka Stockade** had grown greatly from the scale first envisaged, and its budget had increased to around £200 000 — nearly twice that of **Sons of Matthew**. In May 1948, after six months of solid work, shooting was complete. The delays and compromises took their toll on the finished film. Watt had lost the thread of his original intention to have **Eureka Stockade** serve as a statement on national independence; and a crucial factor had been Ealing's insistence that Chips Rafferty be cast as the rebellion's leader Peter Lalor. The portrayal, although earnest, robbed the film of much of its ideological depth, and other attempts to save it brought fragmentation that left little substance apart from spectacle. The regular herding of miners for licence inspections, the burning of the Eureka Hotel and the attack on the stockade are evoked with fine precision. But after the fighting the significance of the events is little

181

examined, and the film limps to its close with the quiet re-emergence of Lalor as a tamed conservative politician in the Victorian Legislative Assembly.

Even before **The Overlanders**, Ealing had decided that absolute commitment to a continuing Australian schedule depended on its ability to find a co-production partner. In February 1948 the company's chairman, Major Reginald Baker, arrived to investigate the extent of his company's operations in Australia and in particular to commence discussions with Greater Union Theatres. One of Ealing's hopes in producing **The Overlanders** had been that if the film succeeded, an organisation like Greater Union could be talked into joint production plans. The proposition Baker put to Norman Rydge was that if Greater Union paid for a quarter of the cost of each film, they would automatically hold rights to Australian distribution and, as preferential security, would obtain a proportion of Ealing's rest-of-the-world returns if an Australian return was not profitable. Rydge, however, remained unreceptive. Reginald Baker remembered:

I found that the idea of being mixed up with production operations here didn't appeal to him, frankly, in the slightest. He would much rather say, ''I'll give you a few hundred pounds advance when you deliver the film to me. Then I'll do my best to get money out of it.'' But he didn't want to take a plunge, and have any money in the production of a film. And I think I went back rather disappointed.[27]

For the second time in six months, Rydge had rejected a co-production proposal. But Ealing, probably caught up in the euphoria and high expectations of **Eureka Stockade**, were prepared to persist. Before his departure, Baker purchased the lease of the Pagewood studio from Greater Union, who the year before had acquired it as part of their first co-production plans with Ealing through Rank. In August, following the production of **Eureka Stockade**, Harry Watt announced that Ealing would establish a permanent unit in Australia, with Pagewood as its headquarters. The company was now to spend £25 000 on further improving the studio and would employ a holding staff of eighteen. Production supervisor Eric Williams announced that Ealing, in investing money that might otherwise have been taken from the country in box office returns, would help to build up the industry and improve the export prospects of other producers. Harry Watt claimed:

We have started to put Australian films on the screens of the world. We've raised the pay of both technicians and actors in Australia by about 100 per cent. And we've given creative work to a lot of people who otherwise were smothering with frustration. And it looks as though they're going to get a bit of continuity of employment now. The Government National Films [sic] Board, under Stan Hawes, is doing excellent work, and many of the young people who started with us are working there. Ealing is continuing. Local feature production is on the increase.[28]

But bad luck continued to plague Ealing's Australian venture. Although **Eureka Stockade** on its world release in early 1949 proved a costly failure, Ealing was already committed to proceed, and in May 1949 began the production of **Bitter Springs** under the direction of Ralph Smart. Again, like a repeated omen, severe rain struck the company soon after its arrival on location in Quorn, South Australia, forcing a reduction in schedule and more dire compromise. For Ralph Smart, compromise had already begun during preproduction with Ealing rewriting his script and the studio insisting that the English comedian Tommy Trinder be cast in a leading role. Smart's story, in line with customary Ealing liberalism, told of white–Aboriginal conflict over the ownership of tribal lands in 1900. Where his original script had ended with the whites' full-scale massacre of the Aboriginals, the new version had the miraculous transformation of determined blacks into easygoing sheep hands.

To counterbalance the blinkered self-interest of settler Wally King (Chips Rafferty), a trooper, played by Michael Pate, was never too far from the action to mediate and, in the Western-style climax, to lead a last minute rescue mission. That **Bitter Springs** manages occasionally to have an impact is due once more to the visual collaboration between Smart and George Heath and the general good intentions shining through what had been, from Smart's recollection, the most frustrating experience of his career.[29]

Ealing now held out for another attempt to set up co-production while its Pagewood studio was rented to the American independent Michael S. Gordon for **Wherever She Goes** (1951) and to Twentieth Century-Fox for **Kangaroo** (1952). In early 1951, definite co-production seemed imminent with Kenhall Productions, in which Ken Hall as producer-director was to be backed by the names of people who had been prominent in the Australian film trade and production for many years. Ealing, as part of the joint investment proposal, guaranteed world-wide distribution through its Rank connection and the first project of the joint undertaking was to be **Robbery Under Arms**.

Neither side had reckoned on intervention from a force more unrelenting than the rains of 1947 to 1949. In December 1949, Ben Chifley's Labor Government was replaced by Robert Menzies's Liberal–Country Party coalition. In mid-1951 the Capital Issues Board of the Department of National Development, attempting to curb inflation, prohibited the formation of public companies for specified undertakings whose capital exceeded £10 000 — and this included the production of films. Despite strong appeals for clemency, Hall's company was prevented from issuing a prospectus and raising capital. In January 1952, Eric Williams, as Ealing's Australian production supervisor, announced to the press:

as it seems that there is no Australian sponsorship for films to be produced at Pagewood, the company's board has very reluctantly decided to close down the Pagewood plant.

A year later, Ealing sold the studio to Associated TV for £27 000.

Influenced by the war, the 1940s had seen the rise of documentary as a creative force, the disappearance of Cinesound as a feature producer and its virtual replacement by Ealing, who for five years were encouraged in various ways by the Labor Government to remain and produce features in Australia. Now that the financial strategies of big business and Liberal–Country Party government were bypassing film production, it seemed as if the industry was facing a blackout once again.

8

Into the void
1951–64

The 1950s saw Australia become part of what Marshall McLuhan was to call the "global village". Ideally, the introduction of television should have guaranteed consistent employment for those fleeing from the void in feature film activity; but, no less than before, it saw a continuing drain of Australian creative talent. Although several former feature-film directors remained to work on sponsored documentaries, actors and writers left in droves for England and America. Many had been put out of work by the body blow dealt by the new electronic medium to radio drama, once a flourishing local industry. Early hopes that the production of Australian television drama would employ the displaced personnel were soon dashed. A government inquiry into television in 1963 reported that:

Our actors are still leaving Australia because they cannot earn a living in Australia. They almost invariably do well overseas. The situation would be Gilbertian if it were not so serious.[1]

As wartime idealism and postwar euphoria died away, fears prompted by the Cold War and its supposed threat of global Communism were used by the Menzies Government as justification for tightening strategic links with America and creating a smokescreen in order to make its own heavily paternalistic policies more palatable.

Throughout the 1950s, Australia's allegiances were gradually transferred from Britain to America — in matters of trade, defence and foreign policy. By the 1960s investment in Australia by the United States exceeded that of Britain, although Prime Minister Menzies continued to emphasise the importance of British Empire ties. During the war and for twenty years afterwards, the introduction of American consumer goods, music, films and television dominated Australia's social and cultural life. Anything Australian was often considered second-rate; the plentiful supply of new American products suited the expanding affluence and sense of well-being that had been absent from the nation for decades.

The maintenance of a stable economy and high standard of living depended increasingly on huge overseas investments in Australian business, and the rate at which the country was repaying its foreign investors reached $300 million a year by 1965-66.[2] The largest sections of the film trade had been overseas-owned for years, and under an agreement in November 1948 with the Federal Government, distributors were allowed to return seventy per cent of their profits to the United States. Six years earlier, the Government had reduced distributors' income tax from thirty to ten per cent and this, together with a high wartime rate of cinema-going, could only help to boost profits. The president of the Motion Picture Association of America, in his Annual Report for 1952-53, looked forward to the continuation of Australia as "a good, stable market for American pictures", and stated:

The American companies have been able to realise from this market a steady flow of earnings, thanks to the cooperative spirit of Australian government officials and their informed interest in American film distribution problems.[3]

Local films suffered from the production industry's general lack of momentum and less support than ever from the film trade. Newsreels and a growing number of documentaries kept an industry of sorts alive, if at subsistence level, but regular production of feature films was a dead issue by the mid-1950s. In the opinion of Margaret Cardin, an experienced film editor who arrived from England to settle in 1950, and who from the 1960s became the industry's leading film negative cutter, Australia had no film industry to even remotely compare with the one she had left. Director Cecil Holmes, with whom Cardin was to work the following year on **Captain Thunderbolt**, wrote in 1954:

However remarkable film production may have been in this country in past years, it is quickly becoming a lost tradition. Australian films make no impact on the Australian people: they have little significance culturally or economically because they are virtually non-existent.[4]

In Holmes's opinion, the question of distribution and control was

fundamental to an understanding of the reasons for the disappearance of stable film production in Australia. It is hard to deny the conclusion that as American capital has extended and strengthened its control of the Australian film business, so have opportunities for production dwindled. After all, why should big organisations like Hoyts and Greater Union, whose connections extend into production in other countries, bother with Australian films?[5]

Hoyts by this time owned or controlled 185 theatres and Greater Union 128, nearly all of them in city or key suburban locations. Out of a total of twenty-five cinemas in central Sydney, only two were independent, two were owned by MGM and the remainder by Hoyts and Greater Union.[6] Three hundred and seventy-six feature films were imported during the 1952-53 financial year, while only three local features were produced, and only one (**The Phantom Stockman**) was released.

Cecil Holmes and Associated TV

Cecil Holmes was one of the most promising of a handful of new directors who might have gone on to contribute much valuable work to Australian narrative cinema under more favourable circumstances. Born in New Zealand, he had joined the National Film Unit there as a newsreel editor and later became a senior director of documentaries. In 1949 he moved to Australia at the invitation of John Heyer who had been appointed as production head of the Australian branch of the Shell Film Unit the year before. Holmes directed a documentary for Shell, **The Food Machine** (1950), before becoming involved in the production activities of Associated TV which was run by a fellow New Zealander, Colin Scrimgeour, in partnership with the theatrical entrepreneur Sir Benjamin Fuller. Holmes's first two films, begun in mid-1950, were puppet shorts intended for American television. Next, he directed three advertising films, again using puppets (and this time in bi-pack colour), for the Wrigley Company. Then, in early 1951, he began **Captain Thunderbolt**.

Cecil Holmes chose the true story of the Australian bushranger Fred "Thunderbolt" Ward in answer to Scrimgeour's request that he prepare an Australian Western. Starting from his own opinion that the best of Australian films had been characterised by their "folk quality . . . recognisable and often authentic"[7], Holmes, working with the scriptwriter Creswick Jenkinson, portrayed Thunderbolt as a folk hero and the victim of class oppression. In view of the left-wing political sympathies held by Holmes and Scrimgeour, it is not surprising that Thunderbolt's chief adversary, a prison-warder-turned-sergeant figure, is presented as something of a ruthless colonial fascist, opposed to all that Thunderbolt stands for. The film, modestly budgeted at £15 000 (provided entirely by Sir Benjamin Fuller), is dramatically uneven, although redeemed by its strong commitment and social context. Another bonus is the vivid, adventurous camerawork of Ross Wood, constantly on the move and making good use of the cloudscapes, strangely shaped boulders and twisted trees of the New England area of New South Wales.

Captain Thunderbolt (previewed January, 1953) was not released in Australia until four years after completion, but within two years had returned its money. After a premiere in London's West End, it was screened in the USA, Canada and New Zealand as well as West Germany, Spain and other non-English speaking countries. The film was initially rejected by the Australian exhibition interests of MGM, Hoyts and Greater Union, and had its first Sydney showing in a two-week season at the Lyric Theatre, described by Holmes as "the dingiest cinema available in downtown George Street".[8]

As "Uncle Scrim", Colin Scrimgeour had been one of New Zealand's leading radio personalities in the 1930s. Later, as New Zealand's Controller of Broadcasting, he was sent to America to study developments in television. In 1943, after a petty disagreement with the Minister for Broadcasting, he was dismissed from his position and in the late 1940s he faced twenty years' deportation for holding Communist views. He travelled to Australia and entered radio production, forming Associated Programmes to specialise in drama and variety shows. In 1949, he established Associated TV, displaying his interest in producing films for the American television market and preparing for the time when local transmissions would begin. The next decade was to bring a continuation of Scrimgeour's bad luck, giving him cause to recall later that almost from the outset, his company's efforts were "blocked by the stubborn obstinacy of the cinema people, and by the newspaper people who wanted to own television if it did come into being".[9]

The introduction of television into Australia had only been achieved after considerable delay. In 1941-42 a Joint Parliamentary Committee on Broadcasting looked into the likelihood of its introduction. After the formation of the Australian Broadcasting Control Board in 1948 the Chifley Government expressed its intention to permit television, at first exclusively transmitted by a national or government-run service. In June 1950 the new Menzies Government announced that television would be introduced more gradually than Labor had proposed, beginning with one station in Sydney for the national service (to be operated by the Australian Broadcasting Commission), and one commercial licence each for Sydney and Melbourne. Early in 1952 the plans were deferred because of the economic recession, but a year later the Government passed its first legislation for the establishment of the stations. At the same time, it set up a Royal Commission to provide "a full opportunity for expression of responsible opinions on the subject of television". The Labor opposition criticised the decision to legislate for commercial stations even before the Royal Commission had commenced its hearings, but in 1954 the Commission recommended a single national station and two commercial stations in Sydney and Melbourne.[10]

Colin Scrimgeour's main objective in entering film production with Associated TV had been to reinforce his credentials as an applicant for one of the two Sydney commercial television licences. The lack of a local release and delayed returns for **Captain Thunderbolt** proved to be a major setback, and he disbanded Associated TV's production crew. In January 1953, partly supported by the viable operations of Associated Programmes, his radio company, he reorganised his television interests by arranging for Sir Benjamin Fuller (his partner and a director of the company, along with Fuller's right-hand man, Lyall Grant) to obtain finance from the Rural Bank and other backers to purchase the lease of the Pagewood film studio from Ealing. The complex was optimistically renamed "Television City", and Associated waited for almost two years for the television hearings while earning good money by hiring the studio to Treasure Island Pictures for their feature film and twenty-six part television series **Long John Silver**.

Before and during the licence hearings which began in January 1955, Scrimgeour attracted wide attention and raised production hopes with his declaration that Associated TV would be heavily involved in local content. Initially, all went well, with Associated TV's application supported by several eminent political figures. But unsavoury publicity continued to dog Scrimgeour, reducing his effectiveness in the competition against the tightly organised lobbying of the powerful media conglomerates. The revelation of a secret underwriting agreement cost him his political support, and his wartime dismissal from New Zealand broadcasting was picked on and publicised during the hearings. In spite of the obvious irrelevance of the latter, it was considered as evidence "useful" to the Australian Broadcasting Control Board, and Associated's application was disallowed. The Board was to recommend to the Government that the granting of Sydney and Melbourne commercial licences go to applicants who, like the Packer and Fairfax–Associated Newspaper groups, had established press and radio broadcasting operations. Two of the investors in the Melbourne applicant, the General Television Corporation, were Hoyts Theatres and the Greater Union Organisation. As Sandra Hall has observed, the Menzies Government "liked to entrust new toys to old friends", and the newspaper proprietors were only too eager to move into television, in the same way they had into radio, as a defensive measure against a new threat to their interests.[11] Smaller and more genuinely production-orientated applicants like Associated TV scarcely stood a chance.

After the completion of **Long John Silver**, Colin Scrimgeour allowed Cecil Holmes to use the Pagewood studio rent-free for the interior and back-lot work on **Three in One**. The facilities were subsequently hired by visiting production units from abroad, but Associated suffered financially when the failure of **Long John Silver** terminated elaborate production plans the company had formulated with Treasure Island Pictures. Scrimgeour's problems were compounded when the death of Sir Benjamin Fuller forced him into heavy corporate liability and near-bankruptcy. Associated TV was liquidated, and its lease on the Pagewood studio was sold to the American-owned vehicle manufacturer, General Motors-Holden. It was the ultimate irony for a studio complex that had symbolised the hopes of an independent Australian film industry.

Three in One

After the abrupt closure of the Associated unit, Cecil Holmes worked for six months in a tyre factory, writing radio verse plays for the ABC between shifts. He also filmed the documentary **Words for Freedom** (1956) for the Waterside Workers' Federation Film Unit and opened a small distribution company, New Dawn Films, which concentrated on Russian cinema. In 1955 he was approached by the author Frank Hardy who was keen to invest the foreign royalties from his novel *Power Without Glory* in a half-hour film adaptation of his short story *The Load of Wood*. The remainder of the £6000 budget was provided by an advertising executive, Julian Rose. "Portmanteau" films were then in vogue and, encouraged by the result, Holmes and Rose decided to press ahead with two more episodes that could, with links by actor John McCallum, be combined with the first film to make a feature-length release under the collective title **Three in One** (1956). With further money supplied by Rose and a team of businesss acquaintances, the remaining

189

episodes were **Joe Wilson's Mates**, adapted from Henry Lawson's short story *The Union Buries its Dead*, and **The City**, scripted by Ralph Peterson from an original story by Holmes. (The other two scripts were by Rex Reinits.)

Three in One is a tribute to mateship and the mourning of lost values. In **Joe Wilson's Mates**, the adaptation reduces some of Lawson's irony for the sake of Holmes's message, and the mates themselves are used to reinforce the bonding of union solidarity. The story shows the impromptu burial and tribute organised for the corpse of a total stranger when a group of bush workers discover he was a union man. The frontier mourners include a tramp, a drunken actor and a brace of shearers recruited from a pub along the route of the horse-drawn hearse. Again working with cameraman Ross Wood, Holmes drags his hot and weary procession across immense hillscapes. The use of the settings, together with the rugged faces and touches of humour, effectively recapture the folk quality that Holmes admired in earlier Australian films.

The Load of Wood is set in the 1930s, a time when the old values, polarised by a world war, were further perpetuated by economic depression. Darky (Jock Levy), the central figure of Frank Hardy's story, is more militant than any of Henry Lawson's heroes, but he shares the winter privations that unite the poor and unemployed of a small country town and is determined to rectify matters in the face of his mates' fears. Darky's resolve to get enough wood for homes that have gone without fires for weeks, becomes part of a classic confrontation between the rich and the itinerant of the bush. Having set the scene with cold and weary town-dwellers demolishing fences and walls for scraps of firewood, the action moves through a clash between Darky and the local member of parliament to the episode's best sequence, where Darky and a mate brave the night to fell the tree of a tight-fisted landowner. The wood-gathering that follows is threatened by a watchdog and the suspense is maintained by a downhill drive, without power, through ghostly trees when the truck's engine fails to start.

The City, the third part of **Three in One**, is influenced by Holmes's high regard for postwar Italian neo-realist cinema, and brings the director's preoccupations up to date. Less optimistic and with less of a developed story than the preceding episodes, it captures the ideals and frustrations of young urban Australians in the 1950s. The city is seen to exert a crucial influence on the personal conflict between a couple who face difficulty in raising money for a home. The loneliness and alienation are heightened when, after Ted and Cathie (Brian Vicary and Joan Landor) argue over their delayed marriage, Ted's gloom contrasts with the jollity of the Luna Park fairground, and Cathie, having run off, encounters a series of weird and embittered night characters. One of these, a taxi-driver, voices the film's underlying frustration by saying: "The game's stacked all along the line; the little bloke just can't win." Away from the solidarity of Ted's fellow workers, life in the city is shown to lack the sense of mateship that has sustained the protagonists of **Joe Wilson's Mates** and **The Load of Wood**.

190

Three in One was highly commended at the Edinburgh Film Festival and won a prize at the 1956 Karlovy Vary Festival in Czechoslovakia as the best work of a young director. Its sale, mostly to art cinemas, in at least eight countries returned half the £28 000 budget, but the film failed to reach the Australian market for which it had been made. After rejection by distribution and exhibition outlets, **The Load of Wood** was released as a short supporting an Alfred Hitchcock revival; then in 1959 the complete film was screened several times by the Sydney commercial television station Channel 9 on the initiative of Ken Hall as the general manager. But **Three in One** never recovered its costs, and Holmes' considerable promise as a feature director went unfulfilled. After several more years distributing foreign cinema through New Dawn Films, he returned to making television and cinema documentaries.

Documentary: new initiatives and old

Sponsored documentaries, industrial and educational training films and commercials — all non-fiction films — experienced upsurge at a time when features production was in decline. During 1961-62, when only one local feature was released, non-fiction film producers completed a total of 610 sponsored short films. Throughout the 1950s and 1960s a growing proportion of these were intended for non-theatrical, frequently specific ''in house'' purposes, but many others were industrial or commercial public relations films supplied without charge to cinema chains as featurettes.

In-house films were usually produced on 16 mm stock for cost saving and screening convenience, and they helped perpetuate the great postwar boom in the use of this gauge already started by film societies. In Sydney, a new laboratory company, Associated Film Printers, was formed by the Commonwealth and Automatic Laboratories for 16 mm processing as well as reduction printing from 35 mm theatrical prints. After 1956, the bulk of AFP's work was provided by local and imported television news stories.

Most documentaries were made by small units with a staff of less than five. Although much of the product was little more than utilitarian, the number and the diversity of the people who made them meant that occasionally a highly inventive work emerged. Little, however, of a recognisable ''movement'' or philosophy developed from these films. One reason for this, perhaps, was that despite the great number of non-fiction subjects being produced, most independent producers still faced a battle for survival.

DOI Film Division

The new style of documentary production started at the Department of Information Film Division in the mid-1940s continued to produce some impressive achievements. This was despite constant attempts by the government to stifle development and one distinct threat of closure when it was felt that not only was the organisation moving beyond its brief, but that it was an extravagance. That the Division managed to survive in the way it did throughout the 1950s was due in no small measure to the defensive stance of the Producer-in-Chief, Stanley Hawes. He found himself frequently resisting suggestions that the body's output revert purely to the type of promotion that the Cinema Branch had handled in the 1930s.

The private-sector Film Producers' Association of Australia (formed immediately after the war) would have much preferred the Division to revert to a limited administrative role, overseeing independently-made documentaries on behalf of the Government, as it had during the war years. For a time, this was a proposal which appeared to be one the Menzies Liberal Government might be only too happy to adopt. On the assumption that it had become a mouthpiece for Arthur Calwell, its former minister under Labor, the Department of Information was disbanded in early 1950 and its functions downgraded to become part of the News and Information Bureau of the Department of the Interior. The status of the Film Division (and its Producer-in-Chief) was diminished, and the Government announced that it was considering the closure of the Division and farming out all its filmmaking activities to independent producers. The Division managed to survive, however, when a government inquiry into its function held in 1950 recommended its continued involvement in production. One reason for the continued high level of achievement at the Division in the early 1950s was the employment of such talented directors as Maslyn Williams, Lee Robinson and Shan Benson. During this period they were to produce some of their own as well as the Division's best work.

Perhaps the most remarkable DOI film of the period was **Mike and Stefani**. Directed by Maslyn Williams and released in 1952 the film set out to counter criticism that selection procedures for immigrants to Australia were not stringent enough, as well as to educate Australians to a more tolerant attitude towards non-British arrivals. The film chronicled the wartime separation of a young Ukrainian couple, followed by their chance postwar reunion in a refugee camp and subsequent application to travel to Australia. Filmed in Germany by Williams and the cameraman Reg Pearse, **Mike and Stefani** built up to an unnerving final sequence, filmed as it actually occurred in Bavaria, of the selection interview by an immigration officer. It was this scene, causing official displeasure back in Australia, which contributed, along with the stark subject matter and unconventional length (sixty-four minutes), to the film's securing only government film library release within Australia, with no screenings through the usual embassy outlets abroad. Like the later work of Cecil Holmes, **Mike and Stefani** showed the director's empathy with Italian neo-realist filmmakers, humane but uncompromising in its portrayal of real events.

Other directors of promise at the Division in the early 1950s were Colin Dean and a former Movietone employee and war correspondent, Hugh McInnes. Both made several films for the Division which were strongly individualistic as well as being impressive achievements as cinema. With **A Matter of Manners** (1951), produced for the Public Service Board, Dean dramatised with wit and sensitivity the difficulties that people faced in dealing with public service obfuscation. In the more ambitious **Capacity Smith** (1951), he portrayed, again using dramatised documentary, the generation gap between father-and-son dairy farmers, culminating in the achievement by the son of the introduction of efficient new agricultural methods. With **The Cane Cutters** (1948) and **The Steelworker** (1953), Hugh McInnes provided his audience with vivid records of the lives of workers in both industries, backing strong images with a subjective commentary from the men themselves. Dean and McInnes might have continued to build on their already considerable achievements at the Division, but by the mid-1950s both had left after disagreements over the content of their films.

In terms of public awareness, the highlight of the Division's work during the 1950s was **The Queen in Australia** (1954), a record of the Royal Tour that included coverage of its impact on ordinary Australians. It was the first feature-length local film to be shot in 35 mm colour (Ferrania) and was warmly received by both audiences and critics around the world. It was also an attempt by the Producer-in-Chief, Stanley Hawes, to revive the national programme of the Division (chosen and funded directly by the Division itself) as opposed to departmental films made on government commission. For the rest of the decade, however, the latter remained all-pervasive, and this was to have an adverse influence on the group's initiative and quality. There was also the persistent feeling in government circles that independent producers might fulfil the function equally well. During the 1950s, the Federal Government conducted two more major investigations into the Division's functions and, not surprisingly, this resulted in a self-censorship that tended to discourage the type of individualism and imagination seen in the immediate postwar years.

In 1962 the Film Division (called the Commonwealth Film Unit from 1956) moved from Burwood to new studios in the northern Sydney suburb of Lindfield. From about this time, and for various reasons that included improved morale and a more sympathetic attitude on the part of the administrators in Canberra, the work again started to become more personal and involving. **From the Tropics to the Snow** (1964, directed by Richard Mason and Jack Lee) is generally regarded as the first film to show the new freedom from official constraints. A scathing parody on the process of bureaucratic filmmaking by committee, it turns the pomposity and pretension of the clichéd travelogue on its head.

John Kingsford Smith, John Heyer, Mervyn Murphy

One talented filmmaker to resign from the Division two years after its foundation was John Heyer who, as mentioned before, became head of production for the Australian branch of the Shell Film Unit in 1948. Heyer's best and most acclaimed work for Shell was **The Back of Beyond** (1954).

In content, if certainly not approach, the film closest to **The Back of Beyond** was John Kingsford Smith's **The Inlanders**, completed five years before Heyer's film in 1949. This was John Kingsford Smith's second film under the auspices of his new company, Kingcroft (formed with Lloyd Ravenscroft, a former Cinesound fellow employee, in November 1946). Kingsford Smith had been eager to shoot a film in the Birdsville Track region in Central Australia for some years when he was approached by the Australian Inland Mission to make a record of the annual 5400-mile patrol taken by the Reverend "Skipper" Partridge. Shot by Gordon Gibson over a six-month schedule from July 1947, **The Inlanders** draws cumulative impact from its observation of everyday human endeavours in a region full of difficulties. Accompanying even the most routine events are constant reminders of the harshness and challenge: transitory visitors to homesteads bring little relief to Inland loneliness, and flooded rivers present just as much of a barrier as the creeping desert sands. The good feelings arising from a sense of community closeness on a bush picnic and at a christening are offset by the sight of bush children with their heads draped in eerie black mosquito netting, an Aboriginal shaving with a broken bottle and a gory tooth-pulling. Josephine O'Neill wrote in the *Sunday Telegraph* following the release of **The Inlanders** through MGM, that it was a "fine human film" and "a lively picture of outback characters".[12] On its British release in 1950, *Monthly Film Bulletin* stated that it was "an interesting picture of a remote and little-known territory, honest, realistically if not imaginatively made".[13]

Acclaim for **The Inlanders** laid a solid foundation for the future of Kingcroft, and under the managing directorship of John Kingsford Smith, the company remained a prolific producer of sponsored documentaries and advertising films for the next two decades. (Lloyd Ravenscroft sold his share to Kingsford Smith in 1949, and Kingsford Smith in turn sold his interests to Terry Ohlsson in 1970.)[14]

Through the Shell Film Unit, John Heyer had made a large number of trade and educational films specifically for the Shell parent company's use. He was able to produce **The Back of Beyond** with complete creative freedom as long as he guaranteed to Shell that the budget would not exceed £12 000.[15] His brief was to make a film reflecting the essence of the Australian character. Where Kingsford Smith's film had ranged far and wide through Central Australia, Heyer specifically covered life along the Birdsville Track, following the fortnightly drive of 300 miles by Tom Kruse, an outback mailman. Feeling that no single production could do justice to the Track, its pioneers and current inhabitants, Heyer planned to give an overall impression that would pay tribute to its people "as representative of all who live in 'the back of beyond'."[16] He prepared his shooting script after a research trip taken with Tom Kruse and began five weeks on location in spring 1952. The unit, consisting of twenty technicians and non-professional actors, accompanied by five trucks of supplies and equipment, was plagued by flies and dust, both of which made their way incessantly into and around the camera. Back in Sydney, the film was edited by Heyer himself at Mervyn Murphy's Supreme Sound studio which, since the Unit's formation, had served as a technical base. Characters were re-voiced using professional actors, and a complex soundtrack was created by Murphy and his associate Gwen Oatley. The resulting film is, as Heyer intended, a romantic and forceful impression of life along the Track, distilling the Australian character and its environment in a way that equals the earlier classic documentaries of Grierson and Harry Watt. The effect of Ross Wood's camerawork, combined with the commentary written by Douglas Stewart and Heyer, carries the greatest impact in a grim scene showing two children starting an ill-fated journey through the desert after the death of their mother. In this, as elsewhere in the film, the approach to the region's hardships is matter-of-fact and unsentimental.

The Back of Beyond was seen by over 750 000 people through Australian non-theatrical screenings in 1954, the first year of its release. It was also screened as the official Australian entry at several film festivals including Venice, where it was awarded the Grand Prix. The British documentary filmmaker Edgar Anstey regarded it as "among the half dozen best documentaries made anywhere since the war".[17]

Another prolific producer who, like John Heyer and John Kingsford Smith, managed to remain in business at a time when feature production had dwindled, was Mervyn Murphy, proprietor and managing director of Supreme Sound Studios (later Supreme Films). In 1951 Murphy began the process of building up a studio and laboratory at Paddington, Sydney, in time providing black and white and colour laboratory facilities, technicians and equipment which could be hired by other producers, while he himself produced (and often directed) a score of documentaries and two-minute cinema advertisements. With Kingsford Smith and other producers, Murphy campaigned often and hard for government support for a revived feature industry, and he was kept going, as his associate Gwen Oatley would remember, on the "smell of an oil rag" and an unshakable optimism that conditions would soon revive.[18] At times the business was only kept afloat by the work of its laboratory, headed by a knowledgeable and dedicated technician, Tom Nurse. Murphy provided technical services for the comparatively few features being made, and sometimes invested in them in return for deferred costs. Remaining very much an individualist, Murphy provided first chances in the business for young technicians, gave new opportunities to older ones, and helped up-and-coming filmmakers with loans of equipment and free studio space. Gwen Oatley, as a long-time employee and ultimate business partner, did much to aid the administrative as well as technical growth of Supreme and with Murphy trained and encouraged many technicians who later became prominent in the industry after its revival in the late-1960s.

WWF Film Unit

The survival of the Waterside Workers' Federation Film Unit, like that of the DOI Film Division, was one of the more remarkable phenomena of local film production in the 1950s. Throughout that decade and in the midst of repressive Cold War conservatism, the Unit produced a dozen documentaries expressing radical viewpoints (with a basis of left-wing ideology) on such issues as worker exploitation, the need for pensions, union solidarity and the problem of housing shortages. The dedication and talent of the Unit's members were certainly factors that helped to keep it alive, but it was sustained also by the militancy of the Waterside Workers' Federation itself and the unified support of this and other unions influenced by an active Communist Party.

Originating in 1952 as one of a series of cultural activities promoted by the Federation's Sydney branch, the Unit had as its nucleus the collaborative team of Jock Levy, Keith Gow and Norma Disher, all of whom had been participants in political theatre (Keith Gow had in addition worked as a freelance film technician). With Levy and Gow working as the only full-time members until they were joined by Disher in 1956, the WWF Unit made films for the Waterside Workers' Federation as well as for other unions whose members were prepared to allocate funds and participate in productions. Four films for the Waterside Workers' Federation, **Pensions for Veterans** (1952), **The Hungry Miles** (1955), **November Victory** (1955) and **Four's a Crowd** were made alongside assignments for the Building Workers' Industrial Union, the Boilermakers' Society, and the Miners' Federation.

The Hungry Miles, probably the most impressive of the Unit's surviving work, chronicled the history of the Sydney waterfront, culminating in a plea for greater unity among waterside workers. The highlight is a reconstruction of the Depression years which used hundreds of wharf labourers to recreate scenes of mass unemployment and scuffles for job tickets, incidents which many of the participants had actually experienced. The style, and that of the later **November Victory**, showed the familiarity of the Unit's team with the work of the Russian filmmakers Sergei Eisenstein and Vsevold Pudovkin. Joris Ivens praised **The Hungry Miles** after its screening at the 1957 Warsaw Youth Festival, where it was awarded a gold medal. Another impressive film by the WWF Unit is **Not Only the Need** (1957), a well-shot and intricately edited documentary about postwar housing conditions.

Due to a general economic recession and other limitations on the activities of the Federation, the WWF Film Unit was disbanded after the production of **Hewers of Coal** (1958). Although the screenings had not extended beyond unions and film societies, the productions were well received and served the purpose for which they were made. As films which passionately cared about their subjects, and as works of cinema, the Unit's projects show a consistency of vision that no other local documentary producers of the period were able to match.[19]

The newsreel

For the ten years between the end of the war and the coming of television, weekly newsreels continued to be an integral part of cinema programmes.[20] They had, after all, presented the only regular motion picture record of national life since the 1910s and from the early 1940s their public esteem had risen with authoritative coverage of the war and aspects of postwar reconstruction.

A large number of single-reel specials were made after the war which often tackled important issues. The controversial topics looked at by **Cinesound Review**, under the supervision of Ken Hall, ranged from wildlife conservation and soil erosion to matters of health, slum clearance and Aboriginal welfare. In March 1948, a Cinesound cameraman was assaulted by one member of a panel of doctors investigating a cancer cure; the incident was recorded by Movietone and Cinesound. The Cinesound slum special (September 1948) followed coverage of filthy homes near industrial areas, with footage of "what type of house the people want!"[21]

Another of the issues reflected by local newsreels was the fear of Communism. After the end of the Royal Tour in April, Cinesound achieved a scoop with the departure from Sydney airport — crowded with demonstrators — of Mrs Vladimir Petrov, whom two Russian diplomatic couriers were attempting to whisk out of the country. A **Movietone News** special in April 1949 entitled "Sharpley on Communists' Sinister Aims" featured the former Communist Party secretary Cecil H. Sharpley saying why he had denounced "the Red Menace in Australia"[22]; a Movietone special of December 1950 included Prime Minister Menzies giving "his impressions of Communism's diabolical activities and threats to peace in various parts of the world".[23] Ken Hall later related:

The newsreels were respected and sought out by many unexpected bodies. In the early 1950s there was a lot of social awakening, unrest, turmoil, street demonstrations, near-riots. Security, with whom we had good relations, were very interested in the footage covering these events. They wanted to know who was on the guest list, so to speak, invited or uninvited. Faces, picking out faces, so many, to them, old "friends". They did a lot of that.[24]

With all hopes of a feature production industry now abandoned, Hall claimed he poured "whatever frustrated creativity"[25] he had left into **Cinesound Review**. Apart from a consistent editorial stance, the reel under his supervision retained its sense of humour and an intention to keep competing with Movietone on subjects such as sport. In August 1950, two **Cinesound Review** staff (Geoff Thompson and Bede Whiteman) were the only Australian cameramen covering the Korean War, and from the late 1940s the **Review** was the first newsreel in the world to start carrying occasional items in colour.

Under the direction of several filmmakers, including William Carty, Bede Whiteman and Howard Rubie, Cinesound was to make around two hundred sponsored "industrial" documentaries in the twenty-five years after the war, and continued to provide training for new talent.[26] Nonetheless, after the departure of Ken Hall in December 1956 to become chief executive of Frank Packer's Television Corporation (which operated Sydney's TCN Channel 9 among others), much of the studio's earlier morale ebbed away.

Chauvel in the 1950s

In his individual way, Charles Chauvel was determined to override whatever antipathy existed towards Australian feature production and see the industry re-established on a businesslike basis. He managed to obtain special exemption from the Federal Government's capital issues restrictions in 1951 and floated his own public company, Charles Chauvel Productions, with capital of £68 000. The stated aim was for continuous production of first-class motion pictures in Australia. The working title of the first production was **The Northern Territory Story** — eventually released as **Jedda** (1955). Filming was scheduled for late 1951 but it was not started until mid-1953 and completed early the following year.

Jedda is a love story of two full-blood Aboriginals, and the plot was partly intended to show how the policy of racial integration could be mishandled. Jedda (Ngarla Kunoth) herself has been brought up amid polite constraint by the wife of a Northern Territory station owner. Although she has been promised in marriage to Joe, a half-caste stockman (Paul Reynall), on a droving trip she is half-willingly drawn to and captured by Marbuck (Robert Tudawali), who takes her on a long and perilous trek to his own tribal region. In time Marbuck is "sung to death" by his tribal elders for daring to take an outsider as his wife. Followed by Joe and the police, Marbuck, half-mad with fear, drags Jedda up into towering, ochre-coloured escarpments. When finally cornered the couple plunge into a deep valley to their deaths.

Chauvel's choice of subject stemmed from the post-production period of **Sons of Matthew** when an American journalist suggested he make a large-scale film featuring Aboriginals. Universal Pictures, Chauvel's previous backer, was not impressed and Elsa Chauvel later recalled that a number of other potential private investors thought her husband had "really gone mad". This view was shared by Prime Minister Menzies when Chauvel approached him personally for Government aid, although the Liberal–Country Party coalition did eventually help defray transport costs with a free supply of petrol.[27]

Chauvel developed his story and surveyed locations during an exhaustive 10 000-mile journey through the Northern Territory. The trip also saw the casting of the two leads. Robert Tudawali, a Melville Island Aboriginal, was recommended by the journalist Douglas Lockwood and Ngarla Kunoth was found at a hostel for Aboriginal girls. Elsa Chauvel later wrote:

Location work meant a long, grinding journey by road into country that only an occasional white man and the wandering blacks had ever seen ... We went [to Northern Australia] as a completely mobile unit, self-supporting, self-contained, on location in places where there would be no store for several hundred miles — so always it had to have a large commissariat of its own. The unit also had to be so organised that when it halted, the cameras could be set up in a matter of minutes ready to roll.[28]

As with almost every other Chauvel film, the location experience became a saga of endurance and achievement to rival the events on screen. Much of the filming took place on Coolibah Cattle Station near Katherine, and the most spectacular of the locations were around Mantaranka and the Katherine River Gorge. At Marrekei several members of the crew, including Chauvel himself, narrowly escaped being seriously burnt when the decoy fire for Marbuck's abduction of Jedda blazed out of control. While the unit filmed along the Roper River, summer temperatures were so extreme that the sensitive Gevacolor film stock was not unloaded from camera magazines until late at night, and stored in small river caves. As no laboratory in Australia could handle Gevacolor, an elaborate procedure was devised for sending exposed film from locations to the nearest small airport, from where it would be consigned to Darwin, and then to the Denham laboratories in England. Several thousand feet of negative containing the last scenes of the production were lost in an air crash, and the material was later re-shot at Kanangra Walls near the Jenolan Caves in the Blue Mountains of New South Wales.

Jedda is Chauvel's least conventional film in terms of subject matter and narrative, and it is also his most intense. The early part, dealing with Jedda's upbringing by the white property owners, the McCanns, is relatively static, although it does give Chauvel the opportunity to have the McCanns argue the rights and wrongs of racial assimilation. Events from the time of Jedda's capture reassert the director's zest for adventure and nonconformity. The build-up to the abduction scene is compellingly choreographed and, aided by the total conviction of Kunoth and Tudawali, acutely defines the torment Jedda faces in choosing between tribal life and comfortable white conventions. Passages of the pursuit and events immediately before the cliffside death are over-wrought, but Chauvel makes up for the shortcomings with his interpretation of the Northern Territory's eerie atmosphere.

Jedda had its premiere in Darwin in January 1955, and commercial results in Australia were at first encouraging. British screenings followed in 1956, and an American release, under the title **Jedda the Uncivilised**, in 1957. Chauvel had hoped to sell the film in the United Kingdom through the Rank Organisation but, anxious for a quick return, his company's Board sold the rights to a smaller British distributor and saw it obtain release only as a supporting attraction.[29] Britain's *Monthly Film Bulletin* reported:

The film has been considerably shortened for showing in this country and the scene in which Marbuck is "sung to death" by the elders is drastically cut, which makes the end seem unduly abrupt.

Even so, the reviewer found:

Judged as a serious attempt to deal with Aboriginal problems, the film is praiseworthy, though its realisation remains decidedly uneven.[30]

Neither overseas sales nor the eventual Australian receipts earned enough money for Charles Chauvel Productions to survive, and the company was sold to a private concern with no interest in film production. Nevertheless, the British Broadcasting Corporation had been impressed by the way the Chauvels had publicised **Jedda** during a half-hour television interview, and commissioned them to film *Walkabout* (1959), a thirteen-part travel series in colour about a journey from Sydney across to South Australia, and into the Northern Territory to Darwin. The series was immensely popular in England. It commanded a weekly viewing public of seven million and was repeated on three occasions. More television and feature work was being planned when Charles Chauvel died on 11 November 1959.

Lee Robinson and Chips Rafferty

Lee Robinson, the most prolific Australian director of the 1950s, was less concerned than either Chauvel or Ken Hall with making films that interpreted national life or character. In recognising a limited local exposure for Australian features, he aimed his output at an overseas B-film market, stressing the exoticism of Australia but making little attempt to clarify the identity of its people. Robinson's priority, and Chips Rafferty's as his partner, was to produce films to the formula most likely to be attractive as well as economic to the markets at which they were aimed. He said in later years:

There was a very strong feeling that features were something the Americans did and we didn't. The general feeling was that Australians couldn't make feature pictures, and shouldn't. And they shouldn't really dabble about too much making documentaries. You know, there used to be a raised eyebrow when somebody produced a documentary that was acceptable.[31]

Having worked earlier with the Army's Military History Unit, Lee Robinson became a member of the staff newly recruited to the DOI Film Division in 1946. Among the DOI films he directed, **The Pearlers** (1949) and **Outback Patrol** (1951) captured authentically the atmosphere of northern and inland Australian locations which he would later incorporate into his feature and television work. He had been interested in feature filmmaking since his earliest days with the DOI and in 1947 collaborated with the English film editor Inman Hunter on the screenplay for a production which, after they were unable to raise backing for it themselves, was to become the basis of Ealing's **The Siege of Pinchgut** (1959). In 1951, on leave from the DOI, he worked as assistant director on the half-hour film drama **I Found Joe Barton**.

Robinson first worked with Chips Rafferty as writer for a radio series of outback yarns featuring Rafferty as a forceful righter-of-wrongs. Rafferty's contract with Ealing Studios was coming to an end and with that company's withdrawal from local production he was determined to keep working as an actor in Australia producing films by himself in which he would appear. In January 1952 his attempt to set up a £120 000 company to produce an ambitious feature and a thirteen-part series for world television had been quashed by the capital issues restrictions. Soon afterwards, in partnership with Lee Robinson and cameraman George Heath, Rafferty side-stepped the financial limitations by setting up Platypus Productions to produce a feature at the £10 000 limit imposed by the Government.

The Phantom Stockman (1953), scripted and directed by Robinson and derived from the radio series of the same name, linked the same central character with a conventional Western format and such exotic touches as thoughts beamed through Rafferty's use of Aboriginal "bush telegraph". Directorially the film is laboured, although its plodding pace suits the moody evocation of inland Australia. Despite its shortcomings, the film had returned its money plus 27.5 per cent within ten months. The *Sunday Herald* reported:

Before Sydney film men had even seen it, Chips had sold his picture to America, Britain and the East for about £23 000 and repaid his backers in full, plus a healthy dividend. Australian revenue is still to come.[32]

Britain's *Monthly Film Bulletin* wrote:

The Australian backgrounds and idiom and the glimpses of the Aborigines (one scene introduces, somewhat irrelevantly, the painter Albert Namatjira) prove the film's most attractive and interesting features.[33]

In talking about documentary and overseas influences on his first three features, Robinson was later to say:

My whole concept at that time was not to superimpose some story on an environment but to find the story within the environment we had chosen. The first three films were all designed to have a documentary feel to them, but the idea was to not let them become too documentary and to keep to the entertainment area.

We were trying to do something that was different to the American picture and the English picture, something that was Australian within an international format. Because we didn't have the "name" artists to play with, we didn't have the top writers, we didn't have the top directors, the thing we had to try and exploit was the one thing we did have — great backgrounds.[34]

Using a new debenture system operated from a series of loans, Rafferty and Robinson formed Southern International (Production and Distribution) Ltd to produce **King of the Coral Sea** (1954). Capital restrictions were still in force, but the debentures allowed a more ambitious budget (£25 000) and a six-week location schedule at Thursday Island, followed by underwater sequences photographed by Noel Monkman off Green Island on the Great Barrier Reef. Robinson's principal theme was the uniqueness of Thursday Island's sail-powered pearling fleet and the conflict between old and new generations of pearlers over the introduction of the aqualung. The more dynamic elements concerned the bringing to justice of pearlers using their operations as a front for smuggling illegal immigrants. More of the Rafferty persona was able to emerge than in the earlier film; the other performances were uninspired, with the exception of Reg Lye as a seedy and sinister crook. The mainstay was again the strong location atmosphere, this time captured in the crisp camerawork of Ross Wood. Three weeks after editing was complete **King of the Coral Sea** had made its money back in overseas sales, and proceeded to do well in the Australian market.

Walk into Paradise (1956) was the first of Southern International's co-productions. Their partner was the French company Discifilm, whose owner-producer Paul-Edmund Decharme offered to link up with them when the film was in an advanced stage of preproduction. Decharme was one of several French producers of the period who followed a trend toward subjects with multi-national casting shot in distant locations. For the Rafferty–Robinson interests it meant that Southern International's output could effectively be doubled. Southern International agreed to provide seventy per cent of the budget in return for which Discifilm would provide two French stars and a director to shoot the non-English version. Discifilm retained the distribution rights for Europe, South America and French-speaking Canada. In future it was planned to have both companies alternate in providing the bulk of finance for each feature, as well as the choice of subject and ''lead-off'' or principal director, whose initiative the other would follow.

In May 1955 *Film Weekly* observed that, ''The Decharme co-production set-up appears to be the most notable forward step in the Australian motion picture industry's progress toward local production'' and that Rafferty and Robinson seemed ''to have all the answers to persistent trade doubts about the practicability of continuous local production''.[35] A month later **Walk into Paradise** started production. Robinson's associate director was Marcel Pagliero and his version — edited and scored in Paris — was released under the obtuse title **L'Odyssée du Capitaine Steve**. The plot carries *Boy's Own*-style exotica further north into New Guinea, featuring Rafferty as Steve McAllister, a District Officer leading a group investigating jungle oil deposits. Travelling with them is a woman doctor, Louise Demarcet (Françoise Cristophe), assigned by the United Nations to conduct malaria research. Arriving at the oilfield location, Steve obtains the cooperation of initially hostile natives in helping to build an airfield in return for the cure of the chief's sick children. The explorers are nearly massacred when witch doctors create trouble, but the children recover in time and disaster is averted.

Walk into Paradise contained more of an emphasis on travel and action than the earlier Rafferty–Robinson films and, whether influenced or not by the collaboration with Marcel Pagliero, it is Robinson's best feature. An explorer's sense of interest and suspense is sustained, and the colour photography by Carl Kayser (which was highly commended at the Cannes Film Festival) helps to keep both the pace and the documentary interest at high pitch. Rafferty, Cristophe and Reg Lye play their leading roles with conviction, supported by French actor Pierre Cressoy, officers and police of

202

the New Guinea administration, and tribesmen of the Asaro and Wahgi Valleys.

Walk into Paradise was given a "splash release" by MGM at a series of Sydney theatres. It impressed the American showman-producer Joseph E. Levine who, having paid an outright sum of £60000 for US distribution rights, proceeded to reap considerable profits from the film under a new title **Walk into Hell**. Southern International, in the meantime, had called for debenture shareholders to finance three more productions, and the Rafferty–Robinson partnership formed an allied company, Australian Television Enterprises, which in May 1956 bought and refurbished the former Cinesound studio at Bondi in anticipation of receiving work from television. But the partnership began to strike financial problems. Australian television brought no immediate upsurge in film production, and the spread of the medium in the United States by the late 1950s had almost eliminated that country's demand for the kind of "B" movies Southern International had supplied.

With their eyes on the world market, Southern International decided that **Dust in the Sun** (1958) should have a budget of £50000 — twice that of **King of the Coral Sea**. Its creative and financial failure (it was not released in Australia and Britain until 1960) was followed by second and third French co-productions budgeted at figures far in excess of what the Australian company could afford. Ironically, both these films, **The Stowaway** (1958) and **The Restless and the Damned** (1959), were on the level of "major" productions in which Rafferty and Robinson had hoped to be involved after the first three years of their partnership. Their contribution to **The Stowaway** came from the sale of **Walk into Paradise** and funds loaned by Herc McIntyre from the superannuation fund of Universal Pictures' Australian branch; £40000 towards **The Restless and the Damned** came from hire of facilities to two overseas films shot in Tahiti and production involvement in several episodes for the American documentary television series *High Adventure*.[36] The absence of Australian locations and characters from the final French co-productions emphasised that the local involvement was more or less token. With the failure of these films, Southern International could undertake no more feature work, and was forced into liquidation. Lee Robinson said later:

We got out of feature production completely because there was a feeling there was no future in it. We came in at the wrong time, Chips and I. We were at our peak when television started in this country. If we'd been at our peak five years earlier, we'd have been consolidated by the time television came in.[37]

Nevertheless television did eventually bring a respite for the partnership. They turned again to the settings of their first three features for the series *Adventure Unlimited*, and in 1964 produced an hour-long documentary, *The Dawn Fraser Story*. Lee Robinson's production work in television (*Skippy*, *Boney*, *Barrier Reef*) and occasional features continued into the

203

1980s, but a disillusioned Chips Rafferty produced no more projects after 1964. However, he continued to appear in other people's films for another ten years.

Visiting productions

In 1958, the Melbourne *Age* commented:

Although Australians are among the world's most assiduous filmgoers, they rarely see a film about themselves; if they do, it will almost certainly be made by American or British companies. For a young country with a sense of national awareness, this is little short of a tragedy.[38]

As the old-style Australian feature industry withered away in the 1950s, the proportion of "visiting" productions — films made by overseas companies — was growing. Most of the thirteen features shot in Australia by visitors between 1950 and 1960 were made after 1956, the year of television's arrival. One reason for this was the decline of the Hollywood and English studio systems and the increasing number of independent producers prepared to travel far and wide for new locations and fresh appeal. Eight of the features were independently made, although sometimes with money from a major studio. Not surprisingly, after Ealing's success in the mid-1940s with **The Overlanders**, just over half of them were British.

Kangaroo and the Smiley films

Twentieth Century-Fox, who had been promising since the early 1930s to invest directly in Australian production, finally put money into three of the "visiting" films. Their main incentive being an attempt to "thaw" and export box office takings frozen in Australia during the war, Fox first spent big money on **Kangaroo** (1952), and several years later co-invested with Treasure Island Pictures on **Long John Silver** (1954) and with the English company, London Films, on **Smiley** (1956).

Kangaroo is a drama of pioneering life with a worn and creaking plot (prodigal son, symbolic breaking of the drought) that echoes several much earlier Australian films and hundreds of American Westerns. Appalled at the script Fox had provided for him, the American director Lewis Milestone (whose credits included **All Quiet on the Western Front** (1930)), tried to persuade his studio that the huge budget should be used instead in an adaptation of two novels by the Australian journalist Brian Penton — *Land Takers* and *Inheritors* — both vividly depicting early convict life. The Fox executive ten thousand miles away refused the request. Milestone salvaged some of his intention by integrating Penton's description of drought-stricken animals into his studio's saga of escaped convicts and a bush family's conflict with the blacks. Working with a combined American-Australian cast and crew, he included in his location work a number of distinctive historic landmarks, to emphasise, the director said, "the fact we were actually in

Australia; out in the wide open spaces you might as well be in Arizona''.[39] The response of the New York preview audience was poor and studio president Darryl F. Zanuck sought to rectify the deficiencies with a new ending. The attempt, made in Milestone's absence, was pointless because **Kangaroo** failed critically and commercially the world over despite its famous director, the £800 000 budget and a cast including Maureen O'Hara, Peter Lawford, Finlay Currie, Richard Boone and Chips Rafferty. In Australia this Technicolor production was greeted by withering critiques and scant attendances. For years afterwards, Fox used its world-wide failure as their reason for not wishing to continue substantial investment in local filmmaking.

Smiley was a far better subject, and one which the British producer-director Anthony Kimmins had been trying to film since the late 1940s. Adapted from the novel by Moore Raymond, the story features the young child of a struggling family whose attempts to raise enough money to buy a bicycle lead him to unknowingly act as an opium courier to outcast Aboriginals on the fringe of his town. In between, the boy, Smiley (Colin Peterson) steals and damages the bicycle of a kindly police sergeant (Chips Rafferty) and knocks out his father (Reg Lye) who has stolen the boy's savings to pay off a gambling debt. The film amalgamates childhood pranks with an unsentimental portrait of Australian outback poverty and racial exploitation. Against Smiley's innocence are set the taunts of the schoolmaster's snobbish son and the manipulation of the publican (John McCallum) who uses him as a courier. While characterisation is simplified, the social context sustains credibility.

Smiley was very popular, and resulted in a sequel, **Smiley Gets a Gun** (1958) which, in following the same basic formula, traded the harsh social background for a string of clichés typified by a pet kangaroo and a hidden cache of gold. *Monthly Film Bulletin* reported that the story was ''written and told entirely in juvenile terms, and is acceptable only on that level''.[40]

Rank and Ealing

In 1957, under the auspices of the Rank Organisation, a sound version of **Robbery Under Arms** finally reached the screen. The film rights to the Rolf Boldrewood novel had been at various times the property of Raymond Longford, Efftee and Cinesound, and the project was considered as part of the ill-fated Cinesound and Rank co-production plans of the late 1940s. Jack Lee, the director of the new version, had shot the final sequences of **A Town Like Alice** (1956) in Australia, and Peter Finch, the co-star of that film, was signed to play **Robbery**'s anti-hero, Captain Starlight. Finch was reportedly unhappy with the script, and Lee wanted to shelve the project and work on a draft that did more justice to the novel. Nevertheless, the Rank Organisation was adamant that the film keep to schedule, and according to one of Finch's biographers, the actor later recalled: ''Off we all went at half-cock with a half-baked project rushed in and out of the oven because that was the chef's orders''.[41] The resulting **Robbery Under Arms** might just as well have been a British Western filmed in Spain and the novel's exuberant spirit was only glimpsed in the closing sequences shot in South Australia's Flinders Ranges. The final shoot-out transcends Western inevitability as Starlight and his men fire at troopers from a towering cliff that serenely counterpoints the scurrying ant-like figures. Finch, despite his misgivings, provides a memorable Starlight, but otherwise an associate cast of English actors roughing it for a world market bear no resemblance to the authentic characters of the novel or to those of Kenneth Brampton's film version of 1920.

Finch's favourite film was **The Shiralee** (1957), filmed in Australia immediately before **Robbery Under Arms** and co-financed by Ealing Studios with the British branch of MGM. The basis for the screenplay was D'Arcy Niland's novel of the same name which concerned the wanderings of a swagman Macauley (Peter Finch) and his "shiralee" (or burden), his five-year-old daughter who is seized by Macauley with spite — and later regret — from an unfaithful wife in Sydney. The girl, named Buster, shares the wanderlust more out of devotion to her father than a real liking for life on the road. When Macauley tries to leave her in the care of friends, she catches up with him and asks, disarmingly, "What if the sky fell on you?''. Macauley places himself above the other drifters they meet along the way — an assortment of shearers, con-men and dithery swaggies. He is a mid-twentieth century successor to the bush drifters of the old *Bulletin* stories, but the romanticism is qualified by cynicism and paternal responsibility. The novel, riding unevenly over its later plot developments, ended commendably with father and daughter's life on the road an open-ended prospect. The film, scripted by Neil Paterson and Leslie Norman, concludes on a safer note for 1950s audiences with the addition of an old flame of Macauley waiting to bring stability to their lives. The mainstays are Peter Finch and Dana Wilson as father and daugher; their relationship has a conviction lacking in other areas of the film. *Sight and Sound* reviewed **The Shiralee** not as an Australian feature, but as "possibly the most individual Ealing production for some time, a film not wholly satisfying but most agreeably even-tempered''.[42]

The following year, Harry Watt returned to direct **The Siege of Pinchgut** (1959), the final film made by Ealing before its closure in Britain and the sale of its assets to ABPC. Both in subject matter and casting it departed markedly from the output of the studio's heyday and what emerged was an American-style crime melodrama starring Aldo Ray. The original story by Lee Robinson and Inman Hunter, written in the late 1940s, evolved from the idea of two German prisoners-of-war holding Sydney under siege from Fort Denison (or Pinchgut as it is also known) in the middle of the harbour while trying to make good an escape to South America. Ealing had known about the Robinson-Hunter script and purchased the rights in the late 1950s. The basic premise was reworked by Watt and the novelist Jon Cleary, changing the prisoners-of-war into a single civilian prisoner escaping unjust incarceration. Lee Robinson later remarked that the change in period and the central character's nationality had made the tale less credible, and indeed the final result is a strange hybrid; Aldo Ray is disastrously miscast and emotions are synthetically overwrought. These contrast unfavourably with the assured documentary-style handling of the exterior locations, particularly Watt's handling of the mass evacuation of harbourside suburbs and the placing of sharpshooters on the city's surrounding vantage points as Ray threatens to use Pinchgut's defence armoury to blow up the waterfront. Away from the urgency of the threatened catastrophe, the social drowsiness of Sydney in the 1950s is evoked with accuracy.

In 1961, the British-based Children's Film Foundation produced their second Australian feature, **Bungala Boys** (director Jim Jeffrey), and although moderately well-received, it had nowhere near the success of the first, the 1947 **Bush Christmas**. The rest of the visiting productions of the period were filmed by American concerns, of which only one, Warner Brothers Productions, who backed **The Sundowners** (1960), was a major company in the old studio sense. **Shadow of the Boomerang** (1960), produced by the motion picture division of the Billy Graham Evangelistic Association, was a "Christian Western" which told of an American cattle station manager who overcomes his anti-Aboriginal prejudice on hearing a radio broadcast of Billy Graham's 1959 Australian crusade. **Summer of the Seventeenth Doll** (1959) and **On the Beach** (1959), although not made by large Hollywood studio companies, might just as well have been because of the approach they took.

American money — whose identity?

Ray Lawler's *Summer of the Seventeenth Doll* became the key Australian stage play of the 1950s soon after its first performances in Melbourne during 1955. It perceived the flaws in. the outward self-assurance of a middle generation of Australians brought up in a relatively unquestioning prewar social climate. At a time when live theatre was dominated by British and American writing and in a nation experiencing its newly acquired comforts against a background of Cold War caution, the play's emotional truth was a rare commodity. The immense success that the stage production was to enjoy in Britain and Europe did much to restore confidence in Australian drama.

The play features two canecutters who for seventeen years have been spending the lay-off season continuing a five-month romance with two barmaids who live in an inner-city boarding house. The upset caused by the marriage of one of the women, and the confrontation with middle age, finally erupts into violence. Although the play ends with the destruction of their romantic dream, the film closes with the reunion of the central couple, Roo and Olive.

The screen rights to *Summer of the Seventeenth Doll* were bought by the American company, Hecht-Hill-Lancaster, who in turn formed a new company, Hecht-Hill-Lancaster (Australia) to make the film. John Dighton's script adaptation brought several significant changes to the Lawler original, the biggest of which — apart from the ending — was the transfer of the main location from Melbourne's inner-city Carlton to harbourside Sydney. Under the direction of Leslie Norman, a potentially fine cast was headed by Ernest Borgnine (Roo), Anne Baxter (Olive), John Mills (Barney) and Angela Lansbury (Pearl), with Ethel Gabriel, the only member of the original stage cast, as Olive's mother. The journalist Charles Higham, having watched some of the filming, wrote that most of Leslie Norman's films

have made his approach to the medium clear: he is a disciplined and tough craftsman, capable of getting the utmost from short commons and restricted schedule, and was thus the obvious choice for the pinchpenny and workmanlike production team of Hecht, Hill and Lancaster. Observed closely, as he handled a number of scenes, Norman appeared to be aiming for no elaborate or subtle effects.[43]

Having dismissed Lawler's original focus on character, the finished film was to weigh too heavily on its altered plot. The performers try hard but have too little effect and the visual direction is uninvolving. The moments that do work show the sadness and humiliation of threatened relationships, principally in the climax where Roo smashes the plastic kewpie dolls he and Barney had bought to celebrate each trip south. *Sight and Sound* judged that "Ray Lawler's play, with virility, nostalgia, and sentiment, could have been made into a successful small film instead of a would-be large one".[44] Another critic wrote: "Too much crispness and freshness obtrudes upon what should be stale, foolish and pathetic", and that generally, "the locale could have been any large seaside town".[45]

In 1959 Sydney served as the setting for a disaster fantasy with **The Siege of Pinchgut**; Melbourne in the same year was to enjoy more than its share of prominence as the last surviving city on earth in Stanley Kramer's **On the Beach**. Setting the story in 1964, Neville Shute's novel depicted Melbourne as the world's last city to be affected by nuclear fallout after the final World War. Stanley Kramer shot most of the film in and around Melbourne but evidence of this location aside, **On the Beach** could give no more of an adequate impression of national identity than **Pinchgut** or **Summer of the Seventeenth Doll**. Although some impact springs from individual moments of truth and the scenes of a population forming long queues in the desolate city for suicide pills, the novel's chilling quality is lost when the film becomes an all-star "problem" movie displaying the worried profiles of Ava Gardner, Gregory Peck, Fred Astaire and Anthony Perkins. *Sight and Sound* commented: "Stanley Kramer is unlikely to convince anyone that this quartet is in imminent danger of any kind of extinction".[46]

With **The Sundowners**, based on the novel by Jon Cleary and directed by Fred Zinnemann, came a worthy successor to **The Overlanders** as a visitor's film that captured some genuine national sentiment without appearing to overreach itself. The story tells of the Carmodys, a shearing family, whose transient existence is called into question by the wife (Deborah Kerr). The relationship with her husband (Robert Mitchum) is mutually sustaining for as long as she continues to tolerate his obsession to keep moving.

Gary Cooper was originally to play the Irish-Australian drifter, but Robert Mitchum was assigned the role, with Deborah Kerr as his wife Ida, and Michael Anderson as their son. Other imported leads were Peter Ustinov, Glynis Johns and Dina Merrill; the Australians Chips Rafferty, Lola Brooks and John Meillon took supporting roles. The scenes of domestic intimacy between Mitchum and Kerr are deeply felt, and even strident confrontations are played with conviction. Only Zinnemann's desire to include innumerable examples of Australia's fauna, making it into a veritable bestiary of the bush, lowers the credibility. Despite this, Robert Mitchum gives one of the best performances of his career. However, it is through Deborah Kerr that the most vivid feelings of the film are expressed, whether in the scene where, hot and dusty, she watches a smart city woman peering at her from a train window, or the disappointment when she sees an ideal farming property (and her chances for stability) slipping away from her.

Well received the world over, **The Sundowners** was one of the last features of any description to be made in Australia for another five years. With the passing of the 1950s, the flow of visiting productions that had kept local actors and technicians in work abruptly ceased. After **The Sundowners, The Bungala Boys** and the local and modest budget children's film **They Found a Cave** (1962) there was to be a gap of three years in which not one Australian feature was released.

Television and the Vincent inquiry

Throughout the late 1950s and early 1960s, television seemed paradoxically to both sound the deathknell of and hold out the promise of regeneration for the film industry. Because a lack of production seemed likely to continue, a new and more sophisticated activism began to stir among producers capable of making narrative films but denied the opportunity to work in either medium. Partly because of this, and because of public concern over the state of Australian television, the year 1960 brought the Federal Government's first sign of real interest in the film industry in more than three decades.

By then it was clear that imported television programmes were dominating audiences' viewing habits at least as much as imported feature films had before television transmission had begun. In October 1963 the Report from the Select Committee on the Encouragement of Australian Productions for Television (the Vincent Report) named the importation of too many television drama programmes from America as one of its "major criticisms" of the current industry position. Out of the total 57.8 per cent of time devoted to drama during one month of 1961, a mere 1.06 per cent had been Australian. In examining the cultural and sociological consequences of this, the Vincent Report commented:

Perhaps the greatest danger lies in its effect upon the rising generation (the adult population having grown up without television), who, day after day, are not only receiving anything but the most inadequate picture of Australia, her national traditions, culture and way of life, but in its place are recipients of a highly coloured and exaggerated picture of the way of life and morals of other countries (mainly the United States of America).[47]

This statement echoed the cultural protectionist arguments of the 1927 Royal Commission, and it was clear that the domestic situation that allowed "cultural imperialism" from abroad was unchanged. What had altered was not so much a concern for defending Australian culture, as one for developing it.

As material affluence had increased during the decade, so had Australians' appreciation of the arts. Many developed a new awareness of painting and invested in works of art in a boom described by one censorious critic as "a cut-throat scramble for culture"; music composition flowered; the Australian Elizabethan Theatre Trust was formed in 1954 in response to fresh calls for a "national theatre"; a National Institute of Dramatic Art was opened in 1958; Australia's first film festivals began in Melbourne in 1952 and in Sydney in 1954. As Geoffrey Serle has acknowledged:

Some time about the late 1950s a decisive change in fashion and taste, a recognition that the arts *mattered*, became evident among both the upper-middle class and the younger educated generation.[48]

The first television station to begin regular transmission in Australia was TCN 9 in Sydney on 16 September 1956. By the end of the year, both Melbourne and Sydney had two commercial channels and one national (ABC) channel each, and both cities were able to watch live coverage of that year's Melbourne Olympic Games. Other cities soon followed suit, and by 1961 over thirty country regions had the benefit of both ABC and commercial channels. Between 1956 and July 1957, a high proportion of local programming had been made possible by a shortage of overseas currency and government restrictions on foreign programme purchases. But by September 1958, total Australian content (including drama) had fallen to below forty-five per cent; Australian television from then on was to reflect the country's national life less than most other developed countries.

The basis of the problem had been predicted by Richard Boyer, chairman of the Australian Broadcasting Commission, when he had warned the 1953 Royal Commission into television that the natural urge of commercial interests was "to fill all possible hours with material of some sort, for time is the product sold". Indeed, in granting city and regional commercial licences, as well as a national ABC licence, the Government scarcely heeded the caution given by the Royal Commission report that the "danger of television is that success depends on an appeal to numbers, and it is difficult to escape mediocrity or vulgar sensationalism". Ten years later, the Vincent Report noted that only the ABC, which accepted its obligations on local content, had "a real understanding of its responsibility". However, the Report continued that, due to inadequate finance, "the extent to which the Commission is

210

succeeding *in* its aim is another consideration".[49]

Despite attempts by several senators to interest the Federal Government in the development of the Australian film industry, it spent the 1950s completely unmoved by the industry's plight. Then, on 17 August 1960, Senator George Hannan (Victoria) initiated a lengthy debate on the film and television industries, asking that the Senate consider four matters: the extent to which foreign films and television programmes were endangering national sentiment; whether a "sound local film industry" was in the national interest; whether and what kind of assistance should be given to the industry; to assess the local market potential for all kinds of television programmes "recorded by predominantly television techniques such as videotape". Although it had been prompted by concern over the four-year performance of local television, most of the debate proceeded to focus on the near-extinction of feature film production. In the debate, which stretched over two days, fourteen senators contributed to it, nearly all of them evaluating the cultural and economic loss. The senators continued to place cultural above commercial objectives as they discussed ways to fortify both industries, and most felt that film was a more crucial area for concern than television. Senator Victor Vincent was the only adamant dissenter; he argued that the scale of the domestic market for television made this medium of more vital interest than film could ever be.

Following the Hannan debate, John Kingsford Smith as president of the Australian Film Producers' Association (a new name for the earlier Film Producers' Association of Australia), had travelled to Canberra to discuss the industry's needs with Senators Hannan and Vincent. Returning to Sydney, Kingsford Smith and other AFPA members embarked on an extended period of research into government assistance to film industries abroad, with the aim of providing the Australian Government with a concrete proposal. The AFPA report was submitted to the Postmaster General in March 1962. Five months later, a Federal Government inquiry was appointed to determine whether government assistance was needed to foster Australian television. Known as the Nimmo Inquiry and appointed by Cabinet on 29 August 1962, it was conducted by representatives from various government departments. Over a hundred submissions were considered, but despite inquiries from the Film Producers' Association and others who gave evidence, the report of the committee, completed in September 1963, was kept secret.

On 29 November 1962, Senator Hannan laid the basis for a second and far more wide-ranging inquiry when he moved that a Select Committee be appointed "to inquire and report on the encouragement of the production in Australia of films and programmes suitable for television, and matters incidental thereto". Senator Victor Vincent's platform — that television was a more pressing field for inquiry — had been a persuasive one.

The new committee, under the chairmanship of Senator Vincent, consisted in addition of Senators Hartley Cant, Samuel Cohen, Thomas Drake-Brockman, George Hannan, Douglas McClelland and Reginald Wright. One hundred and thirty-nine people gave evidence at public hearings in Canberra and all State capitals. Together with members of the general public, the witnesses included Hal Alexander from Actors and Announcers' Equity, television consultant Ray Allsop, Professor Zelman Cowen from Melbourne University, figures in television and film like Hector Crawford, Chips Rafferty, Cecil Holmes, John McCallum, Herc McIntyre, Roger Mirams, Sir Charles Moses, Mervyn Murphy and Eric Porter, and the writers Olaf Ruhen and Morris West. Reflecting Vincent's personal interest in television and live theatre, the Report devoted considerable space to the importance of these areas, with only one section dealing specifically with the Australian film industry. This began with the statement that, whilst the inquiry had not tackled the problems of the film industry as a first priority, the Committee could not

avoid the conclusion that, as in the case of the theatre, an adequate development of drama for television can only be achieved with the building up of a corresponding degree of expansion of the film industry.[50]

But the film section itself was by no means minor. The Vincent Report summarised the industry's dilemma:

This country has already demonstrated that it can make world quality films and export them and the only reason why it did not continue to do so is that the industry was left unprotected and squeezed out of business by an overseas industry which was heavily protected in its own country.[51]

It also forcibly refuted the assumption that the industry was not worth saving:

The rise and fall of the Australian film industry is a melancholy spectacle for contemplation by Australians. One often hears it said that "Australians can never make films" and that the business of film-making is "best left to those countries (meaning the United States of America) who can do it better than we can". The Committee rejects the sentiments so expressed.[52]

The Report added that were it not for a Federal directive from 1960 which virtually prohibited imported commercials, "the film industry would now be extinct".[53]

In its television section, the Committee took the Australian Broadcasting Control Board severely to task for not having penalised commercial stations over what the ABCB itself had long regarded as unsatisfactory programming. The Committee had "no hesitation in concluding that commercial stations provided too many programmes which not only do not have the effect of raising the standard of public taste but have the reverse effect". It gave urgent and high priority to the recommendation that the ABC "should commence upon an increased programme of film production including films for export" and noted grimly that poorly-budgeted ABC television drama had come nowhere near a desirable world standard.

Many recommendations for an improved television system included an Australian drama quota, a reduction of "unsavoury" programmes, and public hearings for licence renewal applications. For the film industry, the

Report recommended government aid in the form of a budget loan scheme, tax concessions for producers, tax incentives for investors and assistance with overseas marketing. These were intended to overcome what the Report divided into economic, artistic, and technical problems faced by the industry. The Committee urged protection for film production, for it was seen to be "entirely at the mercy of unrestricted and powerful overseas competition". In terms of films that could be considered marketable overseas,

the Committee suggests that whilst a strong local atmosphere might be acceptable in other countries, the "theme" must have a basic universality that will render it attractive to other people.[54]

As a government document, the Vincent Report was remarkable for its scope and long-range practicability. The recommendations for film industry aid went considerably further than those of the previous two major inquiries, the 1927 Royal Commission and the New South Wales film inquiry of 1934, and the hearings and Report provoked a wider awareness of media and film issues than had previously existed. Presented to the Senate on 29 October 1963, the Report was released in December, and well received by the public including those whose concern over the state of Australian television had initiated calls for the inquiry in the first place.

The Menzies Government held a different opinion. Parliament showed its complete indifference by adjourning debate on the document in April 1964 and never resuming it. Later in 1964 a major opinion-finding seminar organised by the Producers and Directors' Guild of Australia concluded with a public demand that the debate be resumed. But despite a continuing campaign by the PDGA, AFPA and individual journalists, the Government allowed the Vincent Report to remain buried. Leading newspapers gave little or no publicity to the situation because many were answerable to owners of television stations whom the Report intended to make toe the line. In June 1964, Senator Vincent, when taking part in a Sydney Film Festival forum entitled "The Australian Film Industry: What of its Future?", told the audience that his Report would only be implemented if members of the public and organisations continued to make their wishes known in Canberra. Victor Vincent died on 9 November 1964.

But the petitioning had already begun. The Vincent Report, although never acted upon, focused the problems faced by filmmakers and played a valuable part in gathering their determination that Australian film live down its reputation as a part-time occupation and take its place as a recognised industry.

PART THREE

Revival

9

New stirrings
1965-70

The developments in the film industry of the late 1960s were motivated by the community's deeper regard for film, and initiated by directors trained in documentaries and television, some of whom worked also among the filmmakers creating a new "underground" cinema. Australian film audiences demonstrated for the first time in several decades that they were keen to see evidence of their own culture on screen. But above all, filmmakers wanted to disprove the long-held theory that they were incapable of developing a national cinema, and that even if they could do so, no audience would want to see the results.

Renewed pressure for government support of the film industry was evident within two months of the abandoned debate on the Vincent Report in April 1964. In the total absence of press coverage, the Film Editors' Guild of Australia (FEGA) in June 1964 published a report, *The Conspiracy of Silence*, which told of the way in which the press had ignored the Vincent Report because of its corporate links with television. The FEGA report, distributed widely through the film and television industries and to members of parliament, prompted letters from the Prime Minister's Department, the Federal Treasurer and the Postmaster General. In late September, representatives from the Australian Writers' Guild and Actors and Announcers' Equity conferred with Alan Hulme, the Postmaster General, to propose an increase of Australian drama content on both radio and television to at least one hour per week.

On 11 November, Hulme told the House of Representatives he considered that talent was almost entirely lacking in the film and television industries. He stated:

I do not think we have many good scriptwriters in Australia ... we have not many good actors in Australia ... we haven't producers and we haven't directors of high quality at present.[1]

The following March, the Writers' Guild publicly challenged these remarks at a forum following a National Television Congress which Hulme had attended in Sydney. After the forum, he instructed the Australian Broadcasting Control Board to conduct a further investigation, the result of which, fifteen months later, was a new regulation that television stations should screen in prime time a maximum of thirty minutes of Australian drama per week — only half as much as the Writers' Guild and Actors' Equity had sought the previous September.

Climate of change

The mid-1960s was a time of great change in Australia, both socially and economically. One of the more visible signs was the very high proportion of young people in the population. By 1967, two and a half million Australians were aged between fifteen and twenty-nine. The *Sydney Morning Herald* commented in an editorial on 5 August: "Never have the young been more numerous, more fussed over, more worried about, more envied". Troubled attitudes of a "generation gap" scarcely evident before now challenged what the young saw as the dominant conservatism of the pre-1960s years.

A number of decisions taken in the mid-1960s were to have far-reaching effects during the next decade. Sir Robert Menzies' long innings as the nation's leader was drawing to a close, and sixteen years of political paternalism was to make way for fresher approaches to government. As the economy began to move into a higher gear, fuelled by the prospects of affluence based on mineral wealth, Australia faced a future of reduced isolation and closer proximity to the pressures of the world at large.

Many people regarded the later years of the Menzies Liberal–Country Party coalition governments as a time of unruffled serenity, but others were questioning out-of-date and out-of-touch domestic and foreign policies. Not very far from Australia's northern boundary there was conflict in South-East Asia, and following the passing of an Act in 1964 which allowed for male conscription, Menzies announced in early 1965 that a battalion of Australian regular soldiers would be sent to assist the Americans in Vietnam. This sent shock waves through a society that had come to expect peace, full employment and freedom of choice. An immediate reaction produced demonstrations in the streets, at universities and outside government offices.

Other targets of the mainly youthful protest of this period included what were considered to be the grave inequalities in Australian society including racial discrimination, unwarranted censorship of theatre, books and films, and the increasing use of authority. In January 1966, Robert Menzies was succeeded as Prime Minister by Harold Holt who a few months later accelerated the growing ferment with his announcement that the Australian military presence in Vietnam would include conscripts. "All the way with LBJ" was his catchcry, and normally complacent Australians who had found Menzies' obeisance to the monarchy slightly distasteful, now deplored such sycophantic submission to Amercia and its President.

From the mid-1960s, an underground movement in film production, distribution and exhibition emerged as part of these protests against a

218

conservative society and the old conventions of filmmaking. Differences between underground filmmakers and the old guard of the film trade were considerably wider than the generation gap. Among the works of short and low-budget oppositional cinema produced in Australia at this time were Brian Hannant's anti-conscription film, **Something More** (1965), Kit Guyatt's record of the visit to Sydney by President Johnson, **Vietnam Report** (1966), and the cartoonist Bruce Petty's anti-Vietnam War film, **Hearts and Minds** (1968), which was rejected for local television transmission. As screenings of Australian and imported films took place, censorship was challenged frequently and reacted with its accustomed weight.

At a time when many Australians were sharpening their political and social opinions, the general level of financial support for the arts was still back in the 1950s. But there were a few encouraging signs of change. Developments in poetry, music, architecture and a vigorous national school of painting continued much as they had before, but beside Sydney Harbour, on the site of a former tram depot, Bennelong Point was gradually being transformed from a collection of derelict sheds into a series of vast concrete platforms that one day would become the Sydney Opera House, a proud symbol of the nation's cultural aspirations. In Melbourne, a new State art gallery in the form of a bluestone fortress became the first stage of Victoria's cultural centre. In Adelaide, a biennial Festival of Arts had been established in 1960 and attracted artists and performers from all over the world to a rich cultural *mélange* that could rival the Edinburgh International Festival.

Also in mid-decade, the opera star Joan Sutherland returned to her native land after an absence of fourteen years to be greeted by ecstatic audiences. In Sir Frank Tait's last grand gesture for J. C. Williamson's, the company presented a comprehensive repertoire, in what would be the world's last major season of unsubsidised grand opera. Sutherland arrived on an otherwise arid scene of activity in the performing arts. The Australian Elizabethan Theatre Trust's opera and ballet companies which in the 1970s became the Australian Opera and the Australian Ballet, and earned international reputations, were still in their infancy. The Trust Players, designed to become a national theatre company, after three years had been abandoned. There were sparks in the void like the arrival of Peter Kenna, Alan Seymour and Patrick White as playwrights, but the theatre had failed to continue the 1950s upsurge of optimism and was repeatedly beset by censorship, official and unofficial. There was little evidence of local cinema. After almost a decade of monochrome transmissions, Alan Fairhall, the then Minister for Defence and a radio enthusiast, forecast unofficially in late 1966 that "before very long" Australia would have a colour television system and FM radio — although he would not venture to give an exact date.[2] Both were, in fact, delayed for almost another decade, matching the record delays for the construction of the Sydney Opera House and the Victorian Arts Centre.

By 1966 most Australians could hardly remember when the last truly Australian feature film had been screened, setting aside co-productions and films by visiting foreign production units. Two years later, the Sydney *Sun-Herald* referred to local production as "a perennial damp squib that has been threatening to explode for nearly forty years".[3] The cinema chains were rarely interested in screening Australian-produced short films — particularly those filmed on 16 mm stock — unless they cost little or nothing. A loophole in the film tariffs allowed short educational, children's, and travel or governmental films to enter Australia duty-free. Many were free public relations shorts and they provided the bulk of supporting films at Australian theatres.

To a vast majority of the eleven million Australians, television had now taken over their entertainment and their thoughts — if they thought about it at all. But while Australians saw little of themselves on the cinema screens of the 1960s, they were demonstrating through the television ratings that they were not averse to watching Australian drama and comedy on the small screen. Early drama series such as Artransa's co-production *Whiplash* (1961), Channel Seven's *Jonah* (1962), Crawford Productions' *Consider Your Verdict* (from 1961) and the ABC's *Stormy Petrel* drew varying-sized audiences, but were all noticed. Crawford's police series *Homicide*, which began production in 1963, quickly became the first major Australian television drama success story; it was to be the most popular series between 1966 and 1972, only approached in popularity by the same company's *Division 4*. Television comedy first made an impression with the satirical revue series *The Mavis Bramston Show* (1964-1968), and its success along with some of its ingredients were to carry through to the situation comedy *My Name's McGooley, What's Yours?* (from 1966). But the first international as well as home success came with John McCallum and Lee Robinson's children's series *Skippy* (Fauna Productions, 1967-69) which was sold in eighty countries, including the United States where the price it commanded in late 1968 was the highest ever paid for an Australian television programme.

In the opinion of the British Film Institute's John Huntley, who visited Australia in 1964, an indigenous film industry required a population of eighty million people to become fully self-supporting. His statement, given credibility by the UNESCO auspices under which he travelled, appeared to make sense. Here was an English-speaking country with its social and entertainment traditions rooted in British, and to a fair extent, American values with easy access to the screen products of those nations. In addition, film received little serious attention as an art form.

Consolidation

No industry can be based on a state of enmity with its trade outlets, but in the 1960s the rift between potential producers and the exhibitors remained wide. A conspiracy theory was touted time and again, suggesting that vested overseas interests would go on cruelling the chances for Australian production ever to get off the ground again. It was difficult to disprove.

Distribution and exhibition was flourishing in spite of the severe erosion of cinema attendances by television. In 1965 there were still more than a thousand picture theatres across the nation grossing some $50 million for exhibitors. Of this amount, nearly half was remitted directly overseas through distributors. In 1967, all major film distributors, with one exception (BEF), were wholly-owned from the United States. As Australians, on a per capita basis, were the world's leading cinema-goers, the importance of the local market was obvious.

The exhibition trade viewed the mid-1960s as a period of consolidation, one that saw the demise of many country and suburban outlets but heralded the construction of inner-city showcase cinemas with seating capacities far smaller than the old picture palaces. Various grandiose schemes came to nothing — such as a forty-four-storey building, incorporating cinemas, planned for the heart of Sydney's entertainment district on the Hoyts' Trocadero Ballroom site — but the general mood was one of quiet confidence.

Censorship was a continuing concern throughout the period. Some initial ground-clearing was done in the early 1960s when many people took a stand in support of the satirical magazine *Oz*, whose editors were charged with being in breach of the Obscene and Indecent Publications Act; and in the late 1960s in support of a variety of stage performances barred under State legislation. Film censorship, like its literary counterpart, was plagued by official secrecy and laughable double standards, which from 1965 onwards the press did its best to expose. In 1968, pressure from film festivals led to the Commonwealth Censor's decision that films could be imported uncut by the Sydney and Melbourne film festivals. This decision was reversed the following year when the censors demanded the removal of sexual activity from the Swedish film I Love, You Love, reviving public debate on censorship in general. Senator Malcolm Scott, the Minister for Customs who had upheld the ban, faced public ridicule when the *Sydney Morning Herald* claimed he would not be able to identify sexual intercourse if he saw it. The affair went on to make international headlines, a fact not unnoticed by Scott's successor, Senator Don Chipp, who lifted the secrecy from censorship decisions and from 1970 pressed for the introduction of the ''R'' (restricted) classification that would permit a greater range of films for adult audiences. Exhibitors argued strongly against the ''R'' certificate introduction, largely for the reason that they were traditionally compliant with censorship instructions and hardly wanted the responsibility of policing attendances to restricted films. But Chipp took the unusual step of inviting parliamentarians, church leaders and members of the media to view deleted sections of censored films in order to find out if general community attitudes to the suppression of this material had changed. They undoubtedly had.

There was increasing awareness among filmmakers that the best way to achieve action was through political activism directed at distributors and exhibitors. Filmmakers and sympathetic journalists pointed out the privileges that foreign distribution companies enjoyed as they dominated the Australian film trade. That the foreign film companies with their apparent stranglehold of the Australian industry appeared as the villains of the scenario was not surprising — particularly when they were able to view their opponents as a small, fragmented band of amateurs with little bargaining power. But it was not as if the filmmakers had to start from scratch to rebuild a production industry — either with talent or facilities. There were six small film studios with sound stages — in Sydney, Artransa Park, Ajax Films, Fontana, Eric Porter Productions and Supreme Sound, and in Melbourne, Senior Films. In addition there were a dozen laboratories which, together with the studios, employed a total of around a thousand people.

In the late 1960s, more than fifty film production companies employed from five to over a hundred people each. Their principal activity was making television commercials. The largest employer was the Commonwealth Film Unit, with a staff of more than a hundred at its studio in the Sydney suburb of Lindfield. Among these various film production bodies, along with the television studios, underground filmmakers, filmmakers returning from abroad and individual film critics, the desire for a reborn feature film industry continued to grow.

The Underground film

The beginnings of a substantial revival came, not through the occasional co-production, but from a movement of young people shooting 16 mm underground films that ranged from works of documentary and fiction to the avant-garde. In the face of pessimism about Australian cinema, these young directors were united by a determination to make films. The use of 16 mm equipment, small crews and low budgets (most of them below $1000) meant that the range of subjects and styles could be inexhaustible. Many underground directors aimed at challenging accepted notions of narrative and documentary production and expanding a local awareness of experimental work. All felt confident of being able to attract an audience, and at the outset many of them did.

In some of the more conventional areas of filmmaking, the freedom and relatively low cost of using lightweight 16 mm camera equipment was also employed by surfing and travel documentaries. A number of the surfing shorts and features made by, among others, Bob Evans and Paul Witzig, had ready-made international audiences, and there were lucrative domestic takings for travel subjects shot by adventurer-filmmakers such as Keith Adams, Malcolm Douglas and the Leyland brothers. Few of their films were shown in established cinemas. In the fashion of the early travelling picture showmen, these producers hired arts centres, church halls, town halls and clubs. Sometimes, when the venues were not licensed as cinemas, the screenings were held in defiance of the law.

The success of these showings (especially of the surf movies) was of some encouragement to the early groups of underground filmmakers banding together to show their own films on a cooperative basis. At a time when much of the talk about feature production was accompanied by very little action, they began financing their own films, screened the results themselves, and shared the profits. Some of these directors were to become leading figures in feature film activity after 1970. But for several years in the late 1960s, a flourishing underground cinema co-existed with mainstream films in a manner impossible at any time before or since.

Isolated work in experimental film had been taking place in Australia since the early 1950s, and a significant number of the country's early directors in this field were of non-Australian origin. Beginning in the early 1950s an Italian migrant, Giorgio Mangiamele, made three 16 mm films based on migrant problems (**The Contract** (1953), **The Brothers** (1958) and **The Spag** (1962)), while from 1951 Australian-born Gil Brealey made a series of experimental narrative and documentary films at Melbourne University and later with the Melbourne Repertory Film Unit. At Eltham, near Melbourne, Tim Burstall in 1958 commenced a forty-five minute children's film, **The Prize** (released 1960), which won an award at the Venice Film Festival and began the career of one of the key figures in the industry's revival. In Adelaide, two migrant directors, Dusan Marek, a Czech, and Ludwik Dutkiewicz, a Pole, first made their mark in the early 1960s. In 1961 Marek directed the animated short **Adam and Eve**, which won the first Gold Medal at the Australian Film Awards and was also the first underground film in Australia to adopt a self-analytical approach. Three years later, Dutkiewicz, in collaboration with the photographer Ian Davidson, made the Eisenstein-influenced **Transfiguration**, a reflective montage cut to Bruckner's Ninth Symphony. Dutkiewicz and Davidson were later to make the feature-length **Time in Summer** (1968), a film of stunning visual imagination. The projects of Mangiamele, Marek and Dutkiewicz during the 1950s and 1960s were to be of further significance when one recalls that their essentially European approach was quite unprecedented locally, and their achievements helped lay to rest an assumption that films of artistic worth could not be made in Australia.

Two distinct styles of independent filmmaking emerged in Melbourne and Sydney as the 1960s developed. Melbourne's, centred in the suburb of Carlton, was more traditionalist and serious in tone than the Ubu Films movement in Sydney, which was influenced by the avant-garde in European art and theatre. Carlton cinema, which predated Ubu, took its lead from the French New Wave cinema. Ubu filmmaker Albie Thoms was to emphasise the distinction by stating that the Melbourne independents had ''affinities with those of the British Free Cinema movement of a decade before, more concerned with social conscience than personal expression or aesthetic experiment''.[4]

The year 1964 was one of notable growth for Melbourne's independent filmmaking. Nigel Buesst completed **Fun Radio**, a zanily satirical look at the city's young people moving through a summer weekend to the mood set by station 3UZ. Tom Cowan made his prize-winning **The Dancing Class**, that with precise photographic skill observed ballet training; Giorgio Mangiamele

223

was completing **Clay** (1965), his first feature; and Brian Davies was working on his feature-length **The Pudding Thieves**, released in 1967 after four years in production. **The Pudding Thieves** was Carlton cinema's first major work, heavily French New Wave in influence and constantly re-worked as filming progressed. Phillip Adams, who had seen this tale of two street photographers as a work-in-progress, had feared it might end up as a chronicle of "four years waiting for Godard". But completed and with new footage, he found:

In a very interesting way Australianness has triumphed over influence . . . Its worst failing is a tendency to university-style "in-jokes". Its best quality is an easy-going indigenous informality . . . As it is, **The Pudding Thieves** is more a mood piece than a fully developed feature. The mood, however, is full of interesting ambiguities.[5]

Ubu Films, formed in Sydney during the mid-1960s, was a more numerous and prolific group than the Carlton cinema group, and its avant-garde filmmakers tended to regard the Melbourne efforts as slightly old-fashioned. The foundation members of Ubu were Albie Thoms, Aggy Read, John Clark and David Perry. Others who soon joined the Sydney Filmmakers' Co-operative, the distribution unit which grew out of their efforts, included Bruce Beresford, Garry Shead, Stan Dalby, Michel Pearce, Richard Brennan and David Price. Several were to figure prominently in the feature boom of the 1970s.

Albie Thoms remained the central figure of Ubu Films, and later became "prime articulator, dynamic and documentor"[6] of the Sydney Filmmakers' Co-operative. The origins of Ubu lay in two films Thoms had made for Sydney University stage productions. **It Droppeth as the Gentle Rain**, a short directed by Thoms and Bruce Beresford, was the highlight of *A Revue of the Absurd* which Thoms produced in 1963. Humorous and rough-edged, it was banned by the New South Wales Chief Secretary, whose official injunction was read on stage as part of the night's entertainment. Thoms's second film, **The Spurt of Blood**, paid homage to surrealist cinema and was made as part of another stage production, *Theatre of Cruelty* (itself in turn inspired by the French surrealist playwright and poet Antonin Artaud). Thoms and his collaborators were eager to continue production, and with Ubu Films intended to embark on projects that would advance experimentation, attack repressive authority, rebuff the production pessimists and challenge the prevailing censorship. The ridicule of authority in general and censorship in particular was a repeated aim of Ubu's screenings of local and imported films. Customs Minister Scott even went as far as to declare that Ubu Films itself was obscene when questioned in Federal Parliament as to why he had not reversed a censor-imposed ban on **Relativity**, a film imported by Ubu in 1968.

On 12 April 1966, a team of Sydney filmmakers, including the Ubu members, gave a public screening of their films at the Union Theatre. This event, which marked the actual start of the Sydney Filmmakers' Co-operative movement, had followed a number of meetings at which the filmmakers had viewed each other's work, discussed mutual problems, and decided to distribute and exhibit their own output. Charles Higham wrote of the films at this first programme:

> These are the stirrings. A tone of cynical detachment comes through, suggesting the flavour of a purely Australian avant garde. Personal films should be the expression not only of an individual's psyche, but of a whole range of feelings among the most alive people in the community — Shead, Price and the others are already beginning to convey an Australian quality of physical joy, of sardonic indifference.[7]

But the efforts of Ubu weren't as completely divorced from the vestiges of the earlier Australian film industry as the films themselves suggest. Young Sydney filmmakers had a benefactor in Mervyn Murphy of Supreme Films, who handled virtually all of Ubu's laboratory work and was prepared to suspend credit for several months if necessary. On the basis that a bill could be paid when a film earned its money, Supreme supplied release prints free of initial charge for many films which might otherwise have been halted at work-print stage. While Melbourne's independent filmmakers had for many years received monetary aid from the State Film Centre of Victoria and the Federation of Victorian Film Societies, Supreme's generosity stood as the closest thing to subsidy that Sydney directors had until the advent of the first Federal Government grants for experimental production in mid-1970.

Ubu's projects and other films made available through the Sydney Filmmakers' Co-operative before 1970 included notably, David Perry's **Swansong in Birdland** (1964) and **The Tribulations of Mr Dupont Nomore** (1967), Garry Shead's **Ding-a-Dong Day** (1966), Peter Weir's first film, **Count Vim's Last Experience** (1967), Jim Sharman's first film, **Arcade** (1968), and Mick Glasheen's collage on conceptual thinking, **Evolution of '66** (1966). **The Tribulations of Mr Dupont Nomore** featured Michael Boddy in a surrealist fantasy about a fat man escaping from his wife to fly over Sydney. Albie Thoms' **Blunderball** (1966), intended as a money-raiser for future Ubu films, parodied the conventions of the James Bond features, and cost $1000 at a time when most underground films were budgeted well below that amount. Another exception, costing $5000 raised from private backers, was Christopher McCullough's **Vision for a New World** (1968). It combined elements of conventional film drama with an ambiguous structure depicting suicide and apparent regeneration, and was one of the most impressive Sydney underground films of this period. *Masque* magazine considered that the film's time shifts and thematic juxtapositions gave it "a complexity and depth seldom found in even the professional feature film".[8]

Albie Thoms attributed the success of **Blunderball** and many of the subsequent Ubu shorts to a fresh, youthful interest in Australian films:

People were experimenting with colour and light and sound in the same way as the rock music of the time was going psychedelic. So we were making things that were relevant to the issues of the time, and there was an audience.[9]

Bolero (1967), made by Thoms with a grant from the Royal Belgian Film Archive, was a reaction by the director to the stylistic constraints he faced while concurrently directing episodes of the ABC television drama series, *Contrabandits*. Set to Ravel's familiar music, it consists of a fourteen-minute dolly shot along a North Sydney back street, ending on a close-up of a seated woman's eye. As an exercise in sustained observation, it demands viewer participation while at the same time expanding an awareness of the possibilities of cinema. Explorations of these possibilities were to be made through the three feature-length films made by Albie Thoms during the next ten years. **Marinetti** (1969) was to represent for the director, his disciples and detractors alike, a watershed in the Australian experimental film movement.

Thoms' intention was "first person cinema", a stream-of-consciousness observation of life among friends in inner-city Sydney. Its aesthetic inspiration was the theory of F. T. Marinetti, the Italian founder of the futurist movement in 1909. With conventional plot and characterisation deliberately minimised, **Marinetti** is, right from its ten-minute opening sequence of black spacing, white flashes and a multi-layered soundtrack, another instant challenge to viewer involvement. The film is at its most vivid in a series of jittery "freak-out" impressions of Kings Cross at night. The images finally rain with multiple white scratches which punctuate, re-animate and finally take over from what remains of any conventional image. As surrounding sequences add to the multiple perspective — with frames divided, colour-filtered or seen through a fisheye lens — **Marinetti** becomes a compendium of previous Ubu films and lays down ideas for future expansion.

Although it was to retain a freshness when other local features of the period had quickly dated, the public reaction to **Marinetti** in Australia was cataclysmic. First shown in Sydney the night after the close of the 1969 Sydney Film Festival, it prompted walk-outs and a stormy press. One cartoon showed Albie Thoms as a beret-topped producer presenting "Macaroni" — "ninety minutes of nothing but, boy, it's got the censors worried".[10] A *Sun* editorial noted smugly, "How refreshing the way people walked out in hundreds from that tin-pot film about nothing".[11] Thoms was to attribute the vehemence of critics and confusion of audiences to the very challenges the film presented to "accepted notions of narrative filmmaking and therefore much of the propaganda that had been used so effectively to win government support for the revival of the Australian feature film industry".[12] Depressed by the experience, he spent six months touring **Marinetti** abroad with considerable success. Europeans welcomed it, and their response to the way in which Thoms had interpreted his Sydney environment stimulated ideas for his next feature (**Sunshine City**, 1973). In the meantime, the Ubu Films movement and its allied distribution group, the Sydney Filmmakers' Co-operative was, in Thoms's words, "plunged into despondency".[13] In June 1969, *Masque* quoted Ubu's Aggy Read as saying the local underground film scene was still active and thriving, but the problem, as the magazine put it, was

> ...where can the underground go? It will be a long time, if ever, before there is sufficient profit in short films for many people to make a living from them. Gradually, the commercial cinema is encroaching on underground territory.[14]

On 17 July 1969, a meeting was held to constitute the group as a registered cooperative.[15] Filmmakers now waited to hear the Federal Government's plans for subsidies and the role that underground cinema was expected to play alongside the more traditional areas of production. One film which gave evidence of some Sydney independent filmmakers' desire to work in a more conventional manner was **The American Poet's Visit** (1969), an adaptation of one of Frank Moorhouse's short stories directed by the film editor and critic Michael Thornhill. Although as a critic Thornhill had kindly reviewed some of the underground work, he expressed some of his basic antipathy to the movement when he wrote in *Masque*:

> I wanted to make a short film that wasn't going to be an "aesthetic experience" but rather, I wanted one which would have a discernible narrative structure — if for no other reason than that there are many young men with beards who scratch on film or superimpose shots of naked ladies over the sun sparkling through trees better than I could.[16]

The context of **The American Poet's Visit** was a party run by the Sydney "Push", a broadly-based radical group to which Thornhill and Moorhouse had belonged since the early 1960s. The story satirically charted the differences between a visiting radical poet and the bohemian and anarchist types of the Push who prove to be "armchair philosophers who espouse permanent protest rather than reformism".[17] Marred slightly by selfconsciousness, the film's documentary style (with camerawork by Russell Boyd) crystallises the attitudes of time and place as richly as the better works of Carlton cinema. Rex Cramphorn wrote: "The evocation of derivative, aimless and artificial Australian political attitudes is probably the film's major success."[18]

Mainstream re-emergence

If one were to take evidence of a commercial release as an indication of what Australian films were prominent during this period, it would appear that no truly indigenous Australian feature-length films intended for cinema release emerged until Tim Burstall's **Two Thousand Weeks** in 1969. **They're a Weird Mob** (1966), **Journey Out of Darkness** (1967) and **Age of Consent** (1969) were co-productions, and of the remaining seven features made between 1965 and 1969, two were visiting productions and four were a mixture of spin-offs from television or intended for that market. And yet both the predominantly "art" films **Clay** (1965) and **Time in Summer** (1968) were filmed on 35 mm in the hope that they too would be screened before

227

mainstream audiences. The fact that they were not indicates insular over-confidence by their producers and total reluctance by the trade to handle anything they remotely considered a gamble.

They're a Weird Mob, a much-publicised "rebirth" of Australian cinema, had been planned since the early 1960s. The initiators of the project were the British producer-director Michael Powell and John McCallum, then managing director of J. C. Williamson Ltd. A third of the $600 000 budget came from the Rank Organisation, another third from Britain's National Film Finance Corporation and the remainder from Australian interests, principally J. C. Williamson Ltd. The story, adapted from the 1957 novel by John O'Grady under the pseudonym Nino Culotta, is about Nino, an Italian immigrant, and his endeavours to adjust to the rituals of mateship, learn enough local slang to get by, and win the strong-minded daughter of a building-contractor. The script, by "Richard Imrie" (Powell's long-time collaborator Emeric Pressburger), broadly caricatures Australians but not without affection. Character focus is nowhere near sharp enough to capture the consistent quirkiness of the book, although the hard-working performance of Walter Chiari as Nino manages to make an impact, but only occasional inventiveness recalls the Powell–Pressburger talent so strongly evident in their earlier films **A Matter of Life and Death** (1946) and **The Red Shoes** (1948).

The commercial success of **They're a Weird Mob**, which established an unbeaten record at Sydney's large State Theatre, drew heavily from the continuing popularity of the book and attracted considerable publicity for what was, after all, an unusual event — an Australian feature film. Within a year, the production grossed $3 million from Australian screenings alone but because of the nature of Williamson-Powell's distribution and exhibition agreement, the producers had received only one-sixth of this amount by the end of 1967, and would not recoup production costs until 1974. The box office success, coupled with Williamson-Powell's well-publicised frustration over the distribution deal, led to its prominence as a key film in the drive to re-establish the film industry with government support. Michael Thornhill wrote:

When the Greater Union Theatres Group of companies and the Rank Distributors Ltd are taking $2 500 000 from $3 000 000 and the producers are left with $500 000 the cards are really stacked against the independent producer in Australia.[19]

Early in 1967, amid much industry talk and relatively little action, **Journey Out of Darkness** began shooting around Alice Springs and Darwin. The bulk of the $190 000 budget was United States money arranged through the American daytime television compere Konrad Matthei, who aimed to use this film to establish his reputation as a dramatic actor. **Journey Out of Darkness** was also a first feature for director James Trainor, who had worked predominantly in documentaries, including some early work for the DOI Film Division. Scripted by the veteran Hollywood writer Howard Koch from an idea by Trainor, it told of a white policeman escorting an Aboriginal killer back to a white man's justice and himself nearly dying of thirst. Charles Higham reported that in spite of his own fears that the film would be "a routine B-picture 'actioner' '', the producer Frank Brittain insisted "it will be every bit as much an art picture as a Bergman production".[20] The result — miscast (the white actor Ed Devereaux played a leading role as an Aboriginal blacktracker and the Ceylon-born singer Kamahl the Aboriginal killer), overlong and anything but Bergmanesque both artistically and commercially — confirmed Higham's suspicions.

In 1969, **You Can't See 'Round Corners** and **The Intruders** were made as spin-offs from local television series, while with an eye on the American market, **It Takes All Kinds** was the first of three Australian-American co-productions produced and directed by a former Hollywood second unit director, Eddie Davis. Like its two companion features (**Color Me Dead** and **That Lady From Peking**, both 1970), **It Takes All Kinds** did nothing but quickly dispel euphoria about co-productions being the industry's path to salvation. Michael Thornhill regarded the cinema release under the pretext that it was an A-grade film to be "an imposition on audiences".[21]

Considerably more hope was justified with **Age of Consent** (1969), co-produced by Michael Powell and James Mason, with Michael Pate as associate producer, and backed by British and Australian money. Adapted from Norman Lindsay's novel, **Age of Consent** replaced a 1920s background and evocative New South Wales south coast seediness with a contemporary Barrier Reef setting in Queensland. As he had on **They're a Weird Mob**, director Powell provided some sporadic visual artistry and broad caricatures. Only with the performance of Helen Mirren as Cora, the artist's model, did the free spirit of the Lindsay novel break through. Sylvia Lawson, writing in *Quadrant*, used the film to express her opinion of local co-productions:

The overstrained, manufactured Australianism of **Age of Consent** should be enough to convince any adult filmgoer of the total inadequacy, so far as Australian self-interpretation is concerned, of the British or American-based film project which uses Australia as a location. The fact that this film is doing roaring business here at present does not disprove my point; it further suggests the extent of audience-hunger to see Australian backgrounds, Australian life and performances on the screen.[22]

The following year brought the release of two visiting productions whose box office results were even less encouraging to future visitors. **Adam's Woman** (director Philip Leacock) and **Ned Kelly** (director Tony Richardson) represented, with little new insight, early colonial convict and bushranging sagas costing in each case approximately $2 500 000. **Adam's Woman** featured Beau Bridges as a hippified rebel American convict and **Ned Kelly** presented a miscast and oddly undynamic Mick Jagger as the rebel bushranger. Perhaps inevitably, Australian critical reaction to **Ned Kelly** was severe. Michael Thornhill wrote:

229

Richardson has misunderstood totally the Australian character and temperament. It is no use trying to bring a pseudo-Restoration bawdy approach to a 19th-century colonial disagreement between the Irish Catholic element and the English Protestant Establishment.[23]

Albie Thoms pulled no punches:

... **Ned Kelly** is a cockup. Neither raging pop nor an analytic documentary, it comes across as a token con. People will go to see Mick Jagger and the Ned Kelly trip, but they'll be punished. **Ned Kelly** is half-cocked entertainment and half-arsed history.[24]

Expectations were considerably higher for **Two Thousand Weeks** (1969), the feature debut of Melbourne director Tim Burstall. Following his first film, **The Prize** (1960), Burstall embarked on several other children's projects: the television series, *Sebastian The Fox*, and, for the Commonwealth Film Unit, **Nullarbor Hideout** (1965). In the meantime, he had also made a television series about Australian painters including Arthur Boyd and Sidney Nolan. After his CFU work, Burstall visited America on a Harkness Foundation travel grant and remained there for two years. He studied filmmaking at the University of Southern California and acting under Lee Strasberg at the Actors Studio, then worked as an unpaid assistant with Martin Ritt on **Hombre** (1967). Once back in Australia, Burstall collaborated with Patrick Ryan on the screenplay of **Two Thousand Weeks**.

The advance publicity for **Two Thousand Weeks** stressed that it was the first wholly Australian feature since Lee Robinson's **Dust in the Sun** in 1958, "conceived, written, produced, directed and acted by Australian professionals".[25] Tim Burstall told the *Australian*, "It's got to be a commercial success. If it isn't I would say it probably might be my only go".[26]

The central theme was the desperation of an individual's attempts to prove his professional worth amid the emerging Australian culture of the late 1960s. The film presented a new evaluation of national identity, and threw into relief the eternal decision of whether it was better to travel abroad or to stay at home in seeking professional fulfilment. In several respects, **Two Thousand Weeks** represented for the 1960s feature film revival what **The City** episode of **Three in One** had for the 1950s. Not only were both made at opposite ends of the industry's eclipse, but both endeavoured to capture a contemporary urban identity familiar to many Australians in their time, and featured anti-heroes frustrated by a repressive climate. During production, whatever qualms that may have existed about the film's subject being too esoteric for a mass Australian audience were swept away by a publicity emphasis on Burstall's careful preparation and the impressive credentials of his leading collaborators.

The Burstall–Ryan screenplay was developed from two weeks of taped conversations about their upbringing and present outlook — "things that interested us and are relevant to our generation". According to Burstall, the basis was "someone's life in a state of crisis in relation to his job, his

230

marriage, his friends and family''.[27] **Two Thousand Weeks** tells of Will
Gardner (played by Mark McManus), faced with three crises: the departure
overseas of his mistress (Jeanie Drynan), the slow death of his father, and
coming to terms with his inadequacies as a writer. All take place under the
critical gaze of an old friend and successful expatriate, Noel Oakshot (David
Turnbull).

The best moments, showing Will in open conflict with Oakshot over
Australia's cultural calibre, demonstrate Burstall's commitment to his
subject. Oakshot despises the geographical isolation of Australia which makes
every idea arrive ''secondhand and usually five years out of date''[28], and in
the midst of an argument Will accuses him of being a sell-out expatriate,
aiming to keep Australians as ''second-class Englishmen or Americans . . .
colonists — economically, culturally, in every way''.[29] The brawl that ensues
is a convincing release from mutual claustrophobia and contempt. The film
becomes weighed down, however, by its grave sense of responsibility.
Dialogue becomes pedantic as if to include everything the writers had
discussed, characters lose their spontaneity. Oakshot, the most cynical and
least predictable of the leads, is the only one to sustain genuine interest. The
film also lacks what might have been a redeeming sense of humour, to the
extent that the overwhelming earnestness becomes what some audiences
found laughable.

Two Thousand Weeks opened in Melbourne in early 1969 after
Columbia Pictures had agreed to distribute it. It was mauled by the critics —
especially Colin Bennett of the *Age* — and taken off at the end of two weeks.
In June it was screened to an unfavourable response at the Sydney Film
Festival, and subsequently had a modest season at that city's Gala Cinema. It
fared much better at the Moscow Film Festival of 1969 and was reviewed
favourably by the London *Sunday Times*; by then, however, its commercial
failure was evident. On its home territory, **Two Thousand Weeks** had fallen
prey to much the same kind of expectations that had soured the reception for
Marinetti. Tim Burstall blamed Australian critical response for the film's
failure. He found it particularly galling that widely read critics who advocated
a true Australian cinema should come down so heavily on the first feature of
this kind in more than a decade. He now faced a two year uphill battle to
obtain backing for his second feature.

Other Melbourne initiatives

A number of other Melbourne filmmakers had continued to produce low-
budget films of urban introspection. While still at school, Chris Lofven
attracted attention with his **Forgotten Loneliness** (1965), which depicted the
loneliness of a young Chinese student in Melbourne. In 1968 David Minter
filmed the cinema verité **Hey Al Baby**; its touches of Milos Forman-style
comedy were also shared by Nigel Buesst's **Bonjour Balwyn** (1971), an
episodic satire featuring John Duigan as a magazine editor in trouble with
personal relationships and his creditors. With the benefit of an irreverently

231

witty script by John Romeril, Buesst and Duigan, **Bonjour Balwyn** topped off its nonconformist narrative approach with a spontaneous and hilarious final fifteen minutes as the hero, now broke, is forced into conducting front-door surveys while his employer (Peter Cummins) embarks on a series of back-door thefts. In some ways a further companion piece to **Hey Al Baby** and **Bonjour Balwyn** was Brian Davies's **Brake Fluid** (1970), a comedy co-written by Davies and the playwright John Romeril.

Prior to **Bonjour Balwyn**, Nigel Buesst had made a partly dramatised documentary, **The Rise and Fall of Squizzy Taylor** (1969), which was televised by Channel 9 in Sydney and Melbourne, and **Dead Easy** (1970), a comedy about mass murder. Probably the least typical Melbourne film of this period was **Matuta** (1968), directed by Paul Cox, a professional still photographer. His surreal approach placed it closer to the Sydney underground than to most of his Melbourne contemporaries.

Jack and Jill: A Postscript (1970) by Phillip Adams and Brian Robinson episodically and incisively depicted an ill-fated affair between two people on different social levels: Jill, a kindergarten teacher, and Jack, a bikie. A crisp documentary style captured the varied backgrounds accurately and with frequent satire, while ironic counterpoint was supplied (not always successfully) by the use of ''voice-over'' nursery rhymes. Produced over five years, the final result appeared perhaps too incomplete for the wide audience to which it aspired. The film received encouraging reviews and a small cluster of awards but after 35 mm prints were made (blown up, at the producers' expense, from 16 mm), it was given only limited release as a support.

After making **Jack and Jill**, Phillip Adams told the periodical *Lumière*:

Making serious features in this country is about the most thankless task
imaginable. You tend to think of the drought-stricken farmer as the most
depressed sector of industry in this country. But all they need is a little rain.
What the Australian filmmaker needs is nothing short of a miracle.[30]

Adams at this time was the director of two advertising agencies, had been a television critic and wrote a satirical column which appeared in a number of Australian newspapers. He was a member of a Federal Government Film and Television Committee attached to the Australian Council for the Arts, an interim councillor for the proposed Australian Film and Television School, and a governor of the Australian Film Institute. He was already an important figure in pressing for government support for the film industry. After the experience of **Jack and Jill: A Postscript**, he was to make, with producer-director John B. Murray, a calculated attempt on the mass market with **The Naked Bunyip** (1970).

This two and a half-hour documentary about Australian sexual attitudes was interspersed with comic interludes featuring Graeme Blundell as a market researcher supposedly interviewing a broad spectrum of people including Edna Everage (Barry Humphries), doctors, academics, entertainers, moral reformers, prostitutes, homosexuals, advertisers and pornographers. Adams and Murray chose the subject after their own research into the film industry. Murray wrote:

Careful thought was given to that which we thought the public would support ... To assess the Australian market for locally produced films at this stage in the development of an industry is not as easy as researching the demand for new washing powder.[31]

The gamble, challenging censorship codes as well as accepted patterns of film production and release, paid off for the producers and the industry at large. **The Naked Bunyip**, which had been filmed, like **Jack and Jill**, on 16 mm stock, was toured in that form around Australia for two years ignoring the usual distribution channels. Although Adams later revealed that most of the returns had been made at a few key locations (especially the St Kilda Palais and Playbox in Melbourne)[32], the practice of direct exhibition was to be adopted by other feature filmmakers like Tim Burstall (with **Stork**, 1971) and Michael Thornhill (with **Between Wars**, 1974). A request by the Commonwealth Film Censor that five minutes be deleted from **The Naked Bunyip** boosted press coverage for the film, and this was further stimulated when the producers merely masked the offending footage with a cartoon figure of a bunyip in suggestive poses, and "bleeped" the sound. John Murray's action in screening the uncensored version to the press threw more public debate into the reform of film censorship, and this helped pave the way for the production of subsequent sex comedies: **Stork, The Adventures of Barry McKenzie** (1973) and **Alvin Purple** (1973).

Mounting pressures

From the time of the Vincent Report, the Producers and Directors' Guild of Australia (PDGA) kept up a regular barrage, lobbying Federal and State parliamentarians to act upon the recommendations. This was in spite of the Postmaster General's announcement in 1965 that he could not guarantee that any action would ever be taken on the Vincent Report since the Senate Select Committee which had prepared it had not been appointed by Cabinet.

The following year, the only Australian television drama programme being screened by the commercial networks was Crawford Productions' *Homicide*. By September 1970, there were only two hour-long drama series being made, *Homicide* and another programme from Crawford's, *Division 4*. During the previous month, the TV: Make it Australian Committee had conducted mass protest meetings in Sydney and Melbourne. The actor Terence Donovan, a member of the committee, announced: "If TV drama is cut back any more, we will lose the television industry as we lost the film industry years ago."[33]

Members of the film community continued to organise their own campaign. The editor Anthony Buckley and director Roland Beckett, both committee members of PDGA, were foundation members in 1968 of the

Australian Film Council, formed in Sydney with support from many individuals and all unions, guilds, film society and festival organisations who were interested in the advancement of film production. One of the Council's earliest activities was a screening for Federal parliamentarians of Buckley's **Forgotten Cinema** (1967), an account of the rise and fall of the Australian industry. Impressed by the film and the cause, the Prime Minister, John Gorton, in early 1969 pledged Federal aid at a dinner organised by the Australian Film Council and the PDGA.[34] It was now several months since Gorton had taken over as prime minister following the disappearance at sea of Harold Holt in December 1967. A month before his death, Holt had set up the Australian Council for the Arts, federally funded and with a brief that included film. The various State members of the ACA were appointed by Gorton in June 1968, and at the end of the Melbourne Film Festival that month, Barry Jones, a Victorian member of the Council, announced that he hoped to see Federal Government funds for independent filmmaking within a year. Jones revealed that at the first meeting of the ACA in July, he intended to propose the setting up of a national film board along Canadian lines that would remove the Commonwealth Film Unit from the Department of the Interior. He would also propose a study of the Canadian Film Development Corporation, for the setting up of an Australian equivalent.[35]

Barry Jones was a familiar face to millions of Australians through his repeated triumphs on the television quiz programme, *Pick-a-Box*. He had a background even more colourfully varied than his friend Phillip Adams, for Jones, as *Nation* summarised it, was "Quiz star and historian, university lecturer and travel agent, Methodist lay preacher and dissident member of the Victorian ALP, simultaneously or successively".[36] Since 1967, Jones had been a friend and unofficial adviser on cultural matters to John Gorton, and because of this, both he and Phillip Adams were able to freely discuss film with the Prime Minister. When the Australian Council for the Arts commenced its operations, a Film and Television Committee was appointed under the chairmanship of the New South Wales Liberal politician Peter Coleman. Other members included Jones, Adams, and Stanley Hawes, Producer-in-Chief for the Commonwealth Film Unit. When they were instructed to prepare an interim report on the industry, Jones, Adams and Coleman travelled to study government support of film industries overseas.

Late 1968 brought evidence of a philosophical conflict that was to recur throughout the discussion on government film funding. Although Federal senators participating in the Hannan debate of August 1960 had agreed that cultural results were more important than profits during the industry's reconstruction, opinions on this subject were widely divided. At a dinner in August 1968 organised by the periodical *Quadrant* intended to acquaint the Chairman of the ACA, Dr H. C. Coombs, with the industry's needs, guests were asked how the $500 000 allocated to films might best be used. When John Baxter, Charles Higham and Aggy Read agreed that the promotion of experimental cinema and a meaningful national cinema held high priority, Coombs replied that the money should only be used on productions with the best commercial prospects[37], and that only scripted, part-budgeted films with distribution guarantees should be eligible.[38] During discussion with John Baxter on the need for a film school, Coombs compared the training of filmmakers to that of bricklayers. A report in the *Sydney Morning Herald* stated that guests soon suspected they had been invited along "to act as rubber stamps for his ideas". The same report concluded: "It must have been hard to tell. All hopes of discussion or debate were drowned, then lost, in a growing clamour of voices".[39]

UNESCO and after

More coherent thought was evident at a Sydney seminar organised in November 1968 by the Australian UNESCO Committee for Mass Communication on the professional training of film writers, producers and directors. After six days of debate, the delegates recommended the establishment of a national film school without delay. Two reports were issued. One was on the seminar itself. The other, by Lord Ted Willis, the UNESCO consultant to the conference, reiterated the vital need for a training school and, incorporating impressions gathered on a recent fact-finding tour, commented that the local film industry was restricted by a lack of imagination on the part of employers. Willis commented that the result was widespread stagnation and frustration among employees.

May 1969 saw the Interim Report of the Film and Television Committee of the Australian Council for the Arts and, like the two from UNESCO, it gave top priority to the establishment of a film and television school. But it added that the industry should be further encouraged by the setting up of a film and television development corporation and the provision of an experimental film fund. Overall, the Interim Report was a brief statement supporting a local film industry, but it brought quick results. John Gorton "unconditionally accepted" all of its recommendations, and at the Australian Film Institute Awards on 2 December, confirmed that his Government would establish an Australian Film Development Corporation with a grant of $100 000 for the setting up of the Experimental Film and Television Fund (EFTF), $100 000 for the promotion and distribution of the Fund's films, and a further $100 000 for a start on the film school. For the next four years, the planning and setting up of the school would be supervised by an interim council.

The Australian Film Development Corporation Bill was introduced to the House of Representatives on 5 March 1970, and receiving enthusiastic support from the Government and Opposition parties, it moved quickly through both Houses. Gorton announced that the Corporation would make loans to film and television producers, as well as serving where possible as a joint investor eligible for profits but not being liable for debts incurred. *Nation* commented:

Where unassisted private enterprise has failed, government sponsorship will now have the chance of showing whether its bite is as good as its barkers.[40]

235

The Experimental Film and Television Fund, the "third prong" of the Government's thrust to re-establish the industry, was the first to come into operation. With money from the Australian Council for the Arts, administered by the Australian Film Institute[41], the first allocation was made on 7 July 1970. In the initial batch of loans, seventy-three applicants were granted a total of $111 450. The term "experimental" was to be interpreted so as to include projects that were (a) original in approach, technique or subject matter, (b) technical research projects, or (c) experiments by inexperienced but promising filmmakers. In spite of the fact that the Sydney Filmmakers' Co-operative had for several years previously carried out Australia-wide distribution of the kinds of productions that were expected to result from the EFTF scheme, it was announced that the Australian Film Institute would set up a library to acquire copies of the films and exhibit and market them. The first subject to be completed from EFTF money was **Or Forever Hold Your Peace** (1970), a coverage of thirty-six hours of the anti-Vietnam War Moratorium held in Sydney during May.

Predictably, the commercial distribution and exhibition trade viewed these government initiatives with scepticism. Concerning the Experimental Film and Television Fund, the reactionary *Australasian Exhibitor* fumed:

This industry has long passed the age of experiment by would-be producers and directors.

The Piggy-Bank hand-outs to starry-eyed amateurs by the Australian Council for the Arts borders on the ludicrous but at the same time, dangerous.[42]

Film Weekly, more genuinely concerned for the industry's development, commented in response to John Gorton's AFDC announcement of March 1970:

A move in the right direction, formation of the corporation is nevertheless a small-scale approach to a major problem.

The corporation would seek to encourage the production of box-office successes and to assist in the distribution of them.

This high aim will no doubt be recorded with a degree of cynicism in the industry ... One of the oldest adages in the trade, and one that's still valid is, "if we knew how to make box-office successes, we'd all be millionaires".[43]

The AFDC's first investment was to provide almost a quarter of the budget for Hans Pomeranz's 16 mm feature, **Stockade** (1971), an adaptation of Kenneth Cook's play depicting the historical events at Eureka Stockade. **Stockade**, as it turned out, was to stimulate new and open conflict between producers, the trade and government over the issue of exhibition.

State and federal focus

The first sign of controversy appeared when industry activists and government officials re-examined the provisions of the New South Wales

1938 Theatres and Public Halls Act for the first time in almost thirty years. The Act's requirement that 2.5 per cent of feature films shown in the most populous State should be of local origin, had never been met. In 1968 the Producers and Directors' Guild wrote to the New South Wales Chief Secretary, Eric Willis, and to the State's Theatres and Films Commission, pointing out that if quota provisions of the Act had been enforced over the years, Australia would by now have had a thriving film industry. Roland Beckett, the Guild president, announced to the press:

We feel we can only get somewhere by the public demanding more Australian entertainment, as it has done with Australian television, and by the Government responding to that decision by fully enforcing compliance with the law.[44]

In 1969, Herbert Hayward took over as chairman of the Theatres and Films Commission after almost fifty years in exhibition, distribution and publicity. For the previous twenty-one years, he had been a senior executive of Greater Union Theatres. Like many of his former associates, he was sceptical about the value of Federal Government aid, particularly as the AFDC had invited no film trade opinions while making decisions on its investment. In early 1970, Hayward travelled to study government aid to the British and selected Continental film industries on behalf of the Commission and the New South Wales Chief Secretary. In his report on production, presented to Chief Secretary Willis in October 1970 (along with reports on film censorship and standard forms of distributor–exhibitor contract), he related that the British film industry was being brought to its knees by too many "self-styled producers making the wrong kind of pictures", together with a general lack of overseas marketing strategy, poor story selection and frequent budget extravagance. Hayward stated:

Australia's policy should be considered in the light of the situation in the UK.

Twenty years of assistance by means of the Eady Levy and the National Film Finance Corporation has failed to establish the British film industry on a sound commercial basis. It is now at its lowest ebb ...

The well-meaning intentions of the British Government brought the British film industry, production and exhibition, to the verge of ruin.[45]

Herbert Hayward saw that the future of the Australian feature film lay in co-production, and in 1970 recommended to the New South Wales Government that such films should be counted as part of the State's domestic film quota. Hayward was mindful of the failure of the New South Wales quota in the 1930s and that of Britain in the late 1940s. To give the New South Wales Quota Act what he considered a realistic basis, he also recommended that three documentaries running for a minimum of twenty minutes be counted as a single feature. Part of his rationale was that the ensuing production of documentaries would boost the activity of filmmakers, their technicians and laboratories, but it was a suggestion that alarmed the Australian Film Council and other production bodies.

The Film Council and the PDGA were two groups which had called for enforcement of the Quota Act as it stood, and Chief Secretary Willis had promised to examine the issue after sympathetically receiving the Film Council deputation in 1969. Hopes expressed that the enforcement of the Act could lead to the production of twelve local features in as many months, led distributors and exhibitors to re-state that they had nothing against Australian features, but could hardly fulfil quota conditions in the absence of the required number of films. Hoyts Theatres, through their managing director Dale Turnbull, stated: "We as exhibitors, have always shown Australian films when available; we have never shown any reluctance to screen them." Turnbull claimed that his company had, in fact, exceeded its quota in 1967-68 by showing 4.1 per cent of Australian product, excluding shorts and newsreels. However, the fact remained that fifty-two issues of a local Cinesound or Movietone newsreel counted as an Australian feature-length film. The Australian Film Council's Newsletter commented in September 1970: "It is hard for the New South Wales Government to justify this support for outmoded newsreels."[46]

Producers and fellow activists also pointed out that the Theatres and Films Commission, as the State's supreme authority for cinema licensing, was able to stipulate that screenings would only take place in cinemas approved by them. This, they claimed, discriminated against producers who wished to show their films away from the normal outlets. Under the Theatres and Public Halls Act, the intention of cinema licensing was to ensure fire safety standards were met and to protect registered cinema owners against competition. On the latter point, journalist P. P. McGuinness observed:

... these days such provisions run clearly counter to Commonwealth Government policy, which is to promise competition, and counter to what is now considered generally to be the public interest — free competition.[47]

Herbert Hayward denied that the structure of the existing theatre circuits and the licensing procedures that protected their interests had adverse effects on producers. When in 1969 the president of the PDGA wrote to Willis urging the reconstruction of the cinema chains, Hayward reacted through a memorandum to Willis that this plan warranted "no consideration" and that it showed "a complete lack of understanding and experience of theatre circuit operation in this country".[48] Divisions between the views of the trade and local producers seemed as wide as ever, especially when early the following year, Hayward commented on the Federal Government's million dollar plan for the industry:

Nothing more pathetic or ludicrous has ever come out of Canberra. Firstly a million dollars is less than chicken feed. Secondly it will be in the hands of a bunch of academics, full of high-flown theories but devoid of any real knowledge and experience in feature filmmaking, and local and overseas marketing requirements.[49]

By July 1971, John McCallum, as chairman of the Film Council, was sufficiently disgruntled with rumours that the Theatres and Films Commission was recommending a reduction of quota requirements, to state in the Council's newsletter:

If there is any substance in these rumours, the Film Council will oppose them with all the means at its disposal and will notify the Minister that it has no confidence in the Theatres and Films Commission as presently constituted.[50]

Although minor amendments to the Quota Act were made in 1969 and again in May 1971, the Council's fears about quota reduction were not realised. Instead, an even greater setback occurred in December 1971, when Eric Willis bluntly announced to filmmakers and the press that he would not enforce the provisions of the Act regarding quotas because they were "unenforceable".[51] P. P. McGuinness reported in the *National Times*:

He [Willis] argues that if the quotas were enforced distributors would move to another State, where there was no legislative provision for quotas . . .

Mr Willis further argues that such requirements are better enforced by the Commonwealth government.[52]

December 1971 also brought the premiere of Hans Pomeranz's **Stockade** in Victoria and New South Wales. The Liberal member for Ballarat, Dudley Erwin, denounced the film as "immoral" for its brothel and seduction scenes, but this served as light comic relief compared to the events that followed. As the film had been made on 16 mm and the producers faced the prospect of screening it independently of established outlets, Pomeranz and Kenneth Cook decided to challenge the New South Wales ruling that films could not be screened in unlicensed halls. The announcement that the Quota Act could not be enforced added weight to the portrayal by the press of the **Stockade** producers as small independent Davids locked in combat with the Goliaths of the trade. The Pomeranz–Cook campaign continued to draw public attention to exhibition inequities well into 1972, although the poor quality of **Stockade** undercut some of their arguments. The climax occurred when Pomeranz issued the Chief Secretary with a writ demanding an inquiry into the film trade's attitude to Australian films. Willis was moved to the education portfolio soon afterwards, and *Lumière* reported that "his successor so far has made no impact in this area".[53]

Other producers in New South Wales, Queensland and Victoria continued to fall foul of exhibition laws both old and new. Police in Wollongong nailed up the door of the unlicensed Pioneer Hall when the surfing film **Morning of the Earth** (1971) was advertised for screening there. In July 1972, Cambridge Film and Television Productions were prevented by Queensland's Picture Theatres and Films Act, from screening the documentary feature **Sunbury** as part of a pop concert and light show at Brisbane's Festival Hall. And in early 1972, Melbourne filmmaker Nigel Buesst was charged under Victoria's Films Act of October 1971 with showing an uncensored film in an unlicensed hall and failing to register as a distributor and exhibitor. Buesst was acquitted of all charges but his case only strengthened the impression of local filmmakers that they were an oppressed minority. John B. Murray, as president of the PDGA in Victoria, said the Guild members considered the Films Act to be an infringement of human rights.[54]

In August 1972, Ewart Wade, the editor of *Lumière*, commented that if the Federal Government was to continue to support the film industry through the AFDC, the Experimental Film and Television Fund and the Film and Television School,

then it had better take some action to resolve the situation within the States where overseas interests are dominating the distribution and exhibition situation and making it virtually impossible for any producer to recover his money in this country.

In fact, the Commonwealth was already moving towards such action. In March 1972, the Federal Government under William McMahon (who had replaced John Gorton as Prime Minister in March 1971) instructed the Tariff Board to undertake an inquiry into further assistance required by films and television.

Tariff protection for the industry had long been advocated by the Australian Film Council, and both tariffs and quotas were remedial measures that the Film and Television Committee of the Australian Council for the Arts had recommended be examined by the Tariff Board or another ''specially constituted body''. For some, this had always been the most important of the Film and Television Committee's suggestions.[55] The direction by the then Minister for Trade, Doug Anthony, requested that, following the inquiry, the recommendations of the Tariff Board should be in line with the Government's already stated objective ''to foster and develop an efficient industry producing motion picture films and television programmes and to encourage adequate distribution of the products of this industry within and outside Australia''.

Both sides of the industry, the trade as well as the production sector, now waited to see whether the status quo of distribution and exhibition would be challenged — or granted an approving pat on the head for its long-held complacency.

10

Subsidy and growth
1971 - 75

In early March 1971, the Gorton Federal Government was nearing the end of its term of office. The Prime Minister was hardly talking to his deputy party leader, William McMahon, and Malcolm Fraser as his Minister for the Army resigned, accusing Gorton of personal disloyalty. When an ensuing motion of confidence resulted in a tied vote, Gorton voted himself from office, leaving McMahon to take over the leadership.

For some months, the continuation of Gorton's film industry initiatives appeared to be in doubt, especially as Peter Howson, appointed Minister of a new portfolio, Environment, Aborigines and the Arts, wanted to defer plans for the film school. In protest, Phillip Adams publicly announced his resignation from the Interim Council, but McMahon gave a reassurance that the school was in no danger of being scrapped. Believing that Howson had misled Parliament on its estimated cost, Gorton continued his campaign for the school from the Parliamentary back bench. On 13 October, he urged Parliament to accept the reports and recommendations of the Interim Council "instead of rushing around in circles seeking some way to evade them". In April 1972, following another Interim Council report, Howson stated that his Government was prepared to approve the formation of the school. Its teaching operations would commence early in the following year with an Interim Training Scheme comprising twelve students.

Shortly before the departure of Gorton as Prime Minister, Margaret Jones wrote in the *Sydney Morning Herald*:

1971 may be Year One of the revelation for the Australian film industry.

This is a bold claim, and one which has been made before. Ever since the golden era of cinema in the 1930s, prophets have been forecasting the splendid rebirth of the film industry . . .

The 1970s could be different. For one thing, the industry is being given its first substantial injection of Federal Government money; for another, local backers are beginning to gamble not insubstantial sums on Australian films.[1]

She observed that alongside features still being made without government money, new signs of life were emerging from the Experimental Film and Television Fund and the plans for the Australian Film Development Corporation and the Film and Television School.

If the Australian film revelation does start to take shape this year, part at least of the credit must go to the Federal Government, and to a Prime Minister whose tastes, self-confessed, run to tough private-eye movies and Westerns.[2]

John Gorton himself believed that through the new films, Australians could show the rest of the world that their country contained ''other things than avant-garde kangaroos or Ned Kellys''.[3]

The Australian Film Development Corporation commenced operations in March 1971, the month of Gorton's departure as Prime Minister. Despite Gorton's desire that government aid help develop a cinematic talent the equivalent of a William Dobell or a Russell Drysdale, the AFDC's first objective was to create an industry that was commercially viable. The merchant banker John Darling, as chairman of the AFDC board, announced:

The corporation will be commercially oriented. We have to create the conditions for the industry to grow, and for investors to invest with confidence.[4]

Comedy and anarchy

After the unfortunate **Stockade** (1971) and the interesting **Private Collection** (1972, directed by Keith Salvat), the AFDC's first major investment was the entire $250 000 budget for **The Adventures of Barry McKenzie**. This was to be one of the pivotal films in the early 1970s revival. Together with the earlier **Stork** and later **Alvin Purple** it tapped an enthusiastic market for local sex comedies. All three provided their mass audiences with identifiable Australian types in much the same way that the initial **Selection** and **Hayseed** sound films had forty years earlier. The introduction of the R censorship certificate aided their choice of subject and stimulated box office acceptance.

All three productions owe something to **The Naked Bunyip**, which in late 1970 had played a role in the agitation for relaxed censorship. But it was the success of Tim Burstall's **Stork** (1971) and Bruce Beresford's **The Adventures of Barry McKenzie** (1972) that led to the making of a number of films in the same vein and considerably boosted the morale of other producers and investors. The fact that $7 000 of **Stork**'s $60 000 budget had come from the Experimental Film and Television Fund qualified it technically as the first notable success of the government-funded features.

Burstall had intended to use **Stork** to prove that money could be made from indigenous productions. In late 1971, he wrote:

Surely it's not so difficult to see what the conditions for an Australian industry have got to be. We have to become our own theatre owners, our own distributors and for five years or so we must persist in turning out our own (often disastrous)

242

products until we have slowly built up an audience. It will be a slow process but there is no other way and apart from the industry itself — and the Government — there is no one else likely to undertake the job.[5]

More precisely, Burstall saw audiences for Australian film being nurtured by a combination of time, goodwill, "talent and hard work" and, naturally, "money and some Government help". He anticipated no help coming from the "death-bed scene regularly attended by most of our critics, the film buffs, the festival people, the trendies, the underground". He considered that with technicians and actors having proved their proficiency, the industry's most pressing need was the development of writers.[6]

Since the late 1960s, Tim Burstall had been friendly with the nucleus of writers, directors and actors around the La Mama theatre company in the Melbourne suburb of Carlton. Burstall's wife Betty was La Mama's founder, and although the theatre was to produce such talented actors as Graeme Blundell, Bruce Spence, Peter Cummins and Max Gillies, it was predominantly a writers' workshop. David Williamson, John Romeril and Barry Oakley had their early works staged at La Mama, and Williamson's two-and-a-half-hour urban comedy *The Coming of Stork*, had its first performance there in 1970.

In adapting his play for a ninety-minute film, David Williamson gave greater emphasis to Stork himself (Bruce Spence) as the central character. In the film, Stork is sacked from his draughtsman's job with General Motors-Holden, and moves into a Carlton terrace house with his best mate, two male trendies, and Anna (Jacki Weaver), a diminutive woman whose sexual favours all finally share. Along the way unsuccessful attempts are made to find Stork a steady job and highly successful attempts made by Stork himself to disrupt an art exhibition and Anna's wedding. Stork's neurotic jibes at the establishment provide moments of extreme farce — when, for instance, he strips off to streak wildly around the GM-H plant, or horrifies guests at the art exhibition by jamming an oyster up his nostril. Confrontations between members of the Carlton household are usually observed in a larger-than-life rapidly edited fashion reflecting Burstall's determination to vitalise situations in filmic terms.

When **Stork** was premiered at the St Kilda Palais in December 1971, it was on a direct exhibition basis by Burstall and his production partners who, in distributing the film themselves, wanted to prove to distributors the profit potential of Australian-made films. Little reference was made to the film's Australian origin during the first six weeks of promotion on the advice of a market research company. Over this initial period it netted $20 000, or 33⅓ per cent of the investment. Further screenings around Melbourne increased takings by a further $17 000. Burstall then sold the film to Roadshow Distributors and with 35 mm prints blown up from the original 16 mm material it earned $150 000 across Australia. Critical response was uniformly kinder than that for **Two Thousand Weeks**, a fact that Burstall attributed to the new film's "counter culture" ingredients.[7]

Visually more sophisticated than **Stork** and also more deliberately crude in its language, Bruce Beresford's **The Adventures of Barry McKenzie** (1972) enjoyed an even greater commercial success. Nearly all of its AFDC investment was repaid within three months of release, and its record-breaking screenings at home were followed by a season in London. It met with unprecedented success for an Australian film. Australian reviewers, in quite the opposite reaction to **Stork**, were outraged by **The Adventures of Barry McKenzie**, and particularly by the leading character's predisposition to indiscriminate vomiting. One questioned, "Is the chunder enough to build an industry on?"[8] Others, echoing early 1930s attitudes to the backblocks farces, predicted that the film would reinforce British prejudices about Australia.

Bruce Beresford had worked on experimental films in Australia before travelling to Europe in 1963. A year later he joined the Nigerian Film Unit and in 1966 became supervisor of the British Film Institute's Production Board. The following year, Beresford suggested to the comedian-writer Barry Humphries that the Barry McKenzie cartoon strip he had created for the British satirical magazine *Private Eye*, could be the basis of a good comedy film. Initial response — including that of Sir Michael Balcon — to Beresford's draft script was encouraging, although British investors were reluctant to back a director's first film with such an eccentric subject. Australian investors hardly existed at this time. By late 1971, when both Barry Humphries and the McKenzie cartoon strip were more widely known, the project's producer, Phillip Adams, was amazed to find Australian backers approaching him after a press release stating that the film would be made with government money, regardless of private sector antipathy. Nevertheless, uncertainties over distribution led these backers to withdraw shortly before production began, leaving the AFDC to provide the entire budget. As John B. Murray and Tim Burstall had done previously, Phillip Adams decided to distribute the film himself — a move which earned his company $165 000, or fifty per cent of the box office gross. Adams later told the Tariff Board inquiry that the returns from this process had earned considerably more than if the film had been handled by a conventional distributor.

The Adventures of Barry McKenzie was launched in Melbourne and Sydney in October 1972. The film's now familiar theme of the awkward Aussie overseas is embellished with vulgar double entendres and some encounters with British nymphomaniacs, homosexuals and Jesus freaks. Behind the more sensational aspects, the comedy is almost consistently funny, although it falters towards the end through sheer excess. Many of the better moments benefit from the ebullience and occasional pathos of Barry Crocker as "Bazza" and Paul Bertram as his mate, Curley. Barry Humphries plays his own Edna Everage character, in addition to a rock band leader and a psychiatrist on whose head McKenzie delivers the "chunder" so despised by the reviewers.

Co-productions continue

At a time when the Government and local producers were embarking on their first joint activity, a small number of overseas companies continued to produce features in Australia. In 1972 came the Australian-English-American co-production **Sunstruck** (directed by James Gilbert), for which the AFDC supplied a quarter of the budget. Starring Harry Secombe as a teacher lured from South Wales to New South Wales to run an outback school, it was a mild and amiable comedy that made little box office impact but at least had more entertainment value than the $750 000 Australian-American **Squeeze a Flower** (1970, directed by Marc Daniels), featuring Walter Chiari as an Italian monk fleeing to Australia with a secret recipe for a liqueur.

Quite unexpectedly the partnership of NLT Productions and Group W Films, producers of **Squeeze a Flower**, then made the best of this period's co-productions, **Wake in Fright** (1971). The film, based on a novel by the Australian writer Kenneth Cook, was originally to have been directed by Joseph Losey in the early 1960s. However, after NLT and Group W had set up the project with a budget of $800 000, it began filming under the direction of the Canadian Ted Kotcheff at the Ajax Film Centre in Sydney in January 1970, followed by six weeks on location around Broken Hill in the far west of New South Wales.

The story deals with the abortive attempt of a city-bred schoolteacher, assigned to an outback school, to take a holiday. After losing his money in a two-up game, the teacher (Gary Bond) finds himself caught up in a nightmare of vacuous hospitality and aggressive cameraderie. As incidents of apathy and destruction swirl around him — including a senseless and bloody kangaroo hunt — he finally takes refuge in alcohol. Evan Jones's script and most of the performances — most notably by Donald Pleasence, Jack Thompson and Chips Rafferty, representing the more sinister elements — precisely capture the lethargy, frustration and sudden violent release of the isolated community. Semi-surreal interpretations of two-up games and the kangaroo slaughter provide major set-pieces for the director's view of these national obsessions. The social rituals of this community are just as imprisoning as their actual encirclement by the desert. Beverley Tivey wrote in the *Sunday Australian*:

It's a harsh, jolting movie with an almost physical impact, though its vitality and rough humour prevent it from descending into resigned despair.[9]

Despite excellent reviews around the world and good public response in London and Paris (where it ran for five months), **Wake in Fright** was perhaps too uncomfortably direct and uncompromising to draw large Australian audiences. One of the two executive producers on the production, Bill Harmon, considered that the film had been treated badly by the Australian branch of its distributors, United Artists:

It almost seems nobody wants anything to succeed here. Here we are, wanting to do pictures here, and it's terribly important for the investor to get his money back. But if a good movie can't get any money back here, who the hell's interested?[10]

Wake in Fright represented Australia at the Cannes Film Festival in 1971, the year that also saw the Festival presentation of Nicolas Roeg's **Walkabout**. Adapted by Edward Bond from the novel by James Vance Marshall, **Walkabout** had been filmed for the most part in central Australia during late 1969 with American backing of more than $1 000 000. **Walkabout** presented a more traditional view of the inland than **Wake in Fright**, drawing once more on the theme of the purifying country versus the evil city that had been major ingredients of films of the late 1910s and early 1920s. Roeg and Bond still saw the conflict as irreconcilable, but for the most part examined it away from the city, investing their vast tracts of spectacular and outwardly empty territory with a power of spiritual enrichment that the leading characters embrace or reject according to their conditioning. Entirely different opinions are held by two children, an adolescent girl (Jenny Agutter) and her younger brother (Lucien John) as, following their father's suicide, they trek through the desert with a self-appointed Aboriginal guide (David Gulpilil). The boy easily adapts and is able to communicate with the guide, but his sister, conscious of a racial and sexual barrier, can only see the desert as an alien environment to be traversed as quickly as possible. Director-cameraman Roeg's delicate balance of contrasts is sometimes jarred by excessive symbolism and patches of naivety; but for the most part the film's outlook is infectiously romantic, giving an arid view of Australian cities and lamenting the rejection of greater fulfilment in what lies beyond. In time, **Walkabout**'s sense of enchantment helped to make it a cult film, although not the financial success its backers had envisaged.

The tariff inquiry

By the time the Tariff Board started its inquiry into the film and television industry in September 1972, eight Australian features had been produced with some form of government assistance.[11] Dating the revival from 1965, a total of forty-two feature films had been released at an average rate of five each year. Producers now had more than enough information to present to the inquiry which, according to Michael Thornhill in a *Review* article, threatened "to make the 1927-28 Royal Commission into the Moving Picture Industry and the Vincent Report look like a distributors' convention cocktail party".[12]

The public hearings were held in Sydney, Melbourne and Canberra between 25 September and 29 November 1972. In December, Thornhill noted:

Many people who watched the lingering death of the Vincent Report (1963-64) into the television industry cynically expect this inquiry to also be pigeon-holed, while those who are familiar with the material of the 1927-28 Royal Commission

246

33
34

33
Hollywood sincerity Down Under
in *The Kangaroo Kid* (1950).
Jock O'Mahoney and Veda Ann
Borg.

34
Mike and Stefani (1952). A frame
enlargement showing Stefani at
the black market.

35

36

Filming an escape in *Captain
Thunderbolt* (1953). Director

King of the Coral Sea (1954).
Ilma Adey and Charles Tingwell

37
Ngarla Kunoth as the abducted
and pursued *Jedda* (1955).

38
Robbery Under Arms (1957).
Ben Marston (Laurence
Naismith) and Captain Starlight
(Peter Finch) drive stolen cattle
to market.

39

40

39
Jim Bond (Terrence McMullen)
hunts intrigue in Ubu Films'
Blunderball (1966).

40
Poster for the hugely successful
They're a Weird Mob (1966).

41
Age of Consent (1969). Helen
Mirren and James Mason.

42
Two Thousand Weeks (1969),
promoted as the first wholly
Australian feature in a decade

43
Bruce Spence in *Stork* (1971), a film whose success encouraged investment in Australian features during the early 1970s.

44
Walkabout (1971). A lost child (Lucien John) and the Aboriginal leading him to safety (David Gulpilil).

45
46

45
27A (1974). Bill Donald (Robert McDarra) considers his fate in a mental hospital.

46
The Cars that Ate Paris (1974). The resident mad doctor (Kevin Miles) introduces his patients to townspeople during a fancy dress ball.

47
Between Wars (1974). Günter
Meisner, Corin Redgrave, Judy
Morris and Arthur Dignam.

48
Sunday Too Far Away (1975).
Peter Cummins and Jack
Thompson as rival shearers.

into the moving picture industry suffered from a sense of *déjà vu* while listening to current submissions. Some statements by film producers, distributors and exhibitors were couched in the same rhetoric as was used in that previous inquiry, forty-five years ago.[13]

Many production witnesses were aware of the Report's potential for preventing a recurrence of the problems that had retarded the industry before 1965. All aspects of the distribution and exhibition of overseas and Australian films were to be examined in depth, since part of the Board's brief was to find ways in which the Government could "encourage adequate distribution of the products of this industry within and outside Australia". Methods of possible assistance, tariff or non-tariff, were also to be considered, along with the activities of the Australian Film Development Corporation. Since it was recognised that local and overseas production and distribution costs could not be compared, the Government felt that, "to this extent the term 'economic'... need not be pursued in depth".

The more than a hundred witnesses were divided, not surprisingly, into two main camps: the film and television makers on the one hand, the major distributors and exhibitors on the other. In evidence and in the Board's Report, the producers made a persuasive impact. Virtually every filmmaker shared the view of John McCallum (who gave evidence concerning the release of his 1971 film, **Nickel Queen**) that the deals between distributors and exhibitors were "far too secretive and far too onerous on the producers", especially as information about gross and net earnings was often withheld. Tim Burstall described Australian producers as "in the dark as to what the audience wants" and placed the blame partly on distributors and exhibitors for not knowing either. Evidence repeatedly illustrated that Australian films on their first release were at an immediate disadvantage when screened alongside imports which arrived with a reputation and a proven publicity package. Since the trade was used to making decisions about advertising and publicity expenditure on the basis of overseas results, they were not geared to accommodate local films. Tim Burstall compared the Australian film to a single barrel of oil being offered to a company which had a guaranteed and unlimited flow from another source.

Various producers spoke of how they had avoided standard distribution costs by exhibiting their own films. The financial success of **The Adventures of Barry McKenzie** had been aided by this process, and Phillip Adams advised others to avoid having their product handled by Greater Union and Hoyts Theatres as "they would not have the time or the inclination to handle them properly". Paul Witzig, producer of five surfing features, said that the marketing of his films over six years had been infinitely more difficult in Australia than in the United States, Europe and South Africa. He told of the difficulty in obtaining licensed halls at a reasonable rate, sometimes having to pay as much as half of his takings in theatre hire. Phil Noyce, representing the Sydney Filmmakers' Co-operative, stated that the prohibitive cost of hiring cinemas had led the Co-op to screen regularly at unlicensed premises. He argued that the provision of an exhibitor's quota for Australian short films (other than advertisements or those supplied free) would allow a much wider screening of many of the 208 shorts held at that time by the Co-op's distribution library.

Although most submissions from producers were confined to difficulties with distribution and exhibition, both the Film Producers' Association of Australia (recently formed from a linking of the Australian Motion Picture Studio Association with the Australian Film Producers' Association) and the television producer Hector Crawford called for large production subsidies. The FPAA advocated taxation incentives to encourage private investment. Distributors and exhibitors, on the other hand, opposed any government aid that involved higher duties and taxes on imported films. The Motion Picture Distributors' Association of Australia, while it claimed that the fostering of a production industry was the Government's responsibility alone, wanted distributors to have a say in determining which features would receive government money.

A target for attack from all sides of the industry was the Australian Film Development Corporation. On the production side, FPAA collectively and Tim Burstall individually called for a reconstruction of the AFDC on the basis of its "ivory tower" attitudes, and, as FPAA put it, that "the decisions of the corporation seem to be random and unsatisfactory". Burstall's submission called for a strengthening of the AFDC's role as a project initiator and its employment of assessors not guided by favouritism while allocating funds.

The film trade, which had originally opposed even the idea of such a corporation, was almost unanimous in its attacks. Both Keith Moremon, managing director of Greater Union, and Dale Turnbull, managing director of Hoyts, added to the reconstruction push, and Moremon accused the AFDC of having mounted a smear campaign against distributors and exhibitors. Dr H. C. Coombs, as chairman of the Australian Council for the Arts, took a more conciliatory line, indicating he had modified his approach from the preference for commercial viability he voiced at the film industry dinner of August 1968. Coombs now argued that the AFDC should not be expected to pursue profits during its first ten years, and that the question of profitability had only appeared in the second reading of the Corporation's bill by the then Prime Minister, John Gorton. The original 1970 Bill, Coombs said, had placed greater emphasis on the encouragement of high artistic and technical standards.

Coombs went on to suggest that the "reported restrictive trade practices" of the large distributors and exhibitors should be investigated. This opinion was shared by Michael Thornhill and the economist and journalist P. P. McGuinness, but the trade and the Tariff Board rebuffed it by stating that any judgement on restrictive practices was beyond the Board's province.

Under cross-examination from Board members Richard Boyer and C. H. Grace, the trade expressed a sometimes grudging attitude to Australian production. Eric Davis, the managing director of Twentieth Century-Fox

(Australia) pointed to his company's involvement in **Movietone News, Kangaroo** and **Smiley** but conceded that for an overseas company to invest in an entirely Australian film and have no script involvement would be "very difficult".

Greater Union's Keith Moremon claimed that his company had done much for local production but had lost money on nearly all ventures with the exception of **They're a Weird Mob**. He considered the level of government subsidy to be entirely adequate, but felt Australian films lacked the technical polish of overseas productions. Hoyts' Dale Turnbull thought Australian filmmakers suffered from a "ghetto" mentality, and he advocated subsidies that would encourage foreigners to give local producers the benefit of their experience.

By late November 1972, the tariff hearings had proved yet again that the basic problems faced by Australian producers had hardly changed since the 1920s. At the time of the hearings, distributors and exhibitors appeared to resist as vehemently as ever any possible challenge to their status, and the producers were no less determined to force the Government to make changes they considered essential. One factor, however, gave the Tariff Board inquiry a distinct advantage over earlier investigations: this was an increased awareness of film and the potential for an Australian film culture which had simply not existed before. The evidence of those supporting a local industry showed a new level of sophistication and business sense and in the climate of government reform that followed the Tariff Board hearings, the trade discovered it would have to do considerably more than file the report away.

The Whitlam years

In early December 1972, only days after the end of the Tariff Board hearings, Australians elected a Labor government to power in Canberra for the first time in twenty-three years. Under the leadership of Gough Whitlam, Labor swept into office with an attractive package of social, economic and cultural policies. Filmmakers awaiting the Tariff Board Report were confident that their future, boosted by a new mood of nationalism, was assured. They were only partly right.

The election of Labor brought unprecedented change to a whole range of government priorities including recognition of the People's Republic of China, abolition of conscription and the White Australia policy, new rights for Aboriginals and greatly increased arts subsidies. The AFDC, the Commonwealth Film Unit and the ABC were all placed under a new Department of the Media answerable to the Ministry for the Media under Senator Douglas McClelland. Prime Minister Whitlam himself headed an Arts Ministry which embraced the Film and Television School and the Australian Council for the Arts. With increased funding, the ACA's responsibilities now embraced music, literature, theatre arts, crafts, visual and plastic arts as well as film and television.

An early test for Media Minister McClelland was the visit to Australia in

February 1973 of Jack Valenti, president of the Motion Picture Association of America, the most powerful film lobby in the world. Valenti arrived in Sydney with the stated aim of "paying respects" to the Minister for the Media, but he was also said to be concerned at what a Labor government might do to break the United States' domination of distribution and exhibition. Filmmakers viewed the visit with suspicion. An Australian Film Industry Action Committee (FIAC) was formed in late January under the chairmanship of the producer-director Tom Jeffrey, and announced an anti-Valenti demonstration. FIAC literature highlighted quotes from Chauvel's and Longford's evidence to the 1927 Royal Commission — including the statement by Longford that "I know that if we fail this time we are gone" — and concluded with "Don't fail the Australian film industry this time, Doug." A petition signed by a large number of filmmakers and sent to McClelland, pointed out that foreign-controlled film companies had for many years "persistently and continually attempted to discourage Australian film production".[14]

The protest held on 1 February was attended by representatives of film, theatre and radio guilds, unions and societies. Filmmakers and supporters overflowed the footpath outside the Chevron Hotel in Sydney's Kings Cross, watched by press and police, as the trade representatives arrived. The sentiments behind such signs as "Cut the US Connection" and "We Don't Need a Fairy Godfather", were extended by the arrival in black limousines of one group of filmmakers dressed as Mafia-style gangsters. A one-man band played "Botany Bay" and "Watzing Matilda" as students from the month-old Film School Interim Training Scheme portrayed American movie interests dangling their dollars from fishing lines. The demonstration appeared to make some impact. At an industry luncheon for Valenti the next day, McClelland affirmed the government's determination to defend local production:

Some are saying that he [Valenti] has come here to screw me and I use that expression in the Australian and not the American vernacular.

I welcome Mr Valenti to Australia because it will give me the first hand, man-to-man opportunity to explain to him the Australian Government's determination to build our own film industry.[15]

McClelland expressed the Government's concern "about foreign ownership generally", and he predicted that rigidly enforced quotas would be introduced if each major distributor and exhibitor did not "produce at least one feature film a year in Australia, written, performed and produced by Australians".[16]

The Fate of the Report

On 30 June the Tariff Board Report was tabled in Parliament. A closely-packed document of seventy pages, it contained information and recommendations on the domestic production, distribution and exhibition of film and television programmes. Four of the six recommendations related to the establishment of a new and broader statutory body to replace the AFDC; the fifth called for "legislative provision ... to adjust and regulate the ownership and control of cinemas"; the sixth urged a review after five years of assistance to film and television production. Subsequently, criticisms were made that the Report made "no attempt to delineate the cultural backdrops" and did not "fully rationalise the kinds of filmmaking it supported"[17], but it did offer the prospect of the most sweeping changes ever faced by Australian film and television.

Foremost among the practical issues faced by the Board had been the creation of favourable circumstances for indigenous film production, distribution and exhibition. It identified the factors inhibiting the development of feature production as "uncertain returns and the consequent difficulty of obtaining finance". The marketing of Australian films had been restricted by the favouring of imported films by distributors and exhibitors. As this had encouraged "commercial practices inconsistent with the Board's objectives", government intervention was considered essential to encourage the industry's cultural and artistic development within a free enterprise system. For this reason, Hoyts and Greater Union would be required to divest themselves of a small proportion of their cinemas, and a distribution and exhibition network established to show Australian films on favourable terms. The major distributors would, furthermore, be compelled to invest twenty-five per cent of front money in local productions.

The Tariff Board hearings raised the question of what constituted an Australian film and, more broadly, a film culture; and the matter had been discussed by those interested in local production throughout 1972. The Tariff Board constantly asked witnesses whether films should be made as "Australian in character or, alternately aimed more at international markets". Opinions varied, but the Board reported that "most producer witnesses considered that a film which exhibits both quality and craftsmanship and national characteristics is most likely to achieve international acceptance". In tackling this issue, Professor Jerzy Töplitz (who was later to be the first Director of the Australian Film and Television School) stated:

The kernel of the problem is to make the films which are interesting to others because they are typical, they are original, they are unique in the way of showing a specific kind of life.[18]

Most filmmakers would have agreed that the promotion of a healthy indigenous film culture was impossible under the existing rationale of the AFDC. Several witnesses had been especially critical of the Corporation's policies and administration, and the Tariff Board recognised that investment decisions had been restricted both by the funds available and the objective of profitability. In recommending the AFDC's replacement by an Australian Film Authority, the Board displayed its intention that the new body should provide filmmakers with a direct subsidy, and investment in place of the existing loan system. With the Government assuming more of the burden of

251

risk, it was hoped that private investors would be more adventurous in the projects they backed.

The Australian Film Authority was also intended to operate a Distribution Branch, a Special Funds Branch (whose role would include providing funds for experimental, educational and archival activities), and an Industry Supervision Section (to oversee the divestiture of exhibition interests and be kept closely informed of distribution and exhibition arrangements). The AFA was also expected to administer and control the Commonwealth Film Unit and, as part of its own distribution activity, to handle the centralised purchase of overseas television programmes.

Overall, therefore, the Report sought to restructure the industry's operations and relationships, largely unchanged since before World War I. It also took into account radical changes in national outlook and film production priorities since the early 1960s, providing a blueprint for coexistence with imported film. Most of the recommendations — especially those establishing the relationship between the AFA and the existing film trade — were interdependent.

Considering the vast range of reforms the Whitlam Government had introduced within months of coming to power, it seemed likely that all the Board's recommendations would be implemented. But within twelve months it was obvious that all but one were to be ignored. In the opinion of Phillip Adams, the reasons for this included a threat by American producer-distributors to stop sending feature films and television programmes to Australia if the recommendations were adopted. Adams reported that the Media Minister Douglas McClelland — who counted members of the film trade among his personal friends — had used this "ludicrous" threat

to panic his Cabinet colleagues. He was then able to seize on some constitutional difficulties, and, little by little, the Tariff Report was compromised, dismantled, scrapped.[19]

The only survivor was the proposal for an Australian Film Authority (later known as the Australian Film Commission) to replace the AFDC. Gone was the new organisation's suggested role in distribution — and compulsory divestiture of theatres by the major cinema chains.

Distributors and exhibitors were aware, however, that the Government might yet decide to intervene in their activities, especially as there was talk among producers and small exhibitors of an investigation of the film trade by recourse to the Trade Practices Act of 1974.[20] The three main exhibition companies (Hoyts, Greater Union and Village Theatres)[21] took a searching look at their attitudes to Australian production, and by 1975 Greater Union and Village had begun to invest in local features. When asked to comment on the situation in mid-1974, Graham Burke, managing director of Village Theatres, stated:

The Tariff Enquiry opened up the whole area, and out of it has come an atmosphere where distribution and exhibition are now working with production people in recognition of each other's problems with a view to "building" films.

"Building" being the operative word, because we will only have an industry in Australia if there is cooperation and unity from all sections of that industry — from production through promotion and exhibition.[22]

Alternatives 1971-75

After the first allocation of Experimental Film and Television Fund (EFTF) grants in July 1970, the whole nature of what had been underground film activity in Australia underwent radical change. Government backing meant that this form of activity was no longer truly underground, and alongside the subsidised mainstream feature activity that followed, it assumed the status of an alternative form of production.

Alternative cinema could, and did, embrace a wide variety of low-budget films by those dedicated to exploring stylistic concerns or issues usually impossible in a more expensive film. The alternative films from 1970 were no longer an act of defiance or rebellion against creative and industrial stagnation, as the underground films of Ubu had been. Many of the EFTF films followed the aim of the fund in being either "original in approach, technique or subject matter", or "experiment by inexperienced but promising filmmakers". But the funded films contained much greater potential than that. Sylvia Lawson, in analysing the Government Film and Television Committee's Interim Report in late 1969, thought the term "experimental" was too narrow. The "Short Film Fund", she suggested, would be a more acceptable term, because experimental film would be only one of the many categories the fund would assist.[23]

The most pressing issue, as ever, was distribution and exhibition. Somewhere between John Gorton's late 1969 policy speech on the film industry and the handing out of the first EFTF loans in July 1970, the plan to spend $100 000 on promotion and distribution of the EFTF films (as suggested by the Interim Report) had been dropped. No explanation was given as to why the Australian Council for the Arts could not administer, distribute and exhibit for the EFTF itself, let alone why it ignored the possibility of using the Sydney Filmmakers' Co-operative as the fund's official distributor and exhibitor. The ACA chose instead the Australian Film Institute, which had no prior experience in the field, and which failed to market the films beyond offering them for hire through its Vincent Library. This commenced years of animosity between the Sydney Co-op and the AFI over what the Co-op saw as too stringent control by the AFI over contracts with filmmakers, the undemocratic nature of the AFI itself, and the granting of subsidies to it for distribution and exhibition. The *Bulletin* of 7 November 1970 understated the situation when it referred to "a certain uncertainty about how the films are to be distributed", and Margaret Jones, brusquely assessing the fund for the *Sydney Morning Herald* in March the following year, wrote:

The fund, in fact, is putting money into films which for the most part will never be seen by the general public; partly because there is no showcase for them, partly because the majority will be too experimental to have any popular appeal.[24]

253

The general feeling that the fund would be supporting mostly films "too experimental to have any popular appeal" was to limit the fund, not to say the filmmakers who might otherwise have made a far more concentrated contribution to a truly alternative film culture in Australia. The EFTF was seen as a radical move for the Federal Government, especially in the light of the inflationary spiral of early 1971 and consequent pruning of government expenditure. In March, Margaret Jones reported that the main reason for not reducing the EFTF was that the money was seen as "an investment in the future, not just a piece of conscience-squaring ... Its aim is not to produce commercially viable films but to identify talent and give young filmmakers practice in new techniques."[25] The very general application of the term "experimental" to every kind of funded film except the "commercially" aimed feature within the province of the AFDC, meant that any EFTF film was automatically branded "art" and therefore non-commercial and non-professional. No account was taken of the possibility that funded short films with a discernible narrative structure, be they fiction or documentary, could also be professionally produced with a commercial aim. Where it was quite acceptable for the AFDC to supply an entire $250 000 budget for **The Adventures of Barry McKenzie**, the EFTF funding rationale was guided by an Interim Report recommendation that experimental film loans should be spread thinly among as many applicants as possible. A figure of $1000, the Report suggested, should "rarely" be exceeded. Even before the fund had come into operation, Sylvia Lawson had found this proposal

romantic and, I believe, misguided. Film Fund support should be an index to quality; better one 20-minute piece, possibly involving ... a cost of say $4000 — with a possible result both entertaining and exportable — than the next score or so of five-minute filler exercises in earnestly whimsical montage.[26]

Despite this and other published criticism of the EFTF budgets, the meagre money available usually meant the film had to be made on a part-time basis, with the payment of below-award, frequently deferred wages to technicians and actors, and no salary at all for the filmmaker. Nevertheless, the financial position did improve noticeably (although still not compatible with mainstream production) with the transfer of the EFTF from the Australian Council for the Arts to the Interim Council of the Film and Television School in March 1971. Along with this transfer, production funds were changed from repayable loans to grants. Other new initiatives under the Interim Council were script development grants and funding of up to $15 000 for low-budget features whose subject matter or approach rendered them ineligible for AFDC investment. In early 1973, following the Whitlam Government's election, the fund was transferred back to the ACA, this time under the auspices of the new Film and Television Board. As well as administering the EFTF (in collaboration with the AFI), the Board operated a General Production Fund for experimental filmmakers and a Script Development Fund. It was also to provide finance for Video Access and Resource Centres, travelling film festivals and the filmmakers cooperatives.

The Tariff Board Report of June 1973, in giving major priority to the development of a feature film industry, reconfirmed bureaucratic policy that "experimental" cinema should for the most part serve as a testing ground for talented directors with commercial feature aspirations. For a number of filmmakers subsidised by the EFTF, this may have seemed a logical process. But for others, who, like Albie Thoms, remained committed to the ideal that Australian alternative cinema could co-exist with mainstream production, the Tariff Board confirmation was a distinct loss for their cause. Although the Tariff Report made several recommendations in favour of experimental film, it gave no recognition to the potential for a broader alternative cinema. Looking back at the Tariff hearings, Thoms wrote in 1976 that the failure of the Sydney Filmmakers' Co-operative

to strongly define its position and present a more persuasive case in favour of ["alternative"] cinema can, in retrospect, be judged a missed opportunity of major consequence.[27]

The most consistent outlet for the EFTF product was to be provided by the cooperative movement, both for the films it rented and sold (most frequently to educational bodies, community groups and film societies) and for those it screened in its cinemas. To provide an outlet for the films it held, the Sydney Filmmakers' Co-op began screenings in March 1971 at the University of Sydney. Subsequent seasons were held at the Yellow House artists' commune in Kings Cross and above the Third World Bookshop in Goulburn Street. Constituting the Co-op's most successful seasons for 1971-72 were productions made with at least a proportion of EFTF money: Peter Weir's **Homesdale** (1972), a superb black comedy about ill-assorted visitors to a remote guest house; Bruce Petty's **Australian History** (1971), an animated short whose imagination and humour established Petty (already a pre-eminent cartoonist) as a major filmmaker; Michael Thornhill's **The Machine Gun** (1971), about a would-be revolutionary frustrated by his mundane life; Kit Guyatt's **The Phallic Forest** (1972), showing a woman's retreat into fantasy as her relationship with a lover disintegrates; and Phil Noyce's two-screen **Good Afternoon** (1972), a vibrant record of the events at the 1971 Aquarius Arts Festival in Canberra.

For a short time after the first EFTF films made their appearance, and before the initial fruits of the AFDC's work, Sandra Hall was able to report in the *Bulletin* that "the experimental short film is not a luxury — it's all there is". Covering the appearance of a selection of the first EFTF projects at the 1971 Sydney Film Festival, she stated that most "were as free from bread-and-butter motives as it's possible to get". Drawing a comparison with two superficial mainstream features, Sandra Hall continued that the experimental works

were a far more fascinating field for trend-spotters and national characteristics-hunters than three **Nickel Queens** and four **Demonstrators** put together: since those feature films are revealing more about the difficulties of trying cold-bloodedly to predict and ride the fluctuations of the international movie market than anything about Australian preoccupations.[28]

Early Sydney Filmmakers' Co-op screenings at the Yellow House and Third World Bookshop had been illegal because the premises were not licensed as cinemas. In late 1972, the Filmmakers' Cinema was closed by order of the New South Wales Government, and full-time screenings did not re-commence until May 1973, when (with a grant from the Interim Council of the Film and Television School) a permanent Filmmakers' Cinema opened its doors in St Peter's Lane, Darlinghurst. The new cinema began impressively with a repertoire season of four new Australian features, Jim Sharman's **Shirley Thompson versus the Aliens** (1972), Albie Thoms's **Sunshine City** (1973), Bert Deling's **Dalmas** (1973), and Nigel Buesst's **Come Out Fighting** (1973). With the exception of **Shirley Thompson**, all had been funded by the EFTF, and as they were all individually different from projects attracting AFDC investment, they represented new potential for alternative filmmaking. **Shirley Thompson versus the Aliens** was a combination of pop art, avant-garde, science fiction and naturalistic satire in an allegory about 1950s social numbness; **Sunshine City** was a personal avant-garde and documentary record of Sydney over three years. **Dalmas** began as a genre piece and ended as an exercise in communal self-expression; and **Come Out Fighting** was a documentary-style story of the pressures imposed on an Aboriginal boxer. These four films treated their subjects in a radically different way from the fifteen other local features released in 1972-73. All but one of the four directors represented were to make one or two more features in a related vein, but because of the low funding priority accorded this type of film, gaps between their productions tended to be wider than those of directors working in the mainstream.

Already by March 1973, industry commentator Barrett Hodsdon could observe that the lack of any coherent plan for exhibition and sales meant that the EFTF had functioned in a vacuum. The public was "largely unaware of the vigorous activity in this area", especially since neither the Government, television networks nor commercial distributors were interested in their release.[29] In January 1975, when the Sydney Filmmakers' Co-op screened all the Experimental Film and Television Fund films made to that date, Albie Thoms and other Co-op members were horrified to find the event

ignored by critics, film bureaucrats and filmmakers alike, with no one showing any willingness to draw any conclusions about the quality of independent filmmaking in Australia or the lack of a recognisable aesthetic resulting from five years of funding.[30]

Whether or not it has been influenced by the same "lack of a recognisable aesthetic", the very task of categorising the prolific number and variety of alternative and generally subsidised films made after 1970 is one fraught with contradictions. Year after year from 1970, judges of short film competitions run by the Sydney Film Festival found themselves having to declare films as ineligible for entry into either the fiction, documentary or experimental categories into which they had been entered simply because in their opinion the films failed to conform to those categories. Therefore 1972 brought the most publicised rejection with George Miller's stylish and powerful **Violence in the Cinema, Part 1**. Although the film had been entered in the fiction category, the judges decided it did not constitute a work of fiction, being more in the nature of a documentary. In the same year, the fiction judges referred two further films on to the experimental section, but judging for both documentary and experimental had closed. Extending Sylvia Lawson's earlier statement on experimental film, Joan Long, one of the fiction judges, wrote in a letter to *Lumière*:

Certainly the old divisions of documentary, experimental and fiction are pointless. What is an experimental film? The term has come to be applied to films using certain technical devices, and/or ignoring sequential story patterns. Why should the term be confined to films of this type? They are hardly experimental any more. Many of the great advancements of cinema have come with films which have been made and distributed in the ordinary commercial way.[31]

Subsequently, the festival's experimental section was re-classified as "general". There was no specific mention of the avant-garde.

Documentary and fiction were to be the categories most frequently overlapped among Australian subsidised short films. A number of impressive short dramas of 1971-75, for example James Ricketson's **Limbo** (1972), Ian Macrae's **Love is Hate** (1974) and Nigel Buesst's **Come Out Fighting** (1973), were made in a documentary style. In the same way, certain documentaries — especially Esben Storm's **In His Prime** (1971), the Sydney Women's Film Group's **Woman's Day 20c** (1972) and **Film for Discussion** (1973), and Alessandro Cavadini's **Protected** (1975), — were dramatised recreations that normally used people closely familiar with events they portrayed. For better or worse, the avant-garde remained the most self-contained field of alternative production. But, as we have seen, three of the features that opened the Sydney Filmmakers' Cinema in 1973 contained a mixture of all categories, as did David Jones' **Yaketty Yak** (1974).

The avant-garde

The avant-garde was the least appreciated of all the categories of film available for funding. Although money was still available for avant-garde films, this category after 1970 lost proportionally more of its pre-1970 practitioners than any other. They included leading figures like Gary Shead, Peter Kingston and David Perry whose pre-1970 work had received world exposure, and who now found their ideas being rejected by fund assessors as inadequate. The most prolific of those who remained were Arthur and Corinne Cantrill and Paul Winkler, although impressive films continued to be made by David Perry (**Album**, 1970), Mick Glasheen (the video-work **Teleological**

Telecast from Spaceship Earth: on Board With Buckminster Fuller, 1970), Aggy Read (Far Be It Me From It, 1968-72), Anthony Airey (After Image, 1971), Dusan Marek (And the World Was Made Flesh, 1971), Mike Parr and Peter Kennedy (Idea Demonstrations, 1972), Albie Thoms (Sunshine City, 1973), David Lourie (Fantasies of a Starving Artist, 1975), and Russell Mulcahy (Contrived Mind Flashes, 1975). One of the more widely seen avant-garde works (since it achieved commercial release as a support) was We Should Call It a Living Room (1975), a time-lapse film made through the collaboration of the artists Joan Grounds and Aleksander Danko with the filmmakers David Lourie and David Stewart.

The years after 1970 brought a divergence in the use of avant-garde. On the one hand, the Cantrills and Paul Winkler remained committed to a purist approach popular among the American, British and Australian avant-garde of the late 1960s, disdaining the use of stories and professional actors. There were also others — relatively few at that — who incorporated the avant-garde into feature-length explorations of fiction and documentary forms, as did Albie Thoms with Sunshine City, Bert Deling with Dalmas, David Jones with Yaketty Yak, Gary Patterson with How Willingly You Sing (1975). Ironically, where the output of the Cantrills and Winkler continued well beyond 1975, the concentrated output of this newer movement was relatively short-lived.

Unlike that of the post-1970 experimentalists, Arthur and Corinne Cantrill were familiar with the history of the avant-garde movement and were able to preserve an awareness of their objectives through their publication (from 1971 onwards) of the magazine *Cantrill's Filmnotes*, their teaching activities and discussions with fellow filmmakers. Arthur Cantrill had embarked on the production of experimental films in 1964 and from the following year, continued his experimentation at the Drury Lane Arts Laboratory in London. In 1969-70, the Cantrills received recognition as film artists by being awarded a creative fellowship with the Australian National University. Their enormous output over this period included the feature-length Harry Hooton (1970) and a series of short films in response to the Australian landscape. One of the most highly-praised of these was Earth Message (1970), a twenty-three minute contemplation of the countryside around Canberra which encapsulates the Cantrills' regard for the landscape as "basic to an Australian consciousness".[32] Backed by Aboriginal music, the film alternates repose with frenzied superimpositions to penetrate the outer mood of distant mountains, rounded hillsides and trees.

For this and other subjects, the Cantrills experimented with colour, editing and the hand-printing of film in ways that reflected their response to a subject at the time of filming. Colour filters were used to successively divide an image into each of its primary components, which could then be printed together to present new ways of "reading" that image, while experiments in editing could bring kaleidoscopic complexity, or — as in Earth Message — a simple assembly of shots in the order in which they were taken. The Cantrills' films raised questions of "inner meaning" and "message":

concerns, stated *Cinema Papers*, "which involve expressions of hope, social despair, loneliness and purity".[33] **Harry Hooton** (1970) is a tribute to the Sydney "Push" figure of the late 1950s which develops from straightforward documentary into a chronicle of fifteen months of the Cantrills' Hooton-inspired experimental work. The feature-length **Skin of Your Eye** (1973), consists of impressions of Melbourne which are constantly reappraised by re-filming portions of the projected image.

The Cantrills neither recognised nor sought a mass Australian audience, repudiated analysis and criticism with equal vigour, and were reluctant to define their relationship with other avant-garde filmmakers. So opposed were they to story film's lack of relevance that they published a Cinema Manifesto explaining their approach with statements that included: "Our films have no story, because all the stories have been told and retold on the grey pages of literature until they are meaningless, like a word repeated again and again". Ken Quinnell, writing in *Nation*, regarded this as

bluff and a bit confused ... The Cantrills are not the first artists who, when faced with hostile criticism, have found an assumed egotism a convenient bone for the dogs. But, assumed or not, it has hamstrung them considerably and serves to explain the great gulf that exists between their theory and practice.[34]

Regardless of criticism and just how apart they were from other avant-garde and experimental filmmakers, the Cantrills had by late 1975 completed over fifty projects, constituting one of the most impressive bodies of contemporary avant-garde cinema in the world.

Like the Cantrills, Paul Winkler aimed to explore ways of filmic perception using processes he had developed. Committed to the definition of "a pure cinematic language"[35], Winkler at the same time chose the medium to make comments on issues that moved him personally — for example, urban alienation (**Isolated**, 1968), the Vietnam War (**Neurosis**, 1971), ecology (**Scars**, 1972) and Aboriginals (**Dark**, 1973). Winkler's films were screened abroad and won numerous awards both at overseas festivals and in Australia. **Scars**, the first of his productions to be widely known, angrily comments on the cutting and mutilation of trees with a screaming soundtrack and frenetic zooming. He made **Neurosis** deliberately painful for his audiences by rapidly alternating the frames to convey the pain of wartime killing. With **Brick Wall** (1974), shot frame by frame, he wanted more simply to communicate the process of bricklaying (Winkler's actual trade) — the way in which "you lay them until the sweat starts to run and sits in your eyes, and the bricks seem to shimmer in front of you". **Brick Wall** he considered in late 1975 to be "one of my most satisfying films in terms of pure cinema".[36]

The second stream of the Australian avant-garde between 1973 and 1975, and best exemplified by the feature-length **Sunshine City, Dalmas** and **Yaketty Yak**, used conventional narrative forms to question exactly why the films themselves were being made, how their stories were being told, and their relationship with audiences. While recognisable stories were certainly present in all these films, their telling was a process of "deconstruction", one that went against the normal rules of construction to examine the filmmaking process as part of the narrative. In **Dalmas** one perceives Bert Deling's personal and creative growth as well as an expulsion of uncertainties he had about storytelling over the four years it took him to complete the project. David Jones' **Yaketty Yak** moved into mad comedy as Jones directed, wrote and appeared on screen as a director called Maurice who murders his way through collaborators before using the editing process to remove evidence of their contributions.

Of all three films, Albie Thoms' **Sunshine City** was the one most easily linked to prior and later traditions, for it moved one stage further from Thoms' Ubu films to the structured, albeit complex and experimental narrative of his much later **Palm Beach** (1979). The idea grew from the way in which European audiences had asked him about the Australia they had seen in **Marinetti**. These questions awoke the concept of a film that was

an interrogation of the city I'd grown up in. An interrogation of my own experiences and feelings of what it was like to live there, and to try to extract out of that some sort of hidden meaning that we, as Australians, weren't discovering because it was too familiar to us. I wanted to look at the familiar and make it look unfamiliar.[37]

Thoms interspersed ten interviews with visual contemplations of Sydney, first in a hauntingly sustained dawn ride along the city's expressways which becomes imperceptibly faster to the point of frenzy. Both main components are fractured at key points by a white shimmering effect (achieved in printing) that is at once the heat and glare of the city and the director's desire to impose his perspective. Repetition of this and other unfamiliar devices finally becomes an accepted pattern, to the extent where any entirely "normal" use of image and sound becomes an aberration. The sound for interviews (subjects included Aggy Read, David Elfick, Germaine Greer and Brett Whiteley) repeatedly continues after the uncut camera roll of accompanying image has run out, and on into further montages of image and sound. Even at two hours, the effect is one of unity, and as Ken Quinnell commented in *Lumière*, Thoms' "breadth of subject, his affection for Sydney and the film's variety of attitudes and tones eliminate any inertia".[38]

Documentary and fiction

When one makes a comparison between the number of original and well-crafted fiction films made independently and on low budgets (usually with a proportion of government funding) between 1970 and 1975, and the outstanding documentaries over the same period, the fiction films clearly led the field. It was hardly surprising that most of the funded directors of the early 1970s should concentrate on fiction, since it had always been comparatively easy to set up documentaries in Australia. The real challenge for the maker of documentaries was to tackle subjects that others had shied away from, and those independently made films usually showed the directors' deep commitment to the subject.

Among those who made an impact with documentary in the early 1970s were the Sydney Women's Film Group, which evolved out of Sydney Women's Liberation. The SWFG aimed to produce and distribute films on subjects which conventional media had ignored, and their initial emphasis was on instructing women in production skills. The group's first project, **Film for Discussion** (1973), was commenced in 1971, but one of its first to be released was **Woman's Day 20c** (1972, directed by Margo Knox, Virginia Coventry, Kaye Martyn and Robynne Murphy), a semi-dramatised subject that quietly and despairingly showed the everyday constraints upon a housebound woman living with two small children and addicted to barbiturates. **Film for Discussion** (directed by Martha Kaye (née Ansara) and Jeni Thornley, among others in the SWFG) portrays a young woman frustrated by work and family attitudes which she comes to regard as claustrophobic. Almost painful in its acute observation and restraint, **Film for Discussion** presents situations which the SWFG members felt had shaped them as individuals — the rigid drudgery of office work, the ordeal of a family dinner, and the frustrations of limited conversations with fiancé and parents. **Film for Discussion** was distributed in North America and Britain, and became one of the most widely shown of all Australian short films. The SWFG followed these early films with a series of discussion screenings. A Women's Film Workshop was held in 1974, and in 1975 (International Women's Year), ten films were produced with a grant from the Interim Programme of the Australian Film and Television School. These, like the earlier works, were a mixture of dramatised and straight documentaries. After 1975, films made by women were the fastest-growing category of any entering the library of the Sydney Filmmakers' Co-op.[39]

Other documentaries to attract attention were partly or wholly anthropological studies, like **Tidikawa and Friends** (1973, Jef and Su Doring) and **Niugini: Culture Shock** (1975, Jane Oehr), two films that dealt respectively with traditional and modern aspects of New Guinea existence. Two lucid observations of Australian lifestyles came from the Interim Training Scheme of the Australian Film and Television School. Robynne Murphy's **Bellbrook** (1973) was a series of moody and gentle impressions of life in a small country town, and Phil Noyce's **Castor and Pollux** (1974) intercut the various travels of a hippie drop-out with the maraudings and opposite philosophy of a proudly antisocial bikie. In 1974 a fellow student from the Film School, James Ricketson, also independently (although with help from the ABC) completed **It Wasn't Going to Happen to Me**, a film that took an unflinching look at the final months of a wealthy businessman dying of cancer. It received a large audience when shown in the *Chequerboard* social documentary series on television.

The most successful of the independent documentary filmmakers' work tended toward the unusual or exotic, but many directors of narrative short films drew from everyday subjects which might have been considered the province of the documentarist. The most central of the narrative themes was urban isolation and, allied to this, were films exploring the role of social and ethnic minorities, and the impact of sex-role and media conditioning.

Paul Cox was one director who repeatedly dealt with the theme of alienation in both fiction films and documentaries. In a semi-surreal fashion, he examined the theme with **Time Past** (1966), **Matuta** (1968), **Skin Deep** (1968), **Marcel** and **Symphony** (1969); and more straightforwardly, after 1970, in the documentaries **Phyllis** (1971) and **We Are All Alone My Dear** (1977). Although Cox's notable work as a feature director was to begin after 1975, he had already turned to short feature production with **The Journey** (1972), a sensitive portrait of a middle-aged man haunted by a past love, reflecting on his lack of personal attachments.

Concern for the disabled appeared in two finely-crafted films by John Papadopoulos, **Dead End** (1972) and **Matchless** (1974). For **Love is Hate** (1974), Ian Macrae adopted a documentary approach to gradually reveal that a lonely young male factory worker has a morbidly hilarious obsession with vampires. Although it gained an honourable mention in the AFI Awards, the film received only minimal exposure before gathering undeserved dust. This was a fate shared by Christopher French's equally meritorious **Wake-Ups** (1974), a naturalistic comedy about a telephone ''wake up'' operator. More attention was paid to Gillian Armstrong's film school short **100 a Day** (1973) which employed perhaps the greatest structural complexity of any short narrative film of the period to show how a woman during the Depression has to cope with her factory job and the painful after-effects of a back-room abortion.

Half a dozen of the low-budget features made between 1971 and mid-1975 tackled the theme of alienation with the same uncompromising stance found in many of the shorts. Of these, the most outstanding were by young directors making their first features: **A City's Child** (1971, Brian Kavanagh), **The Office Picnic** (1972, Tom Cowan) and **27A** (1974, Esben Storm).

A City's Child was the first feature to be funded by the EFTF, and was later one of the first to receive AFDC investment to pay for its blow-up from 16 mm to 35 mm. The plot concerns a suburban spinster who is left alone in the world in middle age when her mother dies. Pressured by a salesgirl into buying a plastic doll, she soon builds up an entire ''family'' of dolls including a lifesize ''baby'' around which she constructs a fantasy existence. A young man adds to the ambiguity when he stops by to ask the way and apparently stays to live with the woman. Central to the film's achievement is the performance of Monica Maughan. Whether plodding on endless excursions to the shops, reading escapist novels in her drab home or coming to grips with the presence of the young man (Sean Scully), Maughan portrays with great sensitivity the woman's total defeat by her environment. Although the development of the story does not entirely warrant a running time of eighty minutes, Kavanagh renders the dread emptiness of suburbia with accuracy, carefully sustaining the balance between outward reality and the woman's dream life.

Tom Cowan, like Brian Kavanagh, had a background as a film industry technician (Kavanagh as an editor, Cowan as a cameraman), and had worked on a variety of other people's projects, as well as directing several short films, before embarking on his own first feature. **The Office Picnic** begins by probing the ennui of public service staff at work in a large and mostly empty building. The film then moves on to the annual office picnic, where alcohol allows frustration and bullying to surface. The level of aggression causes a young couple to vanish, never to reappear, and the remainder of the film concerns the effect of the disappearance on several of the staff. John Wood plays the focal role of Clyde, a clerk unable to replace bluff with sincerity despite the shakeup given him by Mara (Kate Fitzpatrick), a typist who has reversed his attempts at humiliation. Colin Bennett, reviewing **The Office Picnic** for the Melbourne *Age*, judged it to be "an intriguing piece of work, witty, meticulously detailed and finally mysterious in its etching of urban life".[40] No other local feature of the period so effectively captured the claustrophobia and hostility to be found in large cities. **The Office Picnic** workers stand as a representative microcosm — unable to forge close bonds or to articulate real feelings, only reaching self-awareness when given a break from bureaucracy and urban chill.

Esben Storm's **27A** contained an even greater indictment of alienation in an uncaring society. The story was based on actual events, following the detention of an alcoholic in a hospital for the criminally insane under Section 27A of Queensland's Mental Health Act. The Act allowed authorities to hold anyone incapable of proving a right to be released. Although Bill Donald (Robert McDarra) initially believes he will be held for a six-month maximum term, he soon learns that Section 27A has made his stay indefinite. Most of the staff listen patiently to his complaints until he makes the first of three escapes. Travelling to the city compounds the despair. Train passengers view him as a derelict; he is embarrassed by meeting an old friend from better times; and his dying wife is unable to talk to him. Simply because he has tried to escape, Donald is regarded as irrational. Marred slightly by an extraneous subplot, **27A** tells its story in a direct, confrontational fashion, rendered all the more authentic by Robert McDarra's performance. Jack Clancy, writing in *Nation Review*, observed that **27A**

is semi-documentary in form, semi-realist in style, and totally honest in conception and purpose ... Let it be added that this is an Australian film that puts to shame a good deal of the commercially successful stuff we have seen so far.[41]

Many other works of fiction employed urban backgrounds in a less specific way. They included two comedies, Gerald Ryan's **The Jumping Jeweller of Lavender Bay** (1971), an exercise in light whimsy of a kind not repeated elsewhere, and John Duigan's debut as a feature director, **The Firm Man** (1974), a surreal fantasy about a businessman trying to unravel the

263

purpose of his job with a mysterious corporation. In a similar but more serious vein to the latter was Michael Robertson's film of Alexander Buzo's play **Rod** (1972), which probed the tensions of business and married life. Gillian Burnett's psycho-drama **Circuit** (1974) concerned the need for personal change after the break-up of a relationship, and featured strong performances by Robyn Nevin and Arthur Dignam. Ken Cameron's first film, **Sailing to Brooklyn** (1975), which deftly charted the growth and limitations of an affair between a schoolteacher and one of his female students, established Cameron as a meticulous director able to draw atmosphere from locations and the nuances of character. In a somewhat heavier tone, Ayten Kuylululu made two dramas involving the problems of Turkish migrants in Australia. **A Handful of Dust** (1973) featured Kuylululu herself as a woman struggling with two jobs and family tensions, and in the feature-length **The Golden Cage** (1975), she showed the effects of culture shock on two young Turkish immigrants, one of whom has a disastrous affair with an Australian woman.

Filmed in Sydney and Istanbul, **The Golden Cage** cost $24 000, with $22 500 coming from the Advanced Production Fund of the Film, Radio and Television Board of the Australia Council. In early 1975, the Board's former Experimental and General Production funds had been restructured to constitute the Basic and Advanced Production Funds, covering, in the first case, the works of promising filmmakers, and in the second, low-budget features, TV pilots and avant-garde works. The maximum grants available through the Advanced Production Fund were at this time $25 000 — quite an advance on the EFTF's 1970 maximum of $1000 but firmly retaining the distinction between what Australia's government film bureaucracies regarded as the kind of "art" productions the Board would fund, and the commercial propositions that would attract investment from the AFDC and its successor, the Australian Film Commission.

After viewing **The Golden Cage**, Lyndall Crisp of the *Australian* considered that its inability to attract a buyer meant the "waste of a good film".[42] But this kind of comment was hardly new for films being made away from the mainstream. As the 1970s progressed, it became clear that the production of low budget, largely government-subsidised alternative films had allowed a reflection of contemporary life styles and attitudes that was generally more direct than that of the costlier features. Government-funded or not, the low budget films were an indispensable part of the Australian scene after 1970. Only limited exposure made them seem less so.

Film Australia

Before the existence of the Australian Film and Television School, Film Australia (from 1973 the name of the former Commonwealth Film Unit) was one of the industry's few training grounds for aspiring filmmakers. Feature film producers and directors who worked there at various times in the 1960s and 1970s, included Peter Weir, Donald Crombie, Joan Long, Anthony

Buckley, Michael Thornhill, Brian Hannant, Oliver Howes, Arch Nicholson and Richard Brennan. Some, like Weir, Crombie, Hannant and Howes, had joined in the 1960s as production assistants. All had come on to the staff when commercial film activity was negligible and the only serious rival for documentary work was ABC television. Many were involved in the industry-wide agitation for a reconstructed film industry, and this was to be reflected in the new types of films being made by Film Australia. From the mid-1960s, an increasing number of films that broke new ground were made by directors who showed that they could treat their subjects intimately as well as with cinematic flair. Films like **Desert People** (Ian Dunlop, 1967), **Shades of Puffing Billy** (Antonio Colacino, 1967) and **The Pictures that Moved** (Alan Anderson, 1968), attracted a new level of critical appreciation and received attention at overseas festivals, while more 16 mm prints of Film Australia's product were being requested than ever before by Australian embassies.

It was a period that was to be viewed in retrospect as Film Australia's "Young Turk" era, when, according to Richard Brennan,

filmmakers were given opportunities to work with unprecedentedly large budgets in what seemed to be the first steps towards feature filmmaking. It was a good period and everything that churned off the assembly line seemed to be a winner: **Bullocky**, **The Gallery**, **Paddington Lace**, **The Line**, **Tempo**, **Seven Days**, **Country Jazz**, soared out of Eton Road, Lindfield, and returned wreathed in laurel and dripping in decorations.[43]

The culmination of these advances was the production of the feature-length, three-part narrative film **Three to Go** (released in 1971). The driving force behind the project was Gil Brealey who, along with fellow producer Richard Mason, had already done much to motivate Film Australia's new spirit. The three episodes, directed and scripted in turn by Peter Weir, Brian Hannant and Oliver Howes, were intended as discussion-starters on the problems of contemporary youth. Each episode was unique, not only because of strong personal commitment on the part of the directors, but also as government films made by young directors confronting audiences with issues relevant to their own generation.

The basis for Peter Weir's episode, **Michael**, was a script called "Rebellion" which he had written unsolicited for the ABC's current affairs television programme *Four Corners*. After the ABC, in Weir's words, "wouldn't touch it"[44], he changed his story idea from a political kidnapping to that of a young, middle-class man (played by Matthew Burton) compelled to choose between the cosy values of well-to-do suburban life and the extremist outlook of radical friends. In the second episode Brian Hannant's **Judy** deals with the problems faced by a teenage country girl (Judy Morris) in her determination to leave her family for a more challenging life in the city. The third episode, **Toula**, by Oliver Howes, shows a young Greek girl (Rina Ioannou) seeking acceptance as an Australian against the wishes of her very traditional parents.

Michael begins impressively enough with a street battle between revolutionaries and the army around Sydney's Circular Quay. This turns out to be part of the central character's dream of revolution. A number of good individual scenes include some genuinely funny satire and a final confrontation when his radical mates turn on Michael with wounding sarcasm. But the story is too slimly developed, a fact emphasised by the use of hectic visuals and pop songs to represent Michael's state of confusion. **Judy** and **Toula**, on the other hand, concentrate diligently and in documentary style on those aspects of community life on which their protagonists are trying to turn their backs. Of the three episodes, **Toula** leaves the most lasting impression, not only for its exploration of Toula's community, but also because her plight is the least likely to be solved.

Three to Go made a considerable impact when first released. **Michael** was awarded the Australian Film Institute's Grand Prix in 1970, and the Channel 7 television network paid around $10 000 for transmission of the three episodes together in early 1971. Commercial cinema screenings of each part, used individually as support programmes, was arranged through BEF Distributors.

Film Australia's staff made plans for further feature production after the success of **Three to Go**. But the ideas were dropped one after another: a film on the explorer Edward John Eyre, because of a potential rights clash; another on a touring theatrical troupe, because of lack of money. Short fiction films, however, continued to be made. Prominent among them were Brian Hannant's mining drama, **Flashpoint** (1972), Cecil Holmes's **Gentle Strangers** (1972), Keith Gow's **Where Dead Men Lie** (1973), and Richard Mason's examination of the consequences of rural poverty, **Moving On** (1974). New documentary initiatives continued to emerge: 1970 brought the start of a major series on Asia as well as Ian Dunlop's ethnographic record of the Baruya tribespeople in the Eastern Highlands of New Guinea. Peter Weir proceeded to make the documentaries **Incredible Floridas** (1972) and **Whatever Happened to Green Valley?** (1973); Joan Long wrote and directed **The Passionate Industry** (1973), the second part of Film Australia's history of the Australian cinema[45], and Jane Oehr directed **Stirring** (1974), a sharp and provocative film on corporal punishment at a boys' high school.

One cause championed more than any other at Film Australia between the mid-1960s and 1975 was autonomy. With the transfer of the organisation to the Department of the Media in December 1972, it was at last attached to a body that had other involvement in film. But complete autonomy was nowhere in the offing — either in the Tariff Board recommendations, or in the final outcome, when Film Australia was transferred in 1975 to the Australian Film Commission, itself a statutory authority. By now, the government funding of independent films was five years old. Some of the Film Australia staff who had hoped to see the organisation involved in regular feature production after **Three to Go**, had left to pursue their careers elsewhere.

Commercial bids

Films that constituted the outline of an alternative cinema were, as we have said, never as much in the public eye as they deserved to be. The films that naturally gained a larger share of attention were those made on higher budgets with a predominantly commercial motive. Key productions, like **Libido, Alvin Purple, Stone, Stork** and **The Adventures of Barry McKenzie** made use of recently liberalised attitudes to on-screen sex and violence to build an awareness of the viability of Australian films.

Least characteristic of these, because of its initial intent, was **Libido** (1973). This was the project of the Victorian branch of the Producers and Directors' Guild of Australia, who were worried about the scarcity of experienced screen writers. PDGA ran several competitions in a vain attempt to solve this problem. Then, with the aim of commercially releasing the end result, they invited a series of established writers to submit material dealing with various aspects of love. From the six scripts submitted four were chosen: **The Husband** by Craig McGregor, to be directed by John B. Murray; **The Child** by Hal Porter, to be directed by Tim Burstall; **The Priest** by Thomas Keneally, to be directed by Fred Schepisi; and **The Family Man** by David Williamson, to be directed by David Baker. All four episodes entered production in mid-1972, backed by $25 000 from the Australian Council for the Arts and approximately $15 000 from PDGA members. The eventual cost, taking into account deferred payments, came to around $120 000.

Despite the film's instant success with the public the deferred production costs meant that financial returns to the PDGA would be a long time coming. Critical response was for the most part encouraging, and the careers of nearly all the directors involved were enhanced. *Nation Review* published two opposing reviews. One, by Max Thomas, attacked it as a display of "eight leading Australian talents scrambling onto the sex bandwagon in an orgy of self indulgence".[46] In the second Bob Ellis said it made him feel "for the first time completely relaxed into the idea that the Australian film business was here to stay".[47]

The best episodes, and certainly the best-received, were Williamson and Baker's **The Family Man** and Porter and Burstall's **The Child**. Despite some resemblance to **The Go-Between** (both the novel by L. P. Hartley and Joseph Losey's film of 1971), **The Child** was Burstall's most technically and dramatically assured film to date, a period piece which drew sensitive performances from its actors, and made splendid use of locations at the historic Werribee Park estate south of Melbourne.

The Family Man contained some of the most perceptive writing, direction and acting of any local film between the mid-1960s and the time of its release. Jack Thompson and Max Gillies portray two predatory businessmen, confident of easy pick-ups in a wine bar. The two women they try to win (played by Debbie Nankervis and Suzanne Bradley) are at first uninterested. When they eventually consent to go to Thompson's beach house their attitudes harden, and they finally horrify their would-be seducers by stripping. Although the portrayal of the women's militancy verges on the pedantic, **The Family Man** for the most part perfectly captures middle-class speech patterns and ocker male vulnerability. The men's performances bounce from bravado to bruised ego with total conviction. Reviewing **Libido** for *Lumière*, Jack Clancy considered Thompson and Gillies's "alertness, timing and sheer control of idiom and mannerism are a revelation".[48] **Libido** in its entirety was Australia's official entry in the 1973 Cannes Film Festival.

After directing **The Child** for **Libido**, Tim Burstall turned once more to comedy with **Alvin Purple** (1973). Its newly-formed production company, Hexagon, comprised Roadshow Distributors in association with Burstall and the production house of Bilcock and Copping — the first production-distribution-exhibition amalgamation to operate in Australia since Cinesound and its corporate links in the 1930s. At various times over the next three years, the existence of Hexagon and its profitability provided hope for those watching developments in the industry. Hexagon's first project was to have been the drama **Petersen** but with its postponement, Burstall began to develop a portmanteau film intended to emulate Pasolini's very popular **Decameron**. One of the ideas submitted from a team of writers was Alan Hopgood's **Alvin Purple**, and Burstall liked the concept sufficiently to drop the **Decameron** idea. As Burstall and Hopgood worked on the screenplay, the serious second half of the script was dropped in order to accentuate the comedy. **Alvin Purple** featured Graeme Blundell as a very average young man who finds himself irresistible to women. The film consists of a series of escapades as the hero is chased from one end of Melbourne to the other, including a sequence in a very shady sex clinic. The exhausted hero finally seeks refuge in a convent — only to find that the nuns have much more than a sisterly interest in him.

The many funny moments draw their impact, like those of **The Adventures of Barry McKenzie**, from slapstick farce and quirky cameos. However, the hurly-burly of incident becomes too repetitive, and the most enjoyable aspects are the performances of Graeme Blundell and others who, like George Whaley as an evil psychiatrist, have a chance to develop their roles. When the film opened in Sydney and Melbourne during the 1973 Christmas season it attracted generally hostile reviews — and long queues of eager patrons. It quickly became the most profitable Australian feature to date. By September 1974 its gross earnings were $1.6 million (of which $94 000 went to the producer).

Petersen (1974), Burstall's next film, was a drama of class conflict written by David Williamson. Tony Petersen (Jack Thompson) is a thirty-year-old electrical tradesman who has decided to put himself through university. In the course of this, Petersen has an affair with a female tutor that ends in betrayal and violent, frustrated revenge. Several of the physical confrontations in the film are wedged incongruously into the plot, but the film tackles the hero's predicament with persuasive force and irony. The reviews were generally favourable, but some critics lashed out with accusations of vulgarity, sexism and senseless violence. Promoted by publicity that stressed these ingredients, **Petersen** proceeded to net a tidy $70 000. Still under the auspices of Hexagon Productions, Burstall began work in January 1975 on a film that was a conscious departure from the ocker syndrome — an adaptation of Russell Braddon's **End Play** (released early 1976).

Somewhat more ambitious than the sex films of this period was Sandy Harbutt's bikie epic, **Stone** (1974). Even though an R certificate removed the film from the under-eighteen age group to whom it might have appealed, it still managed to enjoy considerable commercial success, and quickly returned money to its main investor, the AFDC. The story concerns a plainclothes policeman, Stone (Ken Shorter), assigned to infiltrate a motor cycle gang and find out who is brutally murdering its members. Besides the bikies' protection, Stone is soon involved in heading-off their attempts at recrimination. Sandy Harbutt, directing his first feature, manages to make **Stone** look several times bigger than its $195 000 budget would suggest. The film contains a series of lively action scenes, and the best moments are those exploring the philosophy and loyalties of bikie life. But its over-length and lacklustre central performances lessen the impact. Reviewers, with the notable exception of Bob Ellis in *Nation Review*, were mostly damning in their comments — a fact which, Ellis pondered, might represent a release from "the long constipated frustrations induced by **Barry McKenzie, Alvin Purple** and **Stork**, which they needs must suffer in silence for Australia's sake''.[49] **Stone**, however, became a long-term tenant of Sydney's Forum Cinema and countless drive-ins around the country. Within five years, its Australian gross takings had risen to $2 million and it was still being revived into the 1980s.

New act, new hopes

At the Tariff inquiry in late 1972, the AFDC claimed it had initially chosen to invest only in projects with a reasonable chance of returning the backers' money because its first priority was to prove to the money market that investment in films could be profitable. The AFDC told the inquiry that it now considered the time was ripe for a more flexible approach, and the Tariff Board Report mentioned the Corporation's claim that it would in future assist "projects of quality which would not necessarily have good commercial prospects, and also projects of developmental or innovative value''.[50] Four months after the Report's appearance in June 1973, the first of these films, **The Cars that Ate Paris**, entered production with the AFDC supplying the bulk of the $250 000 budget.

By June 1974, the AFDC had committed a total of $4 350 720 to feature films, television programmes and documentaries. Of this amount, $1 400 720 came from the earnings of earlier projects. At the end of the year, the three most profitable features to which the AFDC had committed money were **Alvin Purple, The Adventures of Barry McKenzie** and **Stone**. But the Corporation's remaining life was limited. Media Minister McClelland stated as early as February 1973 that both the AFDC and Film Australia would become part of a new Australian film authority, and in December he announced Cabinet's approval for the drafting of legislation for an Australian Film Commission. An Interim Board would advise McClelland on the implementation of the Act and the setting-up of the Commission. Under the chairmanship of John Darling (also the AFDC's chairman), the Board held its first meeting in February 1974, and proceeded to prepare a report and recommendations which were delivered to the Minister exactly a year later.[51]

The Interim Board expected that the AFC Act would provide the Commission with a basis for expanded commercial and cultural objectives, and much closer relations with the industry at large. As part of a detailed evaluation of the current and future state of film and television, it balanced the importance of film in thematic, artistic and nationalist terms against the objective of commercial success, stating that among its long-term aims the AFC should demonstrate that "high artistic standards and box office success are not mutually exclusive".[52] With an eye to posterity, the Board felt that encouragement from the Commission should include

the making of those films of high artistic or conceptual value which may or may not be regarded at the same time as conforming to the current criteria of genre, style, taste, but which have cultural, artistic or social relevance.[53]

It recommended that any decision to finance a project should take into account not only commercial potential, but also

thematic importance, Australian content, artistic value and the contribution the project will make to the development of an Australian film industry of high international standard.[54]

While commercial success was an essential aim, it went on to say that its definition had been "elusive throughout the history of the film industry, and it will be no less elusive under the Australian Film Commission".[55]

The Board was emphatic on the point that government assistance, essential for the industry's growth, would be pointless if the Commission did not make "the strongest possible use of its powers in the distribution and exhibition of Australian films". The report firmly stated: "Films do not end with distribution, they begin with it"[56]

Following criticism of the AFDC's "ivory tower" attitude, it was also considered logical that the AFC should embark on a more democratic relationship with the industry it served. Not only should outside consultants be used, it was also suggested that the chairman and full-time commissioners have knowledge of and experience in the arts, and that part-time members be experienced in a wide range of film activities. The Commission was expected to maintain close contact with all areas of the industry, keep it up to date with policy changes, and itself be responsive to change.

The Australian Film Commission Bill, introduced by the Media Minister to the Senate in September 1974, defined the principal function of the AFC as being "to encourage, whether by provision of financial assistance or otherwise, the making, promotion and distribution and exhibition of

Australian films''. This remained in the Act on its assent by the House of Representatives on 7 March 1975, but in the meantime the Bill had been, to quote *Cinema Papers*, ''bounced back and forth through both houses of Parliament for what seemed an eternity''.[57] The Liberal Party in the Senate had rejected the idea of the Media Minister's proposed control over the AFC, insisting instead on statutory status. Another contentious issue was a proposed short film quota which Liberals feared would give free rein to socialist propaganda.

Under the Act as passed in March 1975, the Commission was to consist of a full-time chairman, two full-time and seven part-time members.[58] Outside consultants would be engaged whenever necessary, and the Commission was empowered to make grants in addition to investments and loans. Under the terms of the short film quota, which the Act retained, the Commission could compel any exhibitor — whether a large corporation or an individual — to screen a proportion of short films certified to be Australian. The Commission was to take over the remaining obligations of the AFDC (whose own Act was now repealed) and would therefore be responsible for Film Australia. The new organisation could also help State Government authorities to purchase Australian films ''of an educational nature and of national interest or importance'', and was empowered to encourage film archival activity. Most important, as far as filmmakers were concerned, the Australian Film Commission was to be a statutory body under the Prime Minister's Department.

Media gaffe

Some saw Prime Minister Whitlam's decision to place the AFC under his own control as the start of the dissection of the Department of the Media.[59] Minister McClelland had been under regular fire from the film and television industry and, more recently, from within the ranks of the Labor Party. Producers regarded both McClelland and the Media Department's permanent head, James Oswin, as men insensitive to the needs of their industry, and they remained suspicious of McClelland's apparent friendship with multinational distributors.

Also evident by early 1975 was the failure of the television points system, introduced in August 1973 under Media Department policy, to encourage the transmission by commercial stations of Australian material. The report of the AFC Interim Board revealed that of all programmes transmitted by commercial channels in 1974, local content had accounted for only forty-three per cent, a figure unchanged since 1970. Only 9.2 per cent of television dramas shown in 1974 were of local origin, and this again had changed little in four years.

In the lead-up to the Labor Party's Federal conference at Terrigal on the Central Coast of New South Wales in February 1975, it was announced that Senator James McClelland (no relation to the Minister) would present a completely rewritten platform approved by the Party's arts and media

271

committee. The most important provisions of the draft were the adoption of the 1973 Tariff Board recommendation for the AFC to break down the dominance of major exhibitors; the formation of a statutory authority to administer television station licences; a restructuring of the ABC; and legislation to give the community a wider say in the enforcement of broadcasting laws. It amounted to a repudiation of the Department of the Media's activities over the previous two years. An offended Senator Doug McClelland attacked uninformed critics who wanted to change the policies of his Department "for some cloud-cuckoo-land of heavily weighted élitist fare which could only interest a few".[60] But such sparring was unnecessary. The conference proved to be more concerned with saving the Minister from public denunciation. The reformist arts and media policy was scrapped. Only two substitute provisions were accepted. One called for the progressive build-up of local TV content to seventy-five per cent. The other concerned FM radio.

In April, Douglas McClelland found himself ensnared in a fresh controversy concerning Jack Valenti. Compiling a dossier on the alleged short-comings of the Minister and his Department, film and media groups had taken possession of a six-month-old private letter in which McClelland had invited Valenti to suggest names for the membership of the Australian Film Commission; in the same letter he requested help in finding work for his daughter who had gone to live in Los Angeles. Details of the letter were published on the front page of the *Australian* of 11 April. The newspaper predicted that: "Publication of the letter is certain to create a sensation in the Australian film and television industry". It was no understatement.

Prime Minister Whitlam was reportedly incensed, and the Parliamentary Opposition seized the opportunity for political point-scoring. Despite McClelland's dismissal of the affair as "groundless drivel", he now lost what little industry confidence he had left. Peter Scott, president of the Australian Film Council, predicted that the whole affair would lead to demands for the Minister's resignation, and detected irony in the fact that he could have sent "such a chatty, friendly letter to a man in America while he substantially ignores the local filmmakers".[61] The producer Lee Robinson defended McClelland's action by stating that Valenti himself should be a member of the Commission and Phillip Adams replied: "We need Jack Valenti on the Film Commission like we need Dr Frankenstein to take charge of Medibank".[62]

As Adams, Scott and others pointed out, the letter confirmed that a personal friendship existed between McClelland, Valenti and American-based distributors, when none at all had existed between McClelland and the local film and television industry. There was some difference of opinion over whether McClelland had sought a sufficiently full range of industry opinion on AFC membership prior to the leaking of the Valenti letter. In his own defence, McClelland claimed that between October and December 1974, he and the AFC Interim Board had interviewed representatives of film and television interests including the Australian Film Council, the Sydney Filmmakers' Co-op, the Australian Writers' Guild and PDGA, and that he had invited the Film Council to submit names for consideration as commissioners in September.[63] The Film Council claimed, on the other hand, that telegrams seeking the opinion of key industry unions and associations had been sent out only the day before the letter was published.[64] Many of the unions were said to be opposed to the AFC legislation as it stood, and among concerns voiced by the film industry in general was the strength of the proposed ministerial control over Film Australia. One filmmaker quoted by the *Australian* felt: "If the wrong people are appointed, the Commission could easily work against the interests of the local industry, or neglect it".[65]

On 16 April, the day after McClelland revealed the names of the eight-member Film Commission, the Australian Film Council announced that it was delivering its Media Department dossier to the Prime Minister, and intended also to stage protest rallies against the AFC appointments in four State capitals. In Melbourne, over 800 actors, writers, musicians and television technicians had already demonstrated in support of increasing local television content, and on 21 April a rowdy demonstration against the Media Department occurred in Sydney. On 17 May, Phillip Adams resigned as chairman of the Australia Council's Film, Radio and Television Board, calling McClelland "the biggest Ministerial disaster in the Labor Government".[66]

Soon after this furore, a Federal Cabinet reshuffle brought what the production industry had been seeking — the removal of McClelland from his Ministry. It also confirmed earlier suspicions that the responsibilities of the Department of the Media would be substantially reduced. Under Dr Moss Cass as the new Minister for the Media, the functions were limited to the Australian Information Service, the Australian Government Publishing Service, and the formulation of policies for television and radio broadcasting. In December 1975, one month after Malcolm Fraser's Liberal Opposition was returned to power amidst constitutional convulsions, the Government announced that the Department of the Media would be abolished. By now, all expectations for the film industry's future were centred on the Australian Film Commission, which had met for the first time in early July.

Cannes

According to the evidence of 1974, Australia was again an improving market for American films. In the first half of that year, the nation rose from seventh to second place in America's film earnings, and a total of $US21 million was gained from the screening of its product in Australia. At the same time, the outlook for local features also improved. Between 1972 and 1975, Australian films made good money for distributors and exhibitors who, in their turn, were able to offer the local producers more competitive and favourable contracts. The AFC Interim Board attributed the changed attitude of the trade partly to less reliable film supplies from abroad, and also to "a recent world-wide phenomenon that national films are being sought by people in their own countries".[67]

But it had become apparent that producers of most of the new Australian films were unable to recoup their costs from domestic screenings alone. A concentrated effort to achieve overseas sales was essential and the Cannes International Film Festival, held in May each year, was seen as the most significant marketplace. Producers and government bureaucrats had been encouraged by the success at the 1974 festival of Peter Weir's **The Cars that Ate Paris** and the documentaries **Crystal Voyager** (David Elfick and Albert Falzon) and Jef and Su Doring's **Tidikawa and Friends**. Following that event, *Cinema Papers'* correspondent Antony Ginnane wrote that Cannes presented a vital opportunity for the local producer to assess international market prospects. He continued:

For the moment Cannes is the only world event that manages to combine the artistic and business aspects of cinema so expertly. It is very, very important that as the Australian production output increases, considerable thought be given to the most effective form that governmental and quasi-governmental sponsorship of Australian screenings can take.[68]

Of the Australian films shown independently at Cannes in 1974, **The Cars that Ate Paris** made the biggest critical impact, and headlines back in Australia (inaccurately, as it transpired) announced that it had scored a lucrative deal with American producer-distributor Roger Corman. It was Peter Weir's first feature and progressed thematically from his fifty-two-minute black comedy, **Homesdale** (1971). **The Cars that Ate Paris** concerns the experiences of Arthur (Terry Camilleri), a dazed innocent trapped in a small country town named Paris whose inhabitants make a living scavenging from motor vehicles they have deliberately wrecked. The job to which Arthur is assigned — that of parking officer — finally precipitates a showdown between the older inhabitants and a gang of delinquents who destroy the town with their grotesquely-decorated vehicles. Numerous bizarre and original ideas and a fine balance between low-key and outrageous comedy combine to provide a dark view of an isolated society at war with itself. The film contains an allegory no less significant than **Wake in Fright**, and its international relevance was not lost on overseas critics. Phillip Strick, who admired the film as a work of fantasy, wrote in *Monthly Film Bulletin*:... the film's title in fact works as a metaphor, and Paris could as well be London, New York, or actually Paris.[69] Geoff Brown commented in *Sight and Sound* that

after the boorish and boring adventures of Alvin Purple and Barry McKenzie, it's refreshing and encouraging to find an Australian film which never wallows in its country's inglorious *mores* but uses them tactfully to further an intriguing and compelling narrative of its own.[70]

As stated earlier, **The Cars that Ate Paris** was the first of the AFDC's regular investments in films that combined the aims of quality cinema and innovation. The fact that it was commercially mishandled and generally misunderstood led to financial failure, but it was quickly followed by films of comparable achievement. They were usually made by directors new to big budget film-making and whose results now showed just as much thematic complexity and personal commitment as the short films (many funded by the EFTF) on which they had previously worked. These were to include Michael Thornhill's **Between Wars** and Ken Hannam's feature for the South Australian Film Corporation, **Sunday Too Far Away**, in the immediate future. But not long afterwards other examples followed from Peter Weir, Donald Crombie, Fred Schepisi, Bruce Beresford, Phil Noyce and Gillian Armstrong.

Between Wars drew its perspective from the radical outlook of the Sydney sub-culture, the "Push". Following his first film, **The American Poet's Visit**, Thornhill had made two short films scripted by Frank Moorhouse, **The Girl from the Family of Man** (1970) and **The Machine Gun** (1971). The same writer and director worked for over a year refining a screenplay of **Between Wars**, and the film entered production in February 1974 with its $320 000 budget shared equally between the AFDC and private investment.

Between Wars, set in the interwar period, is the story of a doctor (played by Corin Redgrave) who is repeatedly and unwillingly embroiled in the controversial issues of his time. Dr Trenbow is persecuted at a Royal Commission for his medical practices, branded as a socialist during the Depression and regarded as a fascist at the outbreak of war. Finally, alienated and exhausted, he can raise no opposition to the enlistment of his son. Australian society is shown as mean-minded, with its characters shaped retrogressively by the issues they oppose or support. This view, harsh and sometimes cynically humorous, is always conveyed at a remove, matching the detached perspective of Trenbow himself. Leading Australian reviewers saw this as a courageous point in the film's favour. Mike Harris in the *Australian*, found character development "involving because much of it is handled obliquely"[71], and Bob Ellis gave "full marks" to the "wholly original structure, and the courageous blandness of incident".[72] Although critical favour continued wherever **Between Wars** was screened, its deliberate distancing effect discouraged a wide enough following for financial success. It drew consistent art house audiences, especially in Sydney where it ran for twelve weeks at the Gala Cinema, but poor returns meant that no mainstream feature film with an equivalent radical view of Australian history would be made again until Phil Noyce's **Newsfront** (1978).

International recognition often followed from exposure at Cannes, initially a tentative exercise for Australians but after several years an accepted and polished operation. The first government sponsorship of Australian films and television there occurred in 1975, with the $80 000 bill being shared by the Department of the Media, the AFDC and the Department of Overseas Trade. Despite the fear by journalist P. P. McGuinness that the event might become one of Australia's "crude flag-waving and kangaroo-badge distributing orgies"[73], this first official foray into the international marketplace was relatively profitable. Right at the outset, attention was gained by **Sunday Too Far Away** when it was invited to participate in the festival's prestigious Directors' Fortnight. To promote this and other local films, the Australian Government delegation provided receptions, continuous screenings and press kits, and had twenty-five film producers and twenty-nine television producers on hand to negotiate sales. Brian Trenchard-Smith's **The Man from Hong Kong** was sold to virtually every market, Richard Franklin's **The True Story of Eskimo Nell** to nearly all English-speaking countries, and Tim Burstall's **Petersen** was given a major release in the United States. **Sunday Too Far Away** was bought by Britain and most of Europe, and Michael Thornhill's **Between Wars** by several countries, including Canada.

Looking forward, looking back

In June 1975, **Sunday Too Far Away** had its first public exposure in Sydney on the opening night of the Sydney Film Festival. The festival's afternoon sessions were devoted to a "Salute to Australian Film", a retrospective tribute to local cinema spanning sixty years from **The Romantic Story of Margaret Catchpole** (1911) to **Wake in Fright** (1971). This ambitious event was appropriate for a year that was to bring the release of twenty-five new Australian features, a number unequalled since 1911. Moreover, the retrospective recognised the interest in local film history which had grown from the time of the industry's rebirth. Attitudes to Australian film history had begun to change around 1970, with the growing tally of local features and a newly-emergent nationalism. The first books to be published about Australian film history made their appearance in that year[74], and the following year's Australia-wide transmission on ABC television of virtually all the Cinesound features of the 1930s achieved unexpectedly high ratings. In 1971, after an outcry over the likelihood that all the pre-1951 Cinesound and Movietone newsreels on nitrate stock were to be burnt, the Federal Government allocated funds for copying and preserving them at the National Film Archive of the National Library. Three years later, a pressure group, the Association for a National Film and Television Archive, was formed to urge that existing archival facilities be improved to adequately preserve all other films. By the mid-1970s, educational institutions and film societies were requesting more and more early Australian productions for study purposes from the National Film Library's lending collection.

Among the twenty-five features and more than thirty extracts screened at Sydney's State Theatre for the 1975 "Salute to Australian Film" were **The Sentimental Bloke** (1919), **On Our Selection** (1920), **A Girl of the Bush** (1921), **For the Term of his Natural Life** (1927), **The Cheaters** (1929), **His Royal Highness** (1932), **Mr Chedworth Steps Out** (1939), **Forty Thousand Horsemen** (1940), **A Son is Born** (1946), **Captain**

Thunderbolt (1953) and **Jedda** (1955), along with the visiting productions, **The Overlanders** (1946) and **The Sundowners** (1960). The enthusiastic response to many of the films was heartening to those members of the earlier generation of filmmakers who were able to attend, including the McDonagh sisters, Ken G. Hall, Elsa Chauvel and Cecil Holmes. The retrospective also drew the appreciation of reviewers, and P. P. McGuinness found supreme relevance in the event, "at a time when we are still waiting with some concern to discover whether the current surge will reach take-off, or abort once again".[75]

Perspectives

Sunday Too Far Away was produced by the South Australian Film Corporation, the first of six State Government production bodies to be established over a span of eight years.[76] Under the South Australian Film Corporation Act introduced in 1972 by Don Dunstan's Labor Government, the Corporation was empowered to produce films funded by the State and to borrow money at favourable interest rates to embark on its own productions. By June 1975, the SAFC had been involved in sixty documentaries, two pilot episodes for television series, and a one-hour dramatised documentary, **Who Killed Jenny Langby?** (directed by Donald Crombie). **Sunday Too Far Away** was the Corporation's first feature, and its $300 000 budget was shared with the AFDC.

The writer John Dingwall developed his script from the experiences of his brother-in-law, a shearer in the mid-1950s. Foley (Jack Thompson) plays a top shearer who joins a team headed for a remote outback property. They are initially unified in dealing with a finicky station manager, but once this is resolved they become competitive and edgy. The men are momentarily reunited as the shearers mourn the death of the oldest member of the team, but solidarity of a more permanent kind only returns with strike action over the Government's withdrawal of a bonus "prosperity payment".

Sunday's director, Ken Hannam, had left Australia for London in 1968 after an impressive output of drama for ABC Television. Having broadened his experience with the BBC and commercial companies, he was anxious to return home, and was attracted by John Dingwall's script. Shooting began in March 1974 in the usually arid area of land near Quorn in the north of South Australia. Unexpected torrential rain fell for most of the filming period, and what had been a tight, well-planned script set against a hot and dusty background turned into a seven week ordeal of almost continuous improvisation. After the first cut of the film, the producer Gil Brealey found the result unacceptable and ordered a second and then a third cut in the absence of Hannam. By the third version, the original mood of the production was considerably altered. Hannam was invited to discuss this final form, but was averse to working by committee and left. The resulting success was all the more remarkable in the light of its varied concepts.

Sunday Too Far Away is a study of men in isolation, of camaraderie

277

concealing the essential loneliness of each individual. Its strength lies in the way it examines relationships between the shearers at work, depicting as well the interaction between character and environment. The bush ethos so frequently mythologised in early nationalist literature and Australian films after World War I is replaced by the claustrophobia of isolated work under pressure and a stretching of loyalties to the limit. But the film's structure brings its own problems. Weaknesses either in the original shape, or that created during the drastic reconstruction, make the second half thematically uncertain and several carefully established situations are left suspended. The beginning of a bar-room brawl which should be a climactic affirmation of the men's solidarity leads directly into a closing caption announcing the success of their strike action. The audience is left wanting to know more.

Even before the film's warm reception by large audiences at Cannes, it won four top prizes at the March 1975 presentation of the Australian Film Institute Awards, including best actor (Jack Thompson) and the AFI's Golden Reel. Reviewing the Cannes screening for *Films and Filming,* the British critic Ken Wlaschin compared Hannam's portrayal of male companionship and competition to that of veteran American director Howard Hawks[77] and fellow critics David Robinson and Verina Glaessner drew parallels with John Ford.[78] Andrew McKay of the Melbourne *Herald* felt that, "Australian cinema will really succeed when, as in **Sunday**, we show ourselves as we are and not as we would like to be."[79] By late January 1975, **Sunday Too Far Away** had recouped production costs from its Sydney, Melbourne and Adelaide seasons alone, and within a few years its profit from Australian screenings had climbed to around $120 000.

Sunday Too Far Away and **Between Wars** were among the first of a stream of thirty-one features made over the next six years with period settings. Within a few years, the trend was being attacked by film reviewers as one of nostalgic emptiness and of little relevance to contemporary audiences. But many did present themes, backgrounds and aspects of national character that no filmmaker had previously tackled. While this in itself was not always able to justify a film, the sheer number of historical films increased the possibility that some would interpret their period with a fresh perspective that audiences and critics found appealing.

For more than one reason, **Sunday Too Far Away** was to become a watershed in the development of the Australian film industry. It used the industry's oldest and most consistently popular setting, the bush; it featured mateship, a recurrent theme in films about the bush and war; and it tempered the traditional myth-making of the bush and its ethos with disaffection. The uncertainties of the film's conception were also a reminder that between its earliest days and the present, the creative traditions of Australian cinema had experienced too many breaks. The fact that **Sunday** achieved international status besides a ready market at home meant that the repair and development of these traditions was not only necessary but desired.

In mid-1975, industry observers predicted that the following financial year would indicate decisive trends. Certainly, it was to be a time that brought financial rewards and critical acclaim not only to **Sunday Too Far Away**, but also to Peter Weir's **Picnic at Hanging Rock** and Donald Crombie's **Caddie**. If the response to these was any indication, then perhaps — a very cautious perhaps — the eighty-year-old industry's vicious cycles of growth, euphoria, despair and collapse were about to be broken.

Yet for the industry in mid-1975, an economic recession and the reticence of private investors could still make budget-raising an arduous task. A feature director might still face long periods of frustrating inactivity, and the basic problems of distribution and exhibition remained unresolved. Although 1975 was to be a record year for the tally of Australian features released, those actually in production had declined. By the end of June, even the making of advertising commercials had ebbed. Producer and editor Anthony Buckley wrote:

In 1975, the production of Australian films is the same as it has always been, an ad hoc situation with producers and directors going from one picture to another spending valuable time in trying to raise money for their next, then having made it trying to find a distributor on favourable terms who in turn has to find the right deal from the exhibitor that will return all three parties some revenue, particularly the producer.[80]

Broadly, what was needed was the continued faith of investors and a fresh perspective from filmmakers not easily made complacent by the new acclaim. Since 1975 Australia has seen that faith begin to be rewarded. Within a year one film had won an Academy Award, others had received international recognition at the Cannes Film Festival; the tough American market had begun to open and the British exhibition trade had dubbed that fresh perspective "the new Australian confidence".

The industry in Australia does have a new confidence but today more than ever its cycles of progress, disappointment and renewal over the first eighty years need to be remembered.

Notes

Chapter 1

1. Kevin Brownlow, *The Parade's Gone By*, p. 6.

2. Hertz was not, as he claims in his autobiography (*A Modern Mystery Merchant, the Trials, Tricks and Travels of Carl Hertz*), the first to screen film in New Zealand. That distinction rests with "Professors" Hausmann and Gow at the Opera House, Auckland on 13 October 1896. Hertz visited New Zealand with his "Cinématographe" early in 1897. It should further be noted that Hertz's Cinématographe could only project film, and not — like the Lumière Cinématographe — photograph and print as well.

3. *Age*, Melbourne, 24 August 1896.

4. *Australasian*, 10 October 1896.

5. *Sydney Morning Herald*, 28 September 1896.

6. *Age*, 24 August 1896.

7. *Ibid*.

8. *Everyones*, 9 January 1924, "First Picture In Sydney", published letter from Ted Breen.

9. *Bulletin*, 28 November 1896.

10. *Everyones, op. cit.*

11. *Australasian*, 10 October 1896.

12. *Bulletin*, 3 October 1896.

13. Albert E. Smith, with Phil A. Koury, *Two Reels and a Crank*, pp. 51-68.

14. Robert Sklar, *Movie-Made America*, p. 22.

15. *War Cry*, 18 August 1900.

16. *Evening Post*, Wellington, NZ, 1 December 1898.

17. The complete list of **The Passion Films** (1899) is: 1. **The Saviour's Birth**; 2. **The Flight into Egypt**; 3. **The Raising of the Widow's Son**; 4. **The Entry into Jerusalem**; 5. **The Last Supper**; 6. **The Garden of Gethsemane**; 7. **The Betrayal**; 8. **The Trial before Herod**; 9. **The Scourging**; 10. **The Ascent into Calvary**; 11, 12 and 13. **The Crucifixion**.

18. *War Cry*, 27 January 1900. "The Victorian Contigent" referred to volunteers for the Boer War.

19. **The Passion Play** was screened extensively along the eastern seaboard of the US and may have been seen in Australia before 1900. The *Bulletin* in January 1901 states: "The recent bio. pictures of the genuine Oberammagau [sic] Passion Play set one thinking of the audacious fakes which the late Orpheus M'Adoo introduced to Australia a couple of years ago. *They* professed to have been taken at Oberammagau,

though the latest performance of the *Passion Play* up to that time had happened about three years previous to the invention of the biograph''.

20. Some writers have referred to the presentation as **Early Christian Martyrs**. The mistaken use of this title was originally applied to the feature-length re-make, **Heroes of the Cross** (1909).

21. *New Zealand Herald*, Auckland, 20 May 1901. '' . . . as one thrilling and tragic event succeeded another the narrative became impressed on the mind with vividness, especially when the series of scenes that had been unfolded by the dissolving views were reproduced by the kinematograph.''

Reg Perry later recalled that a film segment showing the martyrs being ''mauled'' by a *papier-mâché* lion was followed immediately by a still photograph of the event. This coloured slide ''was flashed on the screen with blood flowing from the wound, which besides giving a greater impact (to) the audience, enabled (Major) Perry to put his next roll of film on the projector, without a break in the continuity of the show''. (From an unpublished article by Reg Perry, supplied in draft form by Perry to the authors.)

22. *Ibid*. A more accurate screening time for the presentation seems to have been two and a quarter hours.

23. *War Cry*, 22 September 1900.

24. Press advertisements in several Melbourne journals, 13 September 1900.

25. *Argus*, Melbourne, 14 September 1900.

26. *Age*, Melbourne, 14 September 1900.

27. *War Cry*, 22 September 1900.

28. Obituary from unidentified newspaper source, published 27 June 1933.

29. *Bulletin*, 3 January 1907. The Adelaide correspondent reported that, ''a good deal of it would be hard to follow without the help of a closely-printed programme studied beforehand''.

The following is a précis of **The Story of the Kelly Gang**, taken from the synopsis, *The Story of the Kelly Gang by Biograph*. A copy of the booklet is held by the National Film Archive, National Library, Canberra.

The *first scene* opens at the Kelly homestead. Troopers arrive and Mrs Kelly is roughly handled while one of the troopers offers to let Dan go in return for a kiss from the young Kate. Ned comes to Dan's assistance and shoots the trooper in the wrist before disappearing into the bush.

In the *second scene*, the police are camped in the nearby Wombat Ranges. After some of the troopers leave, the remainder are ambushed by the Kelly Gang. Two police troopers, Kennedy and Scanlon, return and are shot down. Ned remarks, ''If we had not shot them, they would have shot us. We had to do it.'' Constable MacIntyre escapes from the camp, and the Government proclaims a £3000 reward for the capture of the bushrangers.

In *scene three*, the Gang stage a hold-up at Younghusband's Station. Ned tells Steve Hart to go through the pockets of the men, but to leave the women unmolested. He remarks, ''We do not rob ladies or children''. The Gang steal the wares of an itinerant hawker, and dressing themselves in new clothes, promptly depart to rob the Euroa bank. Ned poses as a customer, and the Gang escapes with a large haul of gold and notes.

Scene four has Kate Kelly serving as "bush telegraph", taking food to the Gang while Mrs Skillian sends the police on a wild goose chase. Kate learns that Aaron Sherritt has been seen with the police. The Gang later shoots Sherritt in cold blood. Inside Sherritt's house, the police panic. Two of them crawl under the bed, while the others keep Mrs Sherritt as hostage.

Scene five takes place at the Glenrowan Hotel after the Gang has supervised the tearing-up of the railway track. At the hotel, schoolmaster Curnow gains the Gang's confidence and manages to get away. He warns the troopers of the impending train sabotage, and guides them back to the hotel. Shots are exchanged and the troopers set fire to the building. A stray bullet kills a little boy, and Joe Byrne is shot down as he stands at the bar. Dan Kelly and Steve Hart, realising the situation is hopeless, shoot each other simultaneously.

In the *closing scene*, Ned, who has successfully escaped from the hotel, tries to rejoin his mates the next morning. Hampered by the heavy iron-plate armour, he is unable to move quickly enough. The troopers fire at Ned as he advances from the bush, and for a short while the armour protects him. Eventually the troopers bring him down by shooting at his legs. Ned begs the troopers to spare his life. As the synopsis states: "Thus falls the last of the Kelly Gang and with the fall of Ned Kelly, the last of the bushrangers."

30. Reviewing a screening in Wellington of **The Story of the Kelly Gang**, the *New Zealand Times* (4 May 1907) referred to the **Kelly Gang** not as a complete film but as a "series" of films, each depicting a separate highlight of the Kelly Gang's career. The review quotes the duration as "nearly an hour", but a silent film duration frequently varied with the running speed chosen by the projectionist. An advertisement for the film in the same issue of the *New Zealand Times* incorporated a synopsis divided into nine sections.

31. *Age*, Melbourne, 27 December 1906.

32. *Bulletin*, 14 February 1907.

33. *Ibid.*, 2 May 1907.

34. The shorter section of rediscovered Kelly film consists of a few frames from several scenes including a dramatic head-and-shoulders close-up of Dan Kelly in his armour wielding a revolver. The total running time is less than ten seconds. The second discovery is more substantial and the seven shots have a combined running time of approximately two minutes. They are:

Shot 1. Long shot of the Kellys' farmyard. A policeman advances on Kate Kelly and attempts to embrace her. She struggles. There is much exaggerated twirling of bodies and hands and the camera pans to accommodate the action. Kate menaces the constable with her gun and then one of the Gang members nearby shoots him and he falls. Four members of the Gang advance on the fallen constable.

Shot 2. Medium long shot of constable back on his feet, gesticulating at Kate. He is shot again and falls. This is a repeat of *Shot 1*.

Shot 3. Medium shot of Kate Kelly pointing a gun at the constable.

Shot 4. Medium long shot of the four members of the Kelly Gang on horseback in thick bushland. Ned on the left talks to the other three.

Shot 5. Long shot of the Kelly Gang eating a meal in front of trooper's tent in the Wombat Ranges after a raid on the encampment. A policeman with arms upraised stands at the left. Enjoying the meal and the policeman's discomfort, one of the Gang imitates the upraised arms, then rubs his belly and continues to eat.

Shot 6. Gun battle at encampment. Trooper falls.

Shot 7. Brief repetition of *Shot 6.*

35. The Limelight Department under Perry produced short non-fiction films of a general nature from 1900, both for Salvation Army screening and on commission from other exhibitors. Early films included scenes around the Warrnambool coast of Victoria, the Port Fairy fishing fleet putting to sea and a naval contingent leaving Melbourne for the Boxer Rebellion (all 1900). The Limelight Department travelled to New Zealand in 1903 to film various locations including the Timaru breakwater and sequences with the playful dolphin of Cook Strait known as Pelorus Jack.

36. In New Zealand during 1900, Franklyn Barrett produced a series of short comedies based on the adventures of comic strip hero "Ally Sloper". Three years later, in Wellington, Barrett filmed **A Message From Mars**, a ten-minute condensation of a popular English stage drama.

37. Sir Walter Baldwin Spencer, an Englishman, held the Chair of Biology at Melbourne University. He was one of the first to realise the value of film for recording ethnic customs. In 1901 he set out on an expedition into central and northern Australia with an English Warwick Bioscope camera and an Edison cylinder recorder. In the spirit of Muybridge and a handful of others who used photography for scientific purposes, Baldwin Spencer captured in image and sound a unique record of the ceremonies of Aboriginal tribes, including the Aranda. He continued to use film for anthropological records until his death in 1929 at the age of sixty-nine and much of his material is now lodged in the National Film Archive, Canberra.

38. Norman Dawn in correspondence with Graham Shirley, 1970.

Chapter 2

1. *Queensland Jubilee Theatre Album*, 1910.

2. *Lone Hand*, 1 March 1912.

3. *Bulletin*, 27 June 1912.

4. *Argus*, 31 May 1911, 13 January 1912, 25 October 1913.

5. *Bulletin*, 16 September 1909.

6. *Ibid.*, 31 October 1907.

7. Eric Reade, *Australian Silent Films*, p. 38, contends that the studio was located in Kooyong Road, not Khartoum Street.

8. *Bulletin*, 14 July 1910.

9. *Ibid.*

10. *Ibid.*, 17 March 1910.

11. Unpublished autobiographical writings by Alan J. Williamson, January 1951.

12. Radio talk by Alan J. Williamson, *The Romance of the Film Industry* — Part

2: "Logical Developments". Broadcast from 3LO Melbourne, by the ABC, 30 August 1932.

13. Williamson autobiographical writings, *op. cit.*

14. *Ibid.*

15. *Theatre*, 1 January 1915.

16. *Bulletin*, 24 July 1913.

17. (i) *Theatre*, 1 October 1914. (ii) Ruth Megaw: "The American Image: Influence on Australian Cinema Management, 1896-1926", *Journal of the Royal Australian Historical Society*, Vol. 54, Part 2, June 1968. (iii) Andrew Pike: "The History of an Australian Film Production Company: Cinesound, 1932-1970", pp. 2-3.

18. *Theatre*, 1 October 1914.

19. Williamson autobiographical writings, *op. cit.*

20. *Sun* (Sydney), 13 September 1911.

21. *Theatre*, 1 April 1915.

22. *Ibid.*, 1 December 1914.

23. **Home of the Blizzard** (1913) is today the earliest Australian feature-length film to survive in its entirety.

24. Frank Legg and Toni Hurley, *Once More on My Adventure*, pp. 67-8.

25. *Theatre*, 1 February 1915.

26. Ina Bertrand, "Francis Birtles, Cyclist, Explorer, Kodaker", *Cinema Papers*, January 1974.

27. *Everyones*, 9 May 1923.

28. *Theatre*, 1 December 1914.

29. *Ibid.*, 1 May 1915. Henry Fletcher was the author of the series of novels *The Waybacks* which formed the basis of a stage play in 1915 and film in 1918.

Chapter 3

1. *Theatre Magazine*, 1 September 1915.

2. *Ibid.*, 1 December 1915.

3. *Ibid.*, 1 September 1915.

4. *Ibid.*, 1 January 1918.

5. Ina Bertrand, *Film Censorship in Australia*, pp. 114-16.

6. Unidentified clipping from John Faulkner's scrapbook. Faulkner played the part of the principal villain in **The Enemy Within**. The scrapbook is held in the National Film Archive.

7. *Theatre Magazine*, 1 October 1918.

8. *Ibid.*, 1 March 1916.

9. Signed agreement between J. C. Williamson Ltd and Monte Luke, 20 January

1916. Held by Performing Arts Museum, National Gallery of Victoria, Melbourne.

10. Andrew Pike and Ross Cooper, *Australian Film 1900-1977*, p. 83.

11. *Showman*, January 1950.

12. Interview with Mary and Elizabeth Smith (wife and daughter of Gordon Smith), 4 November 1977.

13. *Everyones*, 20 May 1925.

14. *Lone Hand*, 2 September 1918.

15. *Green Room*, 1 August 1918.

16. *Ibid.*

17. *Bulletin*, 6 April 1922.

18. *Everyones*, 20 May 1925.

19. *Green Room*, 1 May 1919.

20. *Ibid.*, 1 June 1919.

21. *Ibid.*, 1 October 1919.

22. Quoted in *Theatre Magazine*, 1 August 1918.

23. *Ibid.*

24. *Ibid.*

25. *Bulletin*, 24 March 1927.

26. *Green Room*, 1 November 1919.

27. *Lone Hand*, 20 March 1920.

28. *Advertiser* (Adelaide), 27 November 1918.

29. *Triad*, 10 November 1919.

30. *Daily Express*, quoted by the *Sun* (Sydney), 21 September 1920.

31. *Referee*, quoted by the *Bulletin*, 3 February 1921.

32. *Daily Mail*, quoted by the *Bulletin*, 25 November 1920.

33. *Kine Weekly*, 1 September 1921.

34. John Ritchie, *Australia: As Once We Were*, pp. 197 and 199.

35. *Smith's Weekly*, 22 August 1931, 4 September 1931.

36. *Sun*, 8 August 1920.

37. *Smith's Weekly*, 7 August 1920.

38. *Picture Show*, 1 April 1921.

39. *Ibid.*, 1 November 1921.

40. Interview with Mrs Marjorie Osborne, 24 March 1980.

41. *Picture Show*, 25 October 1919.

42. *Bioscope*, quoted by *Everyones*, 4 November 1925.

43. *Everyones*, 7 September 1921.

44. *Bulletin*, 10 November 1921.

45. *Everyones*, 8 November 1921.

46. *Sun-Herald*, 21 May 1961.

47. Interview with Fred James, 13 October 1977.

48. *Bulletin*, 20 October 1921.

49. *Everyones*, 11 December 1929.

50. *Theatre Magazine*, 1 September 1915.

51. *Ibid.*, 1 March 1918.

52. *Picture Show*, 1 November 1919.

53. *Ibid.*

54. *Ibid.*, 1 May 1920.

55. *Green Room*, 1 February 1919.

56. *Picture Show*, 1 July 1920.

57. *Bulletin*, 20 July 1922.

58. *Ibid.*, 18 March 1920.

59. *Ibid.*, 20 May 1920.

60. *Everyones*, 21 April 1920.

61. *Bulletin*, 21 October 1920.

62. *Theatre Magazine*, 1 October 1919.

63. *Bulletin*, 9 September 1920.

64. *Evening News*, London, 27 August 1921.

65. *Bulletin*, 24 August 1921.

66. *Smith's Weekly*, 11 November 1922.

67. *Everyones*, 30 March 1923.

68. Review by the *British, Australian and New Zealander*, quoted by *Everyones*, 30 March 1923.

69. Vince Kelly, *Achieving a Vision, The Life Story of P. William Tewksbury*, pp. 153-68.

70. *Sunday Times*, London, 3 June 1923.

71. *Bulletin*, 30 July 1925.

72. *Kine Weekly*, 3 November 1927.

73. Letter from Raymond Longford to Larry Lake of the National Library of Australia, 13 February 1953.

74. *Bulletin*, 28 August 1924.

75. *Ibid.*, 22 December 1921.

76. *Everyones*, 26 April 1922.

77. *Ibid.*, 26 April 1925.

Chapter 4

1. *Daily Telegraph*, 6 April 1927. The De Forest film of Pratten's speech, accompanied by that of the Duke of York's arrival in Sydney, was later placed in a sealed box and cemented into the walls of the company's studio, the former Rushcutters Bay tramshed. The building was demolished during the 1960s. If the film was found, it is not known to have been kept.

2. *Everyones*, 25 May 1927.

3. *Ibid.*, 19 October 1927.

4. Senate Debates, 3 May 1928. pp. 4578-9.

5. *Ibid.*, p. 4576.

6. Ross Thorne, *Picture Palace Architecture in Australia*, p. 19.

7. *Everyones*, 17 April 1929.

8. *Ibid.*, 16 May 1928.

9. *Green Room*, 1 March 1919.

10. *Ibid.*, 1 November 1917.

11. *Sydney Morning Herald*, 30 June 1928.

12. *Smith's Weekly*, article in the McDonagh sisters' scrapbook. Held by the National Film Archive.

13. Much of the information in this section is drawn from Frank Legg and Toni Hurley, *Once More on My Adventure*, pp. 100-139.

14. Letter in *Daily Telegraph*, Sydney, 26 November 1924.

15. *Sydney Morning Herald*, 15 November 1924.

16. *Daily Guardian*, 23 October 1925.

17. *Everyones*, 9 June 1926.

18. *Bulletin*, 10 June 1926.

19. Interview with Herbert Hayward, Film Pioneers Oral History Project, 23 August 1979, held by the National Film Archive.

20. *Sunday Truth*, 6 June 1926.

21. *Everyones*, 18 August 1926.

22. *Ibid.*, 29 June 1927.

23. *Beckett's*, 9 August 1927.

24. *Variety*, 12 June 1929.

25. *Sydney Morning Herald*, 27 June 1927.

26. *Variety, op. cit.*

27. *Ibid.*

28. *Smith's Weekly*, 7 June 1930.

29. John Baxter, *The Australian Cinema*, p. 50.

30. *Everyones*, 26 October 1927.

31. *Ibid.*, 18 April 1928.

32. *Ibid.*, 21 September 1927.

33. Quoted in *Everyones*, 26 October 1927.

34. *Ibid.*, 14 December 1927.

35. *Ibid.*, 9 November 1927.

36. Quoted in Parliamentary Debates, House of Representatives, 4 May 1927, p. 4688.

37. *Everyones*, 19 June 1919.

38. *Ibid.*, 3 October 1928; *ibid*, 27 March 1929.

39. *Ibid.*, 11 December 1929.

40. *Ibid.*, 27 March 1929.

Chapter 5

1. *Sydney Morning Herald*, 4 January 1929.

2. *Everyones*, 25 June 1929.

3. The tariff resulted from one of the 1927 Royal Commission recommendations.

4. *Everyones*, 16 December 1931.

5. *Ibid.*, 14 August 1929.

6. Harry Lawrenson was succeeded at year's end by fellow American Eric Mayell, and with his departure in July 1932, the editorship of Fox Australasian Movietone News passed to Fox's original Australian cameraman, Claude Carter. Under a new board of management (Stanley Crick, Claude Carter and Harry Guinness), Movietone's Australasian activities were expanded with cameramen covering all of Australia and New Zealand. A weekly international Fox Movietone newsreel, edited by Harry Guinness "with due appreciation of Australian values", continued to appear with the local issue. (*Everyones*, 13 July 1932.)

7. The final issue of *Australian Movie Magazine* was released in November 1975.

8. The only known film directly showing the effects of the 1930s Depression was commissioned by the Brisbane City Mission. A copy of the film is held by the National Film Archive of the National Library of Australia.

9. Statement by S. M. Bruce, "Pensions and Luxuries", quoted in House of Representatives, 25 June 1930.

10. *Rydge's Business Journal*, 1 October 1929.

11. Unidentified clipping (3 September 1930) in Raymond Longford scrapbook. Held by the Manuscript Division, National Library of Australia.

12. *Everyones*, 2 September 1931.

13. In 1929 **The Adorable Outcast** was the first Australian silent feature to which sound was added. A music and effects sound-on-disc track was recorded in America before the film was toured through the western states of that country as **Black Cargoes of the South Seas**. This version is not known to survive.

14. *Everyones*, 16 October 1929.

15. *Ibid.*, 10 October 1930.

16. *Sydney Mail*, 27 August 1930.

17. *Everyones*, 22 October 1930.

18. *Ibid.*, 28 May 1930.

19. *Ibid.*, 9 September 1931.

20. *Ibid.*, 16 December 1931.

21. At the 1934 NSW Film Inquiry, Frank Thring revealed he had lost £5000 on **The Sentimental Bloke**.

22. *Everyones*, 25 November 1931.

23. *Ibid.*, 10 December 1930.

24. *Ibid.*, 2 September 1931.

25. *Home*, 1 June 1937.

26. *Ibid.* After 1937, **On Our Selection** went on to earn at least another £10 000.

27. *Sydney Morning Herald*, 15 August 1932.

28. Unidentified clipping from Ken G. Hall's scrapbook.

29. Preceding **On Our Selection**, Frank Hurley's documentaries **Jewel of the Pacific** and **Symphony in Steel** were the first Cinesound productions to be completed and released.

30. *Everyones*, 14 December 1932.

31. **Southward-Ho with Mawson** was released with an effects track only. Hurley's second sound feature covering his 1929-31 Antarctic expeditions, **Siege of the South** (released October 1931), was released with commentary, music and effects skilfully blended "live" by Hurley in the manner of his theatrical presentations, for recording by Cinesound technicians.

32. *Everyones*, 9 August 1933 and 10 January 1934. Frank Thring, quoted by the latter, said of Stuart Doyle's stand on the NSW quota issue:

> He [Doyle] is today in a position to tell independent producers that if they make their films at the Cinesound Studio he will guarantee them release. With the introduction of a Quota Act he would lose that advantage, which is obviously a valuable one. It is not surprising therefore that we find Mr Doyle ranged in opposition to the Quota.

33. Unidentified clipping from the McDonagh sisters' scrapbook. Held by the National Film Archive.

34. *Smith's Weekly*, 30 September 1930.

35. *Ibid.*, 10 February 1934.

36. *Sydney Mail*, 7 February 1934.

37. *Sydney Morning Herald*, 5 February 1934.

38. *Everyones*, 28 June 1933.

39. *Ibid.*, 10 January 1934.

40. The Sydney company was the Mastercraft Film Corporation, formed in October 1934 by Raymond Longford.

41. *Film Weekly*, 2 July 1936.

42. *Everyones*, 16 December 1931.

43. *Ibid.*, 11 December 1935.

44. *Bulletin*, 26 September 1934.

45. *Everyones*, 10 May 1933.

46. *Ibid.*, 25 January 1933.

47. *Ibid.*, 21 February 1934.

48. *Ibid.*, 20 March 1929.

49. This version of the casting of Errol Flynn for **In the Wake of the Bounty** is that of Charles Chauvel (letter to George Frazier, New York, 18 July 1951, held by the National Film Archive) and Elsa Chauvel (letter to Graham Shirley, 21 September 1981). John Hammond Moore (*The Young Errol: Flynn Before Hollywood*, pp. 93-4) quotes John Warwick's account that he had first spotted Flynn on Bondi Beach. A totally different version comes from producer-cameraman George Malcolm (interviewed by Bruce Molloy, 31 May 1977), who claimed that he used Flynn in a suit commercial prior to **Bounty**, and that this was seen by Chauvel.

50. *Everyones*, 23 January 1935.

51. *Ibid.*, 11 December 1935.

52. Interview with writer and producer-director Shan Benson, Film Pioneers Oral History Project, 30 June 1981. Held by the National Film Archive.

53. *Everyones*, 28 October 1936.

Chapter 6

1. Interview with Frederick Daniell, late 1971.

2. *Everyones*, 25 September 1935.

3. *Ibid.*

4. *Ibid.*, 13 December 1933.

5. From late September 1933, Greater Union Theatres used the Civic Theatre, Haymarket (Sydney) as an "All-Australian" cinema, running premiere seasons for **The Squatter's Daughter, Waltzing Matilda, The Hayseeds** and **Two Minutes Silence** among others. Within six months, the cinema was back to screening mostly imported features.

6. *Everyones*, 7 February 1934.

7. *Ibid.*

8. Quoted *ibid.*

9. *Ibid.*, 17 October 1934.

10. *Ibid.*, 25 September 1935.

11. *Ibid.*

12. *Everyones* on 14 February 1934 reported that Australian backgrounds would be part of an "Empire" production policy by Gaumont-British. Besides the Flaherty project, "Portions of a Victor Saville historical film will probably be shot in Australia". Other projects mentioned were **The Camels Are Coming** (Egypt) and **Soldiers Three** (India). *Film Weekly* of 11 June 1936 said that **The Flying Doctor** would be released in America by Gaumont-British, "alongside other Empire productions — notably **Rhodes of Africa, The Great Barrier** (Canada) and **Soldiers Three**".

13. *Today's Cinema*, 14 September 1937.

14. Quoted by *Everyones*, 23 September 1936.

15. *Ibid.*

16. *Sydney Morning Herald*, 21 December 1936.

17. *Everyones*, 28 November 1934.

18. *Ibid.*, 7 August 1935.

19. *Ibid.*, 26 June 1935.

20. *Australasian Exhibitor*, 29 June 1939.

21. *Everyones*, 16 December 1936.

22. *Ibid.*, 18 April 1934.

23. *Ibid.*, 18 March 1936.

24. Charles Merewether, "Towards a radical film practice", Part 1: "Australian Left Film History". *Filmnews*, August 1981.

25. *Everyones*, 18 May 1972.

26. Ina Bertrand, *Film Censorship in Australia*, p. 146

27. *Sun*, 2 September 1926

28. *Everyones*, 15 June 1932.

29. *Ibid.*, 7 February 1934.

30. *Ibid.*, 13 January 1932.

31. *Ibid.*, 22 November 1933.

32. *Film Weekly*, 10 December 1936.

33. *Sydney Morning Herald*, 20 November 1936.

34. Interview with Ken Hall, 2 August 1976.

35. *Everyones*, 7 February 1934.

36. Herbert Hayward was also at this time Greater Union Theatres' Advertising and Publicity Director.

37. Interview with Ken Hall, 28 August 1979.

38. *Cinema Papers*, January 1974.

39. Unidentified clipping in press cutting book held by Mrs Arthur Smith (Dot McConville).

40. Interview with Ken Hall, 28 August 1979.

41. *Daily Telegraph*, 2 May 1935.

42. *Sydney Morning Herald*, 21 December 1936.

43. *Ibid.*, 8 March 1937.

44. According to *Everyones*, 12 December 1934, the Board, which served without pay, consisted "of two producers' representatives, two exhibitors, two distributors, the Commonwealth Chief Censor and four other members of the public, who have no financial interest in the industry and who will be appointed by the Minister".

45. Rupert Kathner, *Let's Make a Movie*, p. 35.

46. *Everyones*, 14 April 1937.

47. Noel Monkman, *Quest of the Curly-Tailed Horses*, p. 169.

48. *Sydney Morning Herald*, 7 April 1941.

49. *Ibid.*, 29 March 1937.

50. *Sun*, 29 March 1937.

51. *Sydney Morning Herald*, 7 April 1941.

52. *Ibid.*, 25 February 1938. The three films mentioned were **Tall Timbers, Lovers and Luggers** and **It Isn't Done**.

53. *Sun*, 17 November 1938.

54. With the opening of the Melbourne Metro in April 1934, Metro-Goldwyn-Mayer followed Fox as the second American-based distributor to commence theatrical operations in Australia. In June the rebuilding of the Cremorne, Brisbane, was completed on Metro's behalf and in July the company acquired the St James Theatre, Sydney. Metro-Goldwyn-Mayer Theatres Ltd was registered as a company in October 1934, with the aim of opening and operating theatres "in any part of the Commonwealth". In July 1971 MGM's Australian operations were bought by the Greater Union Organisation.

55. Letter held among the Daniell Papers, Manuscript Division, National Library of Australia.

56. From notes by Frederick Daniell of a meeting at the Colonial Treasurer's office, 20 October 1939. Held among the Daniell Papers, National Library of Australia.

Ken Hall, in a note to Graham Shirley (15 September 1981) wrote:

> I took next to no part in the so-called Quota Battle chiefly because I did not really believe in it. The operation on behalf of Union Theatres–Cinesound was handled by John Evans who, as Norman Rydge's chief assistant and chairman of the UT management committee, carried a good deal of weight. He was also a long-time close personal friend of mine. Evans and (Fred) Daniell did the work on this matter, and once or twice I made a statement or put my name to something because I was asked to do so. I did not believe that a quota would be effective then, any more than I believe one, if instituted, would be effective today.
>
> I have stated my case on this matter in print and elsewhere, but in essence it boils down to this:
>
> You can legislate to force exhibitors to screen a percentage of Australian films but you cannot force the public to pay to go in and see them. The case will always rest on the drawing power of the film in question.

57. Ken G. Hall, *Directed by Ken G. Hall*, p. 137.

58. Interview with Herbert Hayward, Film Pioneers Oral History Project, 3 September 1979. Held by the National Film Archive.

59. *Everyones*, 28 July 1937.

60. Interview with Ken Hall, 28 August 1979.

61. *Everyones*, 8 September 1937, published the following statement by Norman Rydge:

> Our Australian governments have always protected local industry and will not stand by and allow such a vast organisation as ours to be forced out of business. I am sure no government will hesitate to introduce legislation to protect, if necessary, the jobs of our large army of men and women employees and the interests of about 5000 Australian investors.

62. *Everyones*, 15 September 1937.

63. *Cinema Papers*, March-April 1975.

64. *Herald* (Melbourne), 11 August 1938.

65. *Sunday Sun*, undated clipping from Ken Hall press clipping book.

66. *Cinema Papers*, March-April 1975.

67. Ken G. Hall, *Directed by Ken G. Hall*, p. 146.

68. *Sunday Despatch*, London, 23 July 1939.

69. Interview with Ken Hall, 28 August 1979.

70. *Sydney Morning Herald*, 22 September 1936.

71. Interview with Elsa Chauvel, 12 August 1976.

72. *Everyones*, 7 July 1937.

73. Representing the Hoyts and Herc McIntyre interests on **Forty Thousand Horsemen** was Herbert Hayward, whose brief was to oversee expenditure, ensure "box office value" of the script and coordinate publicity. Hayward (op. cit.) recalled that before production commenced, he worked further on the script with Bill Maloney and playwright Sidney Tomholt, tightening the narrative and working on the pace to stress the prominence of the final charge. Elsa Chauvel, however (in a letter to Graham Shirley, 21 September 1981), wrote: "E. V. Timms was the only one to work with Charles on the script of **Forty Thousand Horsemen**. I helped with some of the scenes affecting Betty Bryant, purely from a feminine angle. Charles was completely responsible for the final script."

74. Elsa Chauvel, *My Life With Charles Chauvel*, p. 80.

75. Ken Hall (note to Graham Shirley, 15 September 1981) stated: "Charles Munro should receive credit for Hoyts' part in **Horsemen**. His personal interest (and he may have had personal money in it) made the film possible."

76. Many of the charge shots (including sustained tracking material) for **Forty Thousand Horsemen** were filmed in the countryside near Bathurst, NSW.

77. Ken Hall (*op. cit.*) related: "**Horsemen** was rejected for distribution by Universal despite a personal appeal Herc McIntyre made to the Board. It was eventually sold, by Herc, to a *member of the same board* for £15 000. He handled

the film independently and made a lot of money with it. These facts are exactly as relayed to me by Herc McIntyre, who was my close friend.''

Chapter 7

1. Basil Wright, *The Long View*, p. 110.

2. *Cinema Papers*, January-February 1979, p. 183 "Stanley Hawes: Interview''.

3. *Smith's Weekly*, 1 April 1944.

4. Interview with Sid Wood, former Movietone cameraman and editor, 5 December 1980.

5. On 23 January 1942, for instance, **Cinesound Review** examined the possibility of Australia becoming a front line with the special, **No Bombs Fall Here Yet**, and the next week's issue urged the formation of a civilian army.

   From mid 1942, cameramen from both newsreels were accredited as official war correspondents. By the war's end, further DOI cameramen included Roy Driver, Reg Edwards, Bill Carty, Reg Pearse and Hugh McInnes.

6. The Australian personnel of the BMI's Far Eastern Bureau were James Pearson, Hugh McInnes and Reg Edwards.

7. Among other early shorts were Argosy's **Innocence at Sea** (the last film directed by Clarence Badger) and **Keeping the Fleet at Sea** (directed by Alan Mill), Mel Nichols' **Fashions for Men**, dealing with factory production, and Ralph Smart's **It's the Navy** (produced through Herschells).

8. Michael Balcon, *Michael Balcon Presents . . . A Lifetime of Films*, p. 150.

9. Harry Watt, "You start from scratch in Australia'', published in *Penguin Film Review, No. 9*.

10. *Ibid*.

11. Ken G. Hall, *Directed by Ken G. Hall*, p. 172.

12. *The Australasian Exhibitor*, 24 October 1946.

13. Ken G. Hall, *Directed by Ken G. Hall*, p. 186.

14. *Ibid*., p. 193.

15. Donald Horne, *The Australian People*, p. 226; and Geoffrey Serle, *From Deserts The Prophets Come*, p.177.

16. Alan Stout, "Making films in Australia'', published in *Australia Today*, 1947.

17. From December 1945 the Documentary Films Committee of New South Wales became that state's advisory committee to the Australian National Film Board. Its name was simultaneously changed to the NSW Documentary and Educational Film Council, and in January 1950 it became the NSW Film Council. The Council was abolished in January 1979 following the formation of the NSW Film Corporation.

18. Alan Stout, *op. cit*.

19. Alan Stout, "Films in Australia'', published in *Media Information Australia*, Issue 6, November 1977.

20. Reprinted in *Film*, February 1947.

21. *Ibid.*

22. Frederick Daniell, the NEI film unit's Officer-in-Charge, later estimated that between 1942 and 1945 the unit produced a total of 160 one-reel documentaries in five languages. Nine were given a world release.

23. *Film*, May 1948.

24. *Ibid.*

25. Harry Watt, *op. cit.*

26. *Ibid.*

27. Interview with R. P. Baker, 6 February 1980.

28. Harry Watt, *op. cit.*

29. Ralph Smart interviewed by David Stratton for the Film Pioneers Oral History Project, 23 October 1979. Held by the National Film Archive.

Chapter 8

1. Report from the Select Committee on the Encouragement of Australian Productions for Television (Vincent Report), p. 16.

2. Brian Carroll, *The Menzies Years*, pp. 108-9.

3. *Sydney Morning Herald*, 18 June 1953.

4. Cecil Holmes, "The film in Australia", published in *Meanjin*, Winter 1954.

5. *Ibid.*

6. Cecil Holmes, *ibid.*, noted with interest that Harold Holt, MHR, was a large shareholder in Hoyts, and that Labor Senator John Armstrong was a director and substantial shareholder of Greater Union.

7. *Ibid.*

8. *National Times*, 17-23 August 1980.

9. Colin Scrimgeour in letter tape to Graham Shirley, 5 October 1981. Further information on Associated TV taken from interviews with radio scriptwriter and producer Creswick Jenkinson (6 August 1976) and filmmaker Cecil Holmes (7 November 1976).

10. Julie James Bailey, "Australian television: why it is the way it is", *Cinema Papers*, September-October 1979. Brian Carroll, *op. cit.*, pp. 129-30.

11. Sandra Hall, *Supertoy*, p. 12.

12. *Sunday Telegraph*, 4 December 1949.

13. *Monthly Film Bulletin*, December 1950.

14. After 1970, John Kingsford Smith remained at Kingcroft as director of the company's Documentary Film Division. By the early 1980s, he had produced a total of over 300 sponsored short films.

15. John Heyer interview, Oral History Project, 6 November 1979. Held by the National Film Archive. Heyer stated that his maximum allowable budget for **Back of Beyond** was £15 000.

16. *Filmnews*, Sydney, December 1975.

17. Quoted in *Sydney Film Society Bulletin*, May 1955.

18. Gwen Oatley interview, Film Pioneers Oral History Project, 20 and 25 July 1979. Held by the National Film Archive.

19. Much of the information on the history of the Waterside Workers' Federation Film Unit has been kindly made available by Brett Levy and John Hughes.

20. Between March and October 1947, thirty-five issues of **Westralian News** (produced and photographed by Leith Goodall), appeared at a theatre in Perth which had commissioned the reel after being unable to obtain supplies of **Cinesound Review** or **Movietone News**. Production was halted when the anticipated statewide release did not eventuate and distributors decided to make the two major newsreels available. From here on, a Cinesound or Movietone reel continued to appear weekly in almost every cinema in Australia.

21. From published summary for *Cinesound Review*, Issue 882, 24 September 1948.

22. From published summary for *Movietone News*, Vol. 20, Issue 21, 29 April 1949.

23. *Ibid.*, Vol. 21, Issue 39, 1 September 1950.

24. Ken G. Hall, *Australian Film, The Inside Story*, p. 165.

25. *Ibid.*

26. For the first nine years of Australian television, Cinesound supplied Sydney's TCN Channel 9 with film segments for its news sessions, along with a number of documentaries and commercials. This brought an increase in the Cinesound staff.

27. Elsa Chauvel in an interview with Graham Shirley, 12 August 1976.

28. Elsa Chauvel, *My Life With Charles Chauvel*, p. 128.

29. Elsa Chauvel interview, *op. cit.*

30. *Monthly Film Bulletin*, September 1956.

31. This quote and background information on the Rafferty–Robinson partnership drawn from Lee Robinson interview with Graham Shirley, 15 August 1976.

32. *Sunday Herald*, 12 July 1953.

33. *Monthly Film Bulletin*, April 1955.

34. Lee Robinson interview, *op. cit.*

35. *Film Weekly*, 5 May 1955.

36. In 1959, Lee Robinson was also employed by the entrepreneur Lee Gordon to direct **Rock 'n' Roll**, a feature-length coverage of a Sydney Stadium concert.

37. Lee Robinson interview, *op. cit.*

38. Quoted in *Sight and Sound*, Autumn 1958.

39. Charles Higham and Joel Greenberg, *The Celluloid Muse*, pp. 166-8.

40. *Monthly Film Bulletin*, June 1958.

41. Trader Faulkner, *Peter Finch: a Biography*, pp. 186-7.

42. *Sight and Sound*, Summer 1957.

43. *Nation*, 14 February 1959.

44. *Sight and Sound*, Spring 1960.

45. *Monthly Film Bulletin*, May 1960.

46. *Sight and Sound*, Winter 1960.

47. Vincent Report, p. 16.

48. Geoffrey Serle, *op. cit.*, p. 181.

49. Vincent Report, p. 11.

50. *Ibid.*, p. 24.

51. *Ibid.*, p. 26.

52. *Ibid.*, p. 25.

53. *Ibid.*, p. 26.

54. *Ibid.*, p. 27.

Chapter 9

1. *Lumière*, September 1970.

2. *Sydney Morning Herald*, 6 October 1966.

3. *Sun-Herald*, Sydney, 11 February 1968.

4. Albie Thoms, *Polemics for a New Cinema*, p. 353.

5. *Bulletin*, 7 October 1967.

6. Barrett Hodsdon in *Filmnews*, Sydney, November 1978.

7. *Bulletin*, 2 April 1966.

8. *Masque*, June-July 1969.

9. Albie Thoms interviewed by Graham Shirley for ABC-TV programme *The Director's Chair*, 3 April 1981.

10. *Daily Telegraph*, 19 June 1969. Cartoon by King.

11. *Sun*, 18 June 1969.

12. Albie Thoms, *Polemics for a New Cinema*, p. 364.

13. *Ibid.*

14. *Masque*, *op. cit.*

15. A Melbourne Filmmakers Co-op was formed in 1970, and an Adelaide Co-op in 1972.

16. *Masque*, *op. cit.*

17. *Ibid.*

18. *Ibid.*

19. Michael Thornhill (uncredited), "The Australian Film?", published in *Current Affairs Bulletin*, Vol. 41, No. 2, 18 December 1967.

20. *Bulletin*, 21 January 1967.

21. *Australian*, 21 June 1969.

22. *Quadrant*, December 1969.

23. *Australian*, 25 August 1970.

24. Albie Thoms, *Polemics for a New Cinema*, p. 101.

25. *Australian*, 11 May 1969.

26. *Ibid.*, 17 March 1969.

27. *Ibid.*, 11 May 1968.

28. Tim Burstall and Patrick Ryan, *Two Thousand Weeks* (screenplay), p. 40.

29. *Ibid.*, p. 146.

30. *Lumière*, October 1970.

31. *Ibid.*, July 1970.

32. *Ibid.*, August 1972.

33. *Ibid.*, September 1970.

34. David Stratton, *The Last New Wave*, p. 11.

35. *Australian*, 17 June 1968.

36. *Nation*, 23 January 1971.

37. *Sydney Morning Herald*, 14 August 1968.

38. Albie Thoms, *Polemics for a New Cinema*, p. 361.

39. *Sydney Morning Herald*, 14 August 1968.

40. *Nation*, 23 January 1971.

41. The Australian Film Institute was established as a non-profit organisation in 1958, with the aim of promoting "an awareness and appreciation of film".

42. *Australasian Exhibitor*, 13 November 1969.

43. *Film Weekly*, 12 March 1970.

44. *Sydney Morning Herald*, 1 October 1968.

45. H. G. Hayward, Chairman, NSW Theatres and Films Commission: Investigation and Report on Film Production in the United Kingdom and on the Continent. Presented to the NSW Chief Secretary on 7 October 1970.

46. Published as supplement to *Lumière*, September 1970.

47. *Australian Financial Review*, 15 June 1972.

48. Quoted *ibid*.

49. *Showman*, 22 February 1970.

50. *Nation*, 21 August 1971.

51. In September 1975, the NSW distributors' quota for Australian films was increased to 4 per cent and the exhibitors' quota to 3 per cent. Australian films had now been well on the increase for five years.

52. *National Times*, 13-18 December 1971.

53. *Lumière*, September 1972.

54. *Age*, 3 March 1972.

55. *Review*, 9-15 September 1972.

Chapter 10

1. *Sydney Morning Herald*, 1 March 1971.

2. *Ibid.*

3. *Ibid.*

4. *Ibid.*

5. *Lumière*, November-December, 1971.

6. *Ibid.*

7. *National Times*, 28 February-5 March 1977.

8. *Lumière*, December 1972.

9. *Sunday Australian*, 17 October 1971.

10. *Australian*, 23 October 1971.

11. These films were **Three to Go, Homesdale, Country Town, Stockade, Stork, A City's Child, Shirley Thompson versus the Aliens** and **Private Collection**.

12. *Review*, 9-15 September 1972.

13. *Lumière*, December 1972.

14. *Australian*, 12 April 1975.

15. *Ibid.*, 3 February 1973.

16. *Cleo*, June 1973.

17. Barrett Hodsdon, "A view of the tariff board report on motion picture films", *Cinema Papers*, January 1974.

18. Tariff Board Report: Tariff Revision — Motion Picture Films and Television Programs, June 1973, Australian Government Publishing Service, Canberra, p. 33.

19. *Sydney Morning Herald*, 19 April 1975.

20. Antony I. Ginnane, "Restrictive trade practices legislation and the film industry: Part 2", *Cinema Papers*, July-August 1975.

21. From its formation in 1954, the Village Theatres Group expanded its operations from drive-in cinemas in Victoria to hard-top cinemas and drive-ins throughout Australia. During the 1960s, the Greater Union Organisation purchased a one-third interest in Village, although the two companies were to remain in day-to-day competition. By early 1975, the company owned approximately eighty-five cinemas and drive-ins.

The allied distribution company, Roadshow, was established by Village in 1968 to acquire direct access to overseas films. It consisted of Roadshow International (handling the franchise for Warner Bros) and Roadshow Distributors (handling films bought from independent producers). The films purchased by Roadshow reflected a greater diversity of world production than those of its traditional competitors, and after 1969, the company virtually outstripped its rivals in the number of feature films it handled. Roadshow provided films to both Village and GUO, and in turn, had access to films distributed through or in association with the Rank Organisation, which still held its 50 per cent interest in GUO.

Aside from its participation (from 1973) in the local production company, Hexagon, the main historic importance of Roadshow was its role as one of a number of newly emergent distributors to challenge the long-held distribution status quo.

22. *Cinema Papers*, July-August 1974.

23. *Quadrant*, December 1969.

24. *Sydney Morning Herald*, 2 March 1971.

25. *Ibid*.

26. *Quadrant*, December 1969.

27. Albie Thoms, *Polemics for a New Cinema*, p. 382.

28. *Bulletin*, 19 June 1971.

29. Barrett Hodsdon, ''The Australian Film Industry — A Case Study'', March 1973.

30. Albie Thoms, *Polemics for a New Cinema*, p. 398.

31. *Lumière*, August 1972.

32. *Cinema Papers*, May-June 1979.

33. *Ibid*.

34. Quoted in *Bulletin*, 19 June 1971.

35. *Cinema Papers*, November-December 1975.

36. *Ibid*.

37. Albie Thoms interviewed by Graham Shirley for ABC-TV programme *The Director's Chair*, 3 April 1981.

38. *Lumière*, May 1973.

39. *A Catalogue of Independent Women's Films*, Sydney Women's Film Group, 1979, pp. 5-7.

40. *Age*, 21 February 1975.

41. *Nation Review*, 2 August 1974.

42. *Australian*, 22 August 1975.

43. Richard Brennan, ''Peter Weir profile'', *Cinema Papers*, January 1974.

44. *Lumière*, February 1971.

45. The first part of this series had been **The Pictures that Moved** (1968, Alan Anderson).

46. *Nation Review*, 13-19 April, 1973.

47. *Ibid*., 19-29 April, 1973.

48. *Lumière*, May 1973.

49. *Nation Review*, 26 July-1 August 1974.

50. Tariff Board Report, p. 36.

51. Other members of the Interim Board were Ronald Elliott, Leonard Beoiley, Graham Burke, Hector Crawford, Joan Long, John McQuaid, James Oswin, Storry Walton, Sir Keith Waller and T. G. Whitbread. The executive officer was Shan Benson.

52. Report of the Interim Board of the Australian Film Commission, February 1975, p. 9.

53. *Ibid.*, p. 7.

54. *Ibid.*, p. 2.

55. *Ibid.*, p. 6.

56. *Ibid.*, pp. 3, 7.

57. *Cinema Papers*, July-August 1975.

58. The Australian Film Commission's chairman was to be Ken Watts, formerly Assistant General Manager of the ABC. Other full-time members were Peter Martin, John McQuaid and Patrick Condon, while part-time members were Anthony Buckley, Graham Burke, Jill Robb and Frank Gardiner.

59. *Age*, 10 June 1975.

60. *Australian*, 31 January 1975.

61. *Ibid.*, 12 April 1975.

62. *Ibid.*

63. *Ibid.*, 16 April 1975.

64. *Ibid.*, 11 April 1975.

65. *Ibid.*, 12 April 1975.

66. *Ibid.*, 18 April 1975.

67. Interim Board Report, *op. cit.*, p. 15.

68. *Cinema Papers*, July 1974.

69. *Monthly Film Bulletin*, May 1975.

70. *Sight and Sound*, Summer 1975.

71. *Australian*, 16 November 1975.

72. *Nation Review*, 24-30 January 1975.

73. *National Times*, 28 April-3 May 1975.

74. These were John Baxter's *The Australian Cinema* and Eric Reade's *Australian Silent Films*.

75. *National Times*, 28 April-3 May 1975.

76. The other state film corporations were the New South Wales Film Corporation, the Queensland Film Corporation, the Tasmanian Film Corporation, the Victorian Film Corporation, and the Western Australian Film Council.

77. *Films and Filming*, August 1975.

78. *Monthly Film Bulletin*, July 1976.
79. *Herald*, Melbourne, 2 July 1975.
80. *Cinema Papers*, March-April 1975.

Bibliography

Books and monographs

Adamson, Judith. *Australian Film Posters, 1906-1960* (Currency Press in joint imprint with Australian Film Institute, Sydney, 1978)

Balcon, Michael. *Michael Balcon Presents . . . A Lifetime of Films* (Hutchinson, London, 1969)

Baxter, John. *The Australian Cinema* (Angus & Robertson, Sydney, 1970)

Bertrand, Ina. *Australian Film Studies: Efftee Productions* (Centre for the Study of Educational Communication and Media, La Trobe University, Bundoora, Vic., 1977)

Bertrand, Ina. *Film Censorship in Australia* (University of Queensland Press, St. Lucia, Qld., 1978)

Brownlow, Kevin. *The Parade's Gone By* (Secker and Warburg, London, 1968)

Burstall, Tim and **Ryan**, Patrick. *Two Thousand Weeks* (Sun Books, Melbourne, 1968)

Carroll, Brian. *The Menzies Years* (Cassell Australia, Sydney, 1977)

Chauvel, Elsa. *My Life With Charles Chauvel* (Shakespeare Head Press, Sydney, 1973)

Dunn, Maxwell. *How They Made Sons of Matthew* (Angus & Robertson, Sydney, 1949)

Everson, William K. *American Silent Film* (Oxford University Press, New York, 1978)

Faulkner, Trader. *Peter Finch: a Biography* (Angus & Robertson, London, 1979)

Hall, Ken G. *Australian Film, the Inside Story* (Summit Books, Sydney, 1980)

Hall, Ken G. *Directed by Ken G. Hall* (Lansdowne Press, Melbourne, 1977)

Hall, Sandra. *Supertoy* (Sun Books, Melbourne, 1976)

Hertz, Carl. *A Modern Mystery Merchant, the Trials, the Tricks and Travels of Carl Hertz* (Hutchinson, London, 1924)

Higham, Charles and **Greenberg**, Joel. *The Celluloid Muse* (Angus & Robertson, Sydney, 1969)

Horne, Donald. *The Australian People* (Angus & Robertson, Sydney, 1972)

Kathner, Rupert. *Let's Make a Movie* (Currawong Publishing, Sydney, 1945)

Kelly, Vince. *Achieving a Vision: the Life Story of P. William Tewksbury* (George M. Dash, Sydney, 1941)

Legg, Frank and **Hurley**, Toni. *Once More on My Adventure* (Ure Smith, Sydney, 1966)

Lyle, Valda, Politis, Tom, and Stell, Ross. *Stanley Hawes: Documentary Filmmaker* (WEA Film Study Group, Sydney, 1980)

MacGowan, Kenneth. *Behind the Screen* (Dell Publishing, New York, 1965)

Manvell, Roger (ed.). *The International Encyclopedia of Film* (Rainbird Reference Books, London, 1972)

Monkman, Noel. *Quest of the Curly-Tailed Horses* (Angus & Robertson, Sydney, 1964)

Moore, John Hammond. *The Young Errol: Flynn Before Hollywood* (Angus & Robertson, Sydney, 1975)

Perry, George. *The Great British Picture Show* (Hart-Davis, MacGibbon, London, 1974)

Pike, Andrew and Cooper, Ross. *Australian Film 1900-1977* (Oxford University Press in association with the Australian Film Institute, Melbourne, 1980)

Reade, Eric. *The Australian Screen* (Lansdowne Press, Melbourne, 1975)

Reade, Eric. *Australian Silent Films* (Lansdowne Press, Melbourne, 1970)

Reade, Eric. *History and Heartburn: the Saga of Australian Film, 1896-1978* (Harper and Row, Sydney, 1979)

Reade, Eric. *The Talkies Era* (Lansdowne Press, Melbourne, 1972)

Rees, Leslie. *The Making of Australian Drama* (Angus & Robertson, Sydney, 1973)

Ritchie, John. *Australia: As Once We Were* (Heinemann, Melbourne, 1975)

Robinson, David. *World Cinema: A Short History* (Eyre Methuen, London, 1973)

Serle, Geoffrey. *From Deserts the Prophets Come* (Heinemann, Melbourne, 1973)

Sklar, Robert. *Movie-Made America* (Random House, New York, 1976)

Smith, Albert E., in collaboration with Phil A. Koury. *Two Reels and a Crank* (Doubleday, New York, 1952)

Souter, Gavin. *Lion and Kangaroo — Australia 1901-1919 — The Rise of a Nation* (Collins, Sydney, 1978)

Spearritt, Peter. *Sydney Since the Twenties* (Hale and Iremonger, Sydney, 1978)

Spearritt, Peter and Walker, David (eds). *Australian Popular Culture* (George Allen & Unwin, Sydney, 1979)

Stratton, David. *The Last New Wave* (Angus & Robertson, Sydney, 1980)

Sydney Women's Film Group. *A Catalogue of Independent Women's Films* (Sydney Film Group, Sydney, 1979)

Thoms, Albie. *Polemics for a New Cinema* (Wild and Woolley, Sydney, 1978)

Thorne, Ross. *Picture Palace Architecture in Australia* (Sun Books, Melbourne, 1976)

Thornhill, Michael (uncredited). "The Australian Film?" *Current Affairs Bulletin*, Vol. 41, No. 2, 18 December 1967

Ward, Russel. *Australia: a Short History* (Ure Smith, Sydney, 1969)

Wasson, Mervyn. *The Beginnings of Australian Cinema* (Australian Film Institute, Melbourne, 1964)

Wright, Basil. *The Long View* (Granada, London, 1976)

Younger, R. M. *Australia and the Australians* (Rigby, Adelaide, 1970)

Periodicals and Newspapers

From the many periodical and newspaper sources of information drawn upon for this book, the following proved to be the most useful: *Australian* (covering the late 1960s and early 1970s), *Bulletin* (covering all periods), *Cinema Papers* (early 1970s), *Everyones* (1920s and 1930s), *Film Weekly* (1920s and 1930s), Melbourne *Herald* (all periods), *Lumière* (early 1970s), *Monthly Film Bulletin* (UK) (late 1940s onward), *Picture Show* (1919-23), *Sydney Morning Herald* (all periods), and *Theatre Magazine* (1910-1920).

(Further details on these and other periodicals and newspapers are contained in the notes.)

Unpublished Theses

Cooper, Ross. "And the Villain Still Pursued Her: Origins of Film in Australia 1896-1913" (MA thesis, Department of History, Australian National University, Canberra, 1971)

Pike, Andrew. "The History of an Australian Film Production Company: Cinesound, 1932-1970" (MA thesis, Department of History, Australian National University, 1972)

Wasson, L. J. "The Quota Question in the Film Industry in New South Wales 1920-1940" (BA (Hons) thesis, Department of History, Australian National University, 1969)

Hodsdon, Barrett. "The Australian Film Industry: a Case Study" (Master of Economics thesis, Macquarie University, 1973)

Government Documents

Federal Senate Debates
Federal Parliamentary Debates (House of Representatives)

Report of the Royal Commission on the Moving Picture Industry (Canberra, 1927)

Minutes of Evidence of the Royal Commission on the Moving Picture Industry (Canberra, 1927)

Report of the Inquiry into the Film Industry in NSW (Sydney, 1935)

Report from the Select Committee on the Encouragement of Australian Productions for Television (Vincent Report) (Canberra, 1963)

H. G. Hayward. Investigation and Report on Film Production in the United Kingdom and on the Continent (Sydney, 1970)

Tariff Board Report. Tariff Revision — Motion Picture Films and Television Programs (Australian Government Publishing Service, Canberra, 1973)

Report of the Interim Board of the Australian Film Commission (February 1975)

Miscellaneous

Unpublished speeches and autobiographical writings by Alan J. Williamson, held by the National Film Archive of the National Library of Australia.

Daniell Papers (consisting of correspondence, reports, notes and clippings), held by the Manuscript Division, National Library of Australia.

Index

Note: Titles in italics refer to books, plays or poems.

314

318

321